FOREIGN MINORITIES
IN CONTINENTAL EUROPEAN CITIES

ERDKUNDLICHES WISSEN

SCHRIFTENREIHE FÜR FORSCHUNG UND PRAXIS
HERAUSGEGEBEN VON EMIL MEYNEN
IN VERBINDUNG MIT
GERD KOHLHEPP UND ADOLF LEIDLMAIR

HEFT 84

FRANZ STEINER VERLAG WIESBADEN GMBH
STUTTGART 1987

FOREIGN MINORITIES
IN CONTINENTAL EUROPEAN CITIES

EDITED BY

GÜNTHER GLEBE AND JOHN O'LOUGHLIN

FRANZ STEINER VERLAG WIESBADEN GMBH
STUTTGART 1987

CIP-Kurztitelaufnahme der Deutschen Bibliothek

Foreign minorities in continental European
cities / ed. by Günther Glebe and John
O'Loughlin. – Stuttgart : Steiner-Verlag-
Wiesbaden-GmbH, 1987.
    (Erdkundliches Wissen ; H. 84)
    ISBN 3-515-04594-5
NE: Glebe, Günther [Hrsg.]; GT

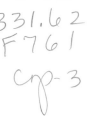

CONTENTS

.c) S m a l l e r E u r o p e a n D e s t i n a t i o n s

PREFACE

This book seeks to make a contribution to the study of the contemporary immigrant situation in the main continental European destination countries. It focuses on immigrant settlement in cities. The question of immigrant settlement in European cities is important for non-academic and academic reasons. More than 15 million people have settled in the western and northwestern European industrial countries since the 1960s and they are located mainly in urbanized areas where industrial employment was concentrated. What was meant to be a short term process of temporary immigration to fill periodical and sectoral labour shortages has, as a result of growing length of stay and continuous family reunification, become more and more a real immigration process. By maintaining the assumption of temporary migration in the early period to 1973, the ethnic minority or 'guestworker problem' was mainly considered under labour market aspects. Based on the myth of a rotation system, which in fact never really existed, it was widely believed that if necessary these immigrant minority problems could be easily solved by state intervention. This belief is still evident in the word 'guestworker' implying the temporary character of their residence, a term still widely used in German-speaking countries.

The gradual qualitative change from labour migration of the early stage of inmovement to immigration was accompanied by shifts in the settlement patterns in many European cities as the migrants had to look for suitable housing for their families. Then they became confronted with the tight housing markets and few vacancies in their price charge that was the case in many countries. At this time, the socio-economic consequences of foreigner immigration became obvious to the general public and ethnic concentration and segregation processes became major issues of public debate. Fears of ghettoization and its social implications were raised in the destinations and were often debated on the basis of emotion than on firm empirical evidence. In recent years in everday life, the economic recession and the associated high unemployment rates in European countries have pushed the immigrant question again to the forefront of political and social debate. Native unemployed workers are resentful of foreign workers in employment, there are social tensions over social benefits, housing and education and rightwing movements have used the immigrant issue to win wider popular support.

On the academic side there has been undue reliance on Anglo-Saxon urban settlement patterns as the basis for theories of immigrant integration and development. The diversity of the immigrant experience in the non-Anglo-Saxon nations of Western Europe was widely ignored in this perspective. Proportionately, the Continental countries have more immigrants than Britain. Yet, because of the language barrier, the false presumption that immigration to Continental Europe would be temporary, and the academic dominance of Anglo-Saxon theories and research themes, the evolving complexity of European immigrant patterns, though not neglected, were nevertheless not a major theme of immigrant research activities.

The first drafts of the papers collected in this book, except the one on Switzerland, were discussed at a symposium organized at the Geographisches Institut of the Universität Düsseldorf in March 1985. Although in recent years many conferences have been concerned with issues related to ethnic minorities who immigrated as a result of postwar labour migration, the Düsseldorf symposium was the first entirely devoted to geographical views of urban migrant communities in the Continental European cities. Previous conferences had either focused heavily on foreigner politics or policies or on specific sociological, sociopsychological, legal or educational aspects of immigrant minorities.

By bringing together researchers from seven different countries it was also hoped to develop an atmosphere that or might lead to more collaboration and intradisciplinary discussion.

The editors whish to thank all participants and contributors for their active participation in the exchange of views and their critical, yet constructive, comments of the papers. The co-operation and continuous efforts of all contributors have made this book possible.

I would like to thank particularly my co-editor John O'Loughlin for his kind assistance in the course of the preparation of the symposium and for performing the exhausting task of polishing the English of those chapters, not written by native English speakers.

However, without the financial support of the Deutsche Forschungsgemeinschaft, the Wissenschaftsministerium des Landes Nordrhein-Westfalen and the Alexander von Humboldt-Stiftung neither the symposium would have taken place nor the book would have been published. We are therefore grateful to all three institutions for their kind assistance. The patience and co-operation of the staff in the Geographisches Institut at Düsseldorf and the sterling assistance rendered by the student workers during the symposium and at various stages of the compilation of the book have eased our task considerably. Finally we like to thank the editors of Erdkundliches Wissen for accepting this co-operative international project into their publication series.

Günther Glebe
Düsseldorf, July 1986

INTRODUCTION :

FOREIGN MINORITIES IN CONTINENTAL EUROPEAN CITIES.[1]

JOHN O'LOUGHLIN (ILLINOIS)

After three decades of immigration into Western Europe and a decade and a half of academic research on the topic of immigrant settlement, the time seems ripe for an overview and evaluation of geographic studies. We need answers to questions like, what do we know, what knowledge do we lack, how useful have our theories been in the light of actual developments and to what extent should the stock-taking result in an overhaul of our general research approaches? Just as the timing of academic research on immigration in North America, Britain and Australia was conditioned by the arrival of large numbers of settlers from abroad, so too in Western Europe, academic research on immigration by sociologists and economists began in the late 1960s and had filtered into human geography by the mid-1970s. Naturally enough, the first major theoretical works emanated from Switzerland with its long history of immigrant labour, (Braun, 1970; Hoffmann-Nowotny, 1973). The profusion of work on European immigration over the past decade seems to have produced an academic „rijstafel", with each academic dish tasty in itself but the whole array of choices must be consumed before a feeling of satisfaction and complete coverage is enjoyed. However, the obvious risk with this pluralist approach is that of academic indigestion and like the patrons of an Indonesian restaurant, we are forced to pick our favorites.

Most academic geographers trained in the positivist heydays of the 1960s and 1970s have attacked research questions on the intraurban settlement of foreigners with the usual barrage of statistical and mapping techniques and theoretical considerations have generally extended only so far as classical urban ecological theory. To their credit, most Continental European geographers have stayed closer to their research subjects than their Anglo-Saxon counterparts, some of whom in their technical excesses have tried to simulate immigrants' intraurban settlement as if city neighbourhoods were similar to Nebraska wheatfields. Like Anglo-Saxon geographers who have switched from positivism to alternative approaches, some European researchers are beginning to question the utility of the spatial approach to urban topics and, taking their cue from structuralist studies, are beginning to probe the social, political, economic and legalistic causes of the observed spatial pattern of foreigner settlement in European cities. It is hoped that this book will make a further contribution to this analysis of the processes leading to the distribution and

---

1 This chapter was written while the author held an Alexander von Humboldt-Stiftung fellowship at the Universität Düsseldorf in 1985.

relocation of immigrants in European cities, with each chapter contributed by a geographer expert on the contemporary local situation.

In addition to the academic survey, the time also seems opportune from a political perspective for a review of the relevance of geographic research to immigration policy. Currently, more than half of all foreigners in Western Europe have been here for over 10 years and sorting of „sojourners" from immigrants among the foreigner population seems to be taking place as return migration has reached new neights since the early 1970s when worker rotation ended. The continued recession has resulted in social stress, produced by the competition for jobs and benefits between native and foreign workers. These trends combine to suggest that we may be entering a decisive period in the history of foreigner settlement in post-war Continental Europe. Public policy at both the local and national levels seems strangely and unnecessarily divorced from academic research. Numerous commentators, for example, have cautioned against the use of spatially-based neighbourhood improvement schemes to tackle the „immigrant problem" but governments persist with this simplistic and misguided policy. Since immigration policy has been debated and implemented much earlier in North America and Britain, a review of the theories of immigrant settlement emanating from these countries is not only useful in the ivory tower debates of academics but is potentially helpful in understanding and evaluating government legislation in Continental European states that has frequently resulted from a (mis)reading of academic work. Beyond this review and in line with the renewed emphasis on process-models in human geography, this book also has the additional aim of examining immigrant settlement in six Continental European nations in relation to the local political, economic, social and housing developments of the past two decades. The utility of general models of immigrant location in cities, derived mostly from the American experience, must be evaluated in the bright glare of urban reality, using published accounts of the foreigner experience in Continental European cities, particularly France and West-Germany. Working through the accumulated mass of data and research reports available in the hundreds of studies of immigrants of Continental European cities is necessary for full understanding of the complexities of policy, temporal trends and national variation.

In this chapter, I hope to introduce some of the major research themes of greater importance, both in the political and research arenas. While each of the individual chapters focuses on a specific topic, certain common themes are repeated from study to study. National policy questions and their repercussions are centerpieces of the chapters by Ogden, Evrensel and Leitner. Peach, Kesteloot, van Amersfoort and de Klerk, Bähr and Gans, and Lichtenberger and Fassmann are concerned with foreigner distribution among and within the major European cities. Gans, and Glebe and Waldorf provide detailed studies of the intraurban movement of foreigners compared to the host German population in attempts to estimate the relative level of foreigner spatial separation. Finally, White examines the retail infrastructure that has developed to serve the needs of foreigner populations in Paris and which serve to promote community identity, and, unfortunately, act as a visible symbol of the foreigner presence for those Europeans who want to reduce this presence.

While this introduction will not attempt to summarize each of these individual studies, it will attempt to review briefly and concisely some general issues that form the background to the individual national patterns and which provided the motivation for the authors to follow their own research paths. In so doing, I hope to paint the broad canvas but the details and interesting specific insights are delegated to the chapter authors. Under the headings of theory in international migration, the contemporary developments in European countries and their imprint on foreigner settlement in cities, I will attempt to highlight some of the current major debates in the social sciences, and especially in geography, on the topic of immigration. Further overwies are provided in the chapters of Part I by Peach on intraurban settlement, Leitner on immigration policies and O'Loughlin on the intricate relationships between the urban social mosaic, housing submarkets and foreigner settlement.

Theory in Immigration Research

An unfortunate gap has developed in immigration theory between the international scale, migration between countries, and the local scale, the settlement of immigrants in towns and neighborhoods. While researchers who focus on the international scale rely on economic theories of development as their guiding framework, research examining immigrant settlement on the local scale look to social-ecological theory. Since both groups of researchers are talking about the same group of immigrants, though at different scales, it would appear that a reapprochment is needed to bridge this unnecessary divide. Such a possibility is provided by Wallerstein's world-systems model with its three spatial scales (Wallerstein, 1979; Taylor, 1982). From this perspective, international migration cannot be separated from global economic trends. Push factors at the origin (periphery and semiperiphery) and pull factors at the destination (core and semiperiphery) work to redistribute workers from areas of capital shortage and labour surplus to countries of capital surplus and labour shortage. Workers have no choice except to sell their labour to the highest bidder and whether workers are directly recruited by the employers, as in Europe to 1973, or indirectly induced by employment differences between core and periphery, as between the United States and Mexico, the result is the same net flow of labour to core economies. In periods of rapid economic growth in the core, immigrant labour provides a necessary dampening influence on wage levels and inflation and allows continued economic growth (Castles and Kosack, 1985) but even in periods of economic stagnation, immigrant labour is still needed by some sectors in the core. Here we must distinguish between oligopoly and non-oligopoly capital (Akinci, 1982; Bach, 1978). While oligopoly capital can reduce its labour costs so as to maintain its competitiveness, by moving plants from the core to the peripheral countries of cheap labour, non-oligopoly capital needs immigrant labour in its industries of food processing, construction, personal services, transportation and agriculture, the „non-footloose" sector. The non-oligopoly sector maintains its profit margins by placing immigrant labour in a marginal position, in effect, into the secondary sector of the dual labour market, characterized by low-skilled, low-paid, insecure and temporary employment. Within the contemporary world economy, the capital accumulation process is maintained by international labour migration (Portes and Walton, 1981; Doherty, 1983). Governments regulate international migration because, even if the core economies are in a recession, certain sectors will demand immigrant labour to reduce their wage bills and undercut prevailing wages of the native working class. Immigrants have traditionally been used as strike breakers, as a force to fight union demands, and capitalists, wishing to divide the native and immigrant working class, oppose more stringent immigration legislation, as proposed currently in the United States. While some governments see immigrant labour as a „Konjunkturpuffer", to be imported in times of growth and expelled in periods of stagnation, Bach (1978) has argued that immigrant labour provides a more basic function in some countries, that is, reproducing capitalist social relations so that immigration solves two problems, the malfunctioning of the peripheral economy and the secondary labour market needs of the core economy (Portes, 1978).

It is at the local level that international economic trends have their most visible effects. The closure of industrial plants, consequent on the switch to cheaper production sites in the global periphery and semi-periphery, and the decline of traditional industries, have set in motion a series of events whose end result is still undecided. For our purposes in this book, the most important effect has been to produce a clear and growing split between the native working class and immigrant labour over competition for jobs, housing and government benefits. In Western Europe and in certain parts of North America, the great wave of immigration of the late 1960s/early 1970s came immediately before or contemporaneously with the massive shift of industrial employment from the core to the periphery and semi-periphery. The working class saw its traditional role in the national economy eroded despite some government efforts to stem the flow of jobs (Pahl, 1980; Friedmann and Wolff, 1982). Forced to turn to poorly-paid service jobs, to the informal sector of the economy or to governmental welfare programs, the native working class turned readily on the immigrant labourers as the source of their woes despite clear evidence that immigrant labourers were also victims and that global circumstances beyond the control of even powerful governments were responsible. In some countries, notably France, Britain and the United States, the anti-immigrant movement has been reflected in support for right-wing politicians. (See the chapter in the book on support for the National Front in France by Ogden.) In most states, resentment has been expressed so strongly that national governments have felt compelled to respond with a barrage of legislation to make immigration more difficult, return migration more attractive and „solutions to the minority problem" more immediate (Leitner, in this book). Immigrants, whose settlement in the urban areas of Northern Europe is the result of earlier core-periphery economic differences, are ironically the victims of a major readjustment in the global economy as a result of the new international division of labour that became obvious in the 1970s. Weakened by the withdrawal of manufacturing from global core to semi-periphery and periphery, native labour naturally defended their balliwicks, including neighbourhoods, certain social infrastructures and social turfs *(Economist,* Feb. 2, 1985, p. 23).

In this book, the focus is the urban residential segregation of natives and foreigners but it must be emphasized that this is only one arena, although a very important one, in which native-immigrant conflicts are played out. Whereas researchers have tended to separate international economic and migration trends from local urban conditions, quite the reverse is true. National governments find themselves fighting a double action to keep social peace at the local urban level while trying to induce multinational capital to invest within their borders. Immigrant labour, caught in a marginal and weak position even in times of general economic prosperity, currently find themselves deprived of their natural allies in the working class and in some cases, (France, for example), find the organizations designed to protect their interests, such as unions, actively campaigning to undermine their employment and social status.

To this point, this chapter has treated the immigration question in general terms and all of the European immigrant nations have been viewed as part of the same global core economy. This discussion will naturally produce charges that the Swiss experience in immigration is patently different from that of France or West Germany. While agreeing that this criticism is accurate in some senses, it should be pointed out that the alternative of viewing each country as unique is equally risky. Our search for a general explanation of international migration should allow for national corrections or deviations. If we accept the notion that international migration is propelled by differences in econmic status between nations and that immigrants are imported by the core economies to meet a certain role, then our examination of the settlement and adjustment of immigrants into the host societies can proceed from this basic foundation. Each immigrant nation has a set of laws controling immigration that reflect its particular needs, its economic and social structures, its political apparatus, its legal tradition and its cultural context. Within each immigrant country, local forces constrain the individual immigrant to a greater or lesser extent in his search for social and employment niches in the host society. At this point, we touch on a critical and controversial question in social science research, the relative freedom of the individual to act within the social, economic and political constraints of a society, a point which is discussed by O'Loughlin in Chapter 3 of this book. Suffice it to say at this point that the experience of immigrants from similar origins has been quite different at different destinations. Thus, Jamaican immigrants in London are evidently poorer than Jamaican immigrants to New York, a fact attributed to the early migration of educated Jamaicans to Canada and the United States and later movement of poor Jamaicans to Britain (Foner, 1979; Petras, 1980). Similarly, the Portugese have built up a cohesive community in Toronto but not in Paris, a difference attributed both to the societies' relative acceptance of immigrants and the attitudes of the immigrants in each destination towards permanent settlement (Brettell, 1981). We clearly need more studies of this nature to reduce current uncertainty over the ability of immigrants to adapt to host environments but in any event, it can be accepted that both immigrant characteristics *and* the social and economic structures of the host societies have to be studied in a dialectical fashion.

Two further points should be made in our discussion of geographic research on immigration and immigrants. While the notion of a „spatial process" may seem ludicrous to some, it is not to some geographers; even textbooks have been written to promote this perspective (Cliff and Ord, 1981). Since Slater's (1967) criticism of the spatial fetish, geographers have been aware of the crucial distinction between spatial patterns and spatial processes and most geographers accept that spatial patterns reflect the operation of underlying social, economic and political processes. Unfortunately, in immigration research, most researchers have been content to stop at basic mapping and do not proceed to investigation of the processes producing the distribution maps. As Johnston (1984b) argues, they have only completed the first stage in any geographic research project. Although maps of immigrant distributions and segregation scores are interesting and important, a full understanding of the patterns and an accurate prediction of how they will change awaits a process explanation, an argument put strongly by Kesteloot in this book. Neither is it enough to examine migration streams of foreigners and natives (see the chapters by Gans and by Glebe and Waldorf in this book) since these migration patterns beg the further question of why they have developed in this fashion which would lead to the examination of housing choices and supply. I am not arguing that a geographic approach is of little utility in modern social science, as the sociologist Saunders (1983) has recently claimed. Rather, I am stating what would appear to be an indisputable contention but one that is rarely carried out by social geographers in their examination of immigrant behavior, that spatial patterns can only be understood through examination of the dialectical relationships between structures and individuals (Jackson and Smith, 1984).

A final theoretical point concerns the structures to which I have alluded but never identified. International migration differs from other forms of migration because it is firmly controlled by the receiving countries, the destinations. A complex series of laws, codes, requirements, permissions, documents, and obligations must be satified or acquired before an individual migrant can move across international borders. These requirements, of course, lead to an increase in clandestine migrants whose numbers are enormous in the U.S. and are estimated to be about 15 percent of the foreigner total in France (Deley, 1983). Even after arriving in the host country, movement between jobs and/or between cities may require further permits and the precarious legal status accorded many foreigners ensures their adherence to social norms and requirements frequently ignored by natives. In the host society, the migrant faces a series of bureaucratic requirements in work and residence which vary in intensity and implementation from country to country. But beyond these legal strictures, the immigrant, like other members of the working class, is severely constrained by income limitations and, usually by racial, ethnic or language differences with the host society. The range of choice in employment is constrained by skill and educational disabilities. Choices in housing are constrained by income level, by family requirements and by legal barriers to municipal social housing. In both employment and housing, foreigners are the victims of massive discrimination (Leitner's chapter in this book). Individual foreigners react to this barrage of constraints by maintaining close ties to fellow countrymen. An example from Paris is discussed by White in this book. It has been a consistent theme in immigration writings since the nineteenth century and in a variety of countries, that small numbers of immigrants need spatial contiguity to maintain a „defensive" community in the face of societal antagonism and overt discrimination. (For reviews of this phenomenon, see Robinson, 1981; Schuleri-Hartje, 1982; and the chapter by Peach in this book.)

The elements of a theory of immigration have now been presented. The theory must have general applicability but be able to take national differences into account; it must recognize the global setting of migration and the role that local class antagonisms have developed as a result of these international economic trends; it must focus on processes, not on spatial patterns, and it must incorporate the interacting relationship between individuals and structures in the host society.

Immigrants in Contemporary European Cities

Because of their marginal position in the host societies, foreigners are strongly affected by the linked local, national and international economic trends and by government policy reacting to these trends. Because of their above-average concentration in central cities, foreigners are also affected by urban redevelopment and private renewal schemes. The segregation of foreigners in European cities must be considered against the background of their major immigration and return migration flows during the past decade since the end of the „rotation" era in 1973/74, as well as contemporaneous developments in housing. Since other papers deal in greater detail with the topic of immigration policy, this review is brief and highlights only major relevant trends (Hammer, 1985; Kritz, 1982; Leitner, Chapter 2 in this book).

As had been the case for both the United States and Britain, little opposition was voiced in Continental Europe against the importation of workers while economies were growing and labour needs in low-skilled industrial and service jobs had to be met from abroad. In most European countries, opposition was even more muted than might be expected because the public expected labour immigration to be temporary, tied exclusively to the labour contract. Switzerland, with its long history of labour — residence contracts for Italian workers, was seen as a model to emulate (White, 1985). Non-employment issues such as education, health service provision and, particularly, housing were hardly discussed as long as most immigrants were single men or married men without their dependents, living predominantly in hostels provided by the employer or in rooms rented on the private market. Without increasingly permanent settlement of foreigner families in the 1970s, native resentment would probably have occurred anyway as a result of the job pressures during the economic stagnation after 1973 and, particularly, during the deep recession of 1981–1983. Resentment in the workplace was increased by resentment in the neighborhoods as foreigner families began to compete with the native working-class for cheap housing and began to use social services, previously the exclusive domain of the native population. The shift in the foreigner composition can clearly be seen in all European destinations so that France, with 4 million foreigners in 1974 of which 1.81 million were workers, had 4.1 million foreigners in 1981, of which only 1.6 million were workers (Mühlgassner, 1984). Similarly, in West Germany, the proportion of workers in the foreigner population dropped from 70.8 percent in 1970 to 50.8 percent in 1981. The most recent data available for the six major destination nations are shown in Table 1.

TABLE 1: Foreigners in Six European Countries (in 1000's)

	ORIGINS	MAJOR DESTINATIONS					
Total	Nationality	W.Germany	France	Belgium	Netherlands	Switzerland	Sweden
823.6	Algeria	6.1	805.4	10.8	0.7	–	0.6
734.0	Morocco	41.7	492.7	105.1	93.1	–	1.4
249.0	Tunisia	25.6	212.9	6.7	2.8	–	1.0
743.5	Spain	158.8	395.3	58.3	23.7	104.2	3.2
1078.3	Portugal	172.1	866.6	10.5	9.4	19.7	–
785.6	Yugoslavia	600.3	68.3	5.2	14.1	58.9	38.8
344.0	Greece	287.1	8.7	21.2	4.1	9.1	13.8
1840.4	Turkey	1425.8	135.0	63.6	148.0	48.5	19.5
1696.1	Italy	545.1	441.0	279.7	21.0	404.8	4.5
3430.1	Other	1101.0	1133.6	317.5	203.3	343.5	331.2
11624.6	Total	4363.6	4459.5	878.6	520.2	988.7	414.0
		(1984)	(1982)	(1981)	(1982)	(1984)	(1981)

Sources: West Germany – *Wirtschaft und Statistik,* March and September 1985: France – *Hommes et Migrations* October, 1983; Belgium-*Annuaire de la Statistique* 1985: Switzerland; White, 1985: Netherlands-van Amersfoort *et al* 1984: and Sweden-Salt, 1985. Data for Austria are not presented because of the lack of reliable estimates of the nationalities of the 291,000 foreigners in that country.

It was clear by the late 1970s that the recession of the 1973–75 period and the oncoming recession that lasted to the mid 1980s were not only a result of a temporary hiccup in economic growth but were also influenced by a deeper and more important trend, the sectional shift in employment in European countries. The movement of manufacturing employment to the periphery and semiperiphery had been underway for decades but the steep decline in employment in traditional industries, such as steel, shipbuilding, textiles and other clothing, and in the coal industry, made in clear that longterm structural shifts in the economies of many European city-regions had taken place. The negative impacts of these shifts fell disproportionately on the native and foreigner working-class. As unemployment rose to post-war records, pressure began on the governments to reduce excess labour by ending immigration and to encourage return home. In some countries, notably France and the United States, the traditional defenders of the working-class, the labour unions, abandoned their immigrant constraints in order to protect the interests of the native majority. Politicians and parties offering the simple solution of "getting rid" of foreigners received surprising support in working-class districts, near districts with large numbers of foreigners, and in which left-wing parties have traditionally drawn their largest support. (See the chapter by Ogden in this book on support for the National Front in France.)

By 1982, all immigrant countries in Europe, including Britain, had adopted a three-pronged policy of immigration. First, severe restrictions against further immigration were put into place, including a reduction in the age of majority to a lowered limit (usually 16) beyond which age, children could not join their parents in the host country; restrictions on the admission of foreigner wives; a near total ban on the issuance of new work permits, and a stronger enforcement against illegal entry, both at the border crossings and by spot checks in the cities. Second, recognizing both the economic need for immigrant labour in the long term and the impossibility of persuading foreigners to leave short of forced removal, governments in Western Europe have debated and, in some cases, introduced legislation to ease the integration into the host society. Attention has been paid, in particular, in the second generation of foreigner children, either born in Europe or who arrived at a very early age. Liberal policies designed to encourage equal opportunity in education, training, social services and housing were introduced by the Mitterand government in France in 1981 and are being considered elsewhere (de Ley, 1983; *Economist*, Nov. 2, 1985). In Britain, the issue of minority policy has, unfortunately, become conflated with innercity policy to the determinent of both (Rex, 1981). In West Germany, the conservative-liberal coalition has not yet finalized its immigration policy despite widespread political interest in the topic and prolonged debate on the question. (See Leitner, Chap. 2 in this book.) Third, to ease the confrontation with the native working-class over the shortage of jobs and to reduce social tensions as well as future integration costs, governments are considering inducements to foreign workers to go back to their origin countries and to take their families with them. Unlike Switzerland where workers are forced to leave upon the expiration of their labour contract, both France and West Germany have opted for financial inducements. A 1985 return programme in France persuaded only 2,000 unemployed foreigners to leave *(Economist,* Nov. 2, 1985). An earlier effort in France in 1977 was unsuccessful. Only 2400 workers applied for the 10,000 French francs offered before the courts ruled it unconstitutional. A total of 45,000 immigrants left France, of which 40 percent were Portugese and, of the total workers who departed, only 13 percent were longtime residents in France. One-half had arrived in France between 1968 and 1972 and another 40 percent between 1963 and 1967. Most significantly, 41 percent had permanent residency rights and only 24 percent were unemployed when they left. It is not clear if the decision to accept the offer of "1 million centimes" was motivated solely by the policy or if the money provided on extra incentive to leave immediately for those who were contemplating return (Poinard, 1979). The most "successful" inducement policy was in West Germany in 1983–1984 when during the policy duration, an estimated 300,000 workers and their families took the 10,500 Deutsche marks offered by the government and left. In addition, most workers cashed their pensions and many were offered additional financial benefits from their employer. An unanticipated result of this national policy was dislocation effects in certain wards in some cities, such as Duisburg, where the rapid departure of a large proportion of the population has had a negative impact on the local infrastructure, both public and private.

The period of mass immigration into Western Europe is over. Estimates of the "pool of immigrants" in the home countries vary but the pool comprises no more than 20 percent of the numbers currently in Europe (Esser, 1982a; Mertins, 1983). Further immigration of family members will be balanced by return migrants so that changes in the foreigner numbers will be predominantly a result of their natural population increase in Europe. While foreigners comprised about 8 percent of the population of the European immigrant nations in the late 1970s, births to foreigners comprised over double that proportion, usually about 20–25 percent. Recent sharp drops in the foreigner birthrates have brought them significantly closer to the level of the native population. Thus, in Duisburg, the number of children born to Turkish women aged between 15 and 44 dropped from 195 per 1000 women in 1976 to 95 per 1000 in 1983; for Yugoslav women from 109 per 1000 to 50 per 1000 and for Italian women from 93 per 1000 to 50 per 1000. For the same years, the German birth rate was 32 per 1000 and 34 per 1000. Predictions by right-wing politicians that the native populations would be swamped by immigrant fertility are clearly both wrong and prejudicial.

The "great unknown" in the prognostications of the number of foreigners in Europe in the future is the strength of the wish to return to the origin countries. Numerous surveys, particularly in West Germany, have tried to estimate the proportions and generally have concluded that most foreigners will stay until at least the age of retirement. Lichtenberger (1984), based on her sample of Yugoslavs in Vienna, estimates the return migrants as 40 percent of the total. Esser (1982) in Duisburg estimates that 40 percent of his Turkish sample will stay while 50 percent will eventually leave. Korte (1980) estimates that 40 percent of the foreigners in the Federal Republic will stay permanently and a recent national survey by Marplan (1984) indicates that 30 percent of the foreigners will settle permanently in West Germany. Estimates of the ratio of foreigners to natives in the year 2000 for the European states vary widely and are of little use, given current uncertainty about the return migration plans of foreigners, government policy and the relative fertility of foreigners and native families. What is clear is that all European immigrant nations must expect to retain a large foreigner population who have all the characteristics of permanence and who have not yet indicated any noticeable movement from their marginal position as a "permanent underclass".

Housing and Social Changes in Continental European Cities

As the postwar immigrations, populations and economic trends evolved, related changes in the character of European metropolitan areas changed the face of Continental cities. Numerous researchers have remarked both on the individual character of European cities, a result of specific historical processes (Lichtenberger, 1976), and the differences between European and Anglo-Saxon, especially North American, cities (Burtenshaw, 1981). However, it is clear that these differences have narrowed over the past two decades leading Friedrichs (1982) to remark that the temporal lag between American and European urban developments had been reduced to 15 years. The stereotypical American experience of city population decline, suburban growth, spatial and social separation of majority and minority populations, central-city decay and renewal, and a decentralization of retail and service functions have been experienced in all Northern European cities to a greater or lesser extent. In this book, the question of the spatial separation of minority and majority populations is paramount.

The levels of spatial concentration of socio-economic and ethnic groups in North American and German cities are different but the gap between cities on either side of the Atlantic was gradually reduced from 1960 to the early 1970s and has probably continued to erode to the present (O'Loughlin, 1983). The period 1960–1975 was marked by a population shift to suburban areas from German cities. It was led by the middle class whose search for homes with gardens was accomodated in developments beyond the city limits (Friedrich, 1982). They were not fleeing the city; their family-style needs could only be accomodated in suburban areas. Working-class families, with or without children, could not afford the skyrocketing prices of suburban homes. The average apartment price in Germany rose from 28300 DM in 1960 to 75920 DM in 1972 and to 170,000 DM in 1980 (Neef, 1981). Within cities, large areas near the centres continued to be the preserves of the middle and upper-classes so that urban differentation was overall less marked than in Anglo-Saxon cities (O'Loughlin and Glebe, 1980). In Paris, the city centre became increasingly the preserve of the rich as prices for apartments in attractive neighborhoods increased beyond the range of all but the wealthy and the poor forced out of "gentrified" neighborhoods (Bentham and Mosely, 1980; Scargill, 1983; White, in this book). Large housing estates were built in demarcated suburban zones to accommodate the displaced urban groups and the growing immigrant populations. Growing spatial separation between the social classes were a result of these processes in both France and Germany, reflecting a trend seen earlier in North American and British cities. By 1980, city populations had shrunk to smaller fractions of the metropolitan populations than was the case in some American cities.

As European cities "Americanized" in the 1960s and 1970s, the hand of government policies and agencies in directing and, in some cases, causing the trends became apparent. As noted by many researchers, the state, (national and local) is usually more influential in directing urban change in Europe through such devices as strict zoning laws, state-supported industrial strategy, public housing and preservation policies. In this introduction, we will concentrate on housing policy as the most important state intervention in the location and segregation of foreigners in European cities. By direct allocation of families to specific homes and by a mortgage subsidy policy through tax deductions for the middle class, the state has directed the urban social processes producing present spatial patterns. If we consider the three general sectors of owner, renter and public housing, the most important

change in most European countries is the sharp drop in the number of renter-oc-
cupied homes, matching the rise in the owner-occupied sector, and the decline in
the 1970s of the number of newly constructed public housing flats. By 1984, the
number of privately-rented dwellings as a proportion of all dwellings was down to
62 percent in Switzerland, 48 percent in the Netherlands, 42 percent in West-Germany, 38 percent in Italy, 27 percent in Sweden, 18 percent in France and only
11 percent in Britain. (The comparative figures for Canada and the U.S. were 39
and 36 percent, respectively.) *(Economist,* Jan. 12, 1985, p. 21).

The reasons behind the shift were the same everywhere although the specific
laws and housing markets operating in each state led to different emphases of home
ownership, from condominiums to single-family detached homes. Some researchers
see the growing "privatization" of housing, termed the recommodification process,
as a result of the general effort by governments in capitalist nations, particularly in
conservative administrations, to reduce the role of the state in society (Martens,
1985, Harloe and Martens, 1985). In Britain, the U.S., Canada and West Germany,
the state has been trying to encourage homeownership through sales of public
housing and easing of rent controls. This has resulted in skyrocketing rents and
displacement and continued subsidy of middle and upperclass purchases of larger
and more expensive homes through mortgage interest deductions on taxes. In many
cities, the authorities have avoided enforcement of eviction laws as building change
from renter to owner-occupied as a result of modernization. (For a review of this
literature in various states, see Neef, 1981; Ipsen and Mussel, 1981; Duclaud-Williams, 1978; Castells, 1977; Fincher, 1984; Adams, 1984; van Weesep, 1984). Harloe (1981) states that the reasons behind the consistent state policy of encouraging
home ownership are threefold namely, to promote adherence to the state, to
promote conservatism (owner-occupiers are generally more conservative than
renters), and to wean the working-class away from class-based politics. Others stress
the general economic importance of the housing sector in capitalist societies and
the deep and extensive interplay of market forces involved in housing supply
(Johnston, 1980).

As states are encouraging home ownership, they have been less willing to build
public housing. One expressed reason for the sharp decline since 1970 in the number of public housing units completed (from 195,000 in 1971 to 99,000 in 1982 in
the Federal Republic) *(Wirtschaft und Statistik,* 1984) has been the end of the post-
war housing crisis. In 1978, the German housing crisis was officially declared over
as the supply of new units matched the number of new households. But, as numerous commentators have remarked (see for example, Kreibich, 1982), this general
matching conceals huge inequities because the supply of cheap and adequate housing remains extremely tight in German cities. Not only did the overall number of
public housing units drop but the cost of the newer, better-equipped social housing
units soared so that by the late 1970s, many of the working class were priced out of
the housing sector that was originally designed to meet their needs and are, as a
result, often forced to remain in the private-rented housing sector. In the Netherlands (Mik, 1983), France (Scargill, 1983), West Germany (Neef, 1981), and Britain
(Taylor and Hadfield, 1982) public housing projects could be categorized on the

basis of rent, and age and quality of the home by the 1970s. High-rise buildings, smaller and poorly-equipped flats, and innercity projects became the refuge of the poorest council-tenants, often "problem families" and, increasingly in Continental Europe, of foreigner households. The better estates became the exclusive domain of the wealthier working-class, who were able to afford higher rents and were knowledgeable about the allocation procedures, allowing them to meet their housing wishes.

In other aspects of housing policy and urban developments, the state has also had direct involvement. As with public-housing supply and allocation and with the "recommodification of housing" generally, the consequences for the housing provision for foreigners are direct and help to understand fully the circumstances behind the location and concentration of foreigners in European cities. As part of the general shift from the renter- and council-housing to owner-occupied, a wave of condominium conversions from private-rental flats has moved through European cities over the past 15 years (van Weesep, 1984). This process is often seen as gentrification of blighted inner-cities but, in addition, to the restoration and improvement of older dilapidated buildings, the trend toward condominiums has also shifted moderate and expensive rental flats into the owner-occupied sector. The trend appears to be most apparent in large cities with growing employment, especially in the rental, governmental and service sectors in the traditional city centre. In Amsterdam, van Weesep (1984) documented the process of conversion in two areas and estimated that, in the city, 6.6 percent of the housing units had been converted to condominiums during the 1970s. In London, Hamnett (1983) documents a similar rate of conversion to luxury flats. Large cities with extensive service sectors tend to have large foreigner populations so that condominium conversions have had a greater impact on foreigner populations than the average rate of conversions would suggest.

The reasons for condominium conversion on the demand side are easy to see, with clear financial benefits accorded to home ownership, especially in a period of high inflation such as the 1970s. Smaller families and couples, both those working and those without children, made condominium living possible, even desirable. On the supply side, a pool of flats built since 1900 and under rent control were evident candidates for conversion since the building owners could not turn a profit on the properties and had allowed the buildings to deteriorate over the years. Despite some government policies reducing the number of rent-controlled flats [in France, from 6 million in 1948 to 3.3 million in 1966 and 1.1 million in 1975 (Duclaud-Williams, 1978)], the 1900—1940 zones of housing in many cities became zones of speculation, squatting, and flight by those who could afford to move. The result was that this zone became the refuge of poor families and individuals. Even though most tenants of rent-controlled buildings are protected against rent increases and eviction, numerous surveys have documented the lack of knowledge by foreigners of their rights and the ease with which they can be removed (Petri, 1984; Kreibich, 1982; Berlin Regierung, 1980; Schuleri-Hartje, 1982). "Condomania", while retaining part of the middle class in the city to the delight of public officials, has had an adverse effect on the weaker segments of society, particular in the removal of affordable rental housing from an already restricted supply.

A final element of state and planning policy, related to condominum conversions, has been the designation and renovation of dilapidated innercity areas. The 1950s and 1960s in Europe were characterized by large-scale clearing projects of older housing and the relocation of poor families to large public-housing projects, frequently on the edge of the built-up area (Burtenshaw, 1981). A scaling-down of renovation to a block by block and house by house basis in the 1970s has continued the removal of cheap rental flats from the private market and, as documented by Holzner (1982) and Hoffmeyer-Zlotnik (1982) for Kreuzberg in West-Berlin, and by Castells (1977) for Paris, the impact on foreigner families has been dramatic and, effectively, led to their departure and replacement by native families. A consideration of foreigner settlement and relocation in European cities that ignores contemporaneous urban housing processes risks the criticism that only description of the surface manifestations is being offered. A true explanation of the apparently simple and general patterns (see White, 1984 for an overview for a large number of Continental European cities) demands analysis of the relationships between housing and population changes.

Immigrant Settlement and Relocation in European Cities

Since many of the chapters in this book discuss the settlement of foreigners in cities in different European states, it is not necessary to summarize this work. A good review of the literature is provided in Paul White's (1984) book on the West European city and by Peach in Chapter 4 of this book. For purposes of this introduction, I will concentrate on four important aspects of foreigner settlement to provide a general background for the specific studies provided later in this book. The relative segregation of foreigners, their geographic distribution within cities, their relocation through intraurban migration and explanatory models of foreigner settlement are briefly reviewed in this section. Since the focus in this introduction is the explanation of foreigner settlement rather than description of its pattern, the emphasis will be on explanatory models. Unfortunately, a gap has developed in research on foreigners in European cities between France and other nations. While we have detailed geographical and longitudinal accounts of foreigner settlement in a large sample of cities in West Germany, Switzerland, Austria, the Netherlands and Belgium, the few studies completed for France have been very cursory and usually report only the general geographic distribution of foreigner groups by arrondissment or quartier (Jones and Johnston, 1985 is an exception). This difference probably reflects not only varied access to data but also the geographic tradition in each country and the extent to which the influence of the Anglo-Saxon ecological research tradition has penetrated the geographic community of each nation.

Repeated application of segregation, concentration and isolation indices to data on foreigner distribution in European cities has shown a consistent pattern of low to moderate segregation. By British or American standards (Peach, Robinson and

Smidt, 1981), foreigners in Vienna (Leitner, 1983; Lichtenberger, 1984), Düsseldorf and Duisburg (Glebe, 1984; O'Loughlin and Glebe, 1984b); Ludwigshafen (Gans, 1984), Brussels (de Lannoy, 1976), Nürnberg (Jones, 1983), Rotterdam (Mik, 1983); Amsterdam (van Ammersfoot, 1981); Utrecht (van Hoorn, 1984) Stuttgart, Bremen and Frankfurt (O'Loughlin, 1980); Frankfurt (Helmert, 1982) and Zürich (Arend, 1982) are not very segregated spatially. It is almost impossible to state precisely the relative degree of segregation between cities because of wide variations in the spatial units on which the indices are calculated, a factor which has a demonstrated effect on the resulting indices. It may be conservatively estimated that, controlling for scale, the segregation of the main foreigner groups in cities in the German-speaking and Benelux countries is less than block segregation in British or American cities. More significantly, residential segregation is increasing very slowly and is even declining in some cities as foreigners return home or move out of their areas of settlement (Lichtenberger, 1984). An important piece of evidence for the notion that housing considerations are the most important determinant of foreigner settlement is the demonstration that, while ward and tract segregation levels are low, the picture shifts dramatically when individual apartment buildings are considered. At this most intimate of all spatial scales, the foreigner segregation scores (IDs close to 90 and sometimes above) indicate near total foreigner separation (O'Loughlin and Glebe, 1984b). We are therefore faced with the prospect of identifying the causal factor(s) which produce(s) near-totally segregated houses but moderate desegration at the ward and neighbourhood scales. Since wards are clusters of houses, the characteristics of individual houses need to be examined to determine why certain houses contain foreigners and others do not. To my knowledge, this approach has not been systematically taken although Lichtenberger (1984) discusses the importance of individual house structure and tenure in her examination of the changing settlement pattern of Yugoslav workers in Vienna.

The second geographic aspect of foreigner settlement concerns their spatial distribution. White (1984), reviewing numerous descriptive studies, concludes that three locations in cities reappear consistently as foreigner concentrations. Most foreigners live in the oldest parts of European cities, in the zones of rental flats built between 1870 and 1940. These apartments are usually subject to rent control and, recently, the scene of condominium conversions, urban renewal and improvement, clearances and house squatting. The most famous foreigner concentrations, such as Kreuzberg in Berlin and La Cage in Marseille, are found in these areas. The second area of concentration reflects the recruitment process. Industrial housing estates have disproportionate numbers of foreigners, especially in these countries where the employer had to provide housing as a condition of residency. Factory housing, such as in Hüttenheim in Duisburg, now provides accommodation for foreigners, since most workers moved out of hostels after family reunification. The importance of factory housing in the Ruhr, as documented by Hottes and Pötke (1977), was rarely matched elsewhere. Thirdly, foreigners also live near industrial zones and on the edge of cities, though they may have no connections with the factory, because of the availability of cheap rental accommodation. These zones are usually located near the city centre or along major transport arteries out of the city.

This third type of foreigner settlement seems to be most important in France and reflects the location of massive public housing projects in the 1950s and 1960s, which are now frequently abandoned by those who can afford to get out. The largest HLM projects (Habitations de loyers moderes) were sited on the cheapest land, on the rural periphery and far from the city centre. Paris, in particular, seems to have experienced the most dramatic increase in the middle class in the city so that the poor population has been displaced to the suburban communes and, frequently, to the HLMs (Bentham and Mosely, 1980; Scargill, 1983). Therefore, contrary to the dominant American models, the outer fringes of the French urban agglomerations have frequently a higher percentage of foreigners than the city itself. White (1984, p. 123) indicates that Lyon had a foreigner proportion of 9.9 percent in 1975 while its suburbs had 13.1 percent and Zürich, 17.5 percent foreigner in 1970, had fewer foreigners proportionately than its surrounding communes (21.1 percent). While the patterns of settlement are generally consistent, their explanation is still incomplete.

Studies of the relocation of foreigners in urban areas has been hindered by lack of adequate data. Most studies have been completed using survey data (Berlin Regierung, 1980) or household registration data (O'Loughlin and Glebe, 1984a). French cities once again are a major gap in our knowledge of the secondary migration of foreigners from the point of initial urban settlement. The question lies at the core of a Burgess-like "invasion-success" models but we do not have adequate material to accept or reject this model for French cities. For German cities, it has been shown that foreigners move more often than Germans, more shorter distances, are slightly more restrictive in the movement fields, frequently move to more segregated blocks after leaving their initial urban home, but that clear and predictable segmented migration fields between Germans and foreigners do not exist on a par with the dual housing and migration systems of American cities (O'Loughlin and Glebe, 1984a; Gans, 1984). On the sociological side, surveys of migrants in German cities (Schuleri-Hartje, 1982; Ipsen, 1981; Berlin, Regierender Bürgermeister, 1980; Esser, 1982a) and in Vienna (Leitner, 1983; Lichtenberger, 1984) have stressed the severe constraints on the housing movements of foreigners, subject as they are to frequent forced relocation, income limitations, family size requirements and general discrimination.

The use of aggregate models in explaining the distribution and segregation of foreigners in European cities has been severely hampered by both theoretical and data considerations. On the theoretical side, the aggregate models which derive from an ecological view of city structure, that is, urban ecological structure determines the location of foreigners, clearly neglect two major sets of explanatory considerations. The characteristics of the foreigners themselves except for nationality, are ignored. Heterogeneity of social status, information sources, assimilation level and return orientation, all of which might be expected to modify the general area characteristics-foreigner percentage relationship, are overlooked (O'Loughlin and Glebe, 1981; Gans, 1983; Weber-Klein, 1980; White, 1984). The data are another major problem since geographers invariably use census data, which not only vary in quality, but are also not generally available at the appropriate scale. Even if researchers use the smallest scale generally available, such as the "quartier" in France, the degree of heterogeneity in foreigner settlement within even such a small area confounds the ecological analysis. As noted by Leitner (1982, p. 63) "an ecological analysis on the scale of census tract is frequently too coarse to provide us with an accurate picture of local conditions affecting the infiltration of migrant workers". Clearly an ecological relationship will be established because foreigners are generally found in areas of poor-quality housing and low social-status but the precise level and direction of relationship cannot be established in the absence of appropriate variables and data at the proper scale of analysis.

The best examples of ecological explanatory models using survey data are found in Esser (1981, 1982b) and Leitner (1983). Both studies clearly are set within an assimilationist framework drawing heavily on American sociological writings for theory and methodology. They sought to incorporate both personal attributes of the foreigners and ecological urban characteristics in comprehensive path models. In each case, the level of assimilation of the individual foreigners, measured by degree of residential segregation (Leitner) and language acquisition, social and occupational status, and inter-ethnic contacts (Esser), is the factor to be explained. Both researchers use as independent variables a mixture of personal (educational level, urban or rural origin, jobs skills in home country, level of interethnic contacts at home and work, ethnic identification, language ability, etc.) and ecological (nature of neighborhood in social and housing status, etc.) variables. Length of stay in the host country appears to be the most important factor in determining integration levels since it is strongly related to language acquisition and, from that, to inter-ethnic contacts with members of the host society and social integration. Most importantly, Esser (1981) found no significant relationships between length of stay of migrants in Köln and occupational status, suggesting that occupational mobility is independent of social integration and providing evidence of the specific sectoral role that foreign workers play in the German economy. Furthermore, Esser (1982b) directly and Leitner (1983) indirectly suggest that personal factors, expecially the level of formal schooling, length of stay in host country and age when entered, are more important than contextual factors (ethnic concentration in neighborhood and quality of housing) in the adaption and assimilation of immigrants in Northern European societies.

This section has reviewed some of the main findings of the past decade on the location, distribution, segregation and relocation of foreigners in European cities. Most geographic studies have derived their methodology and theoretical impetus from American ecological studies of immigrants and have concentrated on empirical identification of foreigner settlement. We can conclude that for most European cities, excepting those in France, we are informed about the patterns of foreigner settlement and their variation from city to city as a result of the different historical develpoment of each place. What is clear is that we still lack a comprehensive theory of foreigner intraurban settlement.

Questions for Further Research[2]

If we return to the questions listed at the beginning of this introduction we may suggest that some important issues in the study of foreigner settlement in Continental European cities have not been examined. As will be evident from this introduction and from the chapter by Peach in this book, most attention by geographers has focussed on mapping the spatial distribution of foreigners, calculating their residential segregation from the host population and almost as an afterthought, attempt to account for the distributions and segregation. The most detailed and numerous studies are for cities in countries with population registration systems and accessible intercensal data. France, in particular, poses a large question when trying to generalize to a continental scale from studies in West Germany, the Netherlands, and Austria.

When we try to understand the level of residential segregation of foreigners, there seems to be general agreement that forcing the explanation into a choice-constraint dichotomy is inappropriate and an intellectual cul-de-sac [See Peach in this book and Brown (1981)]. It is evident that elements of both explanations are present, with the importance of each varying from group to group, from society to society, and even from household to household. Numerous surveys have documented the importance of families, friends and fellow-countrymen in helping newcomers to adjust to life in the new society and other studies have provided details of the constraints of housing, employment, income, law and immigration policy that influence the particular character and pattern of foreign settlement in each city. As discussed in more detail in Chapter 3 of this book, Giddens' structurationist perspective, allowing consideration of individual characteristics and preferences as well as structural elements such as housing submarkets, allocation mechanisms and qualification rules, would appear to offer the best prospect for movement out of the intellectual cul-de-sac that this discussion has entered. Of course, adoption of such a perspective requires detailed survey analysis, an approach that has been avoided by geographers in the past. Alternatives to aggregate data analysis in the study of foreigners and especially their community life, are illustrated in this book in the chapter by White on Paris and by the survey results on Turks in Zürich by Evrensel and on Yugoslavs in Vienna by Lichtenberger and Fassmann. The studies on Vienna and Zürich demonstrative the value of study of a special group in the context of their marginal position in the economic and social life of the host society. Methodologies such as the examination of life histories, diaries, participation-observation, detailed questionnaires on social lifestyles and social interaction mapping offer fruitful methods for further research. The linguistic requirements for these detailed local studies are difficult to meet in practise and, as a result, few geographers have tried to emulate Hoffmeyer-Zlotnick's (1977) detailed local study on Kreuzberg in West Berlin. To succeed in anything like a structurationist study, re-

---

2 This section is developed from the comments made in the concluding discussion at the Symposium "Foreign Minorities in Continental European Cities" at the Universität Düsseldorf, March 20–22, 1985. Thanks are extended to the participants in this useful discussion.

searchers must leave the high ground of aggregate data analysis and descend to the social world of the immigrant communities.

In Anglo-Saxon research on immigrant and minority communities, the relationship between spatial segregation and social isolation has been an important research topic since first formulated by Park (Peach, 1975a). While sociologists and social psychologists have examined the social isolation of foreigners in neighbourhoods, in the workplace and in retail behaviour, geographers have concentrated on spatial segregation at a variety of scales. The two approaches have rarely come together in one work, although the chapters in Friedrich's (1982) book attempt to link the two processes. The results are not convincing since the general model adopted, the invasion-succession model, is not appropriate for use in the particular German context. Research designs for the kind of community-based study advocated here are available in David Ley's (1974) study of an innercity community in Philadelphia. In cooperative research efforts to document the level of adaptation or integration of foreigners into host societies, the contribution that geographers could most usefully make, lies in the study of this important overlap between spatial and social isolation.

An unfortunate reliance on the inappropriate term "ghetto" to describe the relative concentration of foreigners in certain urban neighbourhoods in the popular media has sidetracked the discussion of positive aspects of ethnic concentration. If, for example, the terms "ethnic neighbourhood" or "ethnic community" were substituted for ghetto, the discussion would be brought to a more useful level. The semantics are clearly tied to national policy. Since most destination nations in Europe do not see themselves as countries of permanent immigration, the use of the term "ghetto". with its perjorative overtones, distorts the debate. It allows opponents of permanent settlement of foreigners to point out the negative social aspects of settlement with connotations of separation, foreignness, irreconcilable differences with the host society and, from the American analogy, synonomity with slum conditions. If destination nations were to accept foreigners as permanent settlers, accepting that some will return to the origin countries but that most will stay, and that the immigrants have the right to live where they choose, there is no doubt that ethnic communities will develop, as the second generation of foreigners grows in numbers. In this respect the Continental European experience will repeat that of countries with a longer history of immigration such as Canada, the United States, Israel, Australia and Britain. Ethnic neighbourhoods cannot be classed as good or bad: they are an expected feature of urban settlement by immigrants and only slowly dissolve (Kantrowitz, 1981). Ethnic neighbourhoods offer a host of valuable services to newcomers and provide critical links to other members of the group as well as a protective device against the exclusionary tactics of the host society. Clearly, forced ethnic communities are undesirable but the many positive features of ethnic communities have rarely been discussed or examined in detail in the Continental European nations. Reaearchers and policy-makers have been too concerned to prevent "ghettoes" and they have failed to ask immigrants about their preferred style of neighbourhood and the type and variety of services that they need. A correction of this imbalance is long past due.

It is worth restating that we should not isolate the study of immigrant communities from the host society in which they find themselves. In Kesteloot's study of foreigners in Belgium in this book and from O'Loughlin's account in Chapter 3, the use of a structuralist perspective for studying foreigner settlement, though rare, is not without promise. The roles and positions of foreigners in European nations, that of a marginal group easily victimized in employment and housing, must be accorded adequate attention in any study of their settlement in metropolitan areas. The danger with the structuralist approach, as pointed out in Chapter 3, is that it can become too deterministic. The evidence from conflicts between native and foreign members of the working-class should be cause enough for a revision of the purely economic explanation. An interesting topic directly related to this issue is the question of social movements, particularly within foreigner communities or in those inner-city or industrial areas where foreigners are concentrated. Castell's (1983) recent comparative work offers a model for those interested in taking up the structuralist option, containing as it does a focus on actors, ideas and social movements operating to redefine urban life and character.

In attempting cross-national research, one of two options can be chosen. The preferred option is to standardize subject matter, hypotheses, research questions, and data across nations. It is rarely attempted because of the great variety imposed by international boundaries on data. The alternative, usually forced on those who wish to engage in cross-national research, is to conduct individual studies in the different countries and to compare results in the hope that some comparative conclusions can be drawn. This book is an example of the second approach and the pritfalls of the method will be evident from a reading of all the individual chapters. It is virtually impossible to impose the same research design on researchers in a variety of national settings. Obviously, the editors hope that the individual chapters are not only interesting and important for what they tell us about specific circumstances but, also, for what they offer to those interested in making comparisons and contrasts between nations. Foner's (1979) work on Jamaicans in New York and London and Brettell's (1981) study of Portugese communities in Toronto and Paris are two rare comparative works. Likewise, we could examine the experiences of the wide dispersal of some groups across Continental Europe; Yugoslavs, Italians and Spaniards suggest themselves as candidates for a controlled cross-national study of adaptation and settlement. The difficulties of obtaining the necessary data and of controlling the varied character of the migrants themselves are daunting. A more modest effort, such as the vareful selection of a few destination cities, would provide a guide to the relative value of a controlled comparative study. While the notion is intriguing, the difficulties facing the prospective researcher have discouraged all but the brave few.

After two decades of geographic research on foreigner settlement in Northern European cities, we have accumulated a mass of detail on aggregate patterns but little in the way of explanation. Part of the reason can be attributed to traditional geographic methods which have relied on descriptive mapping techniques and on readily available data sets. Our theoretical weaknesses are clearly visible in our inability to formulate a general theory of migration that will stand up to close empirical scrutiny in a variety of national settings. Recent methodological develop-ments in geography have led to a questioning of accepted research practices and to the introduction of structural approaches to examine both the general socio-eco-nomic role of foreigners and their subsequent intraurban locational arrangement. It is only through further theory-based research and attention to the neglected topics, some of which have been briefly mentioned in this section, that geographers will make valuable contributions to the study of one of the most important politi-cal and social issues in contemporary Europe.

IMMIGRATION AND SEGREGATION IN WESTERN EUROPE SINCE 1945

CERI PEACH (OXFORD)

The purpose of this chapter is to summarise the literature on international migration in Western Europe since 1945 and to examine the extent to which segregation has developed in West European cities. It is divided into three sections: (1) a discussion of the development of migration; (2) an examination of the degree of segregation present in different European cities; (3) a summary and conclusion with a discussion of how these findings relate to the Anglo-American tradition of segregation/Assimilation models.

The area covered comprises France, the Federal Republic of Germany, Great Britain, the Benelux countries, Switzerland and Austria. Attention is concentrated on the Federal Republic, France and Great Britain and some original findings on the latter country are presented. Other chapters in this book deal in detail with the situation in the Netherlands, Belgium, Austria and Switzerland; because of the constraints of space no detailed attention is paid in this chapter to these important cases.

PART 1

IMMIGRATION

Since 1945, Western Europe has experienced international transfers of over 30 million people. These movements have taken place in four overlapping population movements: (1) the return movement of nationals displaced by colonial independence movements or by the over-running of previously national territory; (2) the movement of refugees displaced by war or by political persecution; (3) the movement of elite technocratic or simply rich groups as a result of the greater internationalisation of institutions and trade; (4) the movement of a new working class into metropolitan countries. Categories (2) and (3) are numerically rather small, while categories (1) and (2) each comprise about 15 million people.

Although the main focus of the chapter is on worker migration, this must be seen in the context of two historical processes. The first is the collapse of West European colonial expansion overseas and German expansion in Eastern Europe. This led to the retreat to their metropolitan cores of many expatriates. The second process is the post war European economic re-birth which led to a huge demand for labout articulated through core/periphery relationships. Labour was drawn into the metropolitan cores from an ever-expanding geographical range. France penetrated southwards into Italy, the Iberian peninsula, the Maghreb and even sub-

Saharan Africa. Germany penetrated south and south-eastwards: Italy, Yugoslavia, Greece and, above all, Turkey. In Britain, France and the Netherlands the ambiguous citizenship of former colonial peoples allowed them uncontrolled entry to their former colonial powers so that their arrival was seen as adventitious rather than related to labour demands. In Germany, Switzerland and Austria the links between labour demand and migration were much more clearly defined.

Thus the movement into Europe can largely be divided into two groups, the expellees and the immigrants; they met with very diverging fates. While the expellees were socially accepted and welcomed, despite the economic costs of integration, the immigrants have been socially rejected, despite the economic benefits which they brought. While the expellees were absorbed into the metropolitan countries, the new immigrants produced a colonisation of the cities of the former colonising powers. With time an increasing proportion of the immigration has come from non-European sources. There has been, in particular, an Islamicization of the immigrant populations. Although the immigrants form a small proportion of the total populations, they are notably concentrated geographically in large urban areas which have been losing population. Their male predominance indicates that they have significant potential for growth through family reunification and their young age structures and higher fertility indicates that they contribute a larger proportion of natural increase than their overall proportion of the population of the metropolitan countries would suggest.

Following the growth of non-European immigration into Europe, academic research into the distribution and concentration of immigrants in European cities has also expanded. Initially these researches proceeded in an insular fashion. They tended to be country-specific with little integration into the comparative literature. They lay outside the mainstream of the spatial analysis of social processes developed by Duncan and Duncan (1957), Duncan and Lieberson (1959), Lieberson, the Taeubers (1965) and Kantrowitz (1969) and reviewed by Peach (1975a). Basically, this literature argued that there was a direct relationship between the degree of urban ethnic spatial segregation and the degree of assimilation of that group into the host society. Whatever the limitations of this mainstream, it had the overwhelming merit of producing cumulative social science. It is only in recent years that larger scale efforts have been made to link up the European experiences with each other and with the Anglo-American literature. Paul White's (1984) work was a major step in the direction of synthesis; Jürgen Friedrichs has produced (198 (1982) a comparative perspective; Elisabeth Lichtenberger's (1984) book contains some linkage into the Anglo-American literature as does the work by Helga Leitner (1983). Van Amersfoort and Cortie (1973) pioneered the linkage of the Dutch experience to the mainstream literature and De Lannoy (1975) did the same for the Belgian. O'Loughlin (1980) together with Glebe (1981, 1984a, 1984b) and Gans (1984) have not only linked the literature on German cities to the mainstream, but in their use of new techniques, such as P*, path analysis and entropy analysis have put it at the forefront of the main tradition. Despite a number of individual efforts (Jones, A.M., 1980, 1981; Ogden 1977) the literature on France has continued in a rather insular fashion with little in the methodological approach to tie it to the

Anglo-American literature. This is a great loss because it becomes difficult to integrate extraordinarily detailed pieces of work such as Simon's (1979), dealing with the totality of the Tunisian migratory experience in Tunis and in France, into the rest of the literature.

However, if the literature is being linked together into a single tradition, the experience of immigration and of settlement in European cities shows substantial differences as well as similarities not only with the United States, but with each other. These differences relate to the ethnic groups involved, the distance travelled, the degree of acceptance and permanence of the settlement. Not least, there are substantial difficulties with the data. For example, there are differences of half a million in the estimates of foreign population in France produced by two Ministries (Lebon, 1984,8).

In summary, there is a kind of mainstream of Anglo-American literature on segregation in cities. The European literature has tended to form small isolated inland lakes which are now flowing over and linking up to the mainstream. The purpose of this book ist to strengthen the channels which are being cut. At the same time, the energy of the new literature is producing changes in the direction of the mainstream; there has been a broadening of statistical approaches and a questioning of the assumptions of the relationship between social and geographic distance. We now turn to an examination of the main immigration categories.

(1) RETURN MOVEMENT OF NATIONALS

Belgium, Britain, France, Germany, the Netherlands and Portugal have all experienced return movements of their nationals from abroad since 1945. Although these movements were, in some cases, of very considerable magnitude and concentrated into short time scales, they were nevertheless the movements which seem to have caused the least problems of adjustment and assimilation. On the whole those returned populations contain the totality of society and have the same cross-section of ages and sex balance as the metropolitan population rather than the age and sex selective characteristics of other immigrants.

Germany experienced the most sizeable of these migrations. The Federal German census of 1961 showed just under 9 million people were dispalced there by Russian and Polish annexation of formerly German territory in Eastern Europe. In addition, the Federal Republic received about 3 million refugees, many of working arge, from the DDR before the construction of the Berlin Wall in 1961 (Statistisches Bundesamt, 1966, 22–23). The Federal Government paid the Polish government for the repatriation of Volksdeutsch remaining in that country. From 1968 to 1983 616,438 Aussiedler arrived (Statistisches Bundesamt, 1984, 84). These figures have to be seen in the context of the German total population of 56 million in 1961 and of 61 million in 1983. These very substantial numbers have been absorbed into the population of the Federal Republic with apparently very social resentment although there is some evidence that the contact fields of the latest Aussiedler may be rather restricted (Schwinges, 1980, 56).

The French experience of *pieds noirs* returnees was on a smaller scale than that of Germany, but much of it was concentrated into a very short time after Algerian independence from France in July, 1962. About 1 million non-Muslim French citizens returned to Metropolitan France from North Africa after Algerian independence. (Guillon, 1974, 654). The *pieds noirs* were notably concentrated in the Midi. Just under 50 per cent on the repatriates were found in the regions of Cote d'Azur, Rhone-Alpes, Languedoc and Midi-Pyrenees in 1968 (Guillon, 1974, 647; Brun, 1974, 676). However, although they had a southern regional concentration and made a significant impact on agriculture (Brun, 1974), in their urban distribution, particularly in Paris and the Paris region, they were notable for their dispersal (Guillon, 1974, 663). Thus, rather like the displaced Germans, they were absorbed into the population of the urban areas without producing any notable evidence of spatial segregation. They behaved, in fact, exactly as the social distance/physical distance models would suggest. Like the German expatriates, however, they remain an important political element as the chapter by Ogden in this volume demonstrates.

The Dutch experience of repatriation differed from the French and German situations in several ways. Whereas the German and French repatriated populations were essentially ethnically French or German for the most part, the 250,000 Dutch who returned from Indonesia in four waves between 1948 and 1958 (van Amersfoort, 1974, 86–87) were largely Eurasian (about 180,000 out of the total). Although this group was physically distinctive, its absorption into Dutch society seems to have been complete (van Amersfoort, 1974, 86). Of the Dutch cities, only The Hague has a substantial Eurasian population (van Amersfoort, 1982, 57). Groups such as the 12,500 Moluccans who came to the Netherlands at the same time, because they had allied themselves with the Dutch against the Indonesian independence movement, should be regarded as emigres or refugees rather than repatriates. Unlike the Indonesians, who blended into Dutch society; the Moluccans maintained a high degree of spatial separation.

The conclusion seems to be that the repatriation of the Indonesian population, although ethnically distinct from the rest of the Dutch population, fits into the model of German and French repatriation.

In Britain, although there has been a return population from its former Empire, it is not a significant population and has, on the whole vanished into the domestic scene. There are two main elements to this return population: (1) British-born in India under the Raj numbering at most 107,000 in 1961 and 1971 (Peach and Winchester, 1974, 391). The most notable characteristic of this group is not sociological but that they create complications in trying to interpret the characteristics of the Indian ethnic population. In particular, they may explain the low IDs of Indianborn population in London in 1961 and 1971. (2) The second group, the Old Commonwealth citizens, numbered 153,000 in 1981 (HMSO 1983, 2) Among young Australians and New Zealanders who come to London on world trips as part of the rites of passage, there does seem to be some evidence of spatial patterning. Earl's Court in London is sometimes referred to as 'Kangaroo Valley' but detailed investigation of Asutralian distribution is lacking. The Old Commonwealth population seems to be totally assimilated when it has been resident for any length of time.

I have not been able to locate any literature on returnees to Austria, Belgium or Portugal, all places where in different ways the return population must be quite significant.

(2) REFUGEE MOVEMENTS

This is a highly heterogeneous category, which apart from Austria, does not seem to be particularly numerous. In Britain in 1981, for example, there were 13,000 Vietnamese. More significant were the East African Asians who were expelled from Uganda in the early 1970s. There were 197,000 East African born persons in Britain in 1981, including 46,000 from Uganda. It is thought that the large majority of this East African born population was Asian. In terms of their political status, they were rather similar to the Indonesians who fled to the Netherlands, but unlike the Dutch who welcomed their citizens warmly, the East African Asians received a grudging welcome from the British government. East African Asians, on the other hand, were a well educated and enterprising group who seem to have made substantial economic progress since their arrival. Despite their refugee status on arrival, they are best considered as part of the worker migration to Britain.

(3) MIGRATION OF ELITES

Little research seems to have been done on the movement of foreign elite populations in Europe. O'Loughlin and Glebe (1984, 276–77) have commented briefly on the high degree of Japanese segregation in Düsseldorf. De Lannoy's work (1975) on the 1970 census in Brussels indicated a high degree of segregation for the high class American-born population (an IS of 61.3. using a fine areal unit averaging about 2,000 persons). The French (21.7), Dutch (26.4), Italians (34.9), British (38.6) and the Germans (45.11) showed lower degrees of segregation. De Lannoy attributed the high US figure to the recentness of the group's arrival.

(4) THE MOVEMENT OF THE NEW WORKING CLASS INTO METROPOLITAN AREAS

Very broadly, the international immigration into Europe can be divided into the period of very rapid but fluctuating growth and extending migration fields from 1945 to 1973/74 and the period of freeze, reflux, governmental controls and increasing family reunion in the metropolitan countries since the economic collapse, following the 1973/74 oil crisis. The literature, particularly on the first period is extensive (Castles and Kosack, 1973; Böhning, 1972; Kennedy-Brenner, 1979; Hall and Ogden, 1983; Mühlgassner, 1984). Given the limitations of space only the main features are reported here.

1945–1973

There were in 1983 about 15 million foreign immigrants living in the industrialised countries of northwest Europe. France and the Federal Republic of Germany dominated this distribution with over 4 million immigrants each. The numbers present in 1983 had remained roughly stable since 1973 although with some fluctuations in the ethnic and family composition of the groups concerned. The period from 1945 to 1973 witnessed a massive but irregular in crease in the number of immigrants as the European economies recovered from the devastation of the war. The recovery mainfested itself earliest in France and Britain with Germany acting as a source of migrants until the early 1950s. The German demand for foreign labour surged from just over 100,000 in 1958 to over 1 million in 1966; by 1968 Germany had overtaken France as the largest concentration of foreign labour in Europe (Mühlgassner, 1984, 73).

France set up a national immigration office (ONI) in 1945 and thereafter concluded a series of bilateral agreements with different governments. Between 1945 and 1951 agreements were made for the recruitment of Italian and German workers. Further agreements were made with Greece (1954), Spain (1961), Morocco, Tunisia, Portugal, Mali and Mauritania (1963), Senegal (1964), Yugoslavia and Turkey (1965), (Kennedy-Brenner, 1979, 22–3). These arrangements were in addition to the supply of Algerian labour which was freely available before Algerian independence in 1962 and which continued thereafter. Germany concluded bilateral agreements with Italy (1955), Spain and Greece (1960), Turkey (1961), Morocco (1963), Portugal (1964), Tunisia (1965) and Yugoslavia (1968), (Thomas, 1982, 181). Britain, having already recruited labour for her munitions works in Jamaica during the war, began recruiting labour on a small scale in Barbados in the early 1950s to work in London Transport, British Rail and in the hospital service. She also had some small-scale Italian labour to work in the coal mines and in the Bedforshire brick industry. In summary, France had started recruiting non-European labour in Algeria immediately after the war; Britain began attracting labour from the West Indies in the early 1950s and Germany began attracting non-European labour from the early 1960s.

NON-EUROPEAN LABOUR

In the early 1950s, although one cannot speak with great accuracy, the number of non-Europeans in Europe was probably less than 350,000. Judging from Castles and Kosack's figures, France had less than 200,000 at that time, largely Algerians (Castles and Kosack, 1973, 33); Britain had less than 50,000 (Peach, 1982, 23) and Germany a negligible number.

By the early 1960s there were probably about 1 million non-Europeans in Europe. France, again judging by Castles and Kosack's figures, had about 300,000 (Castles and Kosack, 1973, 33); Britain had about 500,000 (Peach, 1982, 23) the Netherlands, perhaps 250,000 (Amersfoort, 1974, 87).

By the early 1970s, there were probably about 4 million non-Europeans. France had 1.4 million and Germany 1.1 million (Mühlgassner, 1984, 72). Britain about 1.2 million (Peach, 1982, 23) and the Netherlands about 0.3 millions.

By the early 1980s the number had risen to about 6 millions. France had 1.67 million and Germany 1.66 millions (Mühlgassner, 1984, 72), Britain had 2.2 million (Peach, 1982, 23) and there were perhaps a further 0.4 million in the Benelux countries.

1974–1984

Between 1974 and 1981 the overall numbers of foreigners living in Europe stabilized. Generally speaking, the number of foreign workers declined but the number of dependants increased. This is well illustrated by Mühlgassner's (1984, 72) figures for Germany and France. Between 1974 and 1981 the total number of foreign workers in Germany decreased from 2,416,000 to 2,096,000 and in France from 1,813,000 to 1,600,000. On the other hand, the foreign population increased during this period from 4,127,000 in Germany to 4,630,000 and in France from 4,043,000 to 4,148,000. In other words, Germany lost 300,000 workers but gained 500,000 more foreigners; in France the changes were less dramatic. The German figures were dominated by the Turks whose share of the foreign population increased from one quarter to one third. The French figures were dominated by North Africans (35.3%) and the Portuguese (21.4% in 1981). In Britain, the West Indian population showed a very slight decrease during the 1971–1981 decade, but the Asian population continued to grow.

With the greater stability of total figures, political pressure is shifting from immigration to natural increase and citizenship as sources of controversy. However, the pressure for family reunion will remain substantial. In Germany, for example, although the number of women per 1,000 men has increased from 638 in 1974 to 738, it is still some way from unity. The Turkish ratio had risen from 554 to 719 but was still below the average for all foreigners (Statistisches Bundesamt, 1984, 17). In France in the census of 1982 the ratio of women for 1000 male foreigners was 856 compared with 786 in 1968 (Lebon, 1984, 4). This increase in family reunion would be expected to have a profound effect on the housing requirements and therefore the distribution of the immigrant groups in the urban fabric.

PART 2

SEGREGATION IN EUROPEAN CITIES

GERMANY

The foreign-born population of Germany has risen from 686,000 in 1961 to 1,807,000 in 1967, 4,127,000 in 1974 and 4,535,000 in 1983. It is in Germany that the greatest governmental worries about segregation have been expressed and also where the strongest action has been taken to prevent the overdevelopment of concentrations. Action has taken place at three levels: at national level there was the *Anwerbestop,* or halt of immigration recruitment of November 1973 at the local level: municipalities which had over 12 per cent of their populations from abroad have the power to prevent additional foreigners from settling in their administrative areas. This *Zuzugsperre* was available from April 1975 and was by the Kreuzberg and Wedding Districts of West Berlin to prevent further immigrant settlement. Because of legal challenges, the instrument has not been used since 1978. The third level of control has been to designate some of the areas of dense immigrant settlement as urban renewal project areas; urban renewal means immigrant removal (Holzner, 1982; Hoffmeyer-Zlotnik, 1977). This has had the effect in West Berlin of lowering the Turkish IDs, but in Ludwigshafen the greater reductions in the German than the foreign population led to local increases in segregation (Gans, 1984, 97).

The general consensus of the geographical literature, however, is that at the Borough, ward or tract level, very high concentrations do not exist, but that at a very detailed scale, high concentrations can be pinpointed. The foreign-born constitued 7.4 per cent of the German population in 1983. Because of the concentration of job opportunities, immigrants have been concentrated in large cities and now constitute more than 12 per cent of the population of Munich, Frankfurt a.M., Stuttgart, West Berlin, Cologne, Düsseldorf, Duisburg and Nuremberg (O'Loughlin and Glebe, 1984a, 273). In many of the major cities, foreigners composed 30 per cent of the population of certain districts (the Altstadt and the Wiesenviertel of Munich; the Etzelstrasse area of Cologne; Schorndorf in Bochum; Kreuzberg in Berlin and Stadtbezirk in Ludwigshafen). Overwhelmingly the immigrants are concentrated into the inner areas of cities. There are, however, punctiform patterns of high concentration where workers' barracks have been erected on outlying building sites (Jones, 1983, 125) although Hottes (1977) indicates that this type of housing accounted for only a small minority. In contrast to the situation elsewhere in Europe, concentrations also exist in old villages cores and outlying villages (Geiger, 1975; Gans, 1984, 83).

The highest percentage of foreigners found in a block in Kreuzberg in 1973 was 61 per cent (Hoffmeyer-Zlotnik, 1977, 50). In a later study of Kreuzberg, Holzner concluded that there were only 3 blocks where Turks formed over 50 per cent of the population, 7 where they formed 40 to 50 per cent and 13 where they formed 30 to 40 per cent (Holzner, 1982, 67). Jones (1983, 123) shows that over extensive areas of inner Nuremberg the foreign population exceeded 20 per cent of the total in 1980 (at district level) rising occasionally to over 30 to 40 per cent. However, only 13.6 per cent of the foreign population were living in areas where they formed over 40 per cent of the population (Jones, 1983, 128).

Successive reductions of scale increases the degree of observed segregation and O'Loughlin and Glebe's (1984a) studies at Stadtteile (ward about 12,300) Stimmbezirke (voting districts of about 1,500 people), blocks and blocksides (block frontages) indicate a doubling of the indices of segregation between the largest and the smallest units (See tables 2 and 7 in O'Loughlin and Glebe, 1984a).

There are however, some conceptual problems with reducing the scale too far. It is not clear from the paper how many people reside, on average in each blockside. Peach (1981) has indicated that measures of segregation increase not only as areal scale is reduced, but as group size diminishes and that for purely statistical reasons it is possible to achieve very high levels of segregation when very small groups are measured over very fine areal frames. When the number of areal units begins to converge with the number of individuals in an ethnic group randomness will produce high readings.

Holzner (1982), having specifically considered the question of whether Turkish ghettos were forming, concluded that in Berlin's case the situation was exaggerated and that nothing like the north American black ghetto existed. Generally speaking his conclusion seems to conform with that of other geographers although there is a degree of caution in the recent work of O'Loughlin and Glebe and Gans (1984). This slight ambivalence of view by O'Loughlin and Glebe derives from two different approaches in their work. The first is that the small scale statistics show very high degrees of ethnic concentration at the level of individual buildings (O'Loughlin and Glebe, 1984a, 279) and that IDs computed at the blockside scale give some very high values, in the 70s. The second is that through their analysis of small scale migration data they can demonstrate both a purposive regroupment of migrants into ethnic areas while at the same time they can detect a high turnover of Germans and also a net loss of Germans in areas of high ethnic concentration. This, they think, may possibly indicate the beginning of racial transition, ethnic succession and tipping point type development (O'Loughlin and Glebe, 1984b, 20–1). They also show significant increases in the level of segregation in Duisburg from 1970 to 1980, although not for Düsseldorf. Gans (1984, 99) also shows the development of separate housing markets for Germans and foreigners and that despite the beginnings of movement by foreigners into better class areas in Ludwigshafen, the general trend is for slow polarization of the two populations.

One issue which emerges from the recent literature on the German situation is that the Turks do not seem to be as segregated as their position in social distance terms would suggest; on many of the measures the Greeks appear to be more highly segregated. O'Loughlin and Glebe (1984a, 276–7) ascribe this phenomenon to Greek self segregation. This would accord with earlier findings of high levels of Greek segregation in Australia (Peach, 1974) and of Greek Cypriots in London (Peach, Winchester and Woods, 1975). O'Loughlin and Glebe (1984a, 279) however, use the fact of the mismatch between expected and observed degrees of segregation in the case of the Turks to call into question the use of segregation scores as measures of social isolation.

SEGREGATION IN FRENCH CITIES

In the census of 1982, the foreign population of France was 3,680,000 or 6.8 per cent of the population (cf. Ministry of Interior 4.2 millions). This was about the same percentage as in 1931. In 1954, foreigners formed 4.1 per cent; in 1962, 4.7 per cent; in 1968, 5.3 per cent and in 1975, 6.6 per cent (Algerian Muslims are included in these figures Lebon, 1984, 3).

While, in some ways, the pattern of immigrant settlement in French cities shows clear parallels with the situation elsewhere in Europe, in other respects there are unique features. The general features are that run-down inner city areas have traditionally shown high concentrations of immigrants. The unique features are the existence of *bidonvilles* — shanty towns — although their significance has diminished substantially since legislation in 1964. Anne Jones reports, for example (1984, 37) that by July 1975, 34 of the 40 original *bidonvilles* in Marseilles had been removed. Often, however, the *bidonville* inhabitants were placed in *cités de transit* which were only marginally better in amenities and which showed tendencies of permanence despite their name (White, 1984, 133). The effects of clearance policies and also attempts to restrict immigrants, in some cases, to 15 per cent of the subsidised HLM apartments (Jones, 1984), together with the construction of these new *grands ensembles* in the suburbs at some considerbale distance from the centre, has produced some degree of ethnic dispersion.

Kennedy-Brenner reports the pioneering work done on the housing of foreigners by J–P Butaud in 1970 in which he concluded that nationality was the most important single determinant of housing condition. He found that there was a considerable difference in the quality of housing between Italians, Spanish and Yugoslavs on one hand and Portuguese, North and Black Africans on the other. However, a further disparity existed between the Portuguese, who were less exposed to racism and North and Black Africans (Kennedy-Brenner, 1979, 64). Butaud concluded that region and length of stay in France was a secondary rather tha primary determinant of housing conditions, the length of stay being inextricably linked to a whole complex of economic processes concerning the type of permit which in turn conditioned intentions with regard to the degree of permanence of immigration which in turn determined the transfer of savings to families left behind and so on (Kennedy-Brenner, 1979, 64).

Housing type varied considerably between national groups. Kennedy-Brenner, (1979, 63) indicates that in 1968, Italians and Spanish were living principally in rented unfurnished apartments, including HLMs, Yugoslavs were evenly distributed between furnished accommodation and unfurnished accommodation. The Portuguese, while living principally in furnished accommodation were proportionally almost as numerous as the Italians in individual housing and represented the highest proportions in makeshift housing and shanty towns. Maghrebians were found principally in furnished hotels while a high proportion of Africans were living in hostel accomodation (Kennedy-Brenner, 1979, 62).

Studies of segregation in French cities are perhaps too few to make worthwhile generalizations. Detailed statistics seem elusive and may seem to lack credibility. However, it appears that indices of dissimilarity for Paris are very low (Ogden, 1977) and anomalous, while those for Marseille are not only higher, but display the types of pattern that assumed social distance scales would lead us to expect. In 1975, Ogden showed for Paris (Ogden 1977, 32) that at the *arrondissement* level the Portuguese who were of low status, recent arrival and had, at one time, notable concentrations in *bidonvilles* had an IS of 8.17, while the Luxembourgers stood at 30.23, and the Algerians at 24.87.

Anne Jones (1980, 320–321) showed for Marseille in 1975 at the *arrondissement* scale (c. 57,000 residents) that the Portuguese were the most segregated group (IS 52.88), closely followed by the Algerians (51.10), while the Spanish (29.55)

and the Italians (20.65) were much lower. Most importantly, Jones's indirect standardization demonstrates that economic class 'explains' only a quarter of the high
segregation levels of the Portuguese and Algerians, but over a third of the lower
index levels of the Spanish, and nearly half of the segregation levels of the Italians
(Jones, 1980, 409). (See Tables 1 and 2).

TABLE 1

Ethnic Segregation Marseilles 1968–1975
by Arrondissement

	1	2	3	4	5	6
1. French	–	9.30	10.47	19.26	44.50	NA
2. EEC	14.17	–	34.34	26.49	49.61	NA
3. Italian	19.67	5.15	–	21.95	43.40	NA
4. Spanish	30.63	29.78	31.30	–	30.57	NA
5. Algerian	51.49	50.20	51.99	49.48	–	NA
6. Portuguese	51.87	51.58	52.57	52.01	65.03	–

Above diagonal, 1968; below diagonal, 1975
Arrondissement population Average 55,590 in 1968
Average 57,000 in 1975

Source: Jones, A.M. 1980, 320

TABLE 2

Indices of Segregation dervied from indirect standardization
Marseilles 1962–1975

Index of Segregation

	Indirect Standardization	Observed	% segregation due to socio-econ. status
1968			
Algerian	17.42	56.94	30.59
1975			
Algerian	13.18	51.10	25.79
Italian	9.4	20.65	45.52
Spanish	10.17	29.55	34.41
Portuguese	13.0	52.88	24.58

Source: A.M. Jones (1980) 409

Figures for the 1975 census produced by Brettell (1981, 8) for Paris show the
highest concentration of foreigners to be 22.3 per cent in *arrondissement 2* and
20.5 in *arrondissement 3*. Brettell's figures may not be totally reliable (the figure

for Algerians in the 16th is clearly incorrect). However, on this basis the IDs would certainly be low. White, however, can point to studies showing extreme social segregation of Islamic West Africans in Lyon (White, 1984, 122). Simon's work (1979, 186–9) shows high concentrations of Tunisians in the decaying central *arrondissements* of Marseille and Lyon. The 1st, 2nd and 3rd *arrondissements* of Marseille between the Port and the St. Charles Station, contained 50.8 per cent of the Tunisian population of that city in 1970. Lyon showed a similar concentration in the old quarters (3rd, 7th and 8th) on the left bank of the Rhone. Thus, paradoxically, there are substantial proportions of immigrant groups in restricted areas where they do not form outstandingly high percentages of the population. In Paris, at least, there are low IDs.

Most interestingly of all, Simon publishes a map of the distribution of Tunisians according to religion which, despite his comments, seems to suggest a significant degree of segregation of Jews and Muslims outside the central areas (Simon, 1979, 195). Elsewhere in his work (1979, 92–101), he demonstrates the internal segregation of Maghrebians. Similarly the work of Salah (1973, 71–2) showed how chain migration led to the reconstitution of Algerian village communities in parts of the Nord, but such concentrations can be found only at a very small scale.

One problem in the French literature remains unresolved. According to Kennedy-Brenner's research, the Portuguese suffered particularly poor housing conditions and had some notable concentrations in *bidonvilles*. However, according to Brettel (1981) who was attempting a comparative study of Portuguese ethnic areas in Toronto and Paris, " . . . in Paris, I found no little Portugal . . . ". (Brettell, 1981, 1). Brettell's view was that Toronto was horizontally segregated while Paris was vertically segregated. The Portuguese acting as servants or concierges occupied poor apartments, but achieved an even distribution in the city of Paris.

SEGREGATION IN GREAT BRITAIN

In Britain the geographical analysis of immigrant minority groups has been long established (Peach, 1965, 1966, 1968, 1975b; Jones, 1968). Since the late 1960s the literature has burgeoned with important contributions from Lee (1977) and Jones (1978). The net movement of West Indians to Britain in the period 1955–1974 has been shown to be very closely correlated with fluctuations in unemployment in Great Britain ($r = -0.65$) (Peach, 1978/9). The net migration from India and Pakistan shows a similar but weaker relationship. Robinson (1980) found an inverse correlation $r = -0.52$ between unemployment and net immigration from India for the period 1959–1974 and a weaker relationship, $r = -0.49$ for net movement to Britain from Pakistan for the same period. The abandonment by the British government of the counting of departing migrants after 1974 prevents the extension of this investigation. However, the correlations themselves may be suspect because of temporal auto-correlation. Despite the loss of return figures since 1974, it seems that there has been a net outflow of West Indians since that time and a continued net inflow of South Asians. Between the censuses of 1971 and 1981, the

West Indian born population in Britain decreased from 304,070 to 296,913. The Indian figures increased from 321,995 to 389,823 and the combined Pakistan/ Bangladesh population from 139,935 to 235,321. (HMSO 1983, 164).

The total coloured population of Great Britain has shown a very substantial increase since 1945. In 1951 it was less than 50,000; by 1961 it was probably less than 500,000 (or less than 1 per cent of the population); by 1971 there were probably between 1.25 and 1.5 millions (i.e. between 2.3 and 2.8 per cent of the population); by 1980 the figure was probably 2.2 millions or about 4.1 per cent of the population (Peach 1982, 23–4). The uncertainty in the precise figures is due, in part, to the lack of an ethnic question in the Bristish Census and to the increasing proportion of the ethnic population born in Britain. If the ethnic population is assumed to be that usually resident in households headed by a person born in a particilar country (an assumption with decreasing probability as time elapses) then about half of the West Indian ethnic population (273,558 out of 545,744) were born in Britain; about 40 per cent of the Indian population (261,201 out of 673,704) and a similar percentage of the Pakistani population (118,252 out of 295,461) and just over a quarter of the Bangladeshi population (16,938 out of 64,561). The Irish remain, however, the largest single ethnic group with just under 1 million (947,371) persons in households headed by someone born in the Irish Republic (HMSO 1983, 114).

Great Britain presents the calssic case of the black immigrant population as a replacement population. Analysis of 1961 census data revealed a pattern which has not changed in essence since that time. West Indians, Indians and Pakistans were concentrated in regions, which despite their demand for labour were failing to attract or were being abandoned by the white population. Coloured immigrants avoided areas of high unemployment, but, on the other hand were relatively restricted in their penetration of areas which were attractive to whites. The immigrants were particularly concentrated in the conurbations which were losing population and which had been doing so since before 1951. This patterns has continued to the 1981 census. Regressing the absolute numbers of the ethnic population of West Indians given by the NDHS in 1978/9 against the absolute increase or decrease in population by county for the period 1971–1981 yielded a very high inverse correlation coefficient ($r = -0.934$ for the 46 pairs of observations). In other words, West Indians are very concentrated in areas which experienced substantial loss of population and were much less concentrated in areas which had experienced growth. Regressing the ethnic Asian population with the same set of absolute population change figures produced almost as high an inverse correlation $r = -0.891$ (Peach, 1982, 31).

Given that the coloured population is locked into an allocative system that is concentrating them in areas which the white population is abandoning, it seems inevitable that an increasing degree of polarization of blacks and whites should be expected. The parallels with the US situation where the white population is decentralising while the black population continues to centralise are strong. Not only is the immigrant population concentrated into the conurbations, but they are concentrated into the inner areas where the greatest absolute and proportional decreases have taken place (Winchester, 1975; Woods, 1979; Shah, 1980). Inner London, for example, lost 535,000 residents between 1971 and 1981 (18 per cent of the 1971 total) while Outer London Boroughs lost 221,000 or 5 per cent of their population. If one correlates absolute increase or decrease in population between 1971 and 1981 for each Borough with the ethnic West Indian population given by the NDHS survey, there is a marked inverse relationship ($r = -0.714$). In other words, the higher the loss of population, the higher the number of West Indians. Certainly, some of the Boroughs with the highest West Indian numbers, Lambeth, Hackney, Haringey, Lewisham and Wandsworth have some of the largest losses in total population. However, not all Boroughs with large West Indian concentrations have large decreases in total population (Brent, for example). Nor does the correlation between absolute population loss and concentration of ethnic minorities hold for the combined South Asian groups. Only 25 per cent of this combined group were in the Inner Boroughs compared with 69 per cent of West Indians. This reflects, perhaps, the later arrival of the Indians and Pakistanis and also the greater importance of Heathrow airport as the port of entry and source of employment as compared with the railway termini for the West Indians (Peach, 1982, 33–35).

Given that the black population is concentrated in regions, cities and parts of cities which have, for a considerable period of time, been losing population, it seemed inevitable that the degree of concentration and of segregation of these groups would increase between 1961 and 1981. This was certainly the prediction of a book which I published in 1968 which forecast ghettos for the 1980s (Peach, 1968). The detailed 1981 small area statistics for meaningful disaggregated groups have not yet been analysed, but the macro scale statistics suggest that the degree of segragation measured by ID has remained rather stable. Thus, the evidence does not seem to bear out these predictions so far.

Borough level statistics, diaggregated by birthplace groups are available for Greater London for 1981 and IDs directly comparable with earlier work by Woods (1976) have been claculated (Table 3).

TABLE 3

Greater London: IDs for 1971 and 1981
(Borough level)

	1	2	3	4	5	6
1 Total Population	—	20.6*	41.2*	22.5*	37.7*	25.1*
2 Ireland (Republic)	22.28*	—	36.4	22.9	28.7	15.5
3 Malta and Cyprus	40.74*	37.9	—	47.9	36.9	37.9
4 South Asia	30.28*	28.44	48.88	—	40.4	34.3
5 West Indies	38.39*	29.93	37.49	38.94	—	29.0
6 New Commonwealth	25.30*	17.29	34.63	20.22	21.38	—

* Index of Segregation rather than ID
1971 above diagonal (Source : Woods, 1976)
1981 below diagonal (Source : Author's calculations from Census for Greater London)
Column numbers refer to same headings given in rows.

The Borough level units are rather coarse: there are 33 Boroughs in London with an average population in 1981 of about 200,000. Wood's equation for converting Borough level segregation to ward level (wards are about 9,000 persons) for 1971 data was $W = 12.75 + 0.86 B$ and for converting wards to enumeration districts was $ED = 16.04 + 1.09 W$. In real terms West Indians had an IS of 37.7 at the Borough level in 1971 an IS of 49.1 at ward level and IS of 64.5 at ED level in 1971, for example.

These figures show that, with the exception of the South Asian population (India, Pakistan, Bangladesh, Sri Lanka) which increased its IS from 22.5 in 1971 to 30.28 in 1981, there has been relatively little change in the degree of segregation.

Because this table has been produced to make a comparison with Woods' earlier analysis, Woods' birthplace categories have been used. However, these categories are rather unsatisfactory in several cases. For example, Woods combined the Maltese and Cypriot populations which are distinct from one another and the South Asian category conceals the very sharp differences that exist between the Bangladeshis and the other Asian groups. (Table 4)

TABLE 4

Greater London (Boroughs): Segregation Levels of Selected Birthplace
Groups 1981

	1	2	3	4	5	6	7
1 TOTAL	–	21.61	36.53	30.75	35.09	50.15	44.14
2 IRELAND (Republic)		–	29.94	30.37	34.95	46.73	42.48
3 W. INDIES			–	42.72	39.32	51.37	39.92
4 INDIA				–	24.28	59.59	56.23
5 PAKISTAN					–	59.33	57.91
6 BANGLADESH						–	53.08
7 CYPRUS							–

Source: Calculation based on birthplace figures for Greater London Boroughs, 1981 Census

This table demonstrates, despite the coarse areal scale, that disaggregation of the South Asian birthplace groups increases the degree of segregation which they individually display. Bangladeshis stand out as displaying very high levels of separation, being more segregated from the Pakistanis (with whom they shared a nationality in the 1971 census) and Indians than they are from the population as a whole. The Bangladeshis show an extraordinary concentration with 20 per cent of the total population enumerated in Britain located in the one London Borough of Tower Hamlets. The Cypriot population also shows very high levels of segregation, almost as high as that of the Bangladeshis. This is particulary significant because the Cypriot population is largely Greek and white and is not a population that is subjected to any notable discrimination in Britain (a major contrast with the position of the Bangladeshis). The population does include a Turkish Cypriot element of unknown size (but probably about 10 per cent of the total); so if these two groups were dis-aggregated, as were the South Asian populations, the resulting level of segregation might well be even higher.

The Turkish Cypriots do (from sociological evidence produced by Oakley) over-lap the Greek Cypriots. As a check, the small London Turkish population (7,955) was measured against the Cypriot population. This produced the lowest Cypriot ID with any of the groups measured (29.93) — a much lower degree of segregation than the Turks show against the total population (38.00). The Cypriot levels of segregation seem to be the product of voluntaristic self-segregation rather than the result of externally imposed constraints. Although Greek Cypriots would be likely to be a lot closer to the British population on Bogardus type social distance scales, than, say, the Pakistanis, they are significantly more spatially segregated. This finding might help to explain O'Loughlin and Glebe's puzzlement about the higher degree of segregation of Greeks than Turks in Düsseldorf (1984a, 279) when the Turks were regarded by the German population as more socially distant than the Greeks. In studies of immigrants in Sydney, Australia, in the early 1970s, the Greeks were found to be the most segregated and in-marrying of all groups (Peach, 1974). The solution may lie in the attitude of the Greeks rather than in the attitude of the British or the Germans.

The only published work available so far on British 1981 data at the enumera-tion district level is that by D. J. Evans (1984) on Wolverhampton. Unfortunately, only the aggregated New Commonwealth population data were available to him rather than the individual birthplace groups. However, on this basis he has pub-lished a series of IDs at ED level for the four censuses 1961–1981.

There are a number of problems which may make Evans's series of IDs less com-parable than they seem. Apart from the fact that the 1966 census was a 10 per cent sample rather than a 100 per cent coverage (together with the corresponding change of areal scale at the ED level) the New Commonwealth population definition varies from census to census. In 1961 and 1966, the birthplace is taken; in 1971 the popu-lation is that born in the New Commonwealth or with both parents born in New Commonwealth countries while the 1981 data are for those in households headed by a person born in the New Commonwealth rather than for the birthplace groups alone. Definitional shifts are probably less important than the problems of aggre-gating West Indians, Indians, Pakistanis and Bangladeshis together. Evans's maps show that there are significant differences between the West Indians and Asians.

Taking the figures at their face value however, they show a diminution of segre-gation over time and their values accord well with findings from other cities for comparable dates and scales. Until fully diaggregated birthplace data are available however, it will not be possible to establish the true micro level scale of segrega-tion. If, however, the relationship established by Woods (1976) for the different scales on 1971 holds true for 1981, it seems that West Indian ED levels of segrega-tion will remain around the mid 60s with similar levels for Pakistanis in London but with Bangladeshis showing levels in the high 70s. Small area data (largely from electoral rolls) for northern industrial cities with high Asian concentrations suggest that high levels of segregation, in the 70s exist at ED or smaller levels in these cities (Peach et al, 1974; Jones and McEvoy, 1978; Robinson, 1979).

To summarise, the British situation differs considerably from that in most European countries as far as the ethnic composition of its immigrant groups is concerned; only the Netherlands has an equally prominent Caribbean population; the French Antillean population in Metropolitan France numbered only about 160,000 in 1975 (Ogden and Butcher, 1984, 52—5). Unlike France and Germany, where the settlement of immigrant groups at a regional level seems positively correlated with rates of population growth, in Britain, the correlation for West Indians and Asians is negative. There are comparison to be made between the British and German immigrant trend surfaces. In Germany, the surface is highest in the south and lowest in the north (O'Loughlin, 1984) and the same is true in Britain. Similarly, just as the earliest migrants to Germany (such as the Italians) were concentrated near the initial southern entry points and the later migrants such as the Turks, had a more northerly distribution, so the earlier Afro Caribbean migrants to Britain had a more southerly centre of gravity than the later Asian arrivals.

In many ways, Britain approximates more closely to the American model of settlement than do other European countries, though this is not to say that Britain conforms closely to the US model. The levels of segregation of its most highly segregated groups approach those of American blacks. Curiously, British blacks have Hispanic levels of segregation and Asians achieve levels most corresponding to those of American blacks. Despite the larger public housing sector in Britain than the US, there is evidence of ethnic polarization in British housing estates reminiscent of that in some US project housing. The dynamics of suburban growth and inner city decline coinciding with black central city polarization and white peripheral growth is common not only to the British and US situations, but to other European countries.

PART 3

SUMMARY AND COMPARISON WITH US SEGREGATION

The pattern which emerges from these studies of segregation in European cities is that although immigrant groups are often concentrated in the inner city areas of population decrease and poor housing conditions, it is only at the very localised level that they constitute majorities of the population. If very fine areal meshes are adopted for measurement Indexes of Segregation in the 70s may be reached, but, for the most part the readings are in the 30s, 40s, 50s and 60s, much like the situation of European immigrants in US cities in the first half of this century.

The 'ghetto' is a term which is used very loosely in a journalistic fashion. Holzner (1982), for example, goes into considerable detail to refute it in West Berlin but applies it cavalierly to the British situation (Holzner, 1982, 65). For some it is the situation where a high proportion of a group is found in a single area, even if they do not constitute a majority of the polulation (Tiger Bay in Cardiff was thought in the late 1940s to be an example of such a 'coloured quarter'). To others, a ghetto is an area where all of the population is of a given group, even if not all of that group lives in that area. A recent paper has devoted some consideration to the problem of measuring segregation (Peach, 1981); but as a brief working definition, a ghetto is an area in which a very high majority of the population is of a particular group and in which a high percentage of group members live in such concentrations.

European ethnic areas in US cities were very rarely, if ever, ghettos. Philpott's statistics for ethnic concentrations in Chicago demonstrate this point clearly. Not only were the percentages which European formed of local populations small – but generally only small proportions of the ethnic populations lived in such areas. (Philpott, 1978, 141).

On the other hand, the black ghetto in American cities was totally different in kind and in ethnicity. The large majority of American blacks lived and live in areas in which they form a substantial majority of the population (Duncan and Duncan 1957; Taeuber and Taeuber 1965). European ethnic areas in American cities were never as intense as the black ghettos: the black ghetto is not just a voluntaristic temporary phenomenon.

Thus, if our comparison of the European segregation model with that of the American model rests on comparison with Europeans in American cities, similarities can be found. If our comparison is between the black American ghetto and ethnic areas comparisons are much fewer. Some northern British cities have high IDs, for Asian groups; the Bangladeshis and the Cypriots are highly segregated in London. Yet, the high indices that are found in Britain, seem to be more voluntaristic than imposed. European countries seem capable of producing degrees of social distance between their native populations and their immigrants at least as high as those that exist in the US but without the concomitant spatial segregation.

There are, however, three circumstances which make it difficult to speak of a "European" situation with regard to immigrant settlement. Firstly, the ethnic mix differs considerably between the main countries so that they do not confront similar component mixtures. Germany is dominated by Turks and by population drawn from southeastern and southern Europe; France is dominated by North Africans and Portuguese and populations drawn from the south and south west; the British situation is dominated by immigrants from Ireland and from its former colonial empire. The smaller European countries have intermediate positions: the Netherlands is perhaps most like Britain, Belgium and Luxembourg like France and Switzerland and Austria like Germany. Even here, however, the scale and historic specificity of the situations do not allow too may direct comparisons.

Secondly, the attitudes and reasons for immigration differ considerably between the countries. Britain became a country of immigration by default. Immigration took the British by surprise. Her immigrants are, for the very large part, British citizens. France actively sought population both to boost its demographic position and to increase its workforce. It wished, however, to distinguish between the two roles. The Europeans were regarded as assimilable and the North Africans not. Germany,

Austria, Netherlands, Belgium and Switzerland wanted workers but not settlers. The degree of intended permanence, the degree of turnover of the foreign born populations and the degree of family reunification differed significantly between the different countries.

Thirdly, not only did the ethnic mix vary from country to country and the housing needs of the different ethnic groups in different countries vary according to the degree of intended permanence and with the degree of family reunification, but the type and availability of housing varies considerably between the countries. Britain is dominated by single-family houses, has a substantial degree (56 per cent) of owner-occupation and of council housing (31 per cent) and a small and shrinking amount (11 per cent) of private rented property. The French system is dominated by rentals of apartments (producing vertical segregation) and of massive peripheral *cites ouvriers,* relatively unpenetrated by immigrants. France hat the distinctive elements of *bidonvilles* (now largely eliminated), *hotels meubles* and *hotels garnis* as well as the *cites de transit.* Germany has apartment houses, some workers' barracks and little by way of subsidised housing available to immigrants.

In all of the countries, however, certain regularities occur. Immigrants show notable concentrations in inner city arcs around the urban cores and in industrial areas. They are concentrated in areas which the local population is abandoning. Some of the areas of densest settlement have been subject to clearance through urban renewal, partly in order to disperse immigrants. Typically, however, immigrants rarely form majorities over large administrative areas. The highest percentage in a Brussels commune in 1970 was 33.5 out of a total population of 55,055 in St. Gillis; in Paris in 1975, the highest concentration was 22.3 per cent out of 26,225 in 2eme; in Berlin in the late 1970s, the highest concentration seems to have been less than 20 per cent in Kreuzberg; the highest percentage that the overseas born formed of a London Borough in 1981 was 37.2 in Brent's population of 248,092. If the dependants of the overseas born were included, higher concentrations could be shown. In Brent, for example, 53.8 per cent of the population was living in households headed by a person born outside the UK. For the most part, however, immigrants do not achieve the substantial areas of majority presence such as those formed by blacks in the United States. Immigrants can, nevertheless achieve high concentrations in limited areas and some groups manifest high IS and IDs when measured over a fine areal scale.

The picture with respect to the relationship between spatial segregation and social distance is blurred. In studies, such as De Lannoy's in Brussels, there is a strong relationship for most groups. The Turks are highly segregated as are the North Africans; the Spanish and Italians hold a middle position and the French, Dutch, British and Germans show generally low degrees of segregation from the Belgian population and from each other. Only the high degree of American segregation was unexpected on the social distance scale. In Luzern, Good's (1984) analysis of a much more restricted number of nationalitiies produced a fairly close approximation of the expected social distance scale. The Germans show low IDs with the Swiss, the Italians rather higher, the Spanish higher still, and the Yugoslavs highest of all. One surprising finding in Good's work is the low degree of segregation of the Spanish, Italians and Yugoslavs from each other, indicating, perhaps, that pressures of Swiss society are more important than internal desires for self-segregation in explaining immigrant segregation. In Britain high degrees of segregation have been recorded for Asian groups, particularly in industrial cities in the North of England. West Indian levels are lower than the political temperature, particularly between young blacks and the British police and the rash of inner city riots in 1980, 1981 and 1985 would lead one to expect. In the Netherlands, the low degree of segregation of the Surinamese pupulation, so far as it has been successfully measured, is surprising in terms of expected social distance and media comment. The situation in France is more difficult to comment on in the absence of large numbers of observations of IDs. From what is available, however, the degree of North African and Portuguese segregation is much lower in Paris than one might expect, although for certain sub-Saharan groups, very high degrees of encapsulation do obtain. In Marseille, segregation accords more closely with expectations. In Germany, the degree of Turkish segregation measured by IDs seems much lower than expected and there is some evidence in Berlin that the *Zuzugsperre* of 1975 may have spread out the Turkish population more and reduced its ID. The IS fell for the Turks from 49.4 in 1973 to 38.0 in 1979 (White, 1984, 129). Thus, in the European situation, there is not the clear-cut ranking of ethnicities which seems to characterise the American cities over both place and time.

The political consensus seems to be that non-European immigrant workers were economically necessary but socially undesirable. Economically they were integrated into the sectors of the economies which had the greatest difficulty in attracting native labour; socially they were allocated some of the least attractive housing in areas of cities which were often decaying. In the popular consciousness, effect was often identified as cause. It is a short step from recognising that immigrants are living in decaying parts of cities to arguing that parts of cities are decaying because immigrants are living in them. Fears of a black American ghetto-type situation developed. Britain experienced in 1980, 1981 and 1985 a stunning series of riots in which race and ethnicity was a prominent element; all of this was reminiscent of the USA in the 1960s. The political view has become that it is not simply numbers of poor conditions which are important, but the spatial concentration of those conditions. Social geography has become a hot political issue.

The Marxist view of immigrant concentrations is that they are merely the reflection of the capitalistic allocative system. Immigrants are given the worst jobs and get the worst housing; the worst housing is geographically concentrated therefore the immigrant groups are themselves geographically concentrated. Ethnic consciousness is seen as false consciousness and attempts at using ethnicity as an academic category is represented as an attempt to divide the working class solidarity that might otherwise obtain.

The main difficulty of the Marxist proposition is that it allows nothing for ethnicity: it assumes the economic position of the immigrant groups as the main explanation of ethnic concentrations. Economic considerations, however, are only one part of the equation; the desire to settle or return home, religion, language, family size and structure, the whole complex of what we term ethnic identity is another, and it seems, larger part. The problem for social geographers is this: if the poor are segregated from the rich and if immigrants are poorer than the native populations, to what extent are they segregated because they are poor rather than because they are ethnically different?

The view which seems to emerge from my scrutiny of the empirical evidence in the European literature is that economic class explains little of ethnic segregation. Working class immigrants, it is true, live in working class areas; upper class immigrants such as the Americans in Brussels or the Japanese in Düsseldorf live in upper class areas, but neither the working class immigrants, nor all of the upper class immigrants are randomly distributed throughout their respective class areas. Peach, Winchester and Woods showed that economic class explained only 17 per cent of West Indian ward level segregation in London in 1971 and 9 per cent of Indian segregation and 22 per cent of Irish segregation. (1975, 405). In Amsterdam, Amersfoort and Cortie (1973) reported that class standardization of data affected Surinamese segregation hardly at all. Similarly, O'Loughlin and Glebe (1984) indicate rather weak contributions of class to the explanation of immigrant concentrations in Duisburg and Düsseldorf. In Brussels, De Lannoy (1975) has shown that upper class Americans are highly segregated and not dispersed among the upper class. Anne Jones has shown that economic causes explain the least amount for the most segregated groups, the Portuguese and Algerians. However, perhaps the most persuasive evidence ist that in most European cities (Switzerland, perhaps, excepted), working class immigrants are segregated from each other. In other words, the ethnic component in the segregation of working class immigrant groups (and to some extent of upper class groups like the Americans and Japanese) was not 'explained' by their class positions. Ethnicity was a stronger element than economic class in explaining segregation.

If class explains relatively little of immigrant concentrations, the next question is: to what extent are concentrations voluntary and to what extent are they enforced? The answer to this question is paradoxical. In both Germany and France there is evidence that the initial destinations of sponsored immigrants are often dispersed, but that secondary and subsequent moves by immigrants may be to achieve regrouping. Peter de Riz shows this for the immigrant groups which he studied in the Frankfurt area and O'Loughlin and Glebe (1984) demonstrate the marked preference of Turkish migrants for relocating in areas of existing Turkish concentrations. Robinson (1979) shows for Blackburn how offers of suburban council housing are rejected by the Islamic population in favour of remaining close to the Mosque and to the ethnic communal centre. Flett has shown for Manchester how coloured immigrants specified a preference for housing in the conurbation centre while whites showed a preference for suburban housing (Flett, 1977); Anne Jones has shown how Algerian immigrants in Marseille rejected subsidised HLM working class housing in favour of *bidonville* accommodation (Jones, 1984, 35–6)). Evidence from London in 1981 indicated Cypriots remained one of the most highly segregated of immigrant groups, despite the fact that they did not face the racial discrimination confronting West Indians and Asians. Thus, there seems to be substantial evidence that the positive virtues of association play a major part in the formation of ethnic concentrations. There is, on the other hand, considerable evidence of immigrant exclusion from certain areas and the concentration of immigrants into the worst available housing. Work in London by Parker and Dugmore (1977/8) and Peach and Shah (1980) demonstrate this for example and numerous other studies could be cited. Gans (1984, 92) also indicates substantial differences in the degree of social rehousing of German and foreign families in urban renewal areas in Ludwigshafen.

If external factors of constraint were dominant in the explanation of the causation of ethnic residential segregation, immigrants would be segregated as a whole from the host community. In other words, there would be immigrant areas in cities in which the mixture of immigrants would be random. Instead, there is clear evidence of substantial internal sorting of immigrant groups. Similarly, the evidence by O'Loughlin and Glebe on entropy levels of new immigrants and established immigrants supports this patterns of purposeful ethnic grouping (O'Loughlin and Glebe, 1984b, 21). The situation in Europe, as in the USA and in Australia is that immigrant groups are segregated not only from the host populations but from each other. Not only is this the case, but Lichtenberger has produced evidence on increasing lifestyle segregation (Lichtenberger, 1984, 231–2). Ethnic segregation, in other words, is just one aspect of a much larger pattern of urban differentiation which is affecting European cities.

CHICAGO AN DER RUHR OR WHAT?: EXPLAINING THE LOCATION OF IMMIGRANTS IN EUROPEAN CITIES

JOHN O'LOUGHLIN (ILLINOIS)

Despite frequent and severe criticism over the past fifteen years of the "ecological" approach to urban studies, most urban geographers still adhere to the traditionalist school and major texts from a non-ecological tradition have been published only recently (Johnston, 1980; Palm, 1983). It is not my intention here to rehash the criticism that have been leveled at the ecological school from structuralists (Harvey, 1973; Gray, 1975; Bassett and Short, 1980; Badcock, 1983) or to review the contributions of Park, Burgess, and their contemporaries (see Peach, 1975; Jackson and Smith, 1984). Rather, my focus will be whether the interpretation of the process and pattern of migration in early twentieth-century American cities is relevant in late-twentieth century European cities. After examining the utility of the classic ecological models in analysing immigration settlement in contemporary European cities, I will consider a structuralist alternative that examines the role of the housing market and its sub-components as key determinants of the location and intraurban movement of foreigners in European cities. As the papers by Peach, Gans, White, van Amersfoort and de Klerk, and Kesteloot in this volume illustrate for a variety of European settings, the analysis of housing effects is useful in explaining the widely varying levels of foreigner concentration. What is needed is a more formal statement of the relationship and to what extent empirical evidence supports it.

The long American experience with immigration and minority issues, and the resulting voluminous social science literature, naturally caught the attention of researchers examining the later European immigration. European researchers, like most of their Anglo-American counterparts, have emphasized the "spatial sociology" of the Chicago school with its mapping of various indicators of social well-being, urban social structure, neighbourhood boundaries and change and calculation of spatial dissimilarity indices (Burgess, 1926; Lieberson, 1963; Peach, 1975; Theodorson, 1961). The "humanist" perspective of the Chicago school, taking its lead from Robert Park, has been overlooked (Jackson and Smith, 1984). Best known of this latter tradition are the series of ethnographies by Park and his students in the late 1920s and 1930s on city life in Chicago and its constituent neighbourhoods. Only Hoffmeyer-Zlotnick (1980b) on Kreuzberg, West Berlin springs to mind as an exponent of the participant-observer genre.

Factorial ecologists, in their attempts to replicate Hoyt's sectors and Burgess's concentric rings in Europe, found some representation of the ecological models in their sample European cities but with imperfectations caused by the specific historical, land use and legal character of the area. (See the reviews in O'Loughlin and

Glebe, 1980). Given the general socio-economic structure of capitalist societies, with the "segregation of rich and poor not a consequence of each group choosing to live apart but of the rich's capacity to contain the poor within areas where they be exploited and ignored socially" (Engels, quoted in Dennis and Clout, 1980, 20) and the choice of standard census variables to measure these class differences, their consistent results are not surprising. Immigration researchers have generally stayed away from a slavish adherence to American models but despite repeated statements that American ghetto patterns are not reproduced in European cities (O'Loughlin, 1980; Lichtenberger, 1984; Holzner, 1982; White, 1984), the assumptions of invasion-succession, population flight, filtering of housing, ethnic choice leading to ghetto formation and gradual spatial deconcentration as generational change in social status occurs, can all be found readily in numerous European studies of immigrant location and settlement. It is very doubtful that these assumptions are accurate and that the specific locale producing them, large American cities of the early 20th century is duplicated in present-day Europe.

One of the consistent features of European discussion is the improper and frequent use of the term "ghetto", borrowed from the American literature, to describe the disproportionate settlement of foreigners in certain city zones. While the academic debate over the definition of the term is sometimes as confused as the popular press (Peach, 1981), most researchers have carefully stated that a 20—40 percent ratio of foreigners in an area does not constitute a ghetto in the American sense and, more importantly, that slow incremental growth in foreigner concentration is not conclusive evidence of a ghettoization process. In West Germany, both liberals and conservatives argue that "ghettoes" are undesirable features of city life and should therefore be prevented through public policy. Conservatives seem to be arguing that a separate minority society may develop while liberals express the fear that geographic concentrations may reduce future integration options. There is little evidence for this reduction effect (Esser, 1982a, b) and anyway, foreigner concentration may be the result of "voting with their feet" on the part of the minority itself. The conundrum has been expressed clearly by the *Economist* (February 2, 1985, p. 23) in an article on London, although the situation is not so desperate on the Continent. The local authorities in London want to disperse the Asian population among its council housing estates, both to ensure contact with the majority society and "hoping that the odd family here or there will not arouse anger. But isolated Asian families feel terribly vulnerable and may want to live near their cousins and close to the mosque. On the other hand, encouraging the concentration of Asian tenants . . . may mean putting them in bad old flats and encourage the creation of future gehttos".

Surveys have consistently shown that foreigners in German cities would rather live in decent apartments at modest rents and with their fellow-countrymen in a mixed native-foreigner area (Mehrländer, 1981; Esser, 1982a; Schuleri-Hartje, 1982; Berlin, Regierender Bürgermeister, 1980). Policies such as the (thankfully) short-lived prevention of foreign immigration into three Berlin districts greater than 12 percent foreign in 1977—78 (see Leitner's chapter in this book) are impossible to enforce, smack of a police-state mentality, substitute a spatial palliative for a de-

cent solution to an intrinsically social and economic problem, deprive foreigners of
one of their few defense mechanisms against the hostility of the host society and
suggest that the state, under political pressure, is more interested about being seen
as doing something about the foreigner "problem" than in truly understanding the
forces, both constrained and voluntary, leading to the concentration in the first
place.

The term "ghetto", then, has acquired a perjorative meaning in the German context. Politicians can claim that they are acting in society's interest in preventing
"ghetto" development. Bandying the term about is both inappropriate and dangerous. The long American experience with immigration has shown that some groups
retain high levels of spatial concentration long after acquiring social rank equivalent
to that to the wider society and after adopting most of the host society's norms.
Efforts to maintain a certain minority level have been unsuccessful. In Oak Park, Illinois, a Chicago suburb, bordering the large black ghetto of Chicago's West Side, the
experiment of keeping the black proportion less than 30 percent had the unanticipated effect of driving up home prices for black residents and frustrated the wishes
for many black families for a home of their choice. The mechanisms constraining
minorities to a specific geographic zone or to a specific housing type, thereby producing enforced "ghettoes", should be removed. Free choice in residential location
is as much a right of immigrants as the natives and should be as strenously defended.

The concept of "invasion-succession" has been eagerly adopted by those European researchers who would transfer American models to Europe. Friedrichs (1977,
1982) is probably the most ecological of European researchers, and he and his students have followed the Chicago ecological models closely, even to the extent of
reaching conclusions on the basis of flimsy evidence. Thus, Hoffmeyer-Zlotnik
(1982, p. 115) could state that "they (the guestworkers) have settled in etnnic
colonies (i.e., ethnic segregation) preceded, as a rule, by residential succession
(i.e., the emigrant of older residents) which, in turn, is initiated by the process of
invasion". Note the use of the terms and accompanying diagrams indicated the
"stages" of invasion-succession in Kreuzberg, West Berlin. However, at the time the
so-called "tipping point" had been reached, only 9 blocks in the whole district
were more than 50 percent foreign. Similarly, in the same book, Loll (1982) was
able to claim that, based on the assimilation indices of marriage rates, segregated
schooling and occupational skills, the "Italians and the Spaniards are the most
assimilated group. The Turks and the Portuguese are the least assimilated. The
Greeks and the Yugoslavs form the in-between group. This differentiation is quite
clearly identifiable" (p. 134). Those statements fly in the face of other more detailed studies that find no discernible difference between group assimilation (Esser,
1982a, b) and residental segregation scores of the Turks and their interaction with
Germans show that this group is less isolated than the stereotype would suggest
(O'Loughlin and Glebe, 1984b; Malhotra, 1981).

In a participant-observation study of Wilhelmsburg, near Hamburg's harbour,
Bonacker (1980, 102–03) could claim that the district "was undergoing a constant
process of ghettoization which finally leads to the setting-up of a separate subsystem with a more or less institutional completeness" and that "it would seem as if

the older ethnic groups, mainly Italians and Yugoslavs, are slowly being replaced by Turkish families". Other studies, such as Weber-Klein (1980), for Mulhouse, Mik (1983) for Rotterdam, Joly (1980) for Grenoble, Scargill (1983) for Marseille, Ottens and Ter-Welle (1983) for Utrecht and Santana (1980) for Toulouse have reported a slight tendency for foreigners of the first wave of immigration of the 1960s to be more spatially dispersed and to act as pioneers in settling areas that are later settled by foreigners of the second wave (late 1960s-early 1970s). However, Castles (1985, 494) sees a "trend towards increased concentration in innercity districts with low housing standards". The incomplete substitution of later immigrants for some of the earlier immigrants in some areas where the foreigner proportion remains less than 25 percent does not constitute sufficient evidence of an invasion-succession process. The scale and nature of the change in European cities is fundamentally different than that of change in American cities of 50 years ago and to today.

A related research topic that has provoked some debate and study is generally termed the Borris hypothesis (Rist, 1978). Borris (1973), in her foreigner study in Frankfurt, found preliminary indications that the secondary, or intraurban, move of foreigners was frequently to a more segregated area, that is, an area with more foreigners than the area from which they moved. She attributed this trend to the removal of the employer constraint, that determined in large part the primary settlement of immigrant workers by the requirement that employers provide accomodation, usually hostels, for the migrants. Becoming cognizant of the housing options available through the network of information flows among fellow countrymen, the migrant is therefore likely to rely on the informal channels for new accommodation, particularly in the difficult situation caused by family reunion. Since information about housing opportunities generally declines with increasing distance, the overall trend will be a reinforcement of the existing concentrations. Preliminary evidence in Hottes and Pötke (1977) and Rist (1978) for the Borris hypothesis was confirmed by Helmert (1981) for Frankfurt, by O'Loughlin and Glebe (1984a) for Düsseldorf, by van Hoorn (1984) in Utrecht and by contemporary trends in München (Kreibich et. al., 1980). In Vienna (Lichtenberger, 1984 and Leitner, 1983), a trend of Yugoslav settlement from the periphery to the centre would seem to lend further support to the hypothesis. However, the French experience with strong concentration of foreigners in both peripheral housing estates and older inner-city *quartiers* would argue against the general application of the Borris hypothesis. The question is important because if the hypothesis is correct, the European experience would contradict the general spatial deconcentration of immigrants over time in American cities. Further detailed research over a longer timespan is needed before a definite answer can be provided.

We can now list the major structural differences between European cities of the present and Chicago and other American cities earlier in this century that argue against the transfer of classical ecological models across the Atlantic. Dennis and Clout (1980:96), in common with others, list three reasons why the Burgess model is inappropriate for European cities. First, Burgess assumed a succession of immigrant groups and their cultural and economic assimilation over time. In Britain, the

Irish, who have been a major immigrant force for over a century, are still predominantly working-class and living in the same areas as when they first arrived in the
mid nineteenth-century. There is no sign that West Indians, Indians or Pakistans are
assimilating and Doherty (1983:221) claims that "as various government reports
and census analyses have established, the role and position of black workers in the
1970s remained substantially the same as in the preceding two decades". On the
Continent, Mik (1983) in Rotterdam could discern no assimilation trends among
gastarbeiders from Southern Europe in occupational, housing or residential location and Esser (1982a) in Köln and Bühler (1981) for Zürich and Frauenfeld in
Switzerland and Frankfurt and Lippstadt in West Germany found no consistent differences in housing quality, home orientation, contacts with Germans, satisfaction
with home and job, and ability to assimilate between the various immigrant groups.
The reasons are complicated but, basically, are a function of the individual differences among migrants. This latter point is a key element in explaining the apparent
discrepancy between the American and European experiences. European immigrants were recruited specifically and consistently as labour replacement and, despite an average stay of over 10 years in 1985, there has been no deviation from
government policy in Switzerland and West Germany reflecting the purposes of the
initial settlement. As in Britain (Doherty, 1983: 219), immigrants, through victimi-
zation by increasingly restrictive immigration laws and domestic political tensions,
have moved from "potential settler" to "contract labour" status.

Immigrants in advanced capitalist countries facilitate the division of the working-
class into competing native and foreigner segments, thereby inducing a "labour
aristocracy" amongst sections of the native working-class in jobs, housing and education (Castles and Kosack, 1985). In Western Europe, the lack of social mobility
among the immigrant population after two decades reflects this structural division
of labour. A further complication has been stressed by Lichtenberger (1984 and in
this book) in her view that foreigners "live in two societies" because they see themselves and are seen by the host society as only temporary movers into the labour
markets and societies of the destinations. Perhaps distance is an important factor
here since Yugoslav migrants in Vienna (Lichtenberger's study group) can readily
and cheaply travel back and forth and therefore maintain a double set of relationships. The complete break with home that immigrants to the U.S. supposedly make
has been exaggerated and perhaps more than one-third of American immigrants
leave voluntarily and return home (Piore, 1978). In most of Europe, the majority
of foreigners eventually wish to return home. Whether their employment and financial situation and conditions in the host and origin countries will permit this is still
anyone's guess. What is certain is that, unlike European immigrants to the U.S., the
legal certainty of being able to stay as long as desired has not yet been granted to
more than a small proportion of migrants in West Germany, Austria and Switzerland and to larger numbers in other countries. As long as their legal status remains
tenuous, foreigners in European countries can be expected to live in a world of in-
decision and exploitation.

A second major assumption of the Burgess model was the continued growth of
the city with new housing on the fringe of the city provided specifically for the rich

and subsequent filtering of housing down through the social classes. In fact, Burgess' (1926) work was titled "The growth of the city." In Europe, these assumptions are not met. European populations are stagnating and most urban areas are either stable or growing slightly and some are even declining in population. The rapid growth of American cities, specifically Chicago, in the first 30 years of this century has not been duplicated in postwar Europe. Rapid population and economic growth creates a strong demand for housing and in a market with little governmental controls, mobility within the housing sectors is fluid, with some cross-sectoral movement. This point is critical because without a strong rise in the number of dwellings, openings in the housing market for households with less income cannot occur and national populations cannot "abandon" certain areas to immigrants (Cater, 1981). A low level of intraurban mobility has been the case in Europe (White, 1984), especially in the past decade as the post-war housing boom came to an end. This boom had been stimulated by the need to replace housing destroyed during the war and to meet the growing demand for homes by new households formed by the post-war baby boom. It was never mainly concerned to provide bigger, better and more expensive homes for a population that was already adequately housed but who demand more expensive housing so as to maintain their social and economic status and social prestige, as is the case of the U.S. (Adams, 1984). Ghettos cannot form in urban societies that are basically immobile. (See below for more evidence of immobility in European cities). The related aspect of little or no governmental interference is clearly not the case in Western Europe with direct governmental control of about one-third of the housing supply through public housing, a further strong influence through subsidy programs for both rental and owner-occupied housing, and land-use, permit, and sub-division restrictions on all possible housing developments. As Peach and Shah (1980) noted, British cities and by extension, European cities posses, in public housing, the strongest weapon yet devised to promote desegregation. The allocation mechanism in public housing, however, is clearly constrained by the wishes of the minority itself and the racism exhibited by the host society.

A third major factor arguing against the adoption of a Burgess model in European cities is the heterogeneity of most areas, with a mix of rental and owner-occupied housing, some retail and commercial services, and social classes. There is less spatial disparity in housing and socio-economic status in German cities than in U.S. or Canadian ones (O'Loughlin, 1983). Adam (1984) attributes the impostion of zoning laws which codify urban distributions and the strong neighbourhood-based opposition to "negative" externalities in American cities as reflecting a desire to uphold the prestige of owner-occupied areas as a primary sign of social status. Any detailed mapping of census data for Continental European cities would show strong block to block variations within neighbourhoods in the social status of the residents, their composition, housing quality and, even housing style (Friedrichs, 1980: 14– 30; Manhardt, 1977). Natural areas or communities characterized by homogeneity in population and social status and often defined geographically by physical barriers, a feature of American cities, do not exist to any great extent in European cities. The housing and social processes leading to urban change move with glacial speed compared to the fluidity of the American intraurban system. This is not to say that there are no similarities in cities on both sides of the Altlantic. As numerous factoral ecologists have shown, residential differentiation also exists in European cities and it may be becoming more entrenched, especially in large, growing, service cities with a tight and expensive housing market such as Paris (Chauvire and Noin, 1980; Globet, 1980) and München (Kreibich et. al., 1980). Additionally, European cities have retained a larger proportion of the wealthy in the central city than is the case in American cities. Immigrants to American and to European cities, therefore, were confronted with quite different urban structures and processes and their settlement experiences both modified and were moulded by these structures. Until we focus on the complex interaction between immigrants, the host population and the socio-economic and housing structures of the host society, a full understanding of the urban experiences of the European immigrants will remain elusive.

Housing Market Process and Immigration in European Cities

Despite their position in the core of advanced capitalist societies, the American and European experiences of immigrant settlement have been different enough to argue against the transfer of unmodified ecological models across the Atlantic. An alternative theory should tackle some of the issues either ignored by the ecological models or that have arisen because of the shortcomings with them. The time is appropriate for an approach which focuses on the social, political and economic processes that lead to foreign settlement in European cities; in addition, it must be able to take international differences into account within the framework of a general model. An additional requirement is that the model must be testable and either rejected or accepted on the basis of empirical verification. While this approach borrows some of its notions of class conflict and the role of immigrants in industrial societies from Marxist conceptions (Castles and Kosack, 1985; Castells, 1975), its main impetus derives from Weber and his trilogy of conflicts based on class, status, and party (see Jackson and Smith, 1984).

For Marxists, the residential mosaic of the city is a function of the spatial distribution of workers and capitalists in a two-class society. The spatial segregation of classes in cities did not exist before capitalism and the "class-differentiated urban space helps to produce class and status differences within the workforce while serving to fragment class conciousness" (Harris, 1984: 30). Segregation encourages intraclass rivalry, playing off one working-class neighbourhood against another and thereby fragmenting class solidarity. Since immigrants are generally working-class, they comprise part of the lowest stratum of society. "As such, they are priced out of most of the housing opportunities and are constrained to living in the least desirable residential areas which contain most negative externalities. Thus, a consequence of their class position is their residential segregation relative to the city's population as a whole" (Johnston, 1980: 167). Such an instrumentalist view cannot be accepted totally. As well as the role of classes in the production process, urban societal distributions are also the consequence of consumption and consumptive classes. While few would deny a strong relationship between class status and urban intraurban distribution, the Marxist position cannot be accepted in its unaltered form as an adequate explanation of foreigner settlement and redistribution in capitalist cities. This approach conveniently ignores distinctions of religion, culture, ethnicity, origin, and return orientation of immigrants that are independent of their general working-class status. More importantly, it ignores the process of choice by which households distribute themselves within areas dominated by the same social class. Not all immigrant areas have the same character nor are all immigrant areas carbon copies of a general working-class area. And, as has been noted numerous times, the general dual class view of society adhered to by fundamentalist Marxists is not particularly applicable in complex modern societies with large and varied middle-classes and new cadres of managers and operators of the functions of the state, who are neither workers or owners of the means of production (Dennis and Clout, 1980; see also, Johnston, 1984b).

The Weberian view of society, with its consideration of both the productive and consumptive sectors, offers a more attractive prospect for an explanation of foreigner settlement in European cities. Building on Marxian theory, Weber saw conflict as central to the struggle for power in a capitalist society, occurring in a variety of interest areas, not just in the workplace as Marxists see it. In addition to the class relations of production, social relations between native and foreign populations are also affected by cultural, political and bureaucratic processes, especially focussed on housing acquisition. He classified the areas of competition as between classes, status groups and parties. Economic, social and political power can be acquired separately but, generally, there will be some correspondence between the power rankings. With respect to immigration, class differences between immigrants and the capitalist class in the host society have already been noted and have been the subject of detailed study (Piore, 1978; Power, 1977). But many of the host society share a similar class status to that of the immigrants and, yet, conflict is endemic between the two groups of the working class, particularly in employment and housing.

Castles and Kosack (1985) argue that working-class racism is essentially a consequence of the insecure position of wage-workers in capitalist society and they see the growth of hostility to immigrants since 1973, resulting from intensified competition during a prolonged economic crisis, as confirmation of this view. Here Weber's ideas of status groups and parties come into the picture. (For a Weberian analysis of a parallel minority-majority relationship in Belfast, see Boal, 1981). To maintain their weakening position in the face of resource reduction through economic structural changes, such as the decline of traditional manufacturing, the native working-class transcend traditional political boundaries and support parties and pressure groups that claim to protect their interests in the face of a perceived threat from immigrants. Social power can be attained through the rise of parties, promoted for specific needs. A classic example of this transformation in action is the spectacular rise to prominence of the "Front National" party in France under the leadership of Jean-Marie Le Pen. (See the chapter by Ogden in the book.) In

certain towns and arrondissements with high proportions of both native and foreigner working classes, the party got over 25 percent of the vote such as in Toulon,
areas of Marseille, Nice, Perpignan and parts of Cannes *(Le Monde,* 12 March,
1985: 7). In the U.S., pressure has been brought on the government by the trade
unions to stop illegal immigration and to protect the jobs of native union members
from competion from lower-wage establishments, both at home and abroad. Weaker
versions of the French National Front have waxed and waned in Britain, the Netherlands, Belgium, West Germany and Switzerland but none have managed to pene-
trate traditional working class areas like Le Pen's party.

Weber's third element, status groups, "are stratified according to the principles
of this consumption of goods as represented by special styles of life" (Weber,
quoted in Saunders, 1978: 237). It finds its clearest expression in housing conflicts.
Since both immigrant and native labour share similar class and income levels, conflict between the two groups in intensified in the struggle for adequate housing. Because of their political clout and ability to pressure at least one side of the political
structure, the native workers have near total control of the social housing sector,
comprising over 30 percent of the housing in European cities. In fact, social housing is
promoted as a device to reduce working-class antagonism in a two-class society. The
size and security of their income and their ability to meet other requirements such
as length of residency, need, and length of time on the waiting list ensures ready
access by the native working class to council housing. To protect their status and to
maintain their control over a scarce resource, the native working class, through their
influence on the local political establishment and system managers, practice „social
closure", exclusion of foreigners and group solidarity in the face of a perceived
outside treat (Parkin, 1979). While owner-occupiers are exclusionists for both financial and prestige reasons (Adams, 1984; Berry, 1981; Cox, 1983), the native working class are deeply resentful of settlement of foreigners in their traditional areas,
both private-rented and social housing, and they frequently respond with attacks on
the new settlers, as has happened in British and American cities and seems to be
occurring with greater frequency in Continental European cities. This conflict is
exacerbated by rising social tensions resulting from the continuing economic recession.

Housing Sectors in European Cities

Examination of the location and residential segregation of foreigners necessarily
focuses attention on housing and the spatial distribution of various housing sectors.
Debate has raged over the extent to which occupiers of various kinds of housing represent housing classes, with specific views, organizations and positions leading to
conflict between classes, or represent housing sectors, with clusters of households
sharing the same kind of housing (Saunders, 1978, 1980; Pratt, 1982; Leonard,
1982). For orthodox Marxists, these debates are meaningless since they see the only
significant issue in housing as that between the suppliers of housing and its con-
sumers. Conflict is real between housing interest groups but is also intense within

the same housing sector. That housing subsectors exist in every society, including the state-controlled societies of Eastern Europe (Hegedus and Tosics, 1983), is now an article of faith in urban studies.

Since households have some flexibility in allocating family income between various kinds of expenditure, they will never be a perfect correlation between housing sectors and income levels. Among the foreigner population in Europe, some individuals and families may skimp on housing so as to both protect themselves against removal of their work permit and to save for future planned enterprises in the origin country. As families have been united in northern European cities, the level of money sent to the home countries has dropped constantly (Lichtenberger, 1984: 174). Presumably, the trade-off between savings and housing expenditures has moved to greater housing expenditure. Since differences remain among immigrant groups in the strength of their home orientation and return expectations, some differences between groups in the willingness to spend on housing can be expected to continue. However, recent studies in West Germany have shown very clearly that foreigner families are willing to spend nearly as much as Germans for adequate accommodation. Significantly, they are willing to double, on the average, their current expenditure for accommodation that is significantly better than the frequently dilapidated flats that they presently occupy (Marplan, 1984; Berlin, Regierender Bürgermeister, 1980; Esser, 1982a; Schuleri-Hartje, 1982).

Bourne (1981), in his review of housing in several Anglo-Saxon nations, was able to document the consistent division of housing into subsectors. The definition of sectors varied from country to country depending on local political and economic circumstances but the sectors were generally defined by house quality, tenure status, price, mobility of the population and geographic location. Housing markets are segmented by race, income, house price and location into divisions that are formalized by the real estate industry (Palm, 1978). The essential first step in any housing study is to define the housing subsectors for the specific study area. (See, for example, the list in Bourne, 1976: 119). John Rex pioneered the study of immigrant settlement in connection with housing submarkets and, though, he changed his sectoral groups over time, his basic procedure has been followed closely by West German researchers (Rex and Moore, 1967; Rex and Tomlinson, 1979). Rex emphasizes the consumptive side of housing but accepts that change in the housing sectors can only come through change in the nature of housing production. Rex studied innercity areas of Birmingham and he was able to show that Commonwealth immigrants were denied access to the private-owned housing sector by virtue of lower income, a function of their economic role in society, and to good public-housing projects by political subvention. They were thus forced onto the poor private-rented sector which, in British cities, corresponds mostly to the Victorian and Edwardian rings of housing around the center city. Later Rex (1982: 110), in discussing the urban riots of 1981 in Britain. claimed that "Whatever unity there was between black and white workers at the workplace, conflict was likely to occur over housing which was the prime cause of hostility by white workers against blacks". Insisting that groups of households defined by housing sector status are indeed classes, Rex (1981b) remains convinced that what appears on the surface

to be ethnic conflict in British cities between the native workers and Commonwealth immigrants is fundamentally housing class conflict because housing status is
differentiated according to race. Whether termed status groups in the Weberian
sense of the term or classes as Rex prefers, there seems to be little doubt that conflict between groups of households defined by the sectors continues in Britain. Before we can consider the utility of these notions in the continental European context, we must define the sectors of housing and consider two key additional elements in housing allocation and consumption, the role of urban managers and the
role of individual household choice, within the constraints of income and political
power.

    In modern complex urban societies, individual households striving to gain access
to a scarce resource, such as housing, are faced with a barrage of tests, restrictions,
documents and procedures. The fight between groups for housing access makes conflict inevitable and the states have introduced a cadre of managers to relocate housing and to ensure a minimum of urban services. Numerous studies have tried to
document instances of managers' decisions that had geographic impacts but recent
work has turned to the role of managers as the arm of the state, in turn, motivated
by political, social and economic considerations (Pahl, 1975; Lambert et. al., 1978).
While managers have a certain freedom of action in dealing with households on a
one-to-one basis, the overall style and orientation of management serves to enforce
existing distributions of class, power and status. While the local state could direct
immigrant households to particular locations in a spatially-based strategy of desegregation (Peach, 1981), in reality the allocation of social housing to qualifying
households follows ethnic lines. Within the social housing sector, there is a clear
ranking of projects based on quality, location, price, stability and social and physical environment and it has been noted that foreigners generally received accom-
modations in the least desirable houses unwanted by the native households. Moreover, the housing authorities have tended to allocate "problem families" to the
same projects, a situation which exacerbates the simmering social conflict. Finally,
in order to minimize disruption, authorities have tried to keep the proportion of
foreigner families in a project below a specified threshold, taken to represent a
tipping-point. In the private sphere, the managers of factory housing have had the
most direct impact on the allocation of foreigner families. While the patterns of
residential location resulting from the myriad of managerial decisions has been
examined in the aggregate, the micro-level (house) distribution and the process of
allocation, in their policy and strategic elements, await analysis.

    A cursory reading of this section on housing sectors and Weberian theory might
induce in the reader a sense of unease at the deterministic nature of the discussion.
In this view, foreigners comprise a specific class and they are found almost exclusively in a specific housing subsector. Since housing subsectors are well-defined
spatially, therefore, foreigners will be found in certain neighbourhoods only. This
statement, of course, flies in the face of reality since immigrants in European cities
are found in all types of housing and in all areas. It was not my intention to suggest
that individual families have no freedom of action. As mentioned earlier, individual
families may allocate their income as they choose beyond the required minimum

payments for basic necessities and housing choices will partly reflect the operation of a family tradeoff of housing to other expenditures. However, housing sector barriers are relatively impervious so that intraurban movement will be within housing subsectors and rarely across them. A comparison of the housing supply and consumption figures for European countries reveals wide differences in price and supply. Accordingly, the ability to move between subsectors is variable between countries. Filtering theory, which is premised on the idea of a flexible, open and mobile housing system, has been dismissed as inappropriate in the European context by numerous researchers (Dennis and Clout, 1980; Gray and Boddy, 1979; Johnston, 1980; Taylor and Hadfield, 1982; Kreibich and Petri, 1981; Kreibich, 1982; Ipsen, 1981). An approach which falls between "the exclusive enthusiasm for the voluntarism of human subjectivity, and against overemphasizing the autonomy of apparently determining social structures" (Jackson and Smith, 1984: 207) is needed.

In our present example, individual foreigner families operate within the structures of the housing subsectors. Their residential search reflects their weak bargaining position on the housing market, requiring them to rely on their community of fellow immigrants for help in securing adequate accommodation. The combined actions of each foreigner community bring them into conflict with other groups, both native and foreigner. A concerted demand by a large proportion of the foreign population for public housing, for example, would result in raising the level of conflict with native applicants for this housing as well as modifying the nature, demand and supply of both public and private-rented housing. In many European cities, the increasing number of conversions of private-rented accommodation to owner-occupancy has forced many foreigner families to search for council housing, to compete aggressively for the smaller pool of rented flats and, by pooling their resorces, to acquire the cheapest owner-occupied houses for subletting. Urban society is therefore about interaction within and with structures and Giddens' (1979) "structurationist" methodology seems to have widening appeal in human geography. A proper test of its application to the question of foreigner settlement in European cities is still lacking but would seem worthwile in light of the attention given in numerous studies to the role of the housing market.

Eight different housing subsectors may be generally defined for Continental European cities if we consider tenure, age, price, supply, location, mobility and government subsidy as the criteria for subsector definition. They are 1) single and two family, owner-occupied; 2) condominiums; 3) public housing-new, higher-quality, more expensive; 4) pre-1970 public housing, cheaper and higher density; 5) public-subsidized private dwellings, both owner and renter; 6) private rental, good quality and expensive; 7) private rented, poor quality; and 8) lodging houses, hostels and barracks. Numerous surveys of foreigners have shown that the majority now live in category 7, in cheap privately-rented flats, frequently located in housing of the 1870–1940 era and essentially corresponding to Rex's Victorian rented flats. In this sector, foreigners compete with poor native families for the small pool of decent flats of moderate price. Condominium conversions, redevelopment plans and conversions to offices is reducing this pool putting further pressure on existing vacancy chains within this sector. With increasing length of stay, foreigners are now qualifying in greater numbers for public housing but the proportions in public housing are still very small, probably less than 10 percent in all Continental countries (Tribalat, 1982; Laumann, 1984).

Because of the high cost of housing ownership in all countries, particularly in West Germany (Wynn, 1983; Martens, 1985), and the stringent conditions of income and loan qualifications that potential property buyers must meet, the owner-occupancy subsector is all but closed to foreigners in Continental European cities although, in Britain, most Asians have entered this subsector (Phillips, 1981; Doherty, 1983). In the past decade, the number of foreigners living in category 8, rooming-houses and hostels, has dropped precipitously so that only 6 percent of all foreigners in West Germany resided in this category in 1983 (Marplan, 1984). Major reviews (Tribalat, 1982 for France and Marplan, 1984 for Germany) have documented the continued large discrepancies in dwelling size, quality, room density and rent between most natives and foreigners and strong differences between the foreigner nationalities also continue. In all aspects of housing provision, foreigners find themselves victimized by overt discrimination and complicated procedures designed to confine their options. They are pressured by the need to find adquate accommodation for their families and, yet, they are essentially excluded from between one-half and three-quarters of the housing units by income and by discriminatory procedures. Analysis at the aggregate (ward) level will generally replicate earlier studies on the pattern of foreigner location but the variation in foreigner distribution by house and block needs detailed explanation using microlevel housing data that reflect the eight categories listed above. Since the intraward pattern of settlement is highly varied, explanation of the detailed pattern is sorely needed. Because of the general paucity of microlevel housing data, researchers must rely on survey data which give the overall percentages of foreigners in various housing types but do not provide specific geographic locations. A proper test of the housing subsector explanation of foreigner settlement awaits the compilation of the required data sets.

Housing Sectors and Foreigner Settlement in European Cities

No direct test has been completed of the hypothesis that housing sectors are associated with variations in foreigner settlement. Ipsen (1981) offers a flawed analysis since his housing sectors are crudely defined on the basis of rent data and flat-equipment. However, enough information has been gathered by national and local surveys in Europe, particularly in Germany, that a review of this evidence provides a first approximation of the utility of the approach and helps to clarify what aspects of the relationship between foreigner settlement and housing sectors need further detailed work. As mentioned before, the general model must be modified to accommodate the specific national patterns. A review of the evidence is necessarily restricted to those locations in which detailed surveys have occured. Unfortunately, these locations are clustered in the German-speaking nations, with

France in particular offering few surveys beyond the national surveys provided by ONI every year. In the following discussion, six particular aspects of the housing/immigration relationship, namely, 1) the tight nature of the housing supply in European societies; 2) the competition between foreigners and the native working-class for the inadequate supply of cheap and decent accommodation; 3) the comparative quality of housing for immigrants and natives; 4) the role of public and private managers in the allocation of housing; 5) the continued low level of segregation of foreigners, and 6) the expressed view of foreigner families for their preferred social environment are briefly discussed using the available evidence from published studies. Obviously these are not the only topics that merit discussion but they will provide an introduction to the empirical research dealing with housing markets and foreigner settlement in Europe.

It has been an article of faith in urban research that mobility rates are lower and the housing market is tighter in continental European cities than in Anglo-Saxon ones. A yearly migration rate of 20 percent of households in the U.S. can be contrasted with a rate of 10 percent in Britain (Dennis and Clout, 1980) and even lower rates of between 5 and 10 percent on the Continent (White, 1984). Housing prices are generally higher and owner-occupancy much lower in Continental cities. In Germany, Kreibich and Petri (1981) concluded that the overall result of housing policy is "compulsory immobility" with a large proportion of households frustrated in their housing search. A move will usually result in a sizeable increase in rent that exceeds the improvement in flat quality and size (Kreibich et al., 1980). Recent governmental activity has shifted from providing accommodation to those with a weak bargaining position in the market to a greater subsidy for the wealthier sector in an attempt to spur homeownership (Neef, 1981). Foreigners suffer a double disadvantage, hurt both by their nationality and their income. The most distinctive characteristic of their housing search is the "emergency" nature of the decision, prompting the acceptance of the first flat offered in the fear that others will not become available (Marplan, 1984; Petri, 1984; Kreibich and Petri, 1981; Bühler, 1982). Foreigners are realistic about their accomodation with a surprisingly low proportion (26 percent) dissatisfied with their current accomodation. Ipsen (1981) has attributed this apparent paradox, satisfaction with clearly inferior and overpriced housing, to a resignation that their social and economic position will not allow a better option. A search of the housing record in the Stuttgart area revealed that foreigners know little about their legal rights in housing (only a tiny proportion know about the Wohngeld programme, a rent subsidy for poor families), that foreigners suffer a strong negative response from Germans when they reply to housing advertisements, that they have written off social housing as closed to them, and that uncertainty about their legal status and return plans hampers their search for a decent home (Petri, 1984). As the length of stay of foreigners increases, both their satisfaction with the homes and rent payments increases and their fear of racism decreases (Marplan, 1984). Foreigners then, like other weak sections of society, must compromise between the individual household's needs and the objective constraints of the housing market and the usual result is a forced stay in the worst sector (Jessen et al., 1978). Migration within housing subsectors reinforces existing social distributions (Helmert, 1982; O'Loughlin and Glebe, 1984a; Gans, 1984 and in this volume) and should the poor native population abandon this sector, as has happened in Britain and the U.S., the preconditions for innercity ghettos are created.

An important aspect of the housing search is the nature and level of competition between natives and foreigners. A detailed comparison in West Berlin (Berlin, Regierender Bürgermeister, 1980) indicated clearly that the outmigration of Germans from the areas of greatest foreigner concentration is not attributable to a process of invasion-succession but to more attractive offers to Germans elsewhere in the city and in the other housing subsectors. Areas with foreigners remain areas of German immigration (O'Loughlin and Glebe, 1984a; Glebe and Waldorf, in this volume). In München in 1971, a clear economic distinction between movers (middleclass), stayers (working class and old people) and inmovers (single individuals and young families) to innercity areas was documented. (Kreibich et al., 1980). Similarly, in Frankfurt, Germans who can afford better accommodation are leaving innercity areas, but foreigner immigration to the same innercity areas is not the cause of German out-migration (Helmert, 1982). The worst housing area has inmovers divided equally between Germans and foreigners. While Germans rely on a variety of information sources for vacancy search (newspapers, real estate agents, friends, coworkers, etc.), foreigners rely predominantly on informal networks (Berlin, Regierender Bürgermeister, 1980; Schuleri-Hartje, 1982). German landlords have a preference structure with flats only let to foreigners when Germans will no longer rent them due to their poor condition. Turks are less preferred than Italians as renters, a Greek with children less preferred than a Yugoslav without them (Petri, 1984). Mik (1983) in Rotterdam and van Hoorn (1984) in Utrecht concur with these results, as Dutch and foreigners in the oldest neighbourhoods with the worst housing paying rents similar to foreigners and both groups were immigrating to these areas. In Toulouse (Santana, 1980), Marseille (Scargill, 1983) and Vienna (Leitner, 1983; Lichtenberger, 1984), foreigners act as a "replacement" population, filling in slots in innercity housing unwanted by the native population. So, though in a sense, foreigners are competing with the native working-class, the hierarchy of landlord choice suggests that foreigners will generally receive only second and lower preference after the vacancy is rejected by natives. In contradiction to the Burgess model, foreigners are a replacement, not a displacement, population.

So far this discussion has concentrated on the discrimination suffered by foreiners. A counter-argument could be made that foreigners only get what they pay for. In a sense this is true; they pay the lowest rents and receive the worst housing in return but as Reimann (1976), Ipsen (1978, 1981), Berlin, Regierender Bürgermeister (1980), Schuleri-Hartje (1982), Marplan (1983), and Kreibich (1981) show, foreigners receive less housing than native households paying the same rent. The foreigner surcharge is approximately 15 percent. Even more significantly, the same surveys and Esser (1982a) show that foreigners are willing to spend up to 30 percent more on rent for improved accommodation. There also seems to be a willingness to spend even more on housing with length of stay, though factors other than a growing break with the homeland, such as family size, income growth and more contacts with Germans could cause this development. The poor housing conditions of foreigners (see the surveys listed above) are not caused by the inability to pay adequate rents but by the lack of opportunity to do so. In this respect, the role played by real estate agents, public housing officials, housing cooperative agencies and factory housing owners in opening up their facilities to immigrants is important. As noted earlier, the "gatekeepers" only admit foreigners after native households refuse the accommodation. This preference hierarchy has spread to public housing with officials in Toulouse (Santana, 1980, p. 150) publicly stating that no more than 10 percent of HLM housing should be allocated to foreigners for fear of promoting French flight [the threshold is 40 percent in Utrecht (van Hoorn, 1984)] and Scargill (1983: 95) noted that in France "the HLMs have contributed to greater social segregation since it was the policy of the large HLM agencies to build different categories of housing for different tenants". In Stuttgart, most of the social housing that foreigners live in dates from the 1950s and it is also stigmatized by location, environment and social problems. An informal but effective tipping-point seems to be present so that when the foreigner percentage reaches 20, no more German families wish to be allocated to that project (Laumann, 1984).

As well as the allocation side, foreigners are adversely affected by policies on the demand side of housing. A surprisingly large percentage of foreigners have been given notice to leave as buildings are torn down, renovated or converted. In München, 1 in 10 moves in the city were compulsory and of the displaced persons, one-quarter were over 65, 2 in 3 were low-income, and 55 percent of the temporary residents before construction started on the conversions were foreigner (Kreibich et al., 1980). Even though immigrants are often forced to move more than once, they display a lack of knowledge about their legal rights and Petri (1984) concludes that the laws protecting foreigners in this regard are clearly not effective. The system operates generally against foreigners and the cadre of managers, both public and private, are reflecting and implementing the host society's general attributes.

The last two points concern the relative spatial segregation of foreigner groups and their willingness to live in desegregated settings. Given the overall animosity to certain groups of foreigners because of strong differences in language, culture, religion and appearance, it would be expected that Turks in Germany, the Netherlands and Switzerland and Magrebins in France would be significantly more spatially segregated than other immigrants. Such a difference is largely not the case, especially in the Federal Republic (O'Loughlin and Glebe, 1984b). In fact, Turkish segregation is frequently lower than other immigrant nationalities. Surveys of foreigners in all the host countries show consistently that more than half of the immigrants want to live with the native population, rather than with their own countrymen. The figures for Turks in West Germany and Magrebins in France do not differ much from the average but show a slight tendency toward greater self-segregation (Marplan, 1984, Ined, 1974). Also, the class and income status of these two groups is slightly lower than the rest of the immigrant population. Therefore, the three standard predictors of segregation, namely social status, discrimination and selfsegregation (Lee, 1977), have weak relationships with group segregation. The relationship is the reverse of the expected results based on the Anglo-Saxon experience. The explanation may lie in the operation of the housing subsectors. All groups, regardless of background, are subject to the same constraints and opportunities. The early arrivals, like Italians in Germany, have more "freedom of action" in housing choices and so can live together in greater numbers than later arrivals, such as the Turks. Esser (1982b) argues that contextual effects on integration are not nearly as important as individual background variables in determining assimilation, but, in another study, the same author shows that there are some significant differences in the social characteristics and attitudes of Turks in Duisburg based on the overall neighbourhood proportion of Turks (Esser, 1982a). The key questions relating housing subsectors to spatial concentration are only now being asked. Their answers will help resolve many of the remaining ambiguities currently encountered in the geographic approach to immigrant concentration and relocation in European cities.

CONCLUSIONS

This chapter has reviewed the past decade of research on the immigrant settlement question in the context of post-war economic and social developments in cities in European cities. A strong argument was made that the American experience cannot be transferred directly to European cities without modification and that the classical ecological models, based on the American urban experience early in this century, cannot be used in examinations of the contemporary European situation. In particular, the incautious use of the term "ghetto" to describe foreigner distributions in European, particularly German cities, lends itself to the potential danger of repressive measures to stop further foreigner immigration for specific neighbourhoods and stymy the development of foreigner communities. The proposed cure is significantly worse than the supposed illness.

The theory relating foreigner settlement to housing subsectors has its origins in Max Weber's three structural phenomena of power, based on class, status and party. The theory has been applied haphazardly to the minority situation in Britain, North America and Germany but, unfortunately, researchers tend to focus on only one aspect of power and ignore the other two. As was argued in this paper and illustrated using case studies from a variety of European settings, all three aspects of power relations must be considered in an examination of the conflicts and distributions resulting from immigration. There are numerous specific aspects of the theory still to be examined such as the relative importance of class versus status and party, the differences in housing choice and search between "sojourners" and immigrants, the specific procedures used by managers to allocate foreigners to specific housing sites, the exact sequence of moves leading to the changeover to foreigner occupancy (are foreigners a push factor for native households or are they attracted by the gap left by departing native families?), the role of geographic concentration as a protective device for foreigners and as a spatial strategy to encourage the development of community infrastructure, and the locational consequences of foreigner settlement in terms of service demands, public facilities use and urban investment. Issues such as these should occupy the attention of researchers in the geographic community for some time and, hopefully, the results emanating from the research will reach the attentions of our colleagues in Britain and North America so that our existing urban models can be modified in the light of this broader evidence from another part of the modern capitalist core economy.

ACKNOWLEDGEMENT

This chapter was written while the author held an Alexander von Humboldt-Stiftung Fellowship at the Universität Düsseldorf in 1985.

REGULATING MIGRANT'S LIVES: THE DIALECT OF MIGRANT LABOUR AND THE CONTRADICTIONS OF REGULATORY AND INTEGRATION POLICIES IN THE FEDERAL REPUBLIC OF GERMANY

HELGA LEITNER (MINNESOTA)

1. Introduction

The decision to bring in foreigners from the Mediterranean basin as temporary workers to alleviate a shortfall in domestic labour supply was primarily an attempt to provide labour power to fill low prestige and low paid jobs in an expanding economy. Thus the goal was to both meet the needs of individual employers and aid in the expanded reproduction of the national economy. However, the importing of labour power for the economy is not like the importing of other commodities that may be in short supply. This is because labour is not simply a commodity but is embodied in living, conscious human beings; "we asked for workers, and human beings came" (Frisch, 1967, p. 100). Yet the migration policy that was initially implemented did not recognize this. This policy was supposed to provide for a temporary supply of labour ("guestworkers"), who would contribute a requisite number of work hours to the German economy and then return home before they had stayed long enough to require that their needs as human beings be attended to. In only treating labour as a commodity, this policy was bound to become problematic, and be confronted with the consequences of neglecting the other side of the dialectic of the nature of labour.

The contradictions created by this dialectic can be seen in both the conception and the implementation of migration policies. First, there was a misconception of both the degree to which the foreign workers would be needed and would settle for a longer period of time, particularly when joined by their families, and also the difficulties arising from this. This misconception flew in the face of previous historical experiences of foreign labour migration to Germany (such as the Polish labourers in the late nineteenth and early twentieth century). Second, as will be argued in this paper, attempts to deal with the consequences of the above misconception led to the institution of policies to integrate the foreign population. Yet the regulatory goal of securing a flexible labour force meant that full integration could not be pursued. As a result the government resorted to the inconsistent concept of "temporary integration". I shall argue, drawing on elements of a materialist theory of the state (Leitner, 1986) that these problems themselves reflect the deeper contradiction that the state faces mediating between economic growth and human development in capitalist nation states.

The first part of the paper attempts to unravel the forces, interests and conflicts which have shaped policies towards the migrant population. The second part of the paper examines the nature of the regulations and guidelines by which lives of foreign workers (Leitner 1983) are governed, and how these impinge on their lives. My earlier work in the socio-economic integration, spatial segregation and behavioral assimilation of migrant workers left me convinced that in order to better explain these processes and phenomena we have to make the economic and political structures, and public policies, which circumscribe the lives of the foreign population an integral part of the analysis. By the same token, the very process of policy-making is also influenced by these structures, as well as by contradictions that have resulted from earlier policies and from attempts of the foreign population to cope with the impact of state actions. Yet while some mention is made in this paper of the ways that the foreign workers have been affecting the evolution of migration policies, by the actions they adopt to cope with the problems thrown up due to the position assigned to them in West Germany, it has not been possible to provide a full account of the foreigners as conscious agents. The third part is a critical analysis of selected measures adopted at different levels of government to aid the "temporary integration" of the foreign population. Finally I suggest some necessary properties for a coherent migration policy.

2. The state as an economic agent and gatekeeper of social order[1]

In late capitalist societies the state has increasingly adopted the mandate of creating and sustaining the necessary conditions for economic stability, in order to ensure the stability of the socio-economic system as a whole. This involves intervening in the market to correct imbalances and imperfections, ensuring that adequate labour is available at a reasonable cost, and subsidizing necessary capital investments that are too large or insufficiently profitable for private investors. However, since "the late capitalist welfare state bases its legitimacy on the postulate of a universal participation in consensus formation and on the unbiased opportunity for all classes to utilize the state's services and to benefit from its regulatory acts of intervention" (Offe, 1978, p. 396), it is subject to various class and popular democratic struggles. State intervention cannot, therefore, be necessarily directed towards the actual needs of individual capitalists, but must generally reflect a response to political pressure from a variety of sources. These include different branches of capital and labour, the various components of the state apparatus, and political grass-root groups. The form and content of reactions by the state to these pressures depend on the balance of power between these sources as well as on the structure and condition of the economy and society. This implies that there is a significant degree of historical specificity to state action: Depending on the economic situation and the power relationships in society, the means used by the state to try and achieve certain goals will differ in time and place.

---

1   These issues are discussed in detail in Leitner (1986), and a similar argument has been independently developed by Castles *et al.*, 1984.

At a time when the labour necessary for sustained economic growth (particularly in unskilled und semi-skilled occupations in certain sectors of the economy) was no longer available in the domestic labour market, the state supported entrepreneurs' demands for the importation of cheap, flexible labour through a *laissez faire* admission policy combined with regulations facilitating the rotation of the foreign work force. Given the continuously high growth rates and low unemployment rates up until the mid 1960s, the state could at that time equate these needs of entrepreneurs with the national interest. It thus could readily secure popular support for its market oriented policy as well as the acquiescence of organised labour. The latter was achieved by eliminating the threat that foreign workers would undercut wages through guaranteeing foreign workers the same wages. Furthermore unions correctly perceived that the employment of foreigners in menial jobs would result in increased opportunities for job advancement for their members.

When the demand for foreign workers continued to be a necessity at least in certain sectors of the economy, and when individual workers stayed longer than expected and brought their families, the state's policy was challenged on several fronts. The market oriented labour supply policy designed as a solution to the problem of labour shortages has itself created other problems for the state. First, the state had to bear increasing costs of social consumption (education, health services) for the migrant population, reducing their net contribution to the national economy. Secondly, as foreigners came to be perceived not only as economic units, but also as cultural, social and political actors and thus as potential members of the receiving society, issues of integration of the foreign population and of the cultural cohesion of West German society became of concern to the state.

While these developments brought the contradiction between foreign labour as a commodity and the foreign population as human beings increasingly to the fore, decisive state action in response to this did not occur until the economic crises which West Germany experienced in the early 1970s. It was these crises that made it economically necessary to 'stabilise' and even reduce the presence of foreign workers and their families. At the same time, it was during these crises that concerns about preserving the social order and cultural cohesion became especially prominent. As is often the case in times of economic recession, foreign workers, perceived as competing for jobs and scarce societal resources, became a convenient scapegoat to be blamed for unemployment problems; perceptions that were also exploited by right wing and conservative groups for their own political gain. A crisis of mass loyalty then resulted, pushing the state to implement a new restrictive policy that firmly established the priority of indigenous over foreign workers. Such a policy, designed to export unemployment during times of recession, was again clearly directed towards national economic interests even though it ran against the interests of individual employers.

The interventionist strategy adopted by the state consisted of a heterogeneous conglomerate of individual bundles of measures. In addition to a ban on further recruitment of non-EEC foreign workers in November 1973, the West German authorities made full use of the striking amount of administrative discretion given to it in the execution of existing laws regulating the lives of the foreign workers and their dependents from non-EEC member countries. (Foreign workers from EEC countries have a privileged status vis a vis workers from non-EEC countries since the EEC treaty of 1964/65 gives EEC residents the legal claim to work, and settle with their families, in any member country.) Labour offices were instructed to renew work permits only if it would not endanger employment possibilities for indigenous workers, and only for a maximum of 1 year, and for a certain job and employer. The following years saw a further tightening of those regulations. No further work permits were issued for dependents, and the employer had to prove that he/she had offered the job to an unemployed German for a certain period of time, before it could be given to a foreigner.

Table 1: Development of the foreign work force and/or population in the Federal Republic of Germany

Year	Foreign Workers	% of labour force	Foreign population	% of total population
1960	329.356	1,5	–	–
1961	548.916	2,5	686.200	1,2
1962	629.022	2,9	–	–
1963	773.164	3,5	–	–
1964	902.459	4,0	–	–
1965	1.118.616	5,3	–	–
1966	1.243.961	5,9	–	–
1967	991.255	4,6	1.806.700	3,0
1968	1.089.873	5,2	1.924.200	3,2
1969	1.501.409	7,2	2.381.100	3,9
1970	1.948.951	9,1	2.976.500	4,9
1971	2.240.793	10,3	3.438.700	5,6
1972	2.352.392	10,8	3.526.600	5,7
1973	2.595.000	11,6	3.966.200	6,4
1974	2.286.625	10,9	4.127.400	6,7
1975	2.038.779	10,1	4.089.600	6,6
1976	1.920.895	9,5	3.948.300	6,4
1977	1.869.453	9,3	3.948.300	6,4
1978	1.864.051	9,1	3.981.100	6,5
1979	1.947.475	9,3	4.143.800	6,8
1980	2.071.658	9,9	4.453.308	7,5
1981	1.929.700	9,3	4.629.700	7,6
1982	1.809.000	8,8	4.667.000	7,6
1983	1.713.600	8,5	4.535.000	7,4
1984			4.364.000	7,1

Sources: West Germany: Repräsentativuntersuchung '80, p. 3; 1960–1966: Mehrländer, 1974, p. 2; 1981: Korte, Schmidt, 1983, p. 13; 1982, 1983: total foreign population (Sept. 30), foreign workers (June 30) Unterlagen d. Bundesanstalt f. Arbeit, Nürnberg; 1984: Statistisches Jahrbuch 1985 für die Bundesrepublik Deutschland, Statistisches Bundesamt Wiesbaden, p. 69.

It was expected that these actions would reduce the number of foreign workers, without having to adopt an overt repatriation policy. Indeed between 1973 and 1975 the number of foreign workers decreased by about 664.000 and by 1978 the foreign work force had been reduced by 28%. Yet the influx of dependent family members and the high total fertility rate of the foreign population (a rate of 2,3 in 1975, in comparison to 1,4 for the indigenous population. Wirtschaft und Statistik 1978, 3, p. 155) counteracted this numerical reduction in the number of worker and led to a net increase in the foreign population as s whole (Table 1).

The recruitment ban and the displacement of foreigners from the labour market were then effective in reducing the foreign labour force, but at the same time, help-ed by a reduction in child allowances for children who were left in the home coun-try, they sped up the process of in-migration of dependent family members and consequently increased the social problems. The reaction of the government to the continued influx of dependent family members, coupled with increasing unemploy-ment rates among migrant youth, was to impose further restrictions on the entry of dependent family members, to be discussed in section 3.2.

This example shows the reactive and *ad hoc* nature of state intervention, and how these responses created the preconditions for new crises, necessitating in turn new forms of intervention. Indeed the entire history of state intervention with re-spect to foreign workers in West Germany can be characterised as a 'muddling through' policy of crisis management, lacking consistent political planning. This is particularly true for policies adopted to facilitate the integration of the foreign population already present. Rather than introducing a coherent programme for the integration of the migrant population, efforts have been primarily concerned with responding to what were perceived as the most severe problems. The conception behind the various initiatives is that of a temporary integration, which attempts to reduce the potential for conflict by facilitating the adjustment of the foreigners to the receiving society without encouraging them to stay permanently. Indeed, unlike Sweden and France, West Germany has steadfastly refused to declare itself an immi-gration country, despite the reality that almost 60% of the foreigners have already been present in West Germany for more than 10 years (Statistisches Jahrbuch 1985 für die Bundesrepublik Deutschland, p. 69).

Temporary integration essentially attempts to reduce the potential for social problems without fundamentally changing the insecure residence status and the in-ferior economic and political position of foreign workers within the receiving so-ciety. This strategy is inherently contradictory. A large number of studies have shown that a key for the integration of foreign workers is to improve their eco-nomic, social and political position, by granting them, for example, a secure employ-ment and residence status and special political rights (Hoffmann-Nowotny 1973, Esser 1980, Kremer and Spangenberg 1980, Leitner 1983). Only then would the foreign migrants be able to overcome the insecurity which governs their everyday lives and makes long range planning impossible. However, this is obviously not of concern for the policy makers of the receiving countries, at least at the national level. Indeed, insecurity, and political and economic inferiority is consciously main-tained by the state in order to retain regulatory power over the foreigners. This is a necessary result of the economic function assigned to them of acting as a cushion to cyclical economic fluctuations.

Recent government actions with respect to the foreign population confirm, as some authors have put it, " . . . the ruthlessly self-interested way in which West Germany looks at its foreign labour" (Power, Garling and Hardman, 1979, p. 81). The continuing recession and consequent fall in production and increase in unemployment led to legislation in November 1983 (Gesetz zur Förderung der Rückkehrbereitschaft von Ausländern, Bundesgesetzblatt No. 48) designed to further help the Federal Republic 'export' her unemployment. A 10.500 DM return bonus (plus 1.500 DM for each child) was offered to those foreign workers from Yugoslavia, Turkey, Portugal, Spain, Tunisia, Morocco and Korea who had either been laid off because of plant closure or had been working short hours for at least six months. This bonus was granted on the condition that the foreign worker leave the FRG with his or her family permanently before October 1, 1984. In certain parts of West Germany it has induced foreigners to return to their home countries, especially when employers provided additional financial incentives, as was the case in some of the Ruhr cities. Such a scheme has been already in operation in France, but its effectiveness was less than expected (Rogers, 1981, p. 343).

The specific policy instruments adopted to implement the policies described above govern broad areas of the migrants' lives, including: Admission, employment, residence, presence of family members, occupational and spatial mobility, voting and other political rights, access to housing, and the education of children. The following sections will examine these areas in turn, noting details of the instruments used and their origin in the goals of migration policies, and will attempts to assess their impact on the migrants.

3. Government regulations and their impact on migrants' lives

3.1. Residence and work permits

Admission, work and residence for foreign workers from non-EEC member countries are governed by two closely interrelated types of permits: the work permit (issued by the labour offices) and the residence permit (issued by the alien registration bureau). Foreigners wishing to work in West Germany have generally required both permits. Usually the granting of a work permit precedes the granting of a residence permit. Work and residence permits are, however, inter-connected with ohne another. Thus the work permit may be terminated if the residence permit expires, or if the foreign worker leaves the country for more than three months. The interlinking of the residence with the work permit has proved to be a relatively successful tool for keeping the labour force both at the authorities' and the employers' disposal.

The initial work and residence permits are generally issued for one year, on contract to a particular employer, for a certain occupation and a specific location. Thus apart from restrictions on length of stay there are direct restrictions on changing occupation and employer. Both of these may prevent the foreign worker from obtaining better wages and working conditions, and the former also restricts upward occupational mobility. As one might expect, regulations are usually enforced more strictly for a change of occupation than for a change of employer. Again these regulations serve economic interests in the receiving country in many respects. They help keep foreign workers at the bottom of the employment ladder, which is particularly important during an economic recession. When redundancies are necessary, it is these unskilled, foreign workers who can be most easily laid off.

After five years of uninterrupted employment, or after eight years of continuous residence, the foreign worker may apply for a 'special work permit' (Besondere Arbeitserlaubnis), which is issued for a duration of five years. Workers with this permit are free to change their occupation and/or employer, although they may be restricted to a certain locality. After ten years of continued employment aliens may be granted an 'unlimited work permit'. Similarly, after three years the residence permit may be extended for two or more years. An 'unlimited residence permit' (Unbefristete Aufenthaltserlaubnis) may be granted after five years, and a 'permanent residence permit' (Aufenthaltsberechtigung) after eight years, but only if certain conditions (such as sufficient language skills, and adequate standard of housing, and a secure job and income) are met (Verfestigungsregelungen des Aufenthaltsrechtes für ausländische Arbeitnehmer und ihre Familienangehörigen, 1. Oktober 1978). Although this affords greater protection against expulsion, any of these residence permits may be revoked if this is determined to be in the national interest. By 1982 only 30 % of the foreign workers from the non-EEC member countries possessed an unlimited, and less the 3 % a permanent residence permit. Of these two groups only two-thirds (20 % of non-EEC foreign workers) were also in the possession of an unlimited work permit (Reister, 1983, p. 74). These percentage are low by comparison to the number of those workers who have been in West Germany long enough to qualify. The discrepancy is probably due to a combination of lack of information on the part of the foreigners concerning the precise regulations for attaining unlimited and permanent residence permits, and their inability to meet the additional requirements – either in fact or in the opinion of the administrator issuing the permits.

According to Federal law (Alien Act 1965, paragraph 2, section 1), the issuance or renewal of all work and residence permits is conditional on the state of the domestic labour market and on national interest. The nature of these conditions has no precise legal definition. Thus considerable latitude is given to the administrative authorities in granting and renewing work and residence permits, as evidenced by the example of the measures introduced in the FRG since the recruitment ban in 1973 discussed in section two above. This implies that while workers have equal rights *de jure* under the labour and social security laws, this does not imply *de facto* equality because they can be denied renewal of their work and residence permit for reasons that can appear to be *ad hoc* or arbitrary.

Residence and work permits may also be withdrawn if the presence of the foreigner constitutes a threat to public security and order. Generally foreign nationals can be, and often are, deported for minor offences if convicted in court (see Özkan,

1974, p. 17)[2]. Yet according to statistics from the Ausländerzentralregister (AZR) the number of deportations fell by allmost 50%, from 11.236 in 1980 to 5900 in 1983 (Deutscher Bundestag, Drucksache 10/2071, 3.10.1984, Sachgebiet 26, Fortentwicklung des Ausländerrechts, pp. 9–10).

From this description it is clear that the foreign workers have had to learn to live in a restricted environment. Yet in addition it is a highly uncertain environment, due to the reactive and *ad hoc* nature of migration policies. Uncertainty of two kinds must be faced. The short term nature of most permits makes long run planning impossible. In addition, because regulations and their administration may be changed unpredictably and at little or no notice, even careful short plans may be ruined. Taken together, all of this profoundly affects the actions that are possible, and the decisions taken, by the foreign population concerning family reunion, housing, and the degree to which they should participate in West Germany society.

3.2. Admission and employment of dependent family members

Regulations concerning family migration and reunion are not stipulated by law but belong to the discretionary power of the Federal and provincial authorities. They have been changed repeatedly depending on social and economic conditions and vary considerably by province. Generally the provinces governed by the conservative CDU/CSU have adopted more restrictive policies.

Foreign workers are permitted under certain conditions be joined by their immediate family (spouses and children). Residence permits for dependent family members are only issued after a certain time of continued residence (generally three years, or one year for foreigners from 'recruitment countries')[3] and are contingent on the foreign worker being able to prove that he/she is living in adequate housing in West Germany and is currently employed. According to guidelines for foreign workers' housing in the FRG such housing must provide 8 m^2 for each household member (Richtlinien für die Unterkünfte ausländischer Arbeitnehmer in der BRD, April 1973 (BGBl. I, S. 905)). In Bavaria this figure is as high as 12 m^2, and all household members are counted, including those living in the home country.

In the mid 1970s a ban on employment of incoming dependent family members was introduced. In 1979 this was changed into a waiting time after entering West Germany, of two years for children and four years for spouses, before they could obtain a work permit. As with other restrictions, this was justified at the time of its initiation by the existence of increased levels of unemployment as well as by the large number of young Germans who were entering the labour market for the first

---

2 This does not require a court recommendation for deportation since expulsion is a prerogative of the authorities under the foreign employment and alien laws. "(O)nce deportation has been ordered the foreigner is to be taken into custody (Abschiebungshaft). This provisional custody, i.e. imprisonment, can last as long as a year [in West Germany]" (Özkan, 1974, p. 17).
3 Turkey, Yugoslavia, Spain, Portugal, Morocco, Tunisia, and Greece.

time. These restrictions on the employment of dependents reduce the options for additional sources of income, which is important given the migrants' aspirations to build up their financial assets and secure a viable standard of living. The extra burden that these employment restrictions place on the migrant worker who is joined by his/her family can be illustrated with the example of housing. The requirement of providing adequate housing itself makes housing more expensive for those workers wishing to bring their families. These costs are significantly increased when family members are not allowed to work and thus help to defray the costs of housing. Thus the foreign worker who desires family reunion will restrict his housing search to the cheapest rented housing; a sub-market of considerable housing shortage. If such housing can be found at all, it typically means that, at least in the short term, the family will live in dilapidated 19th century housing often located in areas ripe for urban renewal and with insufficient social infrastructure, especially schools. It is then not surprising that the problem of reasonable housing ranks with employment security and childrens' education as one of the most immediate problems as perceived by the foreign population (Repräsentativuntersuchung '80, 1981, pp. 650ff.).

Faced with increasing unemployment rates among both foreign and indigenous youth, the upper age limit for children allowed to come and join their parents was reduced from 18 to 16 years in 1981 (Empfehlungen der Bundesregierung vom 2. Dezember 1981). Recently, representatives of the provinces of Bavaria and Baden-Württemberg have even suggested an upper limit of 6 years. The stated reason behind this move is to avoid the schooling problems experienced by the so called late-entrants (Späteinsteiger); foreign children brought to West Germany only a few years before reaching working age. Children are also no longer allowed to enter the FRG if just one parent is living in the country, and restrictions on the inmigration of spouses of the second generation have been introduced (for details see Reister, 1983, p. 71). Such measures are targeted to reduce the problems associated with incoming dependents, but in all likelihood they will also reduce the total foreign population present. Surveys have shown that most parents, particularly Turks, would not accept a prolonged separation from their children. The trend to lower the age of children who may be admitted runs contrary not only to the guarantee, provided in Article 6 (paragraphs 1 and 2) of the German Grundgesetz (Basic Law), that the family enjoys the particular protection of the state, but also to the resolutions and recommendations of supra-national organizations, such as the ILO and the Council of Europe, that foreign workers should be granted the right to be joined by all their dependent children.

The cumulated effect of all these obstacles is to make the complete reunion of foreign workers' families difficult, expensive and risky. A recent survey estimates that at least 274.000 children who would be eligible for family reunion (up to 16 years) are still living in the sending countries (Gastarbeiter in Deutschland, 1984, p. 19f.). The social and psychological problems generated by keeping the family split can be as severe for those who stay at home as well as for those who move to the receiving country. It has been recognised for some time, and documented for the case of West Germany, that long separation may cause psychological or physio-

logical disorders (Bingemer et al., 1970, Münscher 1979, p. 43ff., Binder and Simoes, 1980). Research on Turkish women has revealed the psychological and
physical trauma they experience because of separation from their children (Baumgartner-Karabak and Landesberger 1978, Münscher 1979). However, much less is
known about the impact of separation on spouses and children left at home, or on
relationships between those moving and those staying behind.

3.3. Restrictions on admission to congested areas

Alarmed by the geographically highly concentrated pattern of destinations of
foreign workers and their families in the industrial centers, and concerned with
'capacity' problems of the social infrastructure in these areas, the Federal government introduced a foreign residence quota for urban regions in 1975. This gave an
urban area the automatic right to declare itself an 'overburdened' area and stop
further in-migration when the percentage of foreigners rose above 12%[4]. This measure was supposed to steer migrants away from the already 'congested' areas and
thus, according to official statements, prevent a further burdening of the local
social infrastructure. Furthermore, in response to the high unemployment rates
at that time in some urban areas, it was thought that such a restriction would increase employment prospects for the indigenous labour force.

As of January 1977, more than fifty five cities in the country had instigated
such a ban, including some of the largest urban areas; Berlin, Frankfurt, Hannover,
Munich and Cologne. In addition to this restriction on entry to particular urban
areas, some cities such as Berlin and Munich also declared certain districts within
their boundaries as areas overcrowded with foreigners. Both types of restrictions
violate the European Human Rights Convention. According to the 4th protocol of
the European Human Rights Convention 1963, which was signed by the FRG,
everybody legally present in a country has the right ot freely choose his or her place
of residence.

Such destination oriented restrictions indicate an association in the minds of
policy makers between the geographical distribution of the foreign population and
the costs accuring from its presence in West Germany. It is assumed that social
infrastructure costs, social tensions and unrest can be minimized by dispersing the
foreign population in space, both at an inter- and intra-urban scale. Put another
way, there is a fear that a high level of concentration of foreigners in certain areas
will create all the various negative manifestations of ghetto life, as captured in the
imagery of the headline from the left-of-center Frankfurter Rundschau: "Harlem
could be on our doorsteps tomorrow" (Frankfurter Rundschau, 9.11.1978, p. 14).
Essentially the spatial distribution is identified as the proximate cause of the problem, and it is believed that the problem can be more adequately controlled by mani-
pulating this distribution rather than by working towards the elimination of social

---

4   The mechanism for achieving this was the right to refuse a residence permit to those who
    request it.

and economic inequalities and discrimination. Furthermore the claim that ghetto formation must be avoided because of its negative effects also neglects its positive role of providing a sense of secutiry for the foreign population. These policies, then, were an attempt to deal with superficial geographical manifestations rather than the real societal causes of inequality, and incorporate the assumption that the German authorities know what is good for the foreign workers and what they need; a supposition which is also characteristic of policies addressing the social integration of the foreign population.

Neither of these measures of settlement prohibition produced the expected results. There are several reasons for this. First, migration continued to occur illegally into these areas. Secondly, employers were opposed to the restriction and lobbied successfully to obtain exceptions in locations where their demand for foreign labour was still high. For instance in Stuttgart and Offenbach, where the percentage of foreigners was as high as 16% or 19%, the ban was never imposed. In addition the restrictions could not be applied to all nationalities of migrant workers, since foreign workers from EEC member countries could not be subject to this restriction. Finally, in 1976 Turks who had been working for more than five years in the FRG were exempted as a result of EEC agreements with Turkey. Spanish and Greek workers were also exempt (Mehrländer, 1978, p. 123). The result was that less than half of all foreign workers were subject to the residence restriction. This last reason was the one officially used to justify the discontinuance of this measure in 1977 for all locations except for the districts of Kreuzberg, Tiergarten and Wedding in West Berlin. Instead, in recent years the local authorities in various West German cities have been adopting a series of other strategies designed to disperse the foreign population within the urban area. These will be discussed in section 5.2.

4. Political rights

Among the possible political rights one might reasonably expect to be granted to resident foreigners, the foremost would certainly be representation in the state institutions which govern their lives. However, the several million foreigners in the FRG, who contribute substantially to the economic well being of the country through payment of taxes and through their participation in the production process, have hardly any such rights. Migrant workers experience the state as a pervasive and frightening power which regulates their lives, but to which they have little or no access.

It is only recently that guestworkers have been allowed to play a minor role in political life and in local government activities. Some of the political parties in the FRG have changed their by-laws allowing foreigners to become party members (SPD, KPD, FDP). Quite a sizable number of cities, including Berlin, Bremen, Darmstadt, Duisburg, Cologne, Nuremberg, have also instituted advisory councils on foreign worker questions *(Ausländerbeiräte, Ausländerausschüsse, Arbeits- oder Koordinierungskreise für Ausländerfragen)* at the city level and/or in some districts within the city. The role of these councils is to inform the city council and administrative authorities about specific problems and needs of the foreign population and to advise them in these matters. However, this is a very limited source of power. The councils have little say in the actual decision-making process, and do not have the power to propose motions to the local authorities. Furthermore representation, participation and the position of foreigners in these councils leaves much to be desired. In many cases the representatives of the foreign population are appointed by political parties, labour unions, and charitable organizations, as opposed to being elected by the foreign population. Given this situation, the councils appear to serve more as an alibi for participation rather than as an effective tool for representing the views of the foreign population.

As a result, a hot debate has raged over whether foreigners should have the right to vote in local and, eventually, national elections. Charitable organizations and some progressive politicans (such as H. Kühn, formerly the government commissioner for foreign worker questions) see the right to vote as one of the most important preconditions for improving the participation of foreigners in the political process. Arguments put forward against the granting of the right to vote center around the fact that it would require a change in the constitution; a long and involved process. In addition, some social scientists argue that the granting of the right to vote should take second priority to securing their work and residence status, because only then will migrant workers be willing to actively participate in the political process. However, while a secure residence and work status is vital, a survey in Berlin has shown that more than two-thirds of the foreign population expressed a desire for increased representation and participation in West German political life. Most of these thought that universal suffrage was the most effective means of achieving this, over and above the right to vote in municipal elections and participation in local advisory councils on foreign worker questions (Schuleri-Hartje, 1984, p. 195).

The granting of citizenship would be one comparatively simple means of providing for political participation, since most political rights are currently tied to citizenship. Some social scientists have argued that making citizenship easier to attain is the only way to meet foreign workers' legitimate concerns that they receive political participation for themselves and their children, and equal treatment in the access to work and housing (Walzer, 1981, p. 30).

There is a long list of conditions that must be met before a foreigner can obtain West German citizenship, including the requirement of ten years residence in West Germany (Reichs- und Staatsangehörigkeitsgesetz, July 22, 1913, see also Özkan, 1974, p. 24)), although there is currently talk of reducing this to eight years for members of the second generation who are between the ages of 18 and 21 (Kommission 'Ausländerpolitik' aus Vertretern von Bund, Ländern und Gemeinden, 1983, p. 124). In contrast to the US, there is also no possibility that a child of a foreign worker born in West Germany can make any legal claim to citizenship.

---

5 Second generation refers to the children of the foreign workers, and third generation to the offspring of the second generation.

On the other hand, many foreigners may not choose to become citizens, given that they maintain close emotional ties to their native land and that they would be required to give up their native citizenship. As one Turkish worker stated: "Dual citizenship would be a feasible option for me, but I would never be able to give up my citizenship because I love my country." The lack of interest among the majority of the first generation of foreign workers has been confirmed in a series of surveys. According to the Repräsentativuntersuchung '80 (1981, p. 554ff.) 93,4% of the foreigners do not intend to give up their citizenship. This predisposition on the part of migrant workers is used by policy makers as an argument against offering them citizenship. It is furthermore argued that the state already has the means to resolve the most pressing problems of foreigners, since it is always possible in principle to enact special measures to improve their rights for everything short of citizenship (Chaney, 1981, p. 54). However, this last position assumes that the appropriate authorities are both aware of the nature of these problems, and are willing to provide the necessary legislation; an assumption that is true of neither the regulatory nor, as we shall see, the integration policies.

5. Measures to aid 'temporary integration'

In the late 1960s and early 1970s the Federal government instituted several commissions *(Sozialpolitische Gesprächsrunde, Bund-Länderausschuß 'Ausländische Arbeitnehmer', Koordinierungskreis 'Ausländische Arbeitnehmer')*, which were responsible for developing suggestions for a coherent 'Ausländerpolitik' including policies which would aid the 'temporary integration' of the foreigners.

However, it was not until the second half of the 1970s that suggestions made by these commission (particularly the Bund-Länderausschuß 'Ausländische Arbeitnehmer'), led to a series of social policy proposals at the Federal level to explicitly aid integration. A variety of measures were introduced by the national authorities, using three complementary strategies: Increased funding to support activities of welfare organizations such as the Deutscher Caritasverband, Diakonisches Werk and Arbeiterwohlfahrt, which had traditionally been active in counselling and helping migrant workers; direct Federal involvement in educating and training the second and third generation; and coordination of Federal actions with those taken by provincial and local governments.

5.1. Education of the foreign children

The primary target of integration policies at all levels of government has become the education and employment problems faced by the second and third generation[5]. It is correctly perceived that the high school drop-out rates and rates of unemployment among the second generation may result in the creation of a permanent underclass that could become a source for social unrest. Only one half of the foreign children successfully complete their compulsory education, achieving a

'Hauptschulabschluß'[6], and about thirty percent of the foreign youth between 15 and 20 years of age are neither in school nor employed (Reister, 1983, p. 73ff.). These rates are particularly high for Turkish youth (Schuleri-Hartje, 1984, p. 134), and for those children who were already partly educated in the sending country and therefore face increased difficulties of integration into the German school system. As a result Federal, and some provincial and local, authorities have increased their efforts in the area of schooling, through educational model programs at the pre-school, elementary and secondary school levels, and in vocational training for the second and third generation.

The principal objective of the educational policy for migrant children as defined by the Standing Conference of Education Ministers (Ständige Konferenz der Kultusminister der Länder, Beschluß zum "Unterricht für Kinder ausländischer Arbeitnehmer" vom 8.4.1976) is to enable them to learn the German language and to obtain German school-leaving certificates. This is supposed to ease their integration into German society, while at the same time allowing them to maintain fluency in the language of the country of origin and knowledge of its culture to ease their reintegration into their home society after their return (for further details on this 'dual strategy' see Castles et al., 1984).

Given the different political complexion of the provincial governments, who have the prime responsibility for implementing policies, there exist considerable differences as to how to achieve this objective. One central difference is whether foreign children should be integrated into the school system or taught in segregated classes. While most provinces pursue an integrationist policy, segregated education is the model in Bavaria, where migrant children are perceived as an essentially transient population who should thus be educated separately because they have different needs. Segregated regular classes exist also in some cities in Baden-Württemberg, and this is also possible in West Berlin if the proportion of foreign students in a class exceeds a predefined threshold. There is public concern that if the proportion of foreign students in integrated classes is too high then the educational progress of indigenous pupils will be held back. As a result official provincial policies attempt to keep the share of foreign students in regular classes below 20%.

Even in localities where there is no segregation *de jure, de facto* segregation can result simply from the uneven geographical concentration of foreign workers. The average proportion of foreign children in elementary schools in the FRG varies generally between 15 and 30%, but in areas of migrant concentration in West Berlin, Bremen and Duisburg, it reaches 50% or more. To alleviate such disproportions some places, such as West Berlin, are discussing the introduction of measures to redistribute students among and between school districts. The city of Duisburg has already introduced busing for schools where the proportion of foreigners exceeds 25–50% (Schuleri-Hartje, 1984, p. 122).

In order to overcome the deficiencies of current educational policies, as manifest in the high drop-out rates, local school authorities in various German cities have

---

6 This is the school leaving certificate; generally a minimum requirement for getting an apprenticeship or any other form of vocational training.

been introducing or are planning to introduce a series of special measures. The types of measures vary from locality to locality. They include: Decreasing the student/teacher ratio in schools with a high proportion of foreign students; providing Turkish as an alternative second language to English; offering classes in the native language; lengthening compulsory education by one year to increase the possibility that pupils might obtain a school leaving certificate: providing additional foreign teachers in schools where more than 60% of the students are foreign; offering special training (Stützunterricht) for pupils once they enter regular classes; supporting homeworkhelp programs arranged by welfare organizations; developing special educational material for foreign students, and; requiring teachers to take continuing education courses on the special problems encountered in teaching foreign students.

It is difficult to determine the degree to which such measures will be able to alleviate schooling problems experienced by foreign children. While there is an observable increase in the number of foreign children successfully finishing secondary education, this might be due to the fact that an increasing number of migrant children have already been born and brought up in West Germany and thus enter the educational system much earlier.

In order to deal with the unemployment rate among migrant children, the Federal government instituted a training program in 1980 (Maßnahmen zur Berufsvorbereitung und sozialen Eingliederung, MBSE — measures for vocational preparation and social integration). It is targeted towards young foreigners who leave compulsory education without a certificate and is supposed to increase their employability.

This measure, directed at aiding the labour market integration of the foreign youth, is tied into regulatory policies for the second and third generation. Foreign youths who take an MBSE course may obtain a work permit upon completion. This complements the special treatment of members of the second and third generation with respect to obtaining an unlimited residence permit (foreign children of the age of 16 and 17 are not subject to the waiting time regulations for an unlimited residence permit, if they can prove their proficiency in the German language) and easier access to citizenship (see section 4). No such special offers have been made to those members of the second and third generation not possessing the requisite education or skills, or to the first generation.

There is no doubt that the migrant children and in particular the adolescents do need special attention. The high unemployment among them, coupled with the stress of growing up and living between two cultures, makes them more vulnerable and marginal than any other group within the foreign population. The problem, as I see it, is not with the measures as such, but with their limited scope and selective effects.

The educational and vocational measures are not comprehensive enough to allow more than a minority of migrant youth to obtain the level of qualification necessary to receive favourable treatment from the West German authorities. For example, the MBSE program provided places for just 15.000 youths in 1981, although almost 90.000 were officially recorded as unemployed that year (Reister, 1983, p. 76). The effect is to polarize the migrant children into the few who satisfy the requirements of being productive workers, and are given a chance to integrate themselves into German society, and the many who are left behind. Furthermore, these measures are piecemeal in nature. Pursuing a policy of encouraging parents to return home while selectively aiding the integration of their children has its own inconsistencies. Surveys among the foreign worker population have shown that the great majority of the parents (particularly among the Turks) are against a separation of their families, and also object to their children becoming German citizens and thus having to renounce their home citizenship (Repräsentativuntersuchung '80, 1981, p. 421ff.). Thus if parents have to leave, West Germany may lose the investment it has made in the children.

5.2. Housing

It has been well documented that foreign workers occupy poor quality housing and are spatially concentrated in inner city locations ripe for urban renewal. It has also been shown that these conditions are closely interrelated and are not only due to the low economic status of foreign workers, but also a result of their insecure legal status and overt discrimination in the housing market (Borris, 1974; Mehrländer, 1974; Schildmeier, 1975; Hoffmeyer-Zlotnik, 1977; Hottes and Meyer, 1977; Zieris, 1977; Ipsen, 1978; Vink, 1980; Glebe and O'Loughlin, 1980, 1981; Gans, this volume, Glebe and Waldorf, this volume).

Problems of housing availability, quality and location are now primarily addressed by the local authorities. A number of measures are currently being tried in selected cities to improve the availability of housing, particularly outside the traditional areas of concentration of migrant workers. In most cases these consist of attempts to increase the supply of affordable housing, and counselling activities undertaken by local housing agencies to assist foreign workers in their search for better housing.

Foreign workers are permitted to occupy public housing, unlike the situation in Austria. However, there are quotas fixing a maximum proportion of these units that can be occupied by foreigners, making the waiting list for public housing longer for them than for indigenous workers. This, along with the sheer complexity of the bureaucracy that has to be dealt with during the application process, acts to discourage many foreigners from seeking out public housing. According to a representative survey in 1980 only 25% of all interviewed families had ever applied for public housing (Repräsentativuntersuchung '80, 1981, pp. 472ff.).

The availability of public or publicly subsidized housing is currently being increased in some cities by raising the maximum allowable proportion of foreign workers from ten to fifteen percent; either in all publicly subsidized housing, or only in certain housing estates. This also serves the purpose of filling vacant housing units in those public housing estates which are not attractive to the indigenous population, and thus have high vacancy rates (for example in Kiel; P. Gans, personal communication). Federal funds for new housing constructions can only be applied for by cities if the currently existing public housing is effectively fully occupied. Public subsidies to housing companies (Gemeinnützige Wohnungsbaugesellschaften) for building new housing estates can be made conditional on the setting aside of a certain percentage of these housing units for occupation by foreign workers, and this is being tried in Berlin and Bremen. Other measures to improve the supply of housing for foreigners and their housing situation include: relaxing minimum size requirements for apartments to accomodate large families, and monitoring rent levels to inhibit the charging of excessive rents (for further details see Schuleri-Hartje, 1984, pp. 83–91).

These kinds of measures, even if successfully executed, can only bring about spatial dispersion and an improvement in housing conditions for a minority of foreign workers. Thus there remains the problem of poor housing conditions in areas of concentration; areas that are the prime target for urban renewal and revitalization in West German cities. While urban renewal and revitalization do indeed greatly improve the quality of the housing stock, they also in many cases lead to dramatically increased rents. As a result, unless special measures are taken, foreign workers (along with the poorer segments of the German population such as the elderly and students) will tend to be displaced as they can no longer afford the housing. According to a listing of housing policy measures in selected West German cities, only in Bremen and Hannover is there an explit attempt to address the problem of displacement of foreigners (Schuleri-Hartje, 1984, pp. 83ff.). In Bremen, a certain portion of the money made available for urban renewal is set aside for the renovation of old housing for migrant workers. In Hannover, replacement housing for households displaced by urban renewal must be made available to households based on their need for such housing, not their nationality. In other cities the likely effect of urban renewal and revitalization is a displacement of foreigners from one problem area to another. If anything, this decreases the housing available to foreigners.

As the above discussion has shown, most cities currently approach the problem of spatial concentration through housing policies rather than geographical restriction on immigration (section 3.3 above). Measures to extend access to subsectors of the housing market other than old dilapidated low-rent housing are clearly important for individual migrant workers. Surveys have shown that many foreign workers would be willing to pay higher rents for better quality housing, but find it difficult to obtain such housing because of discrimination. However, the application of these measures is highly limited. Furthermore, any such housing policies cannot tackle the root cause of poor housing since they are counteracted by regulatory policies governing work and residence status. The insecure status of foreigners from non-EEC member countries clearly acts as a disincentive for them to invest the effort necessary to significantly improve their housing situation. Certainly the currently discussed measure to encourage home ownership has little chance of success unless a more permanent status is granted to foreign workers.

6. Quo vadis migration policies?

West Germany's policy towards foreign workers and their families throughout the history of the migration movement has been and continues to be based on a narrow functional conception of the foreign migrants as economic actors, whose admission, employment opportunities and presence is geared to the needs of the domestic labour market. This in turn has made it all the more difficult for West Germany to come to terms with the fact of permanent immigration. It almost seems that the more West Germany has become a country of *de facto* immigration, the more steadfastly it has been officially denied that this should be the case.

Policies to aid the integration of the foreign population have been subjugated to these economic goals, as is apparent in their limited scope and in the principal objective of 'temporary integration'. Given this situation, and the recent trend in migration policies at the national and provincial level to encourage repatriation of the foreign population, it might seem largely academic to discuss the requirements of a coherent integration policy. However, I would argue this is not the case. Employment of foreign workers in certain sectors of the economy will continue to be a necessity, implying that no drastic short term reduction in the number of foreigners can be expected. Programs to aid integration will therefore continue to be important aspects of state activities, particularly at the local level, in order to reduce the potential for social conflict and unrest.

One of the most important requirements for an effective integration policy is the improvement of the work and residence status of foreigners. However, securing work and residence is only the first necessary step, and must be followed by the granting of basic political rights, which will allow the foreign population to participate in institutions which affect their lives. A permanent status would greatly reduce the uncertainty faced by the foreign population. It would enable them to better plan their lives, and provide them with the motivation to take initiatives and improve their life situation. Once the migrants can take actions on the assumption that they are allowed to stay in the FRG permanently, this will also increase the likelihood that measures to aid integration taken by the state, particularly the local state, will be effective. Under the current legal framework, even the most elaborate and expensive integration measures are unlikely to produce the expected results. In order to overcome this contradiction in migration policies, foreign employment and alien laws, and their administration, should be used not primarily as restrictive regulatory instruments, but as instruments for encouraging integration. This implies that the role of the foreign workers and their families in the West Germany must be rethought (see also Korte, 1982).

One problem of the integration policies as they are currently formulated is their concentration on the second and third generation. Such a strategy does not recognise the distinctive cultures of migrant workers, which include familial structures and bonds that differ greatly from those of the West German population. Many of the Turkish families still have a strong patriarchal structure, which socializes children to be obedient to their father's wishes and emotionally dependent on the approval of their parents. In this context, the offer of a special status, which attempts to effectively separate the lives of children from those of their parents, can impose excessive stress on children who become caught between two social and cultural systems, neither of which fully accepts them. This stress, which will no doubt limit the effectiveness of integration offers to the second and third generation, is a result of ethnocentric bias and a lack of recognition of cultural differences when integration policies are formulated. Such biases also exist in educational and recreational programs offered by the West German authorities; programs which are largely oriented to Western middle class norms and values and do not give sufficient consideration to the special needs of a culturally different low status minority group.

The official pronouncement that the foreigners should be able to retain their own cultural identity is currently little more than a slogan. If this is to be made a reality, the special needs and interests of the foreigners must be taken into account both when formulating the content of, and also when implementing, the integration programs. As I see it, the best way to achieve this is to bring representatives of the foreign population into the design of programs, and to support activities already initiated by the foreign workers.

DEVELOPMENT OF THE GERMAN AND FOREIGN POPULATION IN THE LARGER CITIES OF THE FEDERAL REPUBLIC OF GERMANY SINCE 1970

JÜRGEN BÄHR AND PAUL GANS (KIEL)

1. Introduction, aims and data basis of the study

In and around 1970 there was a turning point in the development of the population in the Federal Republic of Germany. A great decrease in the birth rate among the German population, which was already noticeable at the end of the sixties, resulted for the first time in 1971 that the death rate was greater than the birth rate. Since then a steady decrease in the number of Germans can be observed. The natural growth rate of the German population decreased from 0.4 ^{0}/oo in 1970 to -4.1^0/oo in 1975 and maintained this negative character during the following period (1984: -1.9^0/oo) in spite of the slight increase in births. For this reason the number of Germans decreased during the period 1970–1984 by about 1.6 % to 56.8 m. This is in contrast to the years 1961–1970 when the population rose by just about 4 % from 55.5 m to 57.7 m (since 1962 mainly because of the excess of births).[1]

The decrease was more than balanced out by the enormous influx of foreign workers and their dependents. The figures available for 1984 (4.36 m) surpass those of 1970 (2.98 m) by 46.0 %. As a result the total population in the Federal Republic of Germany increased a further 0.9 % between 1970 and 1984.

The larger cities[2] are greatly affected by these changes, a decrease in the German population, while at the same time the number of foreigners has increased. During the period 1970–1982 German inhabitants decreased in these larger cities by about 5.1 %, and this occured in spite of extensive incorporations of suburbs. At the same time the number of foreigners increased by about 62.4 %. These different types of development are expressed clearly by the percentage of foreigners in the resident population: between 1970–1982 it rose in the larger cities from 6.3 % to 11.3 %, a much more rapid rate than in the Federal Republic as a whole (from 4.9 % to 7.6 %).

---

1   If not otherwise indicated, the figures quoted were taken from the 'Statistical Yearbook of the Federal Republic of Germany' (for the Federal Republic as a whole) and from the 'Statistical Yearbook of German Communities' (for the larger cities): Statistisches Jahrbuch für die Bundesrepublik Deutschland 1972–1985 (Stuttgart/Mainz: Kohlhammer Verlag, 1972– 1985) and Statistisches Jahrbuch Deutscher Gemeinden 1970–1982 (Cologne: Deutscher Städtetag, 1972–1984).

2   In Germany a larger city ("Großstadt") is defined as one with at least 100,000 inhabitants. The missing data base does not allow us to use a metropolitan area concept that includes the larger cities and their suburbs.

The aim of this study is to analyse the demographic changes for the German and foreign population of the larger cities and to identify the components of change (migration and natural increase) between 1970 and 1982. Furthermore the study emphasizes existing differences in population growth between the larger cities and offers explanations for these developments. The information found in the 'Statistical Yearbook of German Communities' was used as the data source. The 66 larger cities of the Federal Republic in the year 1982 are included in this study.

The main problem of temporal analysis is to be found in the incorporations (partly extensive ones) of suburbs into the larger cities. In the cases of Bielefeld, Münster or Braunschweig, their municipal areas more than doubled. Therefore, neither absolute figures nor relative increases or decreases can be used for describing the development of the population. In addition comparison of the population density is not possible because of different dates for areas and number of inhabitants in the yearbooks. For this reason the rates of change concerning the number of inhabitants at the end of the year were based on calculations from the net migration and the natural increase. The details about the population moves refer to the appropriate present-day municipal area in order to exclude, as far as possible, erratic changes brought about by incorporated suburbs. For an analysis of the development of population in the larger cities, the following indices are available, for Germans and for foreigners: 1) rates of population increase or decrease; 2) crude rates of the natural population growth (birth and death rates as well as natural increase rates); 3) in- and out-migration rates and the resulting net migration rates.

2. Recent demographic and economic trends in the Federal Republic of Germany

The employment of foreign workers in the Federal Republic started around 1955, but it was not until 1960 that these immigrant workers became important in the national economy. Before that time the postwar economic reconstruction was mainly based on refugees, displaced persons and returning prisoners of war, who supplied the economy with well trained and specialized manpower in the post World War II period. After a phase of rapid industrial growth, full employment was obtained in the late 1950s. But after 1960, labour became scarce and was a major obstacle for further economic development. There were several reasons for the reduction of the national labour reservoir. Continued economic expansion, the formation of the "Bundeswehr" and introduction of general conscription, longer school and training programmes, the reduction of the regular weekly work time, the age structure of the population and the end of the steady inflow of refugees from the GDR after the erection of the Berlin Wall in August 1961 must be mentioned here to explain the shortage of labour. Even after great efforts to mobilize more people for the economic process the national labour supply was unable to meet an increased demand. A that time possibilities of introducing automatic systems in the production lines were rather limited. On the other hand the Mediterranean countries had a huge reservoir of unemployed labour, and their governments were willing to approve and regulate labour export migrations. Foreign workers were recruited after 1960. Because of the difficult economic and social situation in their home countries they were very willing to come to the Federal Republic. Special Recruitment Agreements were negotiated by the Federal Government with Italy (1955), Spain (1960), Greece (1960), Turkey (1961) and Yugoslavia (1968). This strategy resulted in an ever increasing number of foreign labourers over time. At the end of 1973 the Federal Government decreed a general stop on further recruitment and import of foreign workers, after the oil crisis and related factors had led to a period of economic depression. At that time the number of foreigners in the Federal Republic of Germany was almost 4 million (cf. Table 1). Two main phases of in-migration can be identified: Between 1960 and 1966 the Italians along with Greek and Spaniards in a first wave; afterwards, up to 1973 the recruitment of Yugoslav and Turkish workers became more important in a second phase.

Table 1: Foreign population in the Federal Republic of Germany according to
        nationality 1969–1984

| | Foreign population in thousands (30th Sep.) | | | | | % change |
	1969	1973	1976	1980	1984	1969–1984
Greece	271.3	399.2	353.7	297.5	287.1	5.8
Italy	514.6	622.0	568.0	617.9	545.1	5.9
Jugoslavia	331.6	673.3	640.4	631.7	600.3	81.0
Spain	206.9	286.1	219.4	180.0	158.8	−23.2
Turkey	322.6	893.6	1,079.3	1,462.4	1,425.8	342.0
Total foreign population	2,381.4	3,966.2	3,948.0	4,453.3	4,363.6	83.2

Source: Statistisches Jahrbuch für die Bundesrepublik, Stuttgart/Mainz 1970ff.

As shown by the investigations of Giese (1978), Giese and Nipper (1979) and O'Loughlin (1985), the spatial distribution of the foreign population and structural changes in West Germany may be explained by a model of diffusion. The innovation "recruitment of foreign workers" started in the Labour Office Districts close to the Swiss border in Southern Germany and spread to the Stuttgart metropolitan area in the early 1960s. From there the diffusion wave mainly followed the major communication lines, especially the Rhine-axis, to the Frankfurt (Main) and Cologne/Düsseldorf areas and spread eastwards and to the south to the Nuremberg and Munich regions. This process of spatial diffusion was directed by a spatial information pattern of larger companies concerning their positive experiences with foreign labourers. In addition the national distribution of foreign workers was partly a result of positive information about opportunities in West Germany by foreigners visiting their home countries during the summer vacations. These propaganda effects motivated many friends and family members to follow the example of the "pioneer migrants" and strengthened the existing spatial pattern. This explains the higher percentages of foreign workers in southern German cities as well as the distributions of national groups in Germany. Changes over time between 1960 and 1973 were the result of a complex interrelated information and communication pattern (cf. Table 1). For example, the Turkish segment is much stronger in northern areas than in the South because labour immigration from Turkey began later and was directed to areas far from the innovation cores. It must be mentioned that the pattern that existed in 1973, when official immigration was stopped, did not change very much in either its regional or ethnic structure, although the immigration of close family members continued to some extent in the following years.

At the present time, the percentage of foreigners is considerably higher in the metropolitan areas of southern Germany, and this is an indicator for the higher demand of labour in the years after 1960 (O'Loughlin 1985). The rate of unem--ployment, however, was much the same in the northern and southern Labour Office districts in 1970 (cf. Table 2). It should be noted on the other hand that the urban areas such as Recklinghausen, Mülheim or Kiel, which have less than 10 % below the federal average of per capita gross national product, are located north of the river Main (Heuer 1985, p. 24).

Table 2: Development of unemployment in selected larger cities

Labour offices	Unemployed persons[1]			
	1 9 7 0		1 9 8 3	
	number	% of labour force	number	% of labour force
Hamburg	2,750	0.4	72,484	10.2
Bremen	1,921	0.7	32,567	13.0
Dortmund	2,130	0.7	41,348	15.0
Duisburg	1,441	0.8	30,884	14.7
Cologne	1,355	0.4	49,631	12.4
Frankfurt	1,450	0.3	33,300	6.3
Stuttgart	520	0.1	21,005	5.2
Munich	2,791	0.3	55,329	6.1
Federal Republic	148,846	0.7	2,258,235	9.1

1 Annual average

Source: HEUER 1985, p. 25.

In addition to the traditional rural-urban contrast, an ever increasing difference between North and South is felt in Western Germany, in which the urban centers of the southern metropolitan areas have taken the economic lead. This distribution of economic power is partly based on the history of economic and industrial development in the 19th century, when the old industrial areas of the Ruhr and Saar districts flourished based on coal mining and steel production. The more innovative branches of the industry such as electric engineering, chemicals and car and other vehicle construction settled in southern German centers, such as Munich, Stuttgart, Frankfurt or Mannheim. After the Second World War, some larger companies moved their headquarters, and this has led to even stronger regional disparities in the economic development. For example Siemens moved from Berlin to Munich and concentrated the high technology activities of this company in that area. Since 1973 the disparity between the northern and southern parts of the Federal Republic has become more and more evident in the rates of unemployment (cf. Table 2). The spatial distribution of the crisis ridden, old established sectors of coal mining, steel and shipbuilding in the North and the expanding modern branches of electrical engineering and electronics, aviation and space industries in the South is very profitable for the larger cities in Southern Germany from a financial point of view as well. They thus have a higher potential of flexibility in meeting the technological challenges of the future and it may be predicted that the regional disparities between the North and South will increase in the foreseeable future.

3. Components of Demographic changes in the period of time 1970–1982

Development of the population

All larger cities in the Federal Republic as a whole registered an increase in population for the last time in 1970 (Fig. 1). Since then the rates have been always negative. The lowest values were reached in the midseventies. These trends are caused above all by the development of the German population, which was characterized by losses during the whole period of observation. Only in the last few years has this loss slightly slowed, mainly because of a decline in the suburbanization process. In 1982 the rate of decrease was only half as high as in 1973, the year with the highest rate. The interaction of birth and death rates as well as migration rates is explained below.

In contrast to German population development, the course of the foreigner can be divided into four clearly delimitated phases: 1) the time up to the recruitment ban for guest workers at the end of 1973 with a great increase in the foreign population; 2) the economic crisis after the first oil shock in the midseventies, coupled with a decrease in the number of foreigners; 3) the years between 1977–1980, when the number of foreigners living in the Federal Republic increased once again due to family reunification; and 4) the economic crisis after the second oil shock of 1979 with a renewed reversal of the trend, which again led to a negative foreigner growth rate for the first time since 1976.

In a more modified form these four sections are reflected in a diagram which refers to the whole population. They explain the extremely low rates of change of the years around 1975 as well as the almost balanced rate of change of the year 1980.

A differentiation according to the size of the communities (Fig. 1) basically confirms this picture. The course of the curve is generally the same for all categories, only with regards to their extreme values do they vary. It is noticeable that the relative losses in population are particularly pronounced in the cities with more than 500.000 inhabitants. This is the result of an unusually large decrease in the German population, partly because of disproportionately negative natural growth, partly because of massive suburbanization, which could not be fully balanced by means of higher population gains on the part of the foreigners. (For details, see below).

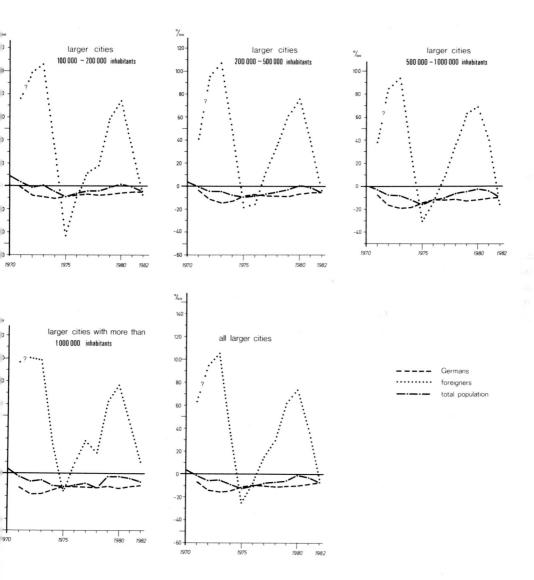

Fig. 1: Population growth rates of the larger cities of the Federal Republic of Germany (1970-1982)

For a better understanding of the development of the population it is necessary to analyse both determining components separately. A comparison of figures 2C and D shows that the decrease in population in the larger cities above all is a result of negative growth in the natural development of the population. There are hardly any migration losses at all; at times, 1979–1981, slight migration gains were achieved.

Natural increase

The total balance of birth and death rates would have been even more unfavourable, if it had not been reduced by the large excess of births among foreigners. At the beginning of the seventies the birth rate among Germans decreased rapidly, then remained almost constant between 1973 and 1979 and has increased again since the beginning of the eighties. Since the mid 1970s, the growth rate for Germans varies only negligibly, with values between $-6^0/oo$ and $-7^0/oo$ per year (Fig. 2A and C).

Extreme contrasts are evident in the foreigner case. Their extraordinarily low death rate, combined with a high birth rate (even if the latter has been constantly and rapidly decreasing since 1974), results in a high excess of births. Occasionally a rate of more than $20^0/oo$ was reached per year and even in 1982 it was at $14^0/oo$. That is why the balance of the natural population moves of the total population, extended over the whole population, never dropped below $-5^0/oo$ during the period of time under study. It has even increased within the last three years to rates of more than $-4^0/oo$ (Fig. 2A and C).

A drawback to using crude rates of the natural development of the population is that to a large extent they are determined by demographic structural components. Age composition especially plays a decisive role. This statement's impact becomes very clear, when the values calculated for foreigners are considered. Due to the fact that only very few elderly people from Mediterranean countries live in Germany, the number of deaths in these groups is consequently reduced. On the other hand, the effects of a greater percentage of women in child-bearing age are clearly seen in the number of foreign children.

If we include some measures of natural population development that are not dependent on structure, some of the results are modified but the basic patterns remain the same. With regard to mortality there is no great difference between the German and the foreign population living in the Federal Republic. If one considers fertility, however, there are large differences between both groups. This is shown in contrasts in the total fertility rate (TFR). The TFR is an expression of the number of births that would occur to a woman during her reproductive period on the assumption of present day age-specific fertility rates. As far back as the end of the nineteen-sixties the TFR for the German population dropped below replacement level (about 2.200). It reached a record minimum in 1979 with 1.301 and in 1981 it was at 1.359. At the same time considerably higher rates for the foreigners were registered. These rates now barely exceed replacement level. During the course of time, one can recognize a behavioural assimilation by foreigners towards the con-

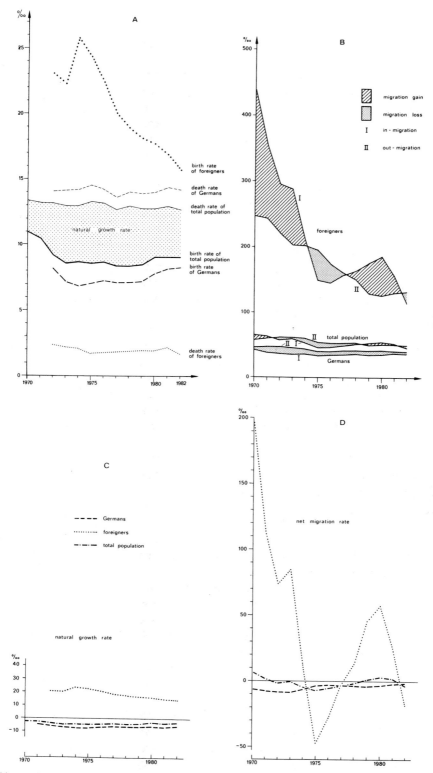

Fig. 2: Natural growth rates and migration rates of Germans and foreigners in the larger cities of the Federal Republic of Germany (1970-1982)

dition already existing among the German population. This is seen in the rapid decrease in the TFR, parallel to the decrease in the birth rates in fig. 2A. In 1975 the foreigners had a TFR of 2.643, whereas in 1981 it was just about 2.278. Quite a few nationalities drop below the threshold value of 2.200 and only the rate for the Turkish population is considerably higher at 3.485 (Hußmanns, Mammey and Schulz 1983, p. 343). Nevertheless, despite this merging, a very different natural population development among Germans and foreigners will remain for the next decade. The reasons are not only persisting behavioural differences but also the higher percentage of young foreigner population. Considering that the larger cities will obtain migration gains of foreigners in addition, it is expected that the percentage of the foreign population in larger cities will increase up to an average of 15 % − 17.5 % by the turn of the century (Bucher and others 1983, p. 1161).

Because of lack of data it is not possible to present a precise comparison between the conditions of mortality and fertility in the larger cities and in other regions of the Federal Republic. However, a few indicators can be deduced from the analysis of regional differences in mortality and fertility. According to Gatzweiler and Stiens (1982) there are considerable regional differences in mortality in Germany. But it is difficult to give a full explanation for this phenomenon. Present-day conditions differ greatly from those for the pre- and early period of industrialization until the second half of the 19th century, when mortality in cities was much higher than in rural areas because of bad living and working conditions. Marked contrasts between the larger cities and rural regions no longer exist. An above average mortality rate is found not only on the one hand in the traditional industrial areas which are densely populated (Ruhr region, Saarland, as well as Berlin), but also on the other hand in areas which are sparsely populated, in particular, the border areas of East Bavaria. In contrast, quite a number of larger cities exist, e.g. Munich, where the mortality rate is relatively low.

For lager cities, more definite findings can be obtained by using a regional differentiation of fertility conditions by means of the net reproduction rate (NRR). The NRR is a measure of the average number of surviving daughters produced by a woman during her reproductive period, assuming that the age- and sexspecific mortality and fertility rates for the current period will continue in future. A NRR of 1.0 corresponds to the replacement level. The spatial pattern of the NRR (for the German population) in 1979 shows remarkable differences between urban and rural areas (Fig. 3). The NRR reaches its peaks in districts like East Bavaria, Swabia, and Weser-Ems and even in isolated cases is above the long-term replacement rate. In contrast, particularly low rates are a characteristic feature of all metropolitan areas, including all the larger cities. Since 1974 no city administered as an independent borough ("Kreisfreie Stadt") has exceeded the threshold value of 1.0. In 1976 the NRR of the German population of the larger cities was, on an unweighted average, only 0.54, which was 30 % below the rate of the rural districts and 24 % below the (unweighted) average for the whole country (Schwarz 1983).

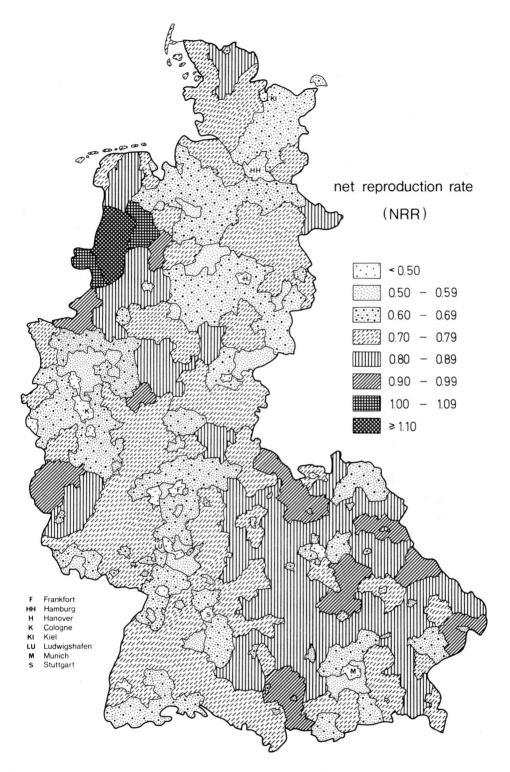

net reproduction rate

(NRR)

	< 0.50
	0.50 — 0.59
	0.60 — 0.69
	0.70 — 0.79
	0.80 — 0.89
	0.90 — 0.99
	1.00 — 1.09
	≥ 1.10

F   Frankfort
HH Hamburg
H   Hanover
K   Cologne
KI Kiel
LU Ludwigshafen
M Munich
S Stuttgart

Fig. 3: Spatial variation of the net reproduction rate (NRR) in the Federal Republic of Germany (1979)

Migrations

If the negative overall population trend is mainly a reflection of the decreasing number of births among Germans, then the variations within the course of the curve clearly can be traced back to migration. A positive net migration for the larger cities calculated for the early seventies as well as for the period around 1980, balances the deficit of births completely or to a large extent. In the intervening years (1972–1978) a negative balance for migration flows into and out cities existed so that the population losses were intensified in the larger cities.

A closer look at migration (differentiating between Germans and foreigners) shows that two opposite trends coexist. In each year of the study period migration losses among the Germans turn the tables round and are in sharp contrast to migration gains among the foreigners (Fig. 2D). Figure 2B points out just as clearly the much higher rate of mobility among foreign inhabitants, that is the balances are a result of the differentiation of similarly high rates of migration into and out of cities. In comparison to the early seventies a decrease in the rate of mobility is evident, even if the foreigner rates today are three times those of the German population (cf. Bähr and Gans 1985).

If one analyses the course of each curve more carefully, concentrating first of all on the German population, then one can ascertain that in the early seventies a great number of people left the larger cities for the surrounding area (Fig. 2B). Since there was no equivalent migration to the cities to offset this loss, increasing migration losses resulted from this trend. Until 1973 these losses contributed to the decrease in the German population in larger cities to a greater extent than the deficit in births (Fig. 2C and D). The tendency towards urban flight declined temporarily as a result of the economic recession after the first oil shock, without however reaching rates similar to those at the beginning of the decade. At present, migration losses are no longer the main factor for the decrease in the German population in the larger cities as it was the case in the early seventies. In 1982 a net migration rate of $-1.6^0/_{00}$ (1972: $-8.4^0/_{00}$) stands in contrast to a negative natural increase rate of $-6.1^0/_{00}$ (1972: $-5.9^0/_{00}$; Fig. 2C and D).

The interplay of migrations into and out of the cities among the foreign population reveals that the phases used to describe the development of the population (see above) can be attributed to changes in attitude towards migration. Maximum gains in migration were recorded until the recruitment ban for guest workers (23rd Nov. 1973). However, at that time the principle of foreign worker rotation ("Rotationsprinzip") operated to a large extent so the out-migration rates from cities reached their highest values as well (Fig. 2B). The recruitment ban of November 1973 temporarily led to a considerable decrease in foreigners arriving in Germany. As a result of continually decreasing rates for urban flight ("Stadtflucht") there were negative net migration rates for the years 1975–1977. The family reunification which followed led to a rise in the immigration rates. This influx was facilitated by legal provisions, for example greater childrens' allowances for the children of guest workers living in Germany from 1st Jan 1975 and easier employment possibilities for relatives from 1st April 1979 (Mertins 1983). This explains the renewed positive balances from 1979 onwards (Fig. 2D).

The development of the past few years is characterized by different measures for controlling the migration of foreigners. On the one hand, making immigration regulations more difficult (limiting the entry of family members to children under 16) has contributed to a clear drop in the foreigner in-migration rate curve after 1980. On the other hand, out-migration rates have increased since 1981 for the first time during the period in question because of increased foreigner remigration to their native countries. As a result the net migration in 1982 was again negative. The latest figures for the Federal Republic as a whole confirm this tendency. The bonus for remigration ("Rückkehrprämie") caused a disproportionately high remigration of foreigners in 1984, so that the migration losses with regard to other European countries (including Turkey) surpassed 200,000 persons compared to 84,000 in 1982. This trend manifests itself in the development of the population as a whole. In spite of slight regressive losses among the Germans, the number of inhabitants in the larger cities here decreased since 1982 to a greater extent than in the years before (Fig. 1).

4. Regional variations of selected components (1972–1982)

The migration balances of the German population and the natural growth of the foreign population were taken as example to demonstrate and analyse regional differences. The explanations given should be interpreted as hypotheses not as final conclusions because up-to-date information about the population of the cities is not available at the present time.

Migration balance of the German population

For the majority of larger cities, the net migration for the German population is negative (52 out of 66). Extremes of $-13^0/oo$ (Duisburg) and $+6^0/oo$ (Heidelberg) per year stand in contrast to the mean of $-3^0/oo$ (annual average of the study period). Those cities with a high negative growth in their population do not present a uniform economic structure. This is seen in figure 4. Here one finds not only the core areas of the two coal and steel industries in Germany (Gelsenkirchen, Oberhausen and Duisburg as well as Saarbrücken), but also cities with a prospering industry and with an extremely high rate of property tax per inhabitant, which reflects an economic strength based on industry and trade as, for instance, Frankfurt, Düsseldorf, Ludwigshafen and Stuttgart (Gatzweiler and Meuter 1983, p. 1101).

From a breakdown of the balances into migration to and from the cities, as is done by way of an example for Duisburg and Frankfurt (Fig. 5), it can be seen that the balances, similar for both city groups, were achieved in completely different ways. In the first case, the lack of attraction of cities dominated by the coal and steel industry is reflected in extremely low rates of migration into the city (Fig. 6),

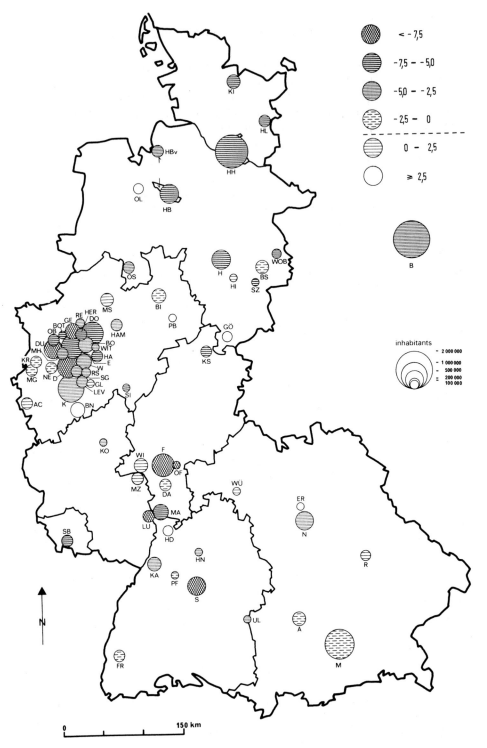

Fig. 4: Net migration rates of the German population in the larger cities of the Federal Republic of Germany (1972-1982 in ‰)

whereas in the second case the high rates of urban flight (especially up to 1975) are responsible for the negative balances. This result indicates a process of suburbanization which began to increase in the early seventies. At that point in time, the number of households (especially those in the higher-income brackets) which left the larger cities and moved to the surrounding areas increased greatly. On the one hand, the reasons are due to an increasing displacement of the residential function by traffic, public services and private. On the other hand, the reasons can be found in the lower land values and in a more varied choice of property in the suburban communities of the surrounding area. Present data point out that this population shift started very early in the large metropolitan areas and continued with an above average intensity. Apart from Munich ($-2.3^{0}/_{00}$), all cities with more than 500,000 inhabitants depict balances of less than $-2.5^{0}/_{00}$ per year.

Between 1972 and 1982 only 14 cities achieved a positive migration balance. To a large extent their economic basis is determined by the tertiary sector (Blotevogel and Hommel 1980, p. 158), i.e. mainly university and/or administration cities. With regards to the tax yield per capita ("Realsteueraufkommen pro Kopf") the cities belonging to this group, with the exception of Mainz, have a middle or even low position. Their particularly broad and varied education opportunities might be one of the main reasons why they are migration destination for those involved. The migration into the city is so high that even a striking flow to the rural surroundings is more than compensated, as is shown for Bonn and Heidelberg in the diagrams of figure 5 (see also fig. 6).

The positive balances of this group of cities are caused partly by the fact that some cities are situated within the suburban area of larger metropolitan areas. Therefore, they attract some of the household migrating from there, acting as suburban destinations. This is probably the case for Bergisch-Gladbach (near Cologne) above all, and in a more modified form for Heidelberg (near Mannheim/Ludwigshafen), Erlangen (near Nuremberg) and Hildesheim (near Hannover; see fig. 6).

To what extent large-scale migration moves influence the distribution pattern in figure 4 can only be answered by means of precise knowledge of the individual migration flows. However, it is striking that the percentage of cities with positive or only slightly negative balances is much higher in Southern Germany than it is in the north or the west of the country. At this point the north-south differential is generally traced which results from calculating the net migrations based on the federal states in Germany. Between 1970 and 1984 positive changes concerning the German population were recorded only in Hessen, Baden-Württemberg and Bavaria, whereas Rhineland-Palatinate, the northern German states as a whole, and, especially North Rhine-Westphalia, were characterized by losses.

The migration balances between the states indicate, as well as the corresponding unemployment rates, that the economic problem areas in Germany are to be found mainly in the north and the west. This contrast between the north and the south has increased in intensity within the last few years. As a result the relative positions of those areas badly hit by the past — 1980 economic crisis deteriorated further (Bucher and others 1983, p. 1173).

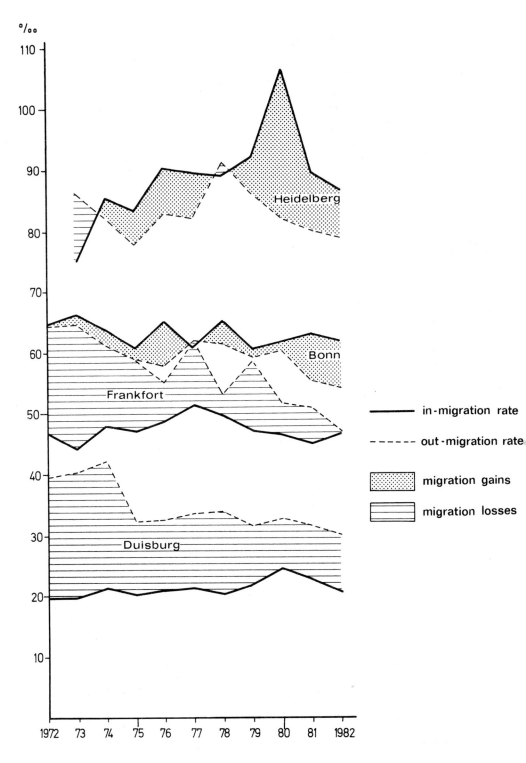

°/oo

Fig. 5: Rates of in- and out-migration of the German population in selected larger cities of the Federal Republic of Germany (1972-1982 in °/oo)

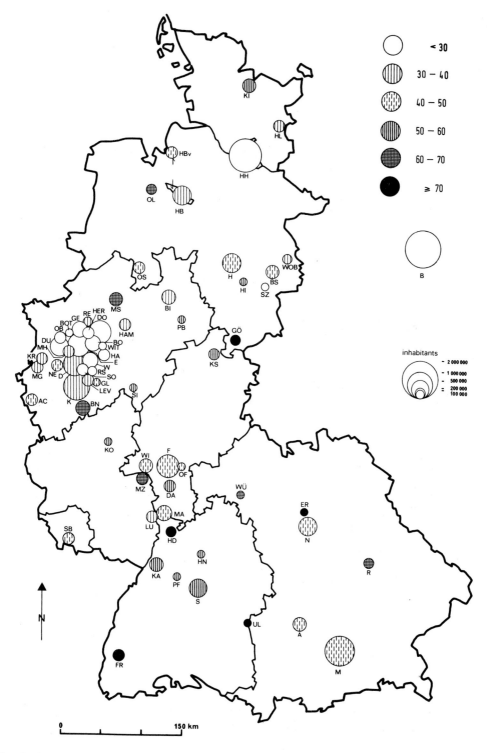

Fig. 6: In-migration rates of the German population to the larger cities of the Federal Republic of Germany (1972-1982 in ‰)

Deficits in births have caused the decrease in the German population to a greater extent than the negative net migration (on average $-5.0^0/oo$ per year in comparison to $-3.4^0/oo$). Only in some cities have the cases of migration excess been sufficient to balance out the regressive number of births and to lead to a positive change in rates among the German population (Fig. 7). During the period of time in question this is true only for Münster, Erlangen, Oldenburg, Göttingen, Heidelberg and Paderborn (which has a positive rate of natural increase). These university cities are preferred destination areas of education-orientated migrations. The higher percentage of younger people in these cities causes less low rates of natural growth, in spite of net reproduction rates which in part are well below the average. (For example, the rate for Heidelberg is 0.33, and for Münster, 0.44 compared to an average of all larger cities of 0.54; Schwarz 1983). In contrast to this, the influence of the age structure results in a decreasing number of German inhabitants despite migration gains for example in Bonn, Aachen and Wiesbaden. Because of the increase in foreigners, the population as a whole has increased in these cities as well (Fig. 7).

Among the cities with a large decrease in the German population (as well as in the total population) there are those, such as Berlin and Hamburg, where the deficit in births exerts the greatest influence. In Berlin, expecially, the high percentage of older persons is critical for understanding the extremely negative natural growth. There are also cities where the negative net migration is the striking feature (Duisburg, Gelsenkirchen, Düsseldorf, Frankfurt, Stuttgart, Mannheim). The relative migration losses in the coal and steel cities with a weak economy are twice as high as the excess of deaths, whereas in Berlin and Hamburg, there is more or less a reversal of these two components (Fig. 7).

Natural population growth of the foreign population

With regards to the foreign population spatial differences are fairly easy to explain. This is true not only for their natural increase, but also for their net migration and consequently for the change in foreigner population as a whole. A conspicuous increase in values from south to north is typical in all. Local characteristics do not play a great part in this general pattern. As an example, the natural growth rate is analysed in greater detail.

All 11 cities which belong to the top category of figure 3 with a natural growth rate of at least $22.5^0/oo$ (annual average 1972–82) are to be found in North Rhine-Westphalia and Lower Saxony (for example (in descending order) Recklinghausen $28.0^0/oo$, Hamm $25.6^0/oo$, Gelsenkirchen $25.3^0/oo$, Herne $24.7^0/oo$, Bremerhaven $23.3^0/oo$, Krefeld $23.2^0/oo$). Of the 28 cities with a relative increase of more than $20^0/oo$, only three lie south of the river Main (Offenbach, Ludwigshafen, Ulm). Two hypotheses can be formulated to explain this striking contrast. First, obvious differences between the different foreign population groups exist concerning their reproductive behaviour. A special position is held by the Turkish population. The average number of children greatly exceeds the average of all foreigners (total fertil-

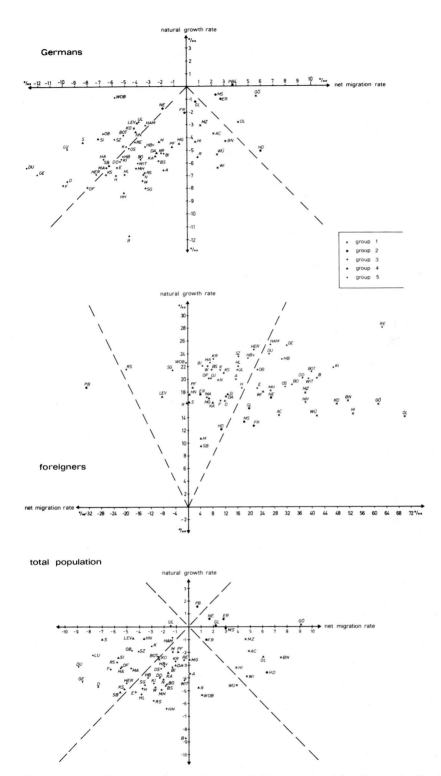

Fig. 7: Components of the population change of Germans and foreigners in the larger cities of the Federal Republic of Germany (1972-1982)

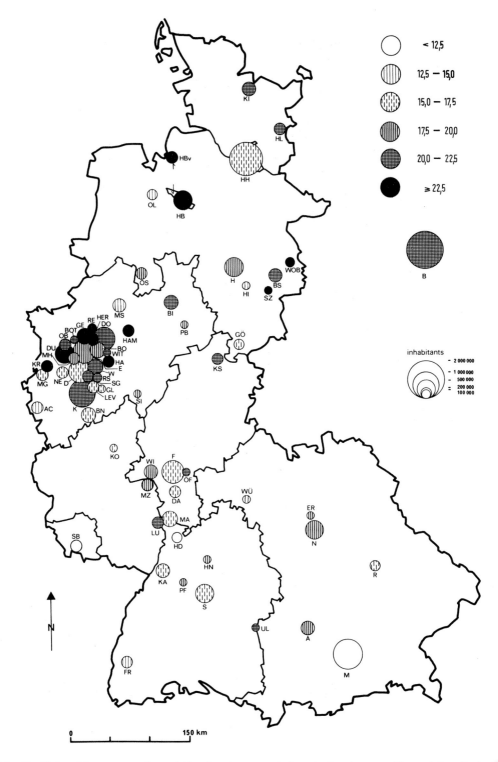

Fig. 8: Natural increase rates of the foreign population in the larger cities of the Federal Republic of Germany (1972-1982 in ‰)

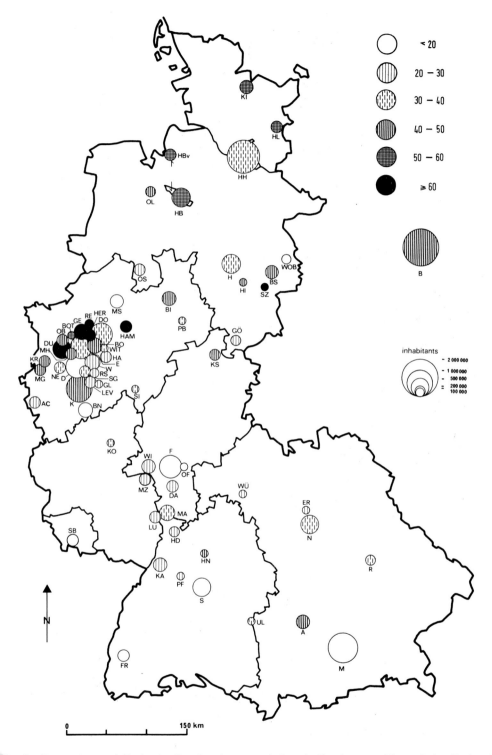

Fig. 9: Percentage of Turks in the foreign population in the larger cities of the Federal
Republic of Germany in 1982

ity rate for the foreign population in 1981: 2.278, for the Turkish population 3.485). As a result larger cities, where the percentage of Turks is more than 60 % of the foreign population, have a natural increase of $22.5^0/oo$ and over. Cities with a Turkish majority among the foreigners register an increase of at least $20^0/oo$. A high percentage of Turks is mainly a characteristic of cities in Northern Germany and in the Ruhr region, since the diffusion of employment of foreign workers from the south to the north is correlated with an increase in the Turkish percentage (Fig. 9). Second, during the study period, there is a noticeable tendency among all groups of foreigners to assimilate their reproductive behaviour to that of the German population. Generally, foreigners south of the River Main have been in Germany for a longer period of time. In addition to that an increasing number of households belong to the following (second) generation. These facts lead one to the supposition that such a process of reproductive assimilation has progressed further in the south and has led to a drop in the natural increase.

Apart from this north-south contrast, in all cities where many foreigners from non-guest worker nations live, only a slight natural increase is recorded. These include typical university cities like Heidelberg ($12.2^0/oo$) and Freiburg ($12.8^0/oo$), but also cities close to the border like Saarbrücken to France with the lowest rate at all ($9.4^0/oo$) and Aachen to Belgium ($14.3^0/oo$). In part this can be explained by the age structure but more decisive is the fact that the reproductive behaviour of foreigners from neighbouring European countries does not vary from that of the German population.

Due to the fact that the net migration and the natural increase in the foreign population have the same reinforcing effects, it is not surprising that the well-known pattern is seen when describing the relative changes among the foreign population. During the time studied the foreign population increased disproportionally mainly in Berlin and in numerous cities in Northern Germany as well as in the Ruhr region. One must keep in mind that most of these cities are not part of the economically important metropolitan areas. Again this seems to indicate a diffusion pattern which at first was of a hierarchical nature and which after the recruitment ban in 1973 was dominated by neighbourhood effects (Giese 1978, Nipper 1983).

Classification of the cities according to natural growth and net migration

We classified the larger cities according to the components of their population development, natural rate of population increase and net migration, each time separating Germans from foreigners. The more similar the values of the cities for the four characteristics, the smaller the distance between the cities in fourdimensional space. Consequently, they are grouped by means of Ward's hierarchical iterative procedure (Bähr 1971). Figure 10 illustrates the result of the classification procedure after the 61st step of grouping (information loss 45 %). The five resulting groups can be subdivided into two categories according to their spatial distribution: the larger cities of groups 1, 2, and 3 are spread over the whole of Germany, where-

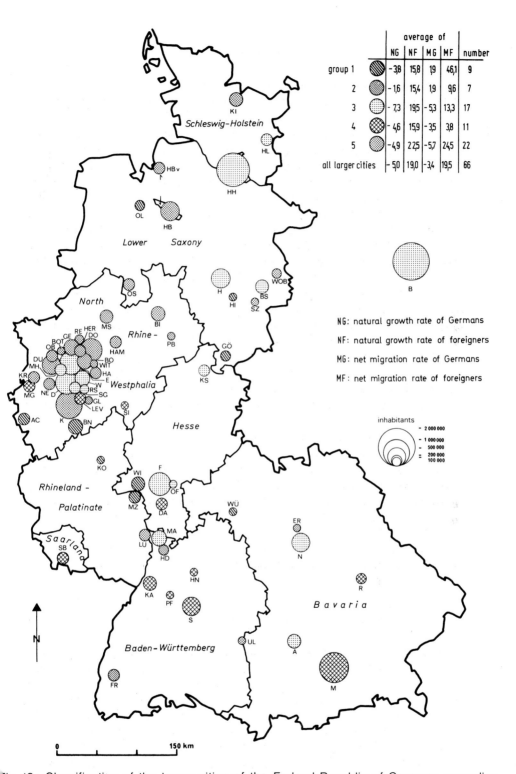

	average of				
	NG	NF	MG	MF	number
group 1	-3,8	15,8	1,9	46,1	9
2	-1,6	15,4	1,9	9,6	7
3	-7,3	19,5	-5,3	13,3	17
4	-4,6	15,9	-3,5	3,8	11
5	-4,9	22,5	-5,7	24,5	22
all larger cities	-5,0	19,0	-3,4	19,5	66

NG: natural growth rate of Germans

NF: natural growth rate of foreigners

MG: net migration rate of Germans

MF: net migration rate of foreigners

inhabitants

Fig. 10: Classification of the larger cities of the Federal Republic of Germany according to the components of the population change (1972-1982)

as those of group 4 are concentrated in the south and those of group 5 in the north.

The cities of classes 1 and 2 differ from each other mainly with respect to the migration gain among the foreign inhabitants. It is nearly five times higher for Bonn, Mainz, Wiesbaden, Hildesheim or Göttingen (group 1) than for Heidelberg, Münster or Erlangen (group 2; cf. 7). Common to both groups is the positive net migration as well as the relatively low deficit in births among the German population, indicating a youthful age structure. With the exception of Neuss and Bergisch-Gladbach, which belong to the suburban area of larger metropolitan areas (Düsseldorf and Cologne respectively), it is a matter of typical administration and/or university cities, where numerous prestigious education opportunities intensify in-migration (Fig. 6). The average in-migration rate for all cities included in the study (43.8 $^0/oo$) contrasts to an average of 58.2 $^0/oo$ for group 1 and that of 63.7 $^0/oo$ for group 2. Figure 6 illustrates that extremely high values were reached in the classic university cities, such as Heidelberg (88.7 $^0/oo$, cf. fig. 5), Freiburg (83.6 $^0/oo$), Erlangen (71.8 $^0/oo$), Göttingen (73.6 $^0/oo$) or Würzburg (69.8 $^0/oo$). On the other hand, cities whose economic structure is not or to a lesser extent based on university employment and attractions had obviously lower rates, but which still were above average (Aachen 48.9 $^0/oo$, Neuss 43.7 $^0/oo$, Wiesbaden 43.0 $^0/oo$, Bergisch-Gladbach 45.3 $^0/oo$).

The cities of group 3, which are also dispersed over the whole country, are characterized by below average values of all variables, except the natural increase in population among foreigners. In particular, the deficits in births and the migration losses among Germans are very high. Obviously the size of the city is a decisive factor for the characteristics of the individual population components. 70 % of the cities in group 3 have a population of more than 200,000 inhabitants and 7 of the 13 cities with at least 500,000 inhabitants are included in it. In this respect it is mainly a question of the larger cities of the important economic areas of the Federal Republic such as Berlin, Hamburg, Hannover, Essen/Düsseldorf/Wuppertal, Frankfurt/Offenbach or Mannheim. The differences in the strength of the local economy of these cities are reflected in the net migration, but rather in the amount of in-migration rates for the German population (Fig. 6). This amount is considerably above the group average (36.4 $^0/oo$) in cities with important administration duties and a favourable industrial structure (e.g. Kassel 52.9 $^0/oo$, Hannover 49.2 $^0/oo$; Frankfurt 47.4 $^0/oo$ (see fig. 5), Offenbach 47.3 $^0/oo$). Cities in the traditional industrial area of North Rhine-Westphalia remain definitely below that level (e.g. Solingen 22.5 $^0/oo$, Essen 22.7 $^0/oo$, Wuppertal 26.1 $^0/oo$, Remscheid 28.4 $^0/oo$).

The cities in groups 4 and 5 show a complementary picture in their spatial distribution. The cities of group 4, with a slight increase in foreigners and comparatively few losses among the German population, are mainly to be found in the south, especially in areas with unemployment rates which are far below the national average. This favourable economic situation is once again reflected in high rates of in-migration for the German population (Fig. 6). Cities with a varied service sector clearly exceed the mean value of the group (49.4 $^0/oo$). Regensburg (66.9 $^0/oo$), Darmstadt (57.6 $^0/oo$) and Stuttgart (54.2 $^0/oo$) are good examples of this type of city. This corresponds with the general movement of population from north to south mentioned above.

In contrast to group 4, the cities of group 5 are mainly concentrated in the north of Germany. The highest migration losses among the Germans and at the same time a high excess of births as well as migration gains among foreigners are recorded in these cities. The positive net migration among foreigners is seen in the process of diffusion, spreading from the south to the north, whereas the negative population changes for Germans are a reflection of structural economic problems. The economic structure of these cities is almost completely based on mining, the steel industry and ship building. On average the intensity of in-migration among the Germans is very low ($34.5^0/oo$, cf. fig. 6). Nevertheless, the values are highly variable and allow a further subdivision of this group into cities which are characterized on the one hand by the coal and steel industry with below average rates (Duisburg $21.2^0/oo$ (cf. fig. 5), Gelsenkirchen $22.8^0/oo$, Herne $24.8^0/oo$, Oberhausen $25.0^0/oo$, Dortmund $25.1^0/oo$) and on the other hand, into cities which contain a broader economic range of activities with an above average rate (Ulm $71.2^0/oo$, Kiel $52.4^0/oo$, Osnabrück $43.9^0/oo$, Bremerhaven $43.7^0/oo$).

SUMMARY AND CONCLUSIONS

The contrast of the north and south of the Federal Republic in the development of the population that appeared again and again in the spatial patterns analysed in this chapter in such a conspicuous fashion may intensify even more in the future. The number of foreign inhabitants in the larger cities will probably not increase much or at all because of further restrictions on in-migration and renewed support for return to their native countries. No changes in German birth rates can be expected in the near future. Therefore, the development of the population in the larger cities depends mainly on success in attracting in-migrants from other areas. Excluding the university cities, this requires sufficient and quite varied employment opportunities and is influenced by the economic development of the country as a whole. Currently there are considerable economic differences within the Federal Republic with a major growth axis in the south illustrated by a low rate of unemployment. For example, in November 1985 the rate of unemployment in Baden-Württemberg and South Bavaria was 5.2 % and 6.4 % respectively, whereas in the low lands of Northern Germany Lower Saxony (11.6 %), Schleswig-Holstein (11.2 %) as well as the city-states Hamburg (12.3 %), and Bremen (15.2 %) it was noticeable above average all prognoses assume that the economic contrast between the north and the south will continue to intensify in the future. The reason for this is that future-oriented expansion industries have located mainly in and around the areas of Stuttgart and Munich (Gschwind and Henkel 1984, p. 995). The subsequent employment demands which exist in these places will attract people from the northern regions and North Rhine-Westphalia and as a result the development of the seventies will continue into the future. Even today this development is seen in above average in-migration rates of the German population in the larger cities situated in the south (Fig. 6).

From the above we can conclude that the population development of larger cities of the Federal Republic of Germany in the future will differ from region to region to an even greater extent than has been the case to date. The larger cities of "attractive metropolitan areas" will continue to be favourite migration destinations for young working people. However, parallel to this regional migration, the urban-suburban migrations will probably continue and in part extend from suburban to exurban rural areas. In contrast, economically mono-structured metropolitan areas in particular the coal and steel regions, will be unlikely to achieve significant migration gains among young working people in the future. For economic reasons suburbanization in these depressed cities will occur less noticeably. However because of the migration away from these cities among older age groups, a comparatively high drop in population can be expected.

Alphabetical List of the Larger Cities Including those Abbreviations that are Used in the Figures
(Register Numbers)

A	Augsburg	Aachen	AC
AC	Aachen	Augsburg	A
B	Berlin	Berlin	B
BI	Bielefeld	Bergisch-Gladbach	GL
BN	Bonn	Bielefeld	BI
BO	Bochum	Bochum	BO
BOT	Bottrop	Bonn	B
BS	Brunswick	Bottrop	BOT
D	Düsseldorf	Bremen	HB
DA	Darmstadt	Bremerhaven	HBv
DO	Dortmund	Brunswick	BS
DU	Duisburg	Cologne	K
E	Essen	Darmstadt	DA
ER	Erlangen	Dortmund	DO
F	Frankfurt/Main	Duisburg	DU
FR	Freiburg/Breisgau	Düsseldorf	D
GE	Gelsenkirchen	Erlangen	ER
GL	Bergisch-Gladbach	Essen	E
GÖ	Göttingen	Frankfurt/Main	F
H	Hannover	Freiburg/Breisgau	FR
HA	Hagen	Gelsenkirchen	GE
HAM	Hamm	Göttingen	GÖ
HB	Bremen	Hagen	HA
HBv	Bremerhaven	Hamburg	HH
HD	Heidelberg	Hamm	HAM
HER	Herne	Hannover	H
HH	Hamburg	Heidelberg	HD
HI	Hildesheim	Heilbronn	HN
HL	Lübeck	Herne	HER
HN	Heilbronn	Hildesheim	HI

K	Cologne	Karlsruhe	KA
KA	Karlsruhe	Kassel	KS
KI	Kiel	Kiel	KI
KO	Koblenz	Koblenz	KO
KR	Krefeld	Krefeld	KR
KS	Kassel	Leverkusen	LEV
LEV	Leverkusen	Lübeck	HL
LU	Ludwigshafen/Rhine	Ludwigshafen/Rhine	LU
M	Munich	Mainz	MZ
MA	Mannheim	Mannheim	MA
MG	Mönchengladbach	Mönchengladbach	MG
MH	Mülheim/Ruhr	Mülheim/Ruhr	MH
MS	Münster	Munich	M
MZ	Mainz	Münster	MS
N	Nuremberg	Neuss	NE
NE	Neuss	Nuremberg	N
OB	Oberhausen	Oberhausen	OB
OF	Offenbach/Main	Offenbach/Main	OF
OL	Oldenburg/Old.	Oldenburg/Old.	OL
OS	Osnabrück	Osnabrück	OS
PB	Paderborn	Paderborn	PB
PF	Pforzheim	Pforzheim	PF
R	Regensburg	Recklinghausen	RE
RE	Recklinghausen	Regensburg	R
RS	Remscheid	Remscheid	RS
S	Stuttgart	Saarbrücken	SB
SB	Saarbrücken	Salzgitter	SZ
SG	Solingen	Siegen	SI
SI	Siegen	Solingen	SG
SZ	Salzgitter	Stuttgart	S
UL	Ulm	Ulm	UL
W	Wuppertal	Wiesbaden	WI
WI	Wiesbaden	Witten	WIT
WIT	Witten	Wolfsburg	WOB
WOB	Wolfsburg	Wuppertal	W
WÜ	Würzburg	Würzburg	WÜ

INTRAURBAN MIGRATION OF FOREIGNERS IN KIEL SINCE 1972 THE CASE OF THE TURKISH POPULATION

PAUL GANS (KIEL)

1. Introduction

When the one millionth foreign laborer, a Portuguese, arrived in the Federal Republic of Germany in 1964, he was greeted with music and gifts. This festivity was typical of the attitude towards "guest workers" at the time (Bundeszentrale für politische Bildung 1984). Government, economy, the news media and the German population were convinced that the immigration of laborers from the Mediterranean countries was a temporary phenomenon. The responsible officials even considered labor migration to be essential for the continued economic expansion and, with it, the steady rise in the standard of living in West Germany. The assumption was that this migration would follow a rotation principle, i.e., after a certain period of time, in which the foreign laborers had saved enough money or possibly learned certain skills, or after the demand for labor had decreased, they would return to their home countries. This immigration policy was confirmed in 1966/67 during the first post World War II recession, when the number of foreign laborers decreased by 400,000 within a period of one year (Table 1).

As the economy began to recover in 1967, the demand for labor also increased again, and by 1973, the number of employed foreigners had increased to almost 2.6 million. The total foreign population had reached almost 4 million (Table 1). At this point the percentage of foreigners who were employed was 65.4%. In the subsequent period, up to 1984, the percentage sank to 36.5% (Table 1). This decrease is an indication of a reorientation among the foreign laborers living in West Germany from temporary to more permanent residence. This change in attitude is a consequence of the recruitment ban proclaimed by the Federal Government in November 1973 as a result of the economic recession (first oil price shock). Foreigner laborers who subsequently returned to their home countries could not expect to later find reemployment in West Germany. With the recruitment ban the rotation principle was deprived of its basis. The proportion of foreigners who had lived in West Germany for at least ten years increased from 16.2 to 57.4%, thus refuting the view held in the 1960's that the employment of foreign laborers was a temporary phenomenon.

The problems involved in the integration of foreign laborers became more and more obvious, especially since there has been a demographic shift in the foreign population since 1973 away from a "guest worker structure" towards an ethnic minority (Esser 1985). The changes have affected not only the percentage of employed persons, as mentioned above, but also the makeup of the foreign population according to nationality with a disproportionately large increase in Turks and a rising number of youths and children. Two other measures taken be the Federal Government have tended to encourage the reuniting of families (Mertins 1983), in addition to the recruitment ban:

— Since 1 January 1975 the subsidies paid to parents of underage children, or children who do not yet have an income of their own, ("Kindergeld") have been raised. Foreign laborers, however, receive the full amount only for children living in West Germany.

— The "Wartezeitenlösung" ("waiting period solution") of 1 April 1979 allows work permits to be issued to children who entered the country as minors after two years of residence and to spouses after three years of residence.

The results of these political measures can be seen in a sudden increase in the proportion of juveniles among the foreign population from 15.7% (1973) to 24.1% (1979), which documents the changes in population structure (Table 1).

Because of the increased trend towards the reunification of families, beginning in 1973, the number of foreigners decreased only slightly until 1978, despite recruitment ban, and then rose again to a level above 4 million (Table 1). The number of foreigners did not begin to decrease again until 1983 during the recession following the second oil price shock, when a disproportionately large number of foreigners was affected by the highest level of unemployment in the history of West Germany. The poor outlook for renewed employment and financial incitements offered to those who returned to their home countries induced many to leave West Germany. The declining numbers, however, do not alter the fact that the proportion of foreigners who wish to remain in West Germany for an extended period of time has been increasing since 1973.

The reunited families needed other housing conditions. Up till then foreign workers had lived mainly in barracks in the vicinity of factories. Now they began to move into residential areas and thus began to compete with the German population on the housing market. From 1973 on the Germans became increasingly aware of the problems entailed in the immigration of foreign laborers. After this date the proportion of Turks among the total foreign population rose from 25% (1974) to 32.7% (1984), and public opinion began to indentify the so-called "foreigner problem" with a "Turkish problem" (Esser 1985).

West Germany today is de facto an immigration country, and the problems involved in integrating foreign residents are going to increase. We must bear in mind that the second and third generation were often born here, or at least grew up here, and only know the country whose citizenship they hold from brief vacation visits. In the following we will investigate problems related to integration using as an example the residential segregation of the foreign residents — particularly the Turkish residents — of the city of Kiel. It can be assumed that the intensity of the contacts between different nationalities — their integration — depends on the spatial distribution of the different population groups within the city. The empirical results of the investigation in Kiel will be preceeded by a brief presentation of data from several other cities in West Germany.

Paul Gans

Table 1: Development of the foreign population in Western Germany since 1961

	foreign population in 1000	employed persons in 1000	employed persons in %	length of residence with at least 10 years in %	less than 15 years old in %
1961	686	549	80.0		15.7
1966	–	1 313	–		18.4
1967	1 807	991	54.8		21.1
1970	2 976	1 949	65.5		22.6
1973	3 966	2 595	65.4	16.2	23.5
1974	4 127	2 331	56.5	17.8	23.7
1975	4 089	2 071	50.6	20.3	24.1
1976	3 948	1 937	49.1	22.8	23.8
1977	3 948	1 889	47.8	23.7	23.6
1978	3 981	1 869	46.9	26.3	23.9
1979	4 143	1 934	46.7	32.2	23.5
1980	4 453	2 072	46.5	37.8	22.5
1981	4 630	1 930	41.7	42.8	
1982	4 667	1 784	38.2	47.5	
1983	4 535	1 714	37.8	54.2	
1984	4 364	1 593	36.5	57.5	

Source: ESSER 1985, S. 121 and Statistisches Bundesamt 1972ff.

2. Residential Segregation and the Housing Market

The problem of integrating foreign residents affects primarily the metropolitan areas. In 1983 the percentage of foreign residents in the large cities was much higher at 11.2% than the national average of 7.4%. Several investigations have shown that foreign residents are not distributed evenly throughout the cities in question. Instead they tend to concentrate in the inner cities, particularly in those areas of the city center with old houses and substandard dwelling units (Clark 1975, O'Loughlin 1980, Helmert 1982, Gans 1981 and 1984, O'Loughlin/Glebe 1984a/b.). The indices of segregation that were calculated for the German and the foreign population, however, lie well below the corresponding values for ethnic minorities in North American cities (Clark 1975, O'Loughlin/Glebe 1984b). In Duisburg, Düsseldorf, or Frankfurt the indices vary from 25 to 35% and show a high degree of temporal stability. Spatial segregation is much more pronounced for certain nationalities than it is for foreigners as a whole. Turks, for instance, are more highly segregated from Germans than are Italians or Jugoslavs (O'Loughlin/Glebe 1984b). Nevertheless, it would be incorrect to speak of ethnic or Turkish ghettos (Holzner 1982). The reason for this is that the inner city housing stock is very heterogeneous with regard to age, condition and ownership. Thus it is mainly individual buildings that are segregated, and it is quite uncommon to find an entire block with more than 80% foreigners (Gans 1979, Jones 1983, O'Loughlin/Glebe 1984a/b). The fact that the housing market in West Germany is not free also contributes to these small-scale differences. Access to many apartments is limited to certain categories of people, because new tenants are expected to fulfill certain requirements. Thus, as Gans (1984) determined, in Ludwigshafen (Rhein) the publicly subsidized development association was not taking foreign households into consideration to the degree that their incomes would have warranted. It would be a mistake, however, to consider the policy followed in choosing tenants to be deliberately discriminatory. Publicly subsidized housing and development agencies are subject to various laws and priority ratings and it is only natural that German households take priority in the search for housing. Foreigners have fewer alternatives for intraurban moves than Germans do. Kreibich/Petri (1982) even discovered that foreign households that attempt to improve their residential situation by moving have no choice. Such limitations are an important factor explaining why the foreign population lives predominantly in substandard residential areas. Nevertheless, their expectations with regard to housing quality are not lower than those of German households with similar income levels, nor or they less willing to pay higher rents (Rothammer 1974). Because of the lack of alternatives foreign families are able to improve their housing standard only step-by-step, and for this reason their intraurban mobility is much greater than that of the German population (O'Loughlin 1980, Bähr/Gans 1985). When they move, they move a shorter distance than Germans do, i.e., the new residential location is generally in the immediate vicinity of the former one (O'Loughlin/Glebe 1984a). One explanation for the differences in the distance moved is the important role that informal contacts play. Foreign families often find new living quarters through information from friends or relatives (Mertens/Akpinar

1981). Results of a study by SOCIALDATA (1980) in Berlin show that informal contacts are more important for Turks than for other nationalities. 45% of the interviewed Greek residents of Berlin, and 40% of the Jugoslavs live in buildings in which all other residents are Germans. For Turks, the figure is only 29%. If other foreigners live in the same building, they are more likely to be of the same nationality in the case of Turks (53%) than of Greeks (22%) or Jugoslavs (33%). A majority of all three nationalities would be willing to move into a ward without other persons of the same nationality if they were offered good housing conditions (SOCIALDATA 1980).

The housing alternatives are not only limited qualitatively, but spatially as well. The result is that foreign households are discriminated against in the urban housing market, the clearest example being that foreigners pay more for their poor quality housing than Germans do even for better quality housing (Zieris 1977, Ipsen 1978). The differences in rent levels can be explained in part by the higher mobility of the foreign households. In part the explanation lies in the fact that, given similar quality, foreigners have poorer chances than Germans do of getting a particular apartment. Their access to the housing market is limited due to mobility barriers existing between different city wards. These barriers are related not only to differences in income, but also to social and psychological factors, such as the social status of a residential area, possible language difficulties, or the landlords' fear of loss of profits. These barriers are an impediment to the unrestricted mobility of all population groups. Because they exist, there is an increased demand for housing in certain segments of the market, leading to a rise in prices (Ipsen 1981). The housing market is divided up into submarkets with varying housing standards, and these submarkets are separated by mobility barriers with varying degrees of permeability, depending on nationality.

The objective of the following study is to analyze changes in the spatial distribution of foreigners in Kiel and to investigate the existing mobility barriers and their effects on the future development of the population.

3. Data

The investigation is based on both individual and aggregate data. We were able to obtain annual data on intraurban migration between all 57 wards in the city of Kiel for both Germans and foreigners for the period of 1972 to 1982. We also had the population figures for the end of each year. For data on housing conditions we had to turn to the building and housing census (Gebäude- und Wohnungszählung) of 1968, and for data on the social status of the population we had to use the census (Volkszählung) of 1970. No more recent data on housing conditions were available for the end of 1980.

In a project carried out for the city of Kiel we were also able to evaluate individual data on the Turkish residents in November 1983: year of birth, sex, date of immigration to Kiel, family status and number of moves. For reasons of protection of personal data (Datenschutz) and to keep costs down we did not evaluate all residential locations since 1976. We first chose those wards with an above average proportion of Turkish residents and then restricted the data for our investigation to the sides of city blocks on which at least 10 Turks lived in November 1983.

The following interpretation of our results, based on the evaluation of the individual data, always refers to the Turkish residents registered as living in Kiel in November 1983. It is not possible to follow up on Turks who lived in Kiel previously but had moved away before the date of our analysis.

4. Intraurban migration of foreigners in Kiel

At the end of 1983 the percentage of foreigners in Kiel was 6.2%, which is much lower than the average for all large cities (11.2%) and even lower than the average for West Germany (7.4%). One reason for this is certainly that in Kiel, the university city and capital of the state of Schleswig-Holstein, the tertiary sector is dominant. Another reason is that Kiel lies so far north that the diffusion of the "employment of foreign laborers", which proceeded from south to north until the recruitment ban at the end of 1973, did not reach Kiel until relatively late (Giese/Nipper 1979). This diffusion was accompanied by changes in the nationality of foreign laborers and the result was that the majority of the foreigners in the city (54%) at the end of 1983 were Turks (of 15 313 foreigners, 8295 were Turks).

Kiel had a population of 248,000 in 1983. It appeared an appropriate subject for investigating whether the various attempts to explain segregative tendencies and intraurban migration of foreign residents also apply under the conditions found in Kiel, with its low proportion of foreigners and the relative homogeneity of its foreign population with regard to nationality.

4.1. Distribution of foreign residents in Kiel at the end of 1983

The average proportion of foreigners, 6.2% in 1983, says nothing about the great differences in the distribution of foreign residents within the city. The values vary quite considerably from 2.0% in Schilksee (24.1)[1] to 19.2% in Gaarden-Süd (13.4). In Figure 1 it is possible to identify certain regularities in the variations in the population figures for foreign residents. Such regularities are also found in other large cities (Gans 1981, O'Loughlin/Glebe 1981). They can be summed up in three points:

1. The percentage of foreigners is influenced by the segregation of socioeconomic groups. This is particularly striking in Kiel, which is divided into two socioeconomically distinct areas east and west of the fjord (Table 5). In the wards east of the fjord not only the proportion of foreigners is high; the absolute figures are also high, as in Gaarden-Süd (13.4), Gaarden-Ost (12.2) and Neumühlen-Dietrichsdorf (21.2). These are all typical working class districts in which much of the

---

1   In the following the number of the statistical ward, which is used in figures and tables, is given in parentheses following the name of the ward.

housing is old and hardly meets present-day standards (Strukturatlas Kiel 1981). Thus in Gaarden-Ost in 1970 52.4% of the residents were blue-collar workers (Kiel: 38.4%), and 37.7% of the apartments did not have private toilets (Kiel: 25.5%). In 1983 most apartments in the urban renewal zone were small with an average of 3.2 rooms (Kiel: 3.7 rooms per apartment).

2. In residential areas that lie in the vicinity of industrial districts the percentage of Turkish residents is high. Thus in Friedrichsort (20), with the engeneering factory MAK, and on the eastern shore of the fjord near the shipyards more than 75% of the foreign population is Turkish. On the western shore of the fjord, where the better residential areas traditionally lie, such as Düsternbrook (6.0) with its many Victorian villas and the location of the university (in Ravensberg 9.2 and 9.3), the majority of the foreigners are of other nationalities. West of the fjord the percentage of blue-collar workers in the total employed population is only 29%. Here the apartments have a higher standard and are larger (3.6 rooms per apartment) than on the eastern side of the fjord (cf. Figs. 6—8 and Table 5).

3. On the whole, the spatial distribution of foreigners is characterized by a decline from the central districts around the fjord towards the outskirts of the city. Thus Spearman's rank correlation coefficient between the variables "distance between ward and city center" and "percentage of foreigners at the end of 1983" has a value of -0.51. This distribution pattern is strongly influenced by the fact that foreigners generally live in rental apartments, and the proportion of rental apartments is much lower in the outskirts than in the center of the city. This also explains in part why a relatively large number of foreigners live in the large residential complex Mettenhof (25. 1/2), where most of them were assigned apartments by the municipal housing authority (Wohnungsamt).

At the end of 1971 this central-peripheral distribution pattern was not yet as pronounced as in 1983. The relationship between the proportion of foreigners and the distance between the ward and the city center was at -0.28 also negative, but the relationship was not as close as it was twelve years later. The changes in the coefficients indicate that the spatial concentration of foreigners in central locations is increasing, and thus population shifts are occurring in the central parts of the city. Thus at the beginning of 1972 60.7% of the foreigners lived in the centrally located wards. At the end of 1983 the figure was just short of two-thirds. In Gaarden-Süd (13.4) the figure rose from 6% (335 persons) to 19.2% (941 persons) and in Gaarden-Ost (12.2) from barely 3% (597 persons) to 14.7% (2,558 persons). These are large increases. Germans, on the other hand, view these inner city residential areas negatively, with their various overlapping and sometimes conflicting forms of landuse and lack of space, and tend to leave them. The result is that the population development of Kiel is characterized by a centrifugal shift of German residents from inner city districts to the periphery and beyond (Gans 1981). Thus in all subdistricts along the fjord there is a decline in the number of Germans that decreases both absolutely and relatively as we approach the periphery. In Schilksee (24.1) and in the western outskirts of the city the number of German residents is even increasing. In comparison with foreigners, the proportion of Germans living in the centrally located wards decreases from 68% at the beginning of 1972 to

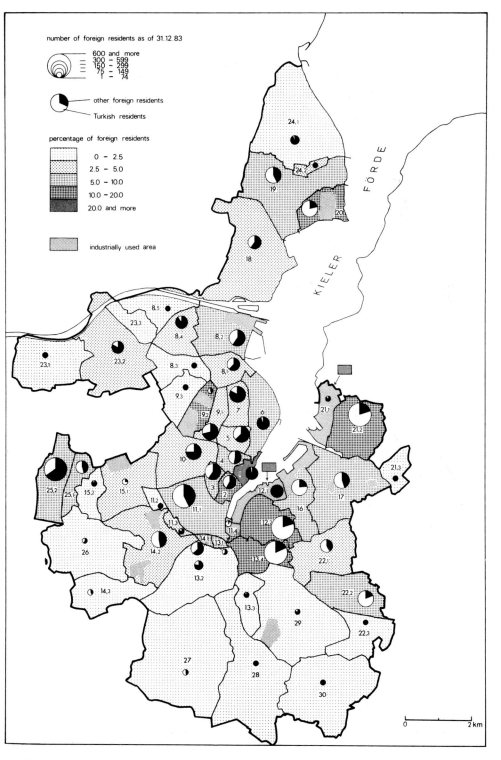

Fig. 1: Percentage distribution of foreigners in the wards of Kiel (31-12-1983)

60.6% at the end of 1983. This demonstrates that the changes in the population distribution of the two groups are moving in opposite directions.

4.2. Reasons for intraurban population shifts

Using multiple regression analysis Bähr/Gans (1985) showed that in Ludwigshafen (Rhein) and Kiel the balances of intraurban moves between 1972 and 1982 have had a profound effect on the spatial shifts in the German and foreign population. The distribution of migration balances depends to a varying degree from group to group on variables that reflect the housing conditions, changes in the same, and the social structure of the wards of Kiel. Figure 2 shows large migration gains for Germans in areas with a lot of new construction activity. At the same time German families are leaving residential areas in which much of the housing is old and not up to modern standards. In contrast, the social structure in the different areas plays a secondary role.

The migration balances for foreigners differ considerably from those for Germans (Gans 1981). The effect of the increasing number of new housing units is definitely lower than for Germans. It is quite obvious that foreign residents profit less from new construction activity. Reasons for this include the lower incomes of

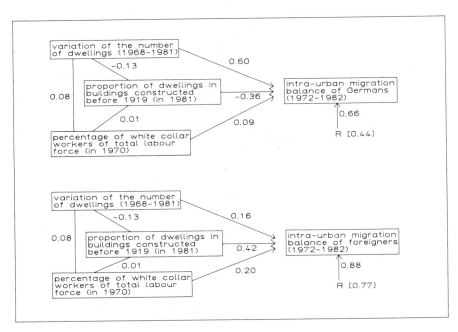

Fig. 2: Path analytical model explaining intra-urban migration of Germans and foreigners in Kiel (1972-1982)

foreigners and their higher savings rates, which continue to limit their available earnings. Foreigners tend to move into areas with relatively old housing stock. They also show a greater tendency than Germans do to move into areas in which a high percentage of employed persons are government employees of office workers. Possibly this must be attributed to a basis effect, i.e., high rates of increase because the initial numbers were particularly low.

When we compare the results of the two analyses we also notice that the three independent variables predict the variability of the migration balances for Germans (56%) much more reliably than for foreigners (23%). Obviously for foreigners other conditions of the housing market play a much more important role. These conditions, which are not described by the variables characterizing the structure, are particularly important for Turkish residents. By tallying all moves the Turks who lived in Kiel at the end of 1983 have made since 1976, it is possible to calculate their effect on the population development in the wards. The correlations between the balances and the variables considered in Figure 2 show certain trends, which are in agreement with the regression analysis:

– At the end of 1983 Turks tended to live in areas where there was a lot of construction during the 70's, such as Mettenhof (25. 1/2).
– An increasing number of Turks also lives in areas with older housing stock, such as the urban renewal zone in Gaarden-Ost (12.2).
– They are leaving working class areas and moving into areas in which a high percentage of employed persons are government employees and office workers, such as Mettenhof, where they are being allocated apartments by the housing authority (Wohnungsamt).

This trend is confirmed by Table 2 which compares the initial residences of Turks with their residences at the end of 1983. This comparison also shows that the spatial distribution of Turkish residents is determined by the increasing importance of a few areas as residential locations. In only two wards, the urban renewal zone in Gaarden-Ost (12.2) and the large residential complex Mettenhof (25. 1/2), are the absolute and relative values for the current residential location higher than for the initial one. In the other residential areas the numbers are decreasing, in some of them quite noticeably. These changes confirm that there is an increased spatial concentration of Turks. Strictly speaking, they contradict the development of the index of dissimilarity since 1978 (Table 3), which is higher between Turks and Germans than between foreigners and Germans, indicating that Turks are more highly segregated than foreigners as a whole are. After 1978 the index drops from 44% to 40%. Thus it appears that the dissimilarity between the distribution of the Turkish and the German population in the city as a whole is decreasing. As Tables 2 and 5 show, this decrease is accompanied by an increase in the number of Turks in a very few areas of the city. The changes in the population figures for both Turks and Germans between 1979 and 1983, expressed in percentages, reach a maximum in the western periphery. This is one of the main reasons for the decline in the dissimilarity index, although if we consider only the Turkish population, we observe an increase in spatial concentration.

Table 2: Turkish inhabitants in Kiel at the end of 1983 by their first and present place of residence in the city

residential area	total number of Turks				male persons older than 16 at arrival date				other immigrants			
	first place of residence		present residence		first place of residence		present residence		first place of residence		present residence	
	tot.	in %	tot.	in %	tot.	in %	tot.	in %	tot.	in %	tot.	in %
urban renewal area Gaarden-Ost (12.2)	1 417	20.9	1 659	24.5	542	22.2	642	26.1	875	20.2	1 017	23.5
high-rise apartment area Mettenhof (25.1/2)	166	2.5	399	5.9	37	1.5	111	4.5	129	3.0	288	6.7
Pries/Friedrichsort (19,20)	601	8.9	484	7.1	261	10.7	210	8.6	340	7.8	274	6.3
Südfriedhof (11.1)	510	7.5	477	7.0	183	7.5	171	7.0	327	7.5	306	7.1
Eastern shore without Gaarden-Ost (13.4, 16, 17. 21)	2 109	31.1	2 003	29.5	701	28.7	673	27.4	1 408	32.5	1 330	30.7
other areas	1 976	29.1	1 762	26.0	719	29.4	649	26.4	1 257	29.0	1 113	25.7
	6 779	100.0	6 784	100.0	2 443	100.0	2 456	100.0	4 336	100.0	4 328	100.0

Table 3: Dissimilarity indices for wards (Statistische Bezirke) in Kiel

Groups	1978	1980	1983
Germans-foreigners	29	27	29
Germans-Turks	44	41	40

If we take the comparison shown in Table 2 and differentiate according to the categories "men who were at least 16 at the date of immigration" and "family members", two regions strike us because of the great differences in their development. The industrial region Pries/Friedrichsort (19/29) played a more important role as initial residential location for males than for family members and the decline, at 19%, was above average for both groups. In Mettenhof (25.1/2) the very high rates of increase that play such an important role in lowering the dissimilarity index reach the extreme value of 1300% for men of at least 16 years of age at the time of immigration. Evidently at the time of immigration older Turks often move into the vicinity of the factory where they work and change their residential location within the city when their families join them in West Germany. Gaarden-Ost (12.2) combines the development patterns of these two regions. Because of its vicinity to the shipyards and its residential opportunities for foreigners both the relative and the absolute numbers increased for both population groups up till the end of 1983.

From the changes shown in Table 2 we can conclude that the increasing importance of only a few areas as residential locations for Turks results from two simultaneous factors. One is intraurban moves. The other is the change in the spatial distribution of the initial residential location of family members, as compared with male immigrants. This hypothesis, based on the comparison of initial and current residential locations, is confirmed by the temporal and spatial differentiation of immigration and intraurban moves shown in Figures 3 and 4.

The recruitment ban, which was pronounced in November 1973, led in Kiel, as in the rest of West Germany, to a definite drop in the influx of foreigners. If we distinguish the Turks living in Kiel today according to sex and age at immigration, we see that the main decrease is in the group of persons 16 and over. In 1975 the number of immigrants in this group decreased to one third of the previous year, whereas the influx of younger Turkish residents increased almost continuously until the second maximum period of immigration was reached in 1980. 65% of the Turkish men who lived in Kiel in 1983 and were at least 16 years old at the time of immigration moved to Kiel before 1975. In contrast, only 31% of the women and children under 16 arrived before this date. After 1973 the transition was made from "migrant workers" to "residential population".

These demographic changes after 1973 also resulted in a spatial shift in the distribution of initial residential locations. Figure 4 shows the differentiation of the development patterns of initial residential location and intraurban migration for selected areas of Kiel. This shows clearly the different significance of Mettenhof (25.1/2) and Pries/Friedrichsort (19/20) for the dynamics of spatial redistribution.

Whereas in Pries/Friedrichsort (19/20) there was a pronounced maximum of immigration of Turkish men before 1974 and the migration balance after 1976 was fairly
even, in Mettenhof (25.1/2) the influx of Turkish residents did not begin until
1977, and it affected young and old approximately evenly. In this period Mettenhof registered considerable migration gains, mainly because of the many persons
assigned apartments by the municipal administration. As the absolute numbers
show, these circumstances do not really contradict the conclusion drawn from
Figure 2 that foreigners in general and Turks in particular are not as able to improve

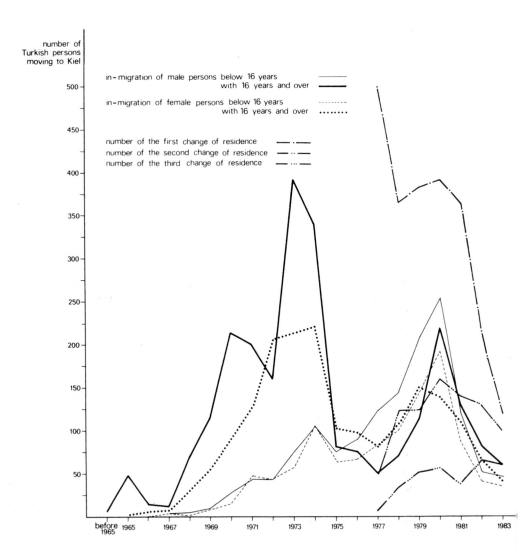

Fig. 3: Development of in- and intra-urban migration of Turkish residents living in Kiel
at the end of 1983

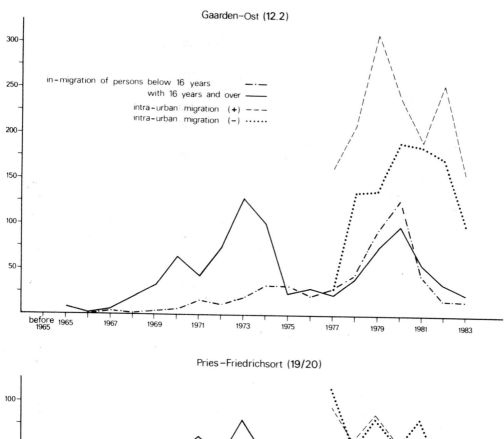

Gaarden–Ost (12.2)

in–migration of persons below 16 years — · —
with 16 years and over ——
intra–urban migration (+) – – –
intra–urban migration (–) ······

before 1965   1965   1967   1969   1971   1973   1975   1977   1979   1981   1983

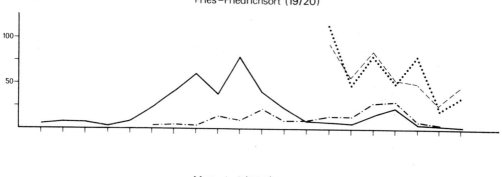

Pries–Friedrichsort (19/20)

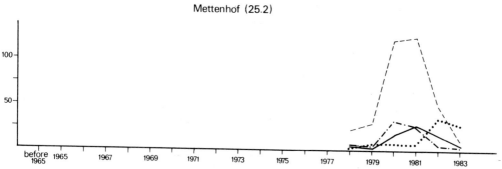

Mettenhof (25.2)

before 1965   1965   1967   1969   1971   1973   1975   1977   1979   1981   1983

Fig. 4: Development of in- and intra-urban migration of Turkish residents living in Kiel at the end of 1983 (selected areas)

their living conditions by moving into new apartments. The Turkish families in Mettenhof (25.1/2) were allocated their apartments by city officies and did not acquire them on the open housing market. Apparently only the housing market in the urban renewal zone in Gaarden-Ost is more readily accessible to Turks. It is the only area with a continuous increase in Turkish residents after 1976 due to intra-urban moves despite a migration development that corresponds to that of the rest of the city.

The results presented thus far are based on the analysis of spatial balances of population movements and demonstrate an increasing spatial concentration of Turkish residents. These results are confirmed by an evaluation of the origin and destination of intraurban moves. The new residential location of Turks is more frequently in the neighborhood of the former one than is the case for foreigners as a whole, which again is more often than for Germans (O'Loughlin/Glebe 1984a). To test this hypothesis, we evaluated intraurban migration between wards according to the distance between the old and the new location. In Figure 5 the relative frequency of migration of Turks, foreigners and Germans at 500 m intervals is represented by polygons. The basis for the comparison is the theoretical distribution of the distance between wards, as represented by the histograms.

In all three population groups short distances clearly predominate. The longer distances are underrepresented, when compared with the theoretical possibilities. This tendency is more pronounced among Turks than among foreigners in general, and there again it is stronger than among Germans.

These facts are demonstrated by Figure 5 as follows:
— the curve representing Turkish residents drops off most steeply within the first kilometer,
— up to the 4.5 km distance ring, the frequencies for foreigners in general are higher than for Germans
— for distances above this the proportion of Germans is generally highest.

This interpretation is also confirmed by the size relationships between the relative frequency of intraward migration and the median distance (Table 4). Only the mean distance is larger for Turks than for foreigners as a whole, because the sudden leap in relative frequency in the 6.5 km distance ring efects the mean, which is particularly sensitive to extreme values.

Table 4: Distances in intra-urban migration in Kiel

	Turks (1976–1983)	foreigners (1972–1982)	Germans (1972–1983)
mean Distance	2 809 m	2 575 m	2 900 m
median distance	1 444 m	2 120 m	2 336 m
intra-ward migration in percentage of all intra-urban migrations	35,3 %	23,3 %	22,5 %

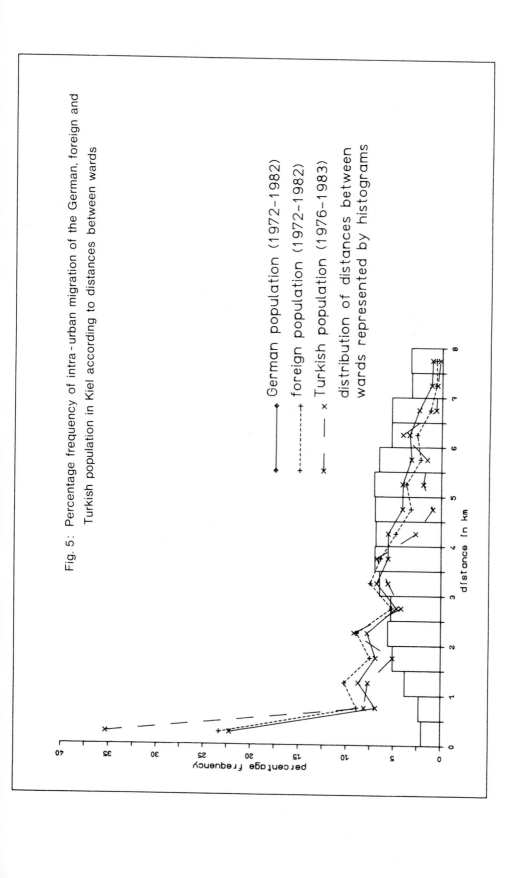

Fig. 5: Percentage frequency of intra-urban migration of the German, foreign and Turkish population in Kiel according to distances between wards

German population (1972–1982)
foreign population (1972–1982)
Turkish population (1976–1983)

distribution of distances between wards represented by histograms

The three characteristic distance distributions demonstrate that Turkish residents in particular restrict their moves to a small area around their former residential location. This limitation is a result of the important role played by informal contacts and is also due to existing mobility barriers of varying degrees of permeability. To determine their spatial location, we investigated the intraurban migration flows by applying a grouping algorithm based on information gains. This procedure takes into consideration the size of the population in the area of destination and clusters areas with strong internal migration links (Gans 1983). The areas with migration links show a high degree of congruence for Germans and foreigners (Figs. 6, 7), based on their intraurban moves between 1972 and 1982. Thus for both population groups we can differentiate between central and peripheral areas, and in an additional step, between the eastern and the western sides of the fjord. Table 5, which is based on the areas with migration links according to migration flows of the total population, shows that there are considerable differences between the different areas in housing standard and in the social status of the inhabitants. At the outskirts of the city the apartments are larger, newer and have a higher standard. In the inner city the differentiation between the western shore and the eastern shore is quite striking with regard to the percentage of foreigners, the proportion of blue-collar workers in the employed population and the size of apartments. Within these areas variations in housing and social status, in some cases quite considerable ones, demonstrate the internal heterogeneity of the linked areas. On the basis of this internal differentiation they can be considered housing submarkets, since

— they are a segment of the housing market of Kiel,
— they offer a certain variety of choice and
— they are fairly secluded from other areas by the high degree of internal migration.

The absolute figures for intraurban migration flows in Figures 6 and 7 clearly show that these housing submarkets play a very different role in the moves of German and foreign residents (Bähr/Gans 1985).

— Germans prefer peripheral residential areas and often change from one submarket to another (Fig. 6). Destinations are chiefly Mettenhof (25.1/2), Hassee (14.2), or Schilksee (24.1). This direction of migration from the inner city to the outskirts also exists in the areas with migration links. Thus Neumühlen-Dietrichsdorf (21.2) registers a positive balance with Gaarden-Ost (12.2). For Germans the eastern and western shores are of equal importance for intraurban moves.

— For foreigners this symmetry makes a definite shift in favor of the eastern shore (Fig. 7). Certainly more foreigners live here than in the other parts of Kiel, (Table 5), however, the central position of Gaarden-Ost (12.2) in the migration flows and the development of its population indicate that foreigners find it easier to enter this housing submarket that to leave it. In general it is difficult for them to overcome the mobility barriers separating the areas of migration links. This discrimination against foreigners in the housing market, compared with Germans, is expressed in the higher intraurban mobility of foreigners and the shorter distance between former and present residential location. This conclusion is strengthened by the moves from Gaarden-Ost (12.2) to Mettenhof (25.1/2),

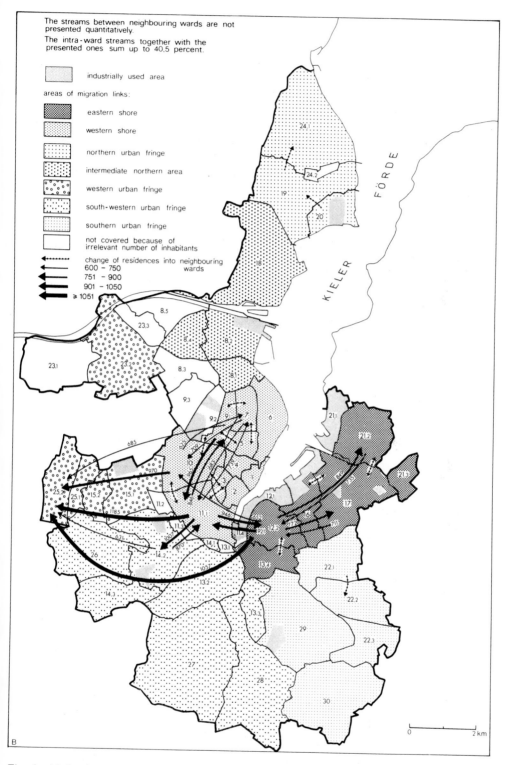

The streams between neighbouring wards are not
presented quantitatively.

The intra-ward streams together with the
presented ones sum up to 40.5 percent.

☐ industrially used area

areas of migration links:

▨ eastern shore

▨ western shore

▨ northern urban fringe

▨ intermediate northern area

▨ western urban fringe

▨ south-western urban fringe

▨ southern urban fringe

☐ not covered because of
irrelevant number of inhabitants

←⋯ change of residences into neighbouring
600 − 750　　　　　　　　wards
751 − 900
901 − 1050
≥ 1051

FÖRDE

KIELER

Fig. 6: Major intra-urban migration streams (≥ 600) for Germans in Kiel (1972-1982)

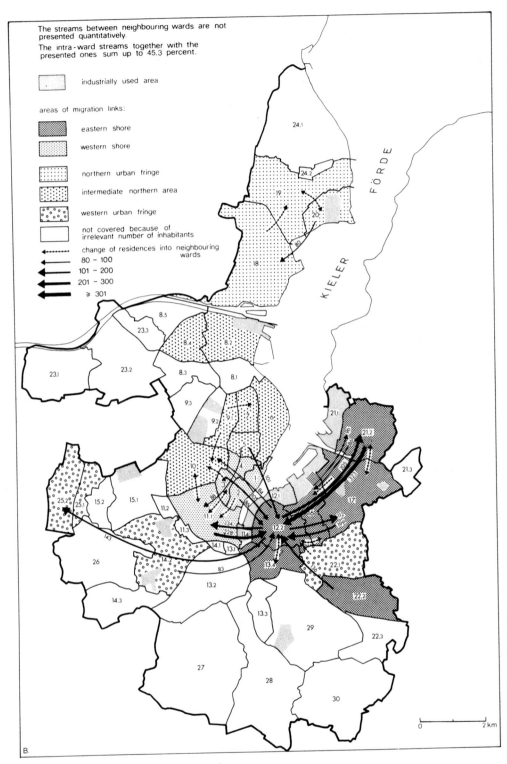

The streams between neighbouring wards are not presented quantitatively.
The intra-ward streams together with the presented ones sum up to 45,3 percent.

industrially used area

areas of migration links:

eastern shore

western shore

northern urban fringe

intermediate northern area

western urban fringe

not covered because of irrelevant number of inhabitants

change of residences into neighbouring wards
80 – 100
101 – 200
201 – 300
≥ 301

Fig. 7: Major intra-urban migration streams (≥ 80) for foreigners in Kiel (1972-1982)

Table 5: Characterization of the areas with intensive internal intra-urban links by housing quality, social structure and population development

areas of intensive internal migration links	workers of total labour force in % (1970)	proportion of dwellings in buildings constructed before 1919 (1981)	dwellings without W.C. in % (1968)	rooms per dwelling (1981)	percentage of foreigners 1971	percentage of foreigners 1983	variation of the foreign population in % German 1971–83	1971–79	1979–83	Turkish 1979–83
inner city										
Western shore (wards: 1.0–7.0, 9.1, 10.0, 11.1)	29.0	42.5	30.5	3.6	2.6	5.2	−20.5	+19.5	+36.1	+25.6
Wik (wards: 8.1, 8.2, 8.4)	23.3	21.4	17.5	3.9	1.7	4.2	−20.0	+68.1	+17.2	+10.2
Eastern shore (wards: 12.2, 13.4, 16.0, 17.0, 21.2, 21.3)	52.1	22.7	24.8	3.5	3.5	11.1	−20.9	+123.3	+20.5	+15.8
urban fringe										
"North"(wards: 18.0, 19.0, 20.0, 24.1)	43.5	18.3	19.3	3.8	4.3	5.3	+1.2	+22.7	1.9	−10.7
"West"(wards: 15.1, 15.2, 23.2, 25.1, 25.2)	35.0	1.8	7.3	4.0	1.8	5.5	+57.4	+140.6	+111.7	+321.3
"South"(wards: 13.2,13.3,14.1, 14.2,14.3,26.0, 27.0,28.0)	39.6	18.3	32.0	3.9	1.9	3.5	−6.4	+34.2	+33.7	+5.5
"East"(wards: 22.1, 22.2, 22.3, 29.0, 30.0)	49.8	9.0	17.2	3.9	2.5	3.5	+0.9	+41.9	−1.3	−7.0

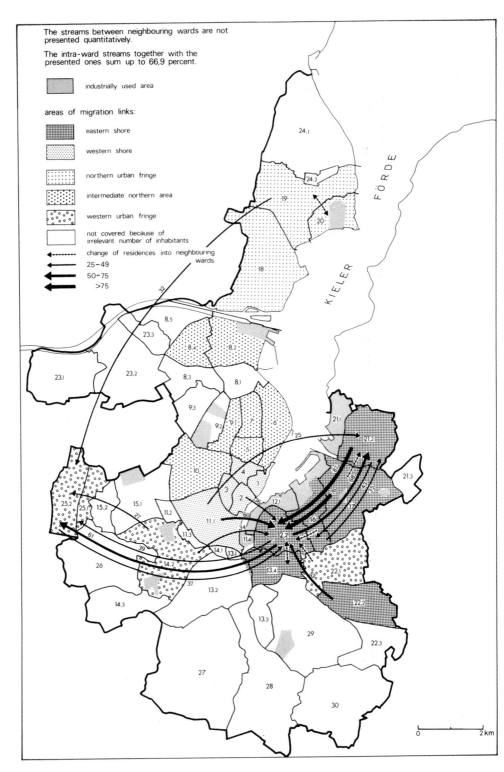

Fig. 8: Major intra-urban migration streams (≥ 25) for Turkish residents living in Kiel
at the end of 1983 (1976-1983)

since most of them are the result of allocation by the municipal housing authority.

The migration flows of Turkish residents between 1976 and 1983 confirm these results. A comparison of Figures 7 and 8 stresses the following points:

— The moves of Turkish residents are much more highly related to the individual areas of migration links than is the case for foreigners as a whole. The migration flows shown in the figures and the intraward moves represent 66.9% of all moves made by Turks, a much higher figure than the 45.3% for all foreigners.

— For Turks the eastern shore plays a predominant role, and there the urban renewal zone in Gaarden-Ost (12.2) is particularly important as a destination. Mobility barriers are less permeable for Turks than for foreigners as a whole.

— Outside of the eastern shore only Mettenhof is an important destination for intraurban migration, and that because of housing allocations.

The results presented in this paper show that foreigners in the city of Kiel have been able to improve their living conditions since 1972 via intraurban moves, but that due to effective housing market mechanisms and the importance of informal contacts they succeeded mainly within the different submarkets. Obviously it is difficult for foreigners — and even more so for Turks — to overcome mobility barriers by moving. Such barriers are only permeable in cases of migration into the urban renewal zone in Gaarden-Ost (12.2). Foreign families manage to leave a given submarket in large numbers only with the aid of municipal housing authority.

5. CONCLUSION

In this paper we have shown, using the example of the Turkish population of Kiel, that the recruitment ban of 1973 was followed by a demographic reorientation from "migrant workers" to "residential population". As families were reunited, the housing needs of foreign households changed, and they attempted to improve their living conditions by intraurban moves. Our results shown, in agreement with previous investigations (O'Loughlin/Glebe 1984a, Bähr/Gans 1985), that the new residential location of Turks is more often in the immediate vicinity of the previous one than is the case for foreigners as a whole or Germans. This spatial confinement results from the varying significance of informal contacts in the search for housing and from mobility barriers with differing degrees of permeability — depending on the nationality of the person making the search — that divide the city into housing submarkets with varying housing standards and social image (Ipsen 1978, 1981). Turkish residents generally improve their housing conditions within a given submarket. They are only able to overcome mobility barriers if the new apartment is in Gaarden-Ost (12.2). Their only chance to move into areas where few foreigners live is via housing allocations by municipal offices.

Presumably the problems Turks have with the housing market will in the future lead to a stronger spatial concentration on the eastern side of the fjord with its less developed infrastructure. It is true that there is a slight decrease of 4% in the dissimilarity index to 40% after 1978, partly as a result of migration links, but mainly due to the tremendous increase of more than 300% in the number of Turkish residents in Mettenhof (25.1/2) Figure 4 shows clearly that in 1983 the migration balance of Turks was already negative. From Figure 8 we can see that most households move to Gaarden-Ost (12.2). The only areas with a higher increase in the number of Turkish residents than the average of 10% for Kiel are the eastern shore and certain areas on the western shore that are likely candidates for urban renewal programs, with 16 and 25%, respectively (Table 5). On the basis of the age structure alone, this uneven distribution will continue to exist. At the end of 1983 31% of the children under 6 in the urban renewal zone were foreigners. 86% of them were Turks, most of whom were born in Kiel. The integration problem continues to exist, even though the number of Turkish residents was retrogressive for the first time in 1984.

MIGRATION OF GUESTWORKERS AND GERMANS: MICROLEVEL ANALYSIS OF NEIGHBOURHOOD CHANGES IN DÜSSELDORF 1981–1983

GÜNTHER GLEBE AND BRIGITTE WALDORF (DÜSSELDORF)

Introduction

In West German cities, migration is the most influential process in the development of city-wide residential patterns. In this regard a study of ethnospecific migration processes promises to yield insight into the dynamics of urban ethnic segregation patterns. This chapter presents the results of an empirical analysis of foreign worker and German migration pattern and processes in three neighborhoods of the city of Düsseldorf, West Germany. Furthermore, the empirical results are related to theoretical concepts of spatial segregation courrently debated, mainly the socio-ecological concept of the Chicago School of Sociology and to a structuralist interpretation of ethnic spatial distributions, based on power relations and their realization within the urban housing market.

This chapter is organized into three parts. The first part presents an overview of the historical and social dimensions of the foreign workers' situation in West Germany, as well as a brief description of theoretical frameworks concerning ethnic segregation. The second part outlines the empirical analysis, data, methodology and a discussion of the results. The final section concludes with an overall evaluation of possible future changes of ethnic segregation patterns within West German cities.

Background

The immigrant minorities, who settled in industrial Western European countries during the last 30 years, have concentrated mostly in larger urban areas. These areas had a sufficient and varied demand for low-income, unskilled and semiskilled labour (Castles and Kosack 1985). Because of their large number, growing length of stay, and changes in their demographic structure, immigrant minorities have become part of the urban social reality in West Germany and other European countries. In the complex network of social, political and economic relations of the capitalist host societies, their position is often determined by social exclusion and economic subordination. One of the most important pervasive and controlling factors of their social and economic situation is the uncertainty that immigrant minorities face, both in the employment and housing markets (Leitner, Chap. 4 in this book). It reinforces their subordinate position, leaves them in a weak position in the network of social power relations and offers feelings of control, superiority and domination to the host society (Castles 1985). This is the basis of many forms of institutionalized and private discrimination against foreigners.

In West Germany, the presence of labour migrants, mostly originating from the Mediterranean countries, is still considered a temporary feature, and this is documented in the prevailing use of the word 'guestworker'. In the period of economic expansion, 1955 to 1973, guestworker recruitment was considered as a necessity for continued economic growth. Guestworker social problems, like provision of housing and education, were largely ignored. The oil crises of 1973 and 1979, and their economic consequences, such as increasing unemployment rates, led to a growing awareness of the social problems that have resulted from the presence of ethnic minorities. However, the situation was evaluated mainly from the perspective of the host society. As a result, the host society substituted neglect, indifference, and exploitation using fears of ethnic conflict and ethnic 'Überfremdung'. For example, local concentrations of foreigners were perceived as the beginning of ghetto formation and a causative factor of social conflicts. In response to these concentrations, local authorities in West Germany implemented restrictions on guestworker migration into so-called 'saturated' areas in cities (Leitner, Chap. 4 in this book).

Since the recruitment ban in 1973, guestworker family reunification constitutes the dominant portion of international migration from the European periphery into West Germany. Often, migration due to family reunification takes place as a stepwise process: the spouse and one or two children migrate first, other children follow at later stages (Schrader, Nikles and Griese, 1979). Whereas the single labor migrant lived in rooming houses or hostels, often supplied by the employer, she/he now had to look for alternative accommodation on the urban housing market, since local authorities require that adequate housing is provided before guestworker dependents are allowed to stay in West Germany for a longer time period. As a result of their social status, low income and restricted access to social housing (Laumann, 1984), guestworkers are confined to the relatively small subsector of private, low quality housing in innercity areas and near industrial locations (O'Loughlin, Chap. 3 in this book). Therefore, from the early seventies, an increasing number of foreigners appeared as competitors of working class Germans in the tight market of low rent housing (Kreibich and Petri, 1982). Hence, housing became the most critical interaction field between ethnic minorities and the host society. With rising unemployment among both native and foreign populations since the late seventies, sensitivity of interethnic relations grew and has been displayed mostly in the housing market. For example, deterioration of innercity housing has often been interpreted as a result of foreign household occupancy. Additionally, ghettoization fears were used for stigmatizing entire neighborhoods. However, low levels of segregation existing in West German cities (Helmert, 1982; Gans, 1984; O'Loughlin and Glebe, 1984b; Glebe, 1984), in comparison to Anglo-American and French cities, show that these fears were widely exaggerated.

The study of segregated structures emerging in European cities with the inmigration of ethnic minorities has been a field of major research. In their search for explanations of the settlement processes, many studies rely on concepts derived from the socio-ecological theory of the Chicago School (Hoffmeyer-Zlotnik, 1977, 1982), like the invasion-succession hypothesis and the tipping point model. In this view, high German outmigration rates and high guestworker inmigration rates into certain neighborhoods are interpreted as flight of the native population from invaded neighborhoods. The applicability of these concepts in the urban historical context of continental European cities seems to be, however, questionable (O'Loughlin, Chap. 3 in this book; Ipsen, 1981; Leitner, 1983; Lichtenberger, 1984).

While the socio-ecological interpretation of ethnic segregation emphasizes the choice component of migratory behavior and the resulting settlement patterns, the second theoretical framework views the constraints imposed by the society on the individual as the main explanatory factor for urban ethnic segregation. For foreign workers in continental European cities, this concept has been elaborated by O'Loughlin (Chap. 3 in this book). Segregation is seen as part of a sorting process which has two dimensions, a spatial dimension (location in space, with resulting spatial segregation) and a social dimension (the development of separate social networks). Segregation takes place within the urban historical framework and is conditioned by the class, status, and party divisions of the society. In the social stratification of the host society, guestworkers are part of the working class. Within the working class, they rank at the lower end (Lichtenberger, 1984), and their ethnic distinctiveness make them more vulnerable to discrimination than other native groups of the lower income sector (Petri, 1984; Laumann, 1984). They will, therefore, settle in those parts of the city, where existing urban structures and the gatekeepers of the housing markets allow access (Ipsen, 1981; Kreibich and Petri, 1982; Leitner, 1983; Gans, 1984; Lichtenberger, 1984; O'Loughlin and Glebe, 1984a; Van Amersfoort and De Klerk, Chap. 10 in this book). The empirical analysis will show that the socio-ecological interpretation does not offer an appropriate explanation for ethnic segregation in West German cities. Rather, by relating housing and migration the empirical analysis will provide some evidence of the influence of housing market mechanisms on ethnic migration processes and the resulting residential patterns.

EMPIRICAL ANALYSIS

Aims, Data, and Methodology

In this chapter, the dynamics of ethnic settlement patterns will be investigated by studying the migration processes of guestworkers and Germans in three different neighbourhoods of Düsseldorf. Furthermore, the appropriateness of currently debated concepts like invasion-succession processes and housing market processes for explaining minority relocation processes in West German cities will be examined. Migration is the most important component of population change within cities. Differential moves of Germans and foreigners have a direct impact upon the levels of spatial segregation. For example, if both groups leave and enter the same spatial units at the same rates, we do not expect significant changes in the degree of segregation. If the movements, however, are complementary, then changes in the degree of segregation are more likely. Therefore, the analysis of guestworker and German migration flows on a microlevel basis is seen as a very promising avenue in the attempt to understand present and future developments of ethnic spatial patterns in West German cities.

The analysis is divided into three steps. First, Germans and guestworkers are compared according to their settlement patterns, migration intensity, and migration patterns. The migration processes will be analyzed at three different scales: intraneighborhood scale, intracity scale, and migration into and out of the city. In this context, a central question will be whether Germans and guestworkers reveal complementary migration fields. A positive answer will indicate further spatial segregation, while a negative answer will indicate the stability of the current settlement patterns. Secondly, the applicability of the housing market concept for an explanation of ethnic segregation in West German cities will be tested by using a microlevel analysis on a neighbourhood basis. Thirdly, answers to the question of future changes in the level of segregation and the development of ghetto-like communities will be suggested.

The analysis is based on three neighbourhoods in the West German city of Düsseldorf (population 579,000 in 1983). The neighbourhoods differ according to locational characteristics, socioeconomic structure, segregation levels and migration patterns. Five criteria were used for the neighborhood selection: foreigner percentage, diversity of nationality, quality of housing stock, the extent of redevelopment processes, and spatial location. The three neighbourhoods finally chosen – Friedrichstadt/Unterbilk, Oberbilk/Flingern-Süd/Lierenfeld, and Gerresheim – border each other and cover an area from the fringe of the Central Business District (CBD) to the eastern boundary of the city (Map 1).

Friedrichstadt/Unterbilk consists of two densely populated wards south of the CBD (Table 1). It was built during the late 19th century and the first decade of the 20th century. Although residential land use dominates, a mixture of housing and office space is typical for blocks close to the CBD. Workshops of local craftsmen and some small industrial premises in the inner courtyards of the housing blocks are characteristic of this innercity neighbourhood. Because of its closeness to the CBD the neighbourhood has been affected by urban renewal, modernization of its older housing stock, and conversion of rental housing into condominiums since the late 1970s.

Oberbilk/Flingern-Süd/Lierenfeld differs from the former neighbourhood by its physical isolation from the CBD through raised railway tracks, its location adjacent to heavy industry, a lower social status and a higher foreigner proportion. In general, it displays typical transition zone characteristics (Table 1). Gerresheim, the third neighbourhood, is located at the city fringe and is structurally divided into two different parts. The south of Gerresheim consists mainly of older factory housing near a large glass producing factory. The northern part displays a suburban character with middle-class status and a high percentage of owner-occupied single family houses. In the past, all three neighbourhoods have experienced heavy population losses. The main reasons for this erosion were high urban outmigration rates for

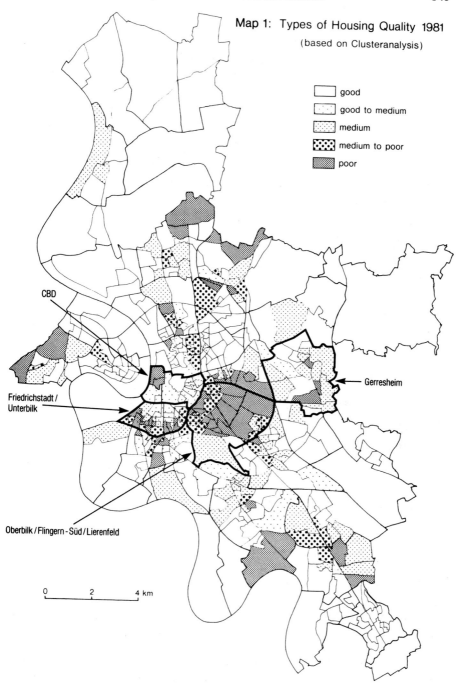

Map 1: Types of Housing Quality 1981
(based on Clusteranalysis)

good
good to medium
medium
medium to poor
poor

CBD

Gerresheim

Friedrichstadt /
Unterbilk

Oberbilk / Flingern - Süd / Lierenfeld

0   2   4 km

Günther Glebe and Brigitte Waldorf

Table 1: Population (1983) and Population Development 1960—1983

	Friedrichstadt/ Unterbilk		Oberbilk/Flingern-Süd Lierenfeld		Gerresheim	
	total	%	total	%	total	%
total Population	40.466		44.494		26.607	
Foreigners	7.107	17.6	11.208	25.2	2.932	11.0
Guestworkers	4.930	12.2	9.042	20.3	2.136	8.0
Turks	1.205	24.4	3.116	34.5	226	10.6
Yugoslavs	1.502	30.5	2.204	24.4	507	23.7
Greeks	941	19.1	1.354	15.0	85	4.0
Italians	533	10.8	1.162	12.9	1.159	54.3
Spaniards	539	10.9	432	4.8	51	2.4
Moroccans	210	4.3	774	8.6	108	5.1

Average Annual Population Change (%)

1961—1970	−1.8	2.4	−1.0
1971—1980	−2.2	2.3	−1.7
1981—1983	−0.8	0.2	+0.4

Average Annual Population Change (%)

Foreigners

1971—1980	+3.3	+4.2	+0.7
1981—1983	−0.6	−0.9	+1.7

Source: Statistische Jahrbücher Stadt Düsseldorf

Germans coupled with a dramatically declining birthrate since the early 1970s. This development has given guestworkers and their families the opportunity to settle in the resulting vacancies in these neighbourhoods.

This study is based on data provided by the Amt für Statistik of the city of Düsseldorf, including migration data, population data, and housing data. The migration data contains information on nationality, age, sex, and marital status of each individual migrant for the three year period, 1981—1983. The three years were combined to create a data set amenable to statistical analysis. This aggregation can be justified, since the year to year changes are minimal. Aggregate population data were available for the same time period and the analysis refers to Germans and the total of six guestworker nationalities (Turks, Greek, Yugoslavs, Spaniards, Italians, and Moroccans). Although is can be assumed that the group of all guestworker nationalities is not homogeneous and that single nationalities are unevenly distributed among the three neighbourhoods, this aggregation has been justified for statistical reasons. Furthermore, if it can be shown that the sample neighbourhoods do not differ in terms of migration, then the analysis yields some evidence that there are no significant differences between the guestworker nationalities.

The housing data are an update of the 1968 housing census. Unfortunately, the housing statistics offer only information on housing quality, size, and age, whereas rent and ownership data are not available. All data were aggregated to the voting districts basis (Stimmbezirke). The voting districts in Düsseldorf have, on average, 1268 inhabitants with a standard deviation of about 400. Although smaller spatial units like individual houses are likely to be a more appropriate basis for the interpretation of migration processes, the selection of voting districts is seen as a compromise in response to data restrictions and requirements of a statistical analysis.

In order to get a better understanding of residential relocation processes, the definition of housing markets is an important task. For reasons of data paucity and technical difficulties, most studies avoid the task of defining housing submarkets. The studies offered so far for West German cities are based on macrolevel and surrogate variables (Ipsen, 1981). Given the limited data on housing, the solution presented in this study defines housing subsectors solely on aggregate housing variables. Five housing variables were used in the classification procedure: two variables of housing size (housing units with two or less rooms and with four or more rooms) and three variables of housing quality (housing units without bath, without kitchen, without central heating). To avoid bias resulting from the specific characters of the sample neighborhoods, a hierarchical clustering procedure was performed for the voting districts of the entire city. A five cluster solution was finally accepted as a good approximation for the city's housing space.

Table 2: Characteristics of the Housing Quality Clusters

	Average Percentage of Housing Units				
Quality Indicator	good I	good/ medium II	medium III	medium/ poor IV	poor V
2 or less Rooms	16	38	27	32	39
4 or more Rooms	55	30	39	26	23
Units without Kitchen	11	30	16	21	27
Units without Bath	17	16	34	20	64
Units without Central Heating	42	46	65	75	77

Table 2 shows the five housing quality types and their characteristics. Voting districts of type I are characterized by an above average share of large and well equipped housing units. Type II voting districts contain good quality housing units but a higher percentage of small housing units as type I districts. Areas with medium housing quality are categorized as type III, and areas with medium to poor housing are assigned to type IV. Type V voting districts are dominated by small, poorly equipped housing units.

The spatial distribution of the quality types over the city (Map 1) reveals a clustering of poorer housing districts in parts of the inner city and — though not immediately obvious from the map — close to industrial areas. Better housing areas are mainly concentrated along the outer-city fringe and along a sector stretching out north from the CBD along the Rhine. However, the high quality housing areas shown on Map 1 have to be interpreted with care since they contain both owner-occupied, high quality, single-family housing and good quality social housing built in the late 1970s. This displays one of the critical limitations using quality types as proxies for housing market sectors. Social housing covers about 30 percent of the housing stock of the city and it cuts across many of the housing quality classes. In the case of our three study areas, however, we can dismiss this intervening factor as the proportion of social housing in these neighborhoods is relatively small.

Table 3: Number of Voting Districts in each Housing Quality Type by Neighbourhood

			Housing Quality Types				
Neighbourhood		good I	good/ medium II	medium III	medium/ poor IV	poor V	Total
Oberbilk/ Flingern-Süd/ Lierenfeld	tot.	1	–	3	16	16	36
	%	2.77		8.33	44.40	44.40	
Friedrichstadt/ Unterbilk	tot.	–	11	4	7	11	33
	%		33.30	12.12	21.21	33.33	
Gerresheim	tot.	6	1	9	–	3	19
	%	31.50	5.26	47.36		15.78	
Total		7	12	16	23	30	88

Table 3 shows the distribution of the voting districts over the five housing quality types in our neighbourhoods. As could be expected by their location and history, poor housing quality is dominant in the innercity neighbourhoods. Oberbilk/Flingern-Süd/Lierenfeld especially has a high percentage of voting districts in the poorer housing categories, whereas the more suburban ward, Gerresheim, offers the best housing conditions.

Migration Patterns and Residential Distribution

After decades of continuous heavy population losses in the three sample neighborhoods, the overall ratio of German inmigration and outmigration is nearly balanced or even slightly positive since the early 1980s (Table 1). On the other hand, the guestworker population is now declining in the inner city neighbourhoods. This decrease in the number of guestworkers since 1982 is mainly the result of remigrations to their home countries. Increasing unemployment, an insecure future in West Germany and additional financial incentives from the West German government have induced the remigration process (Leitner, Chap. 4 in this book). In West Germany, the total net outmigration rate for the six guestworker nationalities has increased constantly since 1982: a total of about half a million have left West Germany within this period, with Turks contributing almost two thirds of the total (Bähr and Gans, Chap. 6 in this book). The situation in Düsseldorf is similar to the overall national development. Between 1982 and 1984, the guestworker population were reduced by 15.9%, while the Turkish population decreased by 21.9%.

Table 4: Indices of Dissimilarity (ID) and Guestworker Percentage by Neighbourhoods

	Friedrichstadt/ Unterbilk	Oberbilk/ Flingern-Süd/ Lierenfeld	Gerresheim
ID	17	30	35
Guestworker (%)	12.2	20	8

In spite of these changes, the citywide segregation patterns remained stable (Glebe, 1984). Furthermore, the level of segregation is very low both for the entire city as well as for the single neighbourhoods. However, the indices of dissimilarity (Duncan and Duncan, 1955) display some interesting variations between the three neighbourhoods (Table 4). Gerresheim, the neighbourhood with the lowest proportion of guestworkers has the highest segregation score. This reflects their concentration in the former factory houses in the southern part of the neighbourhood. The lower dissimilarity indices in the innercity neighbourhoods indicate a more dispersed settlement of guestworkers.

These inter-neighborhood variations become visible when mapping the location quotients: values larger than 1.0 indicate guestworker overrepresentation, values less than 1.0 indicate guestworker underrepresentation in comparison to the citywide level. Although some minor concentrations can be distinguished in each neighbourhood (Map 2), the overall variations of the location quotients are low. In Friedrichstadt/Unterbilk, slightly higher values can be found in the western and southwestern voting districts, where a high proportion of older housing exists. A spatially more differentiated distribution exists in the second inner city neighbourhood, Oberbilk/Flingern-Süd/Lierenfeld. Higher concentrations appear in districts surrounding industrial areas and in high density areas near the main station. Gerresheim shows a strong North-South contrast in its ethnic residential pattern. Guestworkers are clustered in the southern part of the neighbourhood but are underrepresented in the northern part.

The inter-neighbourhood variation as revealed in the settlement patterns is also existent in the migration processes. The neighbourhood with the lowest segregation level, Friedrichstadt/Unterbilk, has the highest mobility rates for both Germans and

Map 2

Types of Housing Quality 1981　　　　　Location Quotients of
　　　　　　　　　　　　　　　　　　　Guestworkers 1981

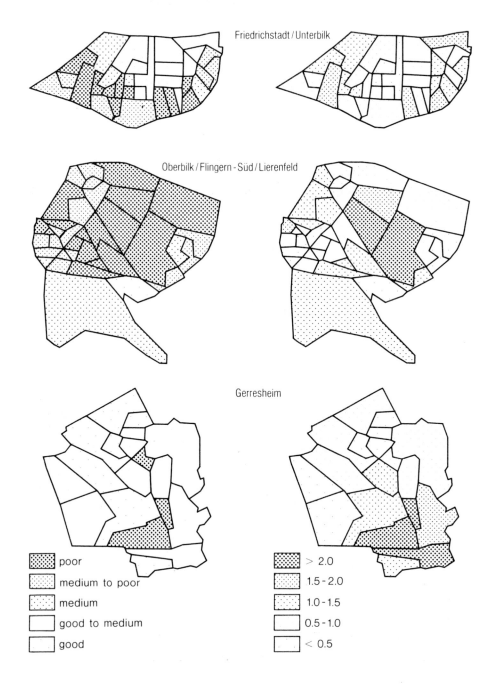

Friedrichstadt / Unterbilk

Oberbilk / Flingern - Süd / Lierenfeld

Gerresheim

poor
medium to poor
medium
good to medium
good

> 2.0
1.5 - 2.0
1.0 - 1.5
0.5 - 1.0
< 0.5

Table 5: Average Annual Mobility Rate of Germans and
Guestworkers by Neighbourhoods 1981–1983

Neighbourhoods	Average Annual Mobility Rate (%)	
	Guestworkers	Germans
Friedrichstadt/ Unterbilk	35	25
Oberbilk/ Flingern-Süd/ Lierenfeld	29	23
Gerresheim	27	16

guestworkers. Vice versa, the highly segregated peripheral neighbourhood, Gerres-heim, displays the lowest mobility rates. These differences in the mobility rates are stronger for Germans than for guestworkers (Table 5). Both the inter-neighbourhood variations and the ethnospecific differences exist also in each migration subsystem (Figure 1). From Figure 1, the following regularities can be observed. First, inde-pendent of the specific neighbourhood, guestworker intraward mobility rates are higher than German intraward mobility rates. The literature suggests that these dif-

Fig. 1: Migration flows at different scales by neighbourhood

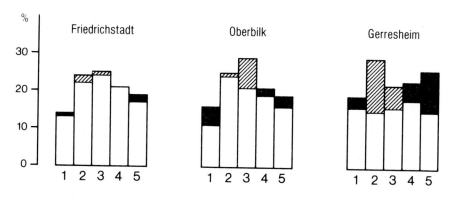

1 % intraward mobility
2 % intracity inmoves
3 % intracity outmoves
4 % inmoves from outside the city
5 % outmoves to outside the city

■ % of guestworkers' moves is greater than % Germans' moves
▨ % of guestworkers' moves is less than % Germans' moves

ferences result from differences between the ethnospecific residential search processes. Many surveys confirm that guestworkers find new housing mainly through informal channels like friends, neighbors and relatives (Berlin, Regierender Bürgermeister, 1980; Esser, 1982; Lichtenberger, 1984). Therefore, the guestworkers residential search space is often confined to the neighbourhood of the current residence.

Secondly, Germans have a higher intracity mobility than guestworkers, suggesting that long migration distances are less common for guestworkers as a result of their restricted residential search process (O'Loughlin and Glebe, 1984a). Thirdly, with the exception of Gerresheim guestworker migration into the city is stronger than guestworker migration out of the city. This is a function of the cumulative effect of both, high immigration due to continuing family reunification and growing out-migration due to return migration to the home countries in the early 1980s.

From this general description of the ethnospecific settlement and migration patterns, we can conclude that the degree of guestworker segregation is relatively low and does not support the notion of ghetto formation in our study areas. The migration rates indicate ethnic variations as well as differences between the innercity neighbourhoods and the suburban neihgbourhood. Ethnospecific variations in the migration patterns at different scales can be taken as evidence for ethnospecific search processes on the housing market due to different constraints facing the two groups.

Ethnospecific migration patterns within the neighbourhoods

One of the most important issues of segregation research is to assess the intensity of ethnic spatial replacement processes. Replacement processes may lead to the development of ethnic communities or even ghetto-like settlements. Since migration can be seen as a link between replacement and ghetto formation, the comparison of ethnic movement patterns by origin and destination may offer some insights into the spatial mechanisms of segregation. Correlation analysis was used to test the hypothesis that the current migration processes do not involve the replacement of Germans by guestworkers and, therefore, do not foster a ghetto formation.

The correlations between the ethnospecific migration rates, totally and at the different scales of intraward, intracity, and migration into and out the city, confirm our hypothesis for all three neighbourhoods (Table 6). For Oberbilk/Flingern-Süd/ Lierenfeld and for Gerresheim the correlation coefficients between the German out-migration rates and the guestworker in-migration rates are non-significant of the .05 level. Similarly, the correlations between German in-migration and guestworker out-migration are non-significant. This lack of a systematic association between the ethnospecific migration flows suggests that replacement processes do not take place in the two neighbourhoods, Oberblik/Flingern-Süd/Lierenfeld and Gerresheim. For the innercity neighbourhood, Friedrichstadt/Unterbilk, positive correlations between the in-migration rates of one group and the out-migration rates of the other group can be observed. However, these values do not indicate replacement processes

Table 6: Correlation Coefficients for German and Guestworker In- and Out-Migration Rates 1981–1983

	Friedrichstadt/ Unterbilk	Oberbilk/ Flingern-Süd/ Lierenfeld	Gerresheim
In-Migration Rate Germans/Guestworkers	.53*	.02	−.20
In-Migration Rate Germans Out-Migration Rate Guestworkers	.50*	.02	.07
Out-Migration Rate Guestworkers In-Migration Rate Germans	.56*	.06	.05
Out-Migration Rate Germans/Guestworkers	.40*	.01	−.12

* significant for $a = .05$

and shorting processes within the neighbourhood since they are joint with positive correlations between the ethnospecific in-migration rates as well between ethnospecific out-migration rates. Hence, the correlation analysis suggests a stronger similarity between German and guestworker migration flows in this neighbourhood. This result, again, must be interpreted within the broader context of the structural changes taking place in this neighbourhood. As has been mentioned before, Friedrichstadt/Unterbilk is affected by extensive revitalization processes. They are a dominant causative factor for the migration process. Since the segregation in this neighbourhood is weak, we can conclude that the chances of being affected by urban renewal are equal for Germans and guestworkers. Particularly, the conversion of rental housing into condominiums forced both, low-income Germans and guestworkers to leave their residences.

Further support for our hypothesis that the migration processes do not involve ethnospecific replacement processes is given by the scattergrams in Figure 2. They show the link between the Geman and guestworker ratios of in- and out-movements. This ratio has a value greater than 1.0, if there is a migration gain and a value less than 1.0 otherwise. The point patterns do not reveal any systematic relationship between the German and guestworker ratios. Therefore, migration gains of one group can not be explained or predicted by migration losses of the other group. Finally, evidence for the lack of ethnospecific replacement processes is also given by the high positive correlation coefficients of inmove rates and outmove rates, both for Germans and for guestworkers (Table 7). This means that migration

Fig. 2: Scattergrams of ethnospecific migration ratios by neighbourhoods

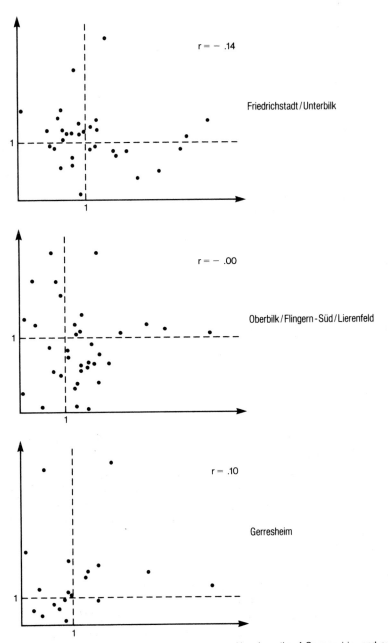

X-axis: ratio of guestworker's in- and out-moves ; Y-axis: ratio of Germans' in- and out-moves

Table 7: Correlation Coefficients of Out- and In-Migration Rates of Germans and Guestworkers 1981–1983

Neighbourhood	Germans	Guestworkers
Friedrichstadt/ Unterbilk	.72*	.71*
Oberbilk/ Flingern-Süd/ Lierenfeld	.92*	.60*
Gerresheim	.76*	.65*

* significant for a = .05

Table 8: Correlations of German and Guestworker Migration Rates at Different Scales 1981–1983 by Neighbourhood

Type of Movement	Friedrichstadt/ Unterbilk	Oberbilk/ Flingern-Süd/ Lierenfeld	Gerresheim
Total Movements	.57*	.03	.00
Intraward	.18	.10	.20
Intracity	.35*	.11	.24
to and from the city	.65*	.13	−.17

+ significant for a = .05

processes are predominantly intragroup exchange processes: there is a high probability that if a member of a group leaves, another member of the same group will enter the area.

The division of the total migration flows into the subsystems of intraward, intracity and in- and out-migration yields similar results (Table 8). The spatial patterns of the intraward migration can be made visible in flow maps (Map 3). To obtain an interpretable picture, only flows with five or more moves for guestworkers and ten or more moves for Germans are shown. The overall impression from these maps is that spatial overlaps between the guestworker and the German migration systems are the most obvious characteristics in the two innercity neighbourhoods while in Gerresheim the guestworker flows are more separated from German flows. Germans show the most intensive flows in the northern districts and guestworker movements are mostly confined to the southern parts of Gerresheim. This spatial division is a reflection of the structural differentiation in this neighbourhood between foreigner and German areas, as discussed earlier in this chapter. In Oberbilk/Flingern-Süd/ Lierenfeld, Germans show predominantly short distance moves. Accordingly, several small migration fields exists. The guestworker migration flows cover the whole neighbourhood refelcting the current residential pattern of guestworkers in this neighbourhood. An even stronger overlap of guestworker and German migra-

Map 3   Intraward Mobility 1981-1983

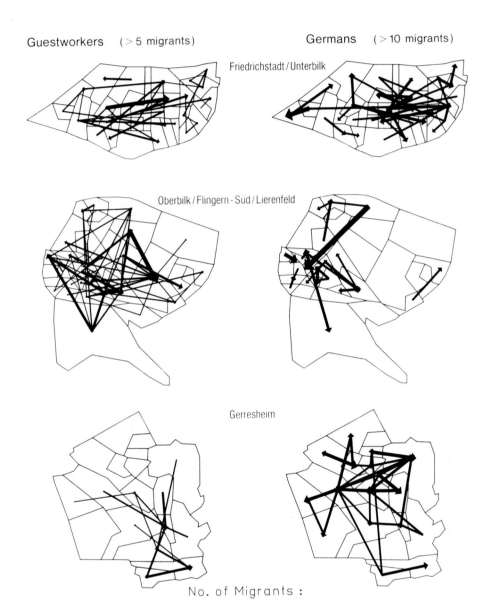

Guestworkers   (> 5 migrants)   Germans   (> 10 migrants)

Friedrichstadt / Unterbilk

Oberbilk / Flingern - Süd / Lierenfeld

Gerresheim

No. of Migrants :

2   4   6   8   10 12 14 16 18 20

tion flows exists in Friedrichstadt/Unterbilk. Here, a concentration of German moves into the more central voting districts and a slight dominance of guestworker moves from the western part of the neighbourhood can be observed. As has been mentioned before, the migration processes in this neighbourhood must be seen on the background of structural changes due to urban renewal. As a result, the strongest guestworker flows originate from voting districts with many conversions of rental housing into condominiums (Thomas, forthcoming). The flow maps confirm that at the scale of intraneighbourhood migration, sorting processes of German and guestworkers do not take place. Additionally, they display the intraethnic exchange character within the existing residential patterns.

Summarizing the results of this section we can state: First, in two neighbourhoods – Oberbilk/Flingern-Süd/Lierenfeld and Gerresheim – there is no systematic link between the guestworker and the German migration systems. In the third neighbourhood, Friedrichstadt/Unterbilk, a stronger similarity between the migration patterns of the two groups can be observed. A further increase of spatial segregation is not likely since in all cases the ethnospecific migration patterns are not complementary.

Migration Patterns and Housing

To find evidence supporting the conclusion of non segregation we now attempt to isolate some of the causes underlying the migration patterns of Germans and guestworkers. However, one has to keep in mind that aggregate data pose certain limitations upon the interpretation of our results. Aggregate analysis offers insight only into the more general aspects of the migration processes and their relations with social and physical aspects of the neighbourhoods. We will confine our analysis to a test of the hypothesis that the housing market influences the ethnospecific migration patterns.

In a previous section, we have defined five housing quality types. Although they do not reflect satisfactorily the complex situation of the German housing market, they will be used as a basis for our analysis. The housing quality types are interpreted as segments of the housing market for which different access and demand by social and ethnic groups exist. Kreibich and Petri (1982) argue that, particularly, in the subsector of cheap rental housing, where guestworkers mainly have to satisfy their housing needs, residential choice is highly restricted or even non-existent. The constrained housing market discriminates against low income groups in general and low class ethnic groups in particular. Höllhuber (1981) demonstrates that even for most German households a residential relocation leads only to marginal improvements of their housing situation. Guestworkers have to reduce their housing aspirations even more. Several surveys show that the majority of guestworkers would leave their present location if they had a chance to find alternative affordable housing elsewhere (Berlin, Regierender Bürgermeister, 1980; Esser, 1982). The restricted access of guestworkers to the German housing market becomes particularly obvious in the social housing sector. Here, guestworkers are generally underrepresented al-

Table 9: Index of Dissimilarity of Germans and Guestworkers Based on Types of Housing Quality 1983

	Friedrichstadt/ Unterbilk	Oberbilk/ Flingern-Süd/ Lierenfeld	Gerresheim
I D	11	24	18

Table 10: In-Migration of Guestworkers as Percentage of Total In-Migration into Housing Quality Types 1981–1983

Housing Quality	Friedrichstadt/ Unterbilk	Oberbilk/ Flingern-Süd/ Lierenfeld	Gerresheim
1 good	–	19.94	12.19
2 good to medium	17.25	–	6.57
3 medium	13.50	23.31	11.41
4 medium to poor	16.62	18.26	–
5 poor	20.71	34.86	29.61

though most of them are eligible for social housing by their income and family status. In the past, the mechanisms of allocation, controlled by private owners and public housing bureaucracies who act as social 'gatekeepers' (Pahl, 1975), have prevented that guestworkers and their families found adequate access in the social housing sector (Laumann, 1984; Kreibich, 1985).

Although ethnospecific settlement patterns are well documented for many cities, their genesis is still controversial (Borris, 1973; Hoffmeyer-Zlotnick, 1977, 1982; Esser, 1982; Gans, 1984; O'Loughlin and Glebe, 1984a). It is generally accepted that guestworker migration is predominantly oriented towards low areas with higher quality housing. The results of our analysis as described below are somewhat tenuous, suggesting that housing quality alone cannot adequately explain guestworker migratory behaviour. The analysis comprises the comparison of housing quality, settlement pattern and migration flows of Germans and guestworkers. Considering first the relationship between housing quality and location patterns, we can find only a weak correspondence between guestworker location quotients and types of housing quality. Particularly in the innercity neighbourhoods, Oberbilk/Flingern-Süd/Lierenfeld and Friedrichstadt/Unterbilk, several poor housing districts do not coincide with high foreigner concentrations, while better housing districts are not necessarily characterized by low foreigner percentages (Map 2). Further, it is interesting to note that this ethnic mix in the residential distribution corresponds with low segregation, calculated on the basis of the five housing quality types (Table 9). Again, the inner city neighbourhood Friedrichstadt/Unterbilk sticks out with a particularly low value.

Secondly, ethnospecific migration patterns and housing quality types reveal a weak correspondence. As could be expected by previous studies (Gans, 1984;

O'Loughlin and Glebe, 1984a), the poorer housing districts received the highest guestworker percentage of all inmovers (Table 10). However, Table 10 also shows that guestworkers are not entirely confined to the poorer housing sectors. Between six and twenty percent of all movers into districts with good and medium quality housing were guestworkers. The net migration figures (Table 11) show an even more complex picture. In the better housing sectors of Friedrichstadt/Unterbilk and Gerresheim, the number of guestworkers leaving the area slightly exceeds the number of guestworkers entering the area, while the German migration flows are characterized by migration gains. In Oberbilk/Flingern-Süd/Lierenfeld, a nearly balanced net migration exists for both guestworkers and Germans in the better housing districts. In the poorer housing districts, Gerresheim has marginal losses for Germans as well as for guestworkers, while in the two innercity neighbourhoods, the figures in Table 12 might suggest the existence of an ethnic replacement process in terms of housing categories. However, both German losses and guestworker gains are extremely low, considering that they are based on a three year period.

The total migration figures, however, hide some interesting variations in the migration flows at different scales. First, the residential relocation process within neighbourhoods is characterized by a dominance of movements originating and ending in the same housing category. This trend suggests the existence of mobility barriers between the submarkets as suggested by Ipsen (1981) and Gans (1984).

Secondly, Germans show a tendency to leave the poorer housing categories while moving within the neighbourhood and within the city. On the other hand, German migration from outside the city into these neighbourhoods is strongly attracted to poor housing areas. The data do not allow to assess whether this documents a transition zone effect in the sense of the Burgess model or whether it marks a new trend of Germans moving back into central city areas (Kreibich, 1985; Droth and Dangschat, 1985). In the first case, high German losses in poorer housing categories at intracity level has to be interpreted as a residential adjustment process. That is, the transition zone is left with a resident's better knowledge of the city's housing market. In the second case, this process has to be seen in connection with recent social and demographic trends, in particular changes in the household composition and its effect on the housing market. Droth and Dangschat (1985) and Kemper (1984) indicate that some household types like younger singles, childless couples, divorced women and one-parent families increasingly demand housing in innercity areas.

Summarizing the results of this section, it can be concluded that first, the relations between the ethnospecific movement patterns and housing quality subsectors are very complex. The relatively weak correlations suggest that in addition to housing market variables, other factors have to be considered in order to provide a better explanatory framework. Secondly, as other studies and surveys have indicated, the strong guestworker movement into poor housing is likely not to be primarily a function of voluntary segregation but mostly of guestworkers' constrained access to and modernization of the older housing stock. For example, the extension of tax subsidies for modernization of older housing has accelerated the conversion of private rental housing into condominiums. As a result, the supply of cheap rental housing has been and will be further reduced, particularly in innercity areas. In

Table 11: Absolute Number of Germans and Guestworkers Entering and Leaving good and poor Housing Quality Types at different Migration Scales by Neighbourhoods 1981–1983

Housing Quality Types

Scale	Group		FRIEDRICHSTADT/UNTERBILK good/medium (I–III)	±	poor (IV/V)	±	GERRESHEIM good/medium (I–III)	±	poor (IV/V)	±	OBERBILK/FLINGERN-SÜD/LIERENFELD good/medium (I–III)	±	poor (IV/V)	±
Intra-Neighbourhood	Germans	out	1573		1638		1671		257		275		2474	
		in	1609	+36	1552	−86	1697	+26	231	−26	296	+21	2453	−21
	Guest-workers	out	413		333		262		101		142		1157	
		in	352	61	394	+61	225	−37	138	+37	105	−37	1194	+37
Intra-City	Germans	out	3298		3177		2339		250		763		6256	
		in	3250	−48	2838	−339	3178	+839	269	+19	668	−95	5522	−734
	Guest-workers	out	690		632		240		69		183		1551	
		in	527	−163	653	+21	231	−9	52	−17	176	−7	1796	+245
to/from the City	Germans	out	2363		2092		1578		243		460		3426	
		in	2922	+559	2299	+207	1876	+289	206	−37	523	+63	3990	+564
	Guest-workers	out	561		509		314		197		140		1441	
		in	637	+76	533	+24	338	+24	107	−90	154	+14	1550	+109
total Movement	Germans	out	7234		6907		5597		750		1498		12156	
		in	7831	+597	6689	−218	6751	+1154	706	−44	1487	−11	11965	−191
	Guest-workers	out	1664		1474		816		367		465		4159	
		in	1516	−148	1580	+106	794	−22	297	−70	435	−30	4539	+380

recent years, there has also been a shift in the provision of social housing to private owneroccupied housing, thus favoring housing construction for middle class groups, while construction of social housing has nearly come to a standstill. The situation is additionally worsened by extremely high rents in more recently built social housing and a resulting high vacancy rate in this subset of social housing. Housing authorities now attempt to reduce the price of units by further subsidies and to relocate emergency cases into these units, including an increasing number of guestworker households.

Other factors counteracting the growth of segregation and the formation of ghettoes are related to structural changes in the German and guestworker household composition and the resulting changes in the demand for housing. On the German side, one and two person households become more dominant and they predominantly prefer housing in innercity areas. In the past, German middle class families left or avoided innercity neighbourhoods because of environmental and housing deficiences. Now, innercity areas have been rediscovered by private investors and

Table 12: Intra-Neighbourhood Migration by Housing Quality Types

Type of Moves	Nationality	Friedrichstadt/ Unterbilk	Oberbilk/ Flingern-Süd/ Lierenfeld	Gerresheim
% of Moves within the same Category	Germans	39.60	55.70	54.71
	Guestworkers	37.30	68.70	48.48
% of Moves into the next better Category	Germans	31.73	24.48	21.42
	Guestworkers	26.80	16.55	19.28
% of Moves into the next poorer Category	Germans	28.65	19.75	23.85
	Guestworkers	35.79	14.70	32.23

Table 13: In-Migration and Out-Migration Rates of Germans in Areas with above and below Average Proportions of Guestworkers

	Guestworker Proportion	
	above Average	below Average
Friedrichstadt/Unterbilk		
In-Migration Rate	45.4	41.2
Out-Migration Rate	45.1	39.6
Oberbilk/Flingern-Süd/Lierenfeld		
In-Migration Rate	43.0	36.8
Out-Migration Rate	44.8	37.1
Gerresheim		
In-Migration Rate	26.0	31.6
Out-Migration Rate	24.5	26.4

revalued as residential locations by new household types (Kemper, 1984; Droth and Dangschat, 1985). Unfortunately, our data do not allow us to assess whether this process is accompanied by an upfiltering of housing. On the other side, a trend of gradually dècreasing guestworker movements into the city can be observed. The inmigration of guestworker dependents, the main contributors to the growth of the guestworker minorities since the recruitment ban in 1973, is slowing down. Furthermore, as a result of restrictive administrative regulations (Leitner, Chap. 4 in this book) it is very unlikely that new household formations of second and third generation guestworkers will initiate a new wave of inmigrating dependents. Given these conditions, the research results presented here indicate that the development of ghettolike communities in West German cities is very unlikely.

better quality housing. Thirdly, the differences in the ethnospecific migration patterns are the result of limited supply of cheap housing and guestworkers' limited access to housing markets. Even if guestworkers are financially able to improve their housing situation, their chances in the housing market are still limited since they are always 'second choice' in a competitive situation (Berlin, Regierender Bürgermeister, 1980). Many guestworkers are prepared to pay more rent if an adequate flat was offered to them. The migration into better housing categories may therefore document guestworker households' attempts to improve their housing situation with the realization that after family reunification, they will stay in West Germany for a long time. Drawing from previous studies on housing and housing policies (Höllhuber, 1981; Ipsen, 1981; Kreibich and Petri,1982; Kreibich 1985) one can assume that low income Germans face similar barriers in the housing market like guestworkers, thereby preventing a complete ethnic segregation process in terms of housing.

CONCLUSION

Ethnic Concentration through Migration: Evidence from Düsseldorf

If press articles and public discussions can be taken as evidence then the formation of ghettolike ethnic communities is well on the way in West German cities with a high percentage of guestworker population. Recent studies (Hoffmeyer-Zlotnik, 1977 and 1982; Bonacker, 1982; Bade, 1984) that rely on the socio-ecological theory have given support to such an opinion. Other studies, however, have doubted that the present concentration of ethnic minorities in West German cities will culminate in ghetto formations in the North American sense (Holzner, 1982; O'Loughlin and Glebe, 1984b; Glebe, 1984; Friedrichs, 1985). They argue that the urban-historical, socio-economic and housing market conditions in West German cities are quite different from North American conditions. Hence, the uncritical adoption of North American concepts and their application to continental European cities is not appropriate (O'Loughlin, Chap. 3 in this book). This final section will give some further evidence for the promotion of a more differentiated approach for interpreting and predicting residential patterns in West German cities.

The previous sections have shown that the degree of segregation is of limited influence on the strength and direction of German and guestworker migration flows. Furthermore, the notions of German flight from or German avoidance of districts with high proportion of foreign population could not be supported, thus rejecting the tipping point model and the invasion-succession hypothesis as postulated for ghetto formations in North American cities. Further evidence for this rejection in the West German context is given in Table 13, showing that areas with high guestworker proportion are very similar to areas with low guestworker proportions in terms of German migration rates.

The main factor counteracting a ghetto development is the specific situation of the German housing market. The growing number of emergency cases on the waiting lists of the housing authorities are indicative of a still tight housing market for low income groups (Neef, 1981). In this situation, low income Germans do not leave their cheap apartments in the older housing stock unless they are forced to move out. German immobility exists also in the older social housing stock with low rents (Kreibich and Petri, 1982; Kreibich, 1985). Although many social housing occupants are no longer eligible for social housing, they are still protected by rent and housing laws. On the other hand, high proportions of outmoving Germans is not a function of the number of foreigners living in the neighbourhood but a response to poor housing and negative environmental conditions (O'Loughlin and Glebe, 1984a). Even in those voting districts where complementary flows might indicate a sorting process, as for example in parts of Oberbilk/Flingern-Süd/Lierenfeld, the number of migrants leaving and entering the voting districts are extremely low.

It is very unlikely that the situation on the low rent housing market will improve in the near future. On the contrary, encouraged by a supporting tax policy private investments tend to shift from the construction of new housing to urban renewal and modernization of the older housing stock. For example, the extension of tax subsidies for modernization of older housing has accelerated the conversion of private rental housing into condominium. As a result, the supply of cheap rental housing has been and will be further reduced, particularly in innercity areas. In recent years, there has also been a shift in the provision of social housing to private owner-occupied housing, thus favoring housing construction for middle class groups, while construction of social housing has nearly come to a standstill. The situation is additionally worsened by extremely high rents in more recently built social housing and a resulting high vacancy rate in this subset of social housing. Housing authorities now attempt to reduce the price of units by further subsidies and to relocate emergency cases into these units, including an increasing number of guestworker households.

Other factors counteracting the growth of segregation and the formation of ghettoes are related to structural changes in the German and guestworker household composition and the resulting changes in the demand for housing. On the German side, one and two person households become more dominant and they predominantly prefer housing in innercity areas. In the past, German middle class families left or avoided innercity neighbourhoods because of environmental and housing deficiences. Now, innercity areas have been rediscovered by private investors and revalued as residential locations by new household types (Kemper, 1984; Droth and Dangschat, 1985). Unfortunately, our data do not allow us to assess whether this process is accompanied by an upfiltering of housing. On the other side, a trend of gradually decreasing guestworker movements into the city can be observed. The inmigration of guestworker dependents, the main contributors to the growth of the guestworker minorities since the recruitment ban in 1973, is slowing down. Furthermore, as a result of restrictive administrative regulations (Leitner, Chap. 4 in this book) it is very unlikely that new household formations of second and third generation guestworkers will initiative a new wave of inmigrating dependents. Given these conditions, the research results presented here indicate that the development of ghettolike communities in West German cities is very unlikely.

IMMIGRATION, CITIES AND THE GEOGRAPHY OF THE NATIONAL FRONT IN FRANCE

PHILIP OGDEN (LONDON)

The political success of the extreme-right National Front in France in the early 1980s, based partly on its virulent anti-immigrant platform, has brought the role of foreign populations in French society to the centre of the political stage once more. Indeed, the last decade as a whole has seen fundamental changes in the volume of immigration, in the demographic and social structure of the resident foreign population and the attitudes of successive governments to immigration policy. Like other European countries which imported labour during the 1950s and 1960s (see, for example, Tapinos, 1975; Freeman, 1979; Castles, 1984) without a great deal of thought for long-term consequences, France has found difficulty in coming to terms with a large permanently-resident population of foreign origin. The mid-1980s are perhaps best characterised by both statistical and political confusion over the immigrant question and a very misty vision emerges of the likely role of immigrants up to the end of the century. Recent trends in the volume and national composition of the foreign population, reflecting its particular place in the country's economic structure, have re-emphasised the importance of the cities and the emergence of distinctive residential communities.

The purpose of this chapter is, first, to outline recent trends in immigration to France and to pinpoint the role of the cities; and secondly, in the light of policy changes under Presidents Giscard d'Estaing and Mitterrand, to illustrate the strength of the urban immigrant issue by reference to the rise of the National Front and, in particular, its pattern of votes at the European Parliamentary elections in 1984.

I. Recent trends in immigration

It is not possible to be precise about the number of immigrants and their families living in France (Wisniewski, 1983, 1984). The most recent population census in 1982 put the number of foreign nationals at 3.6 millions but this may be compared with the Ministry of the Interior figures for the end of 1981 of 4.22 millions. The census undercounts among certain nationalities whilst the Ministry takes insufficient account of departures in drawing up its annual estimate (see the comparisons in Table 1a and the recent estimates of return migration by Zamore and Lebon, 1985). Both sources have difficulties over the number of illegal residents. Despite its limitations, the 1982 census does provide useful data: despite governmental control, the number of foreigners has increased by 7% between 1975 and 1982, but this compares with an increase of some 40% over the previous eight years. There has

Tabe 1a: Foreigners resident in France by nationality 1982
(Census count compared to Ministry of Interior estimates)

Major Nationalities	Census of 7 March 1982	Ministry of Interior 31 December 1981
Algerian	795,920	816,873
Portuguese	764,860	859,520
Moroccans	431,120	444,558
Italians	333,740	452,066
Spanish	321,440	416,372
Tunisians	189,400	193,203
Total (all nationalities)	3,680,100	4,223,928

Source: Recensement général de la population de 1982. Sondage au
1/20. France métropolitaine. Les étrangers. (Paris, INSEE),
p 41.

Table 1b: Evolution of foreign population by origin 1975−1982

Major groups	1975	1982	change 1975−82
Maghreb and Turkey	1,161,310	1,539,980	+378,670
% of total foreign population	33.7	41.8	(+ 32.6%)
'Latin' sources (Italy, Spain, Portugal)	1,719,345	1,420,000	−299,305
% of total foreign population	49.9	38.6	(−17.4%)

Source: Actualités-Migrations (Office National d'Immigration, Paris) No. 16,
February 1984, p 13.

been an increase in the number of family members and a decline in the number of
foreigners in employment (by some 11.5% between 1975 and 1982). The number
of unemployed foreigners has tripled from 73,100 in 1975 to 218,140 by 1982.
The national origins of immigrants have also changed significantly. Six nationalities
(Algerian, Portuguese, Moroccan, Italian, Spanish and Tunisian) make up more than
75% of the foreign population and there has been a rapid increase in the numbers of
immigrants from the North African countries (see Table 1b). It remains the case,
however, that although the political debate is dominated by the 'Arab' question,
these groups still account for only two out of five foreigners.

The detailed census figures reflect the change in government policy during the
1970s. The data do not support the 'official' government figures of net migration
balance of zero in every year since 1974, but they do reflect general controls on
numbers, particularly of new workers, and a change in the immigration stream in

favour of families of already-resident workers (Blanchet, 1985). Figure 1 shows the changing structure of immigration for new arrivals in 1974 and 1980.

Over the longer term the percentage of females in the foreign population grew from 38.2% in 1962 to 42.8% by 1982 and the percentage of under 25s from

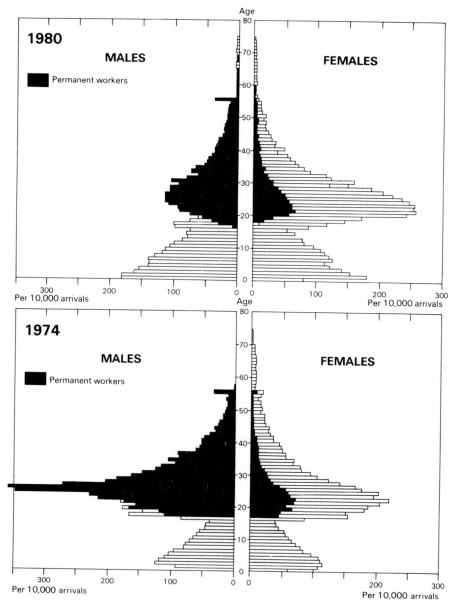

Fig. 1: Age and sex structure of foreign immigrants entering France in 1974 and 1980 (Source: Tribalat, 1983, p. 138)

28.70% to 40.6%. If we look not simply at the strictly − defined population of foreign nationality, but at the population living in households headed by a foreigner, the total number rises to 4.06 million, of whom 1.39 million were under 16 (Ogden and Winchester, 1986). Household sizes vary considerably by nationality: for example, 2.66 for households whose head was French by birth, to 3.99 when he or she was Algerian. These reflect variations in the number of children per family (see Table 2). Foreigners continue to contribute substantially to population growth: in 1982, 86,600 or 11.06 of all births were to foreign mothers (Desplanques, 1985, 37; and see also Lebon, 1981). The census also confirms the relatively inferior status of immigrant households with respect to tenure, facilities and overcrowding (Ogden & Winchester, 1986, table 7.9);

Table 2: Demographic characteristics by nationality 1982

	Average household size[1]	Average No of children[2]
Total Population	2.70	0.90
French: (1) by birth	2.66	0.86
(2) by naturalisation	2.77	0.75
Foreign: Total	3.34	1.54
Italian	3.06	0.91
Spanish	2.99	0.93
Portuguese	3.63	1.51
Algerian	3.99	2.46
Moroccan	3.91	2.52
Tunisian	3.60	2.03

1 In 'ordinary' households where 'person of reference' (head of household)
   is of that nationality.
2 Per family in households as defined in 1.

Source: Recensement général de la population de 1982 (a) Principaux résultats.
        Sondage an 1/20 ème. France métropolitaine p 86; (b) France métropolitaine. Structure de la population totale, pp 88−89. (INSEE, Paris).

The employment pattern of immigrants remains heavily orientated towards certain sectors: while they accounted for 6.2% of the total labour force, immigrants made up 3.4% of those employed in agriculture, 8.1% in industry, 17% in building and public works and 4.3% in services. The recession has affected immigrant employment disproportionately: for example, by 1982 some 22% of all Algerians living in France were unemployed (Tribalat, 1985, 148), and the unemployment rate for every age group and both men and women is higher for foreigners than for the total labour force (SOPEMI, 1985, 26).

The pattern of settlement of the foreign populations displays distinct geographical variations which are crucial to an interpretation of their social and economic impact. Some 58% of all foreigners in 1982 were in the three regions of the Ile de

France, Rhône-Alpes and Provence — Côte d'Azur, that is in the urban regions of
Paris, Lyon and Marseille. There has certainly been an increasing tendency towards
urban concentration and the general picture at the departmental level is shown in
figure 2. Geographical distributions vary markedly by nationality too, the newer
arrivals having particularly marked urban concentrations. For example, whilst only
18.5% of Italians and 26.7% of Spaniards were to be found in the Ile de France region in 1982, this figure rose to 39% for Tunisians, 37% for Algerians and 44% for
Portuguese. Paris does not invariably attract, however: only 28% of Moroccans
and 15% of Turks are to be found in the region, their distribution being more
closely related to their occupation in the heavy industrial sectors. Figure 2 shows,
of course, that certain regions have very few foreigners: Lower Normandy, the
Loire, Brittany and Poitou-Charentes all have under 2% in their total population.

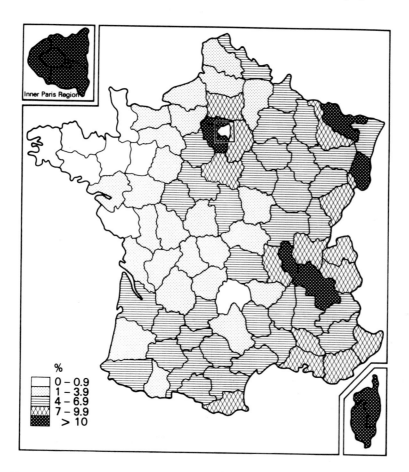

Fig. 2: Percentage of population foreign at 1982 census
(Source: INSEE, 1984, Recensement général de la population de 1982.
Principaux résultats. Sondage au 1/20 e, France métropolitaine, Paris, p. 91)

Table 3: Foreign population of the Ile de France 1962–1982
      a) Evolution of foreign population

	1962	1968	1975	1982
Total population(m)	8,486	9,234	9,877	10,071
Foreign population(m)	.575	.817	1.156	1.340
as % of regional population	6.8	8.8	11.7	13.3
as % of all foreigners in France	26.5	31.2	33.6	36.3
Selected nationalities (as % of total foreign)				
Italian	18.70	12.90	7.37	4.86
Spanish	15.35	17.67	10.97	6.40
Portuguese	3.18	15.12	27.55	25.18
North African*	28.73	30.88	33.28	36.59
Others	34.08	23.43	20.82	26.98

* Algerians, Moroccans, Tunisians. In 1962 all Algerians (even if of French nationality) counted as foreigners; from 1968, only those of Algerian nationality counted as foreign.

      b) Characteristics of the foreign population by department 1982

	TOTAL POP % Foreign	FOREIGN POP % Male	% N African	% FOREIGN IN EMPLOYED POPULATION Agricul	Industry	Bldg[1]	Services[2]
City of Paris	16.6	57.3	29.7	12.0	19.6	45.2	14.5
Seine et Marne	9.0	54.2	25.1	8.4	10.6	24.1	4.9
Yvelines	11.0	55.3	35.5	11.7	12.5	26.8	6.7
Essonne	9.0	56.5	29.3	10.8	8.1	27.8	5.8
Hauts de Seine	13.8	58.6	45.0	15.3	16.0	31.5	10.2
Seine St Denis	17.4	57.8	48.1	19.6	18.1	39.7	9.7
Val de Marne	12.9	57.3	32.5	19.0	12.8	40.0	8.4
Val d'Oise	11.2	56.2	41.9	13.1	11.0	29.1	6.2
Ile de France	13.3	57.0	36.6	10.9	14.3	34.0	9.5

1   Building and public works
2   Commerce, transport, services

Source: INSEE Recensement général de la population de 1982.
        Résultats du sondage au 1/4, Ile de France.

Tables 3 a and b provide further detail for the Ile de France region which, over-all, has 13.3% foreigners in its population and accounts for 36.3% of France's total foreign population. Table 3 a shows how sharply both of these proportions have risen over the last two decades and how the balance of nationalities has shifted towards the North Africans. It nevertheless remains the case that these groups make up only slightly over a third of the total foreign community. Within the region, there are marked contrasts among the eight departments. The city of Paris and the immediately adjacent districts have the largest proportions of foreigners (figure 3) and the highest rates of masculinity amongst the foreign population. Other varia-tions are shown in Table 3b, from which we may draw particular attention to the high proportion of North Africans in the inner departments of Hauts de Seine and Seine St. Denis and the remarkable dominance of foreigners generally in the build-ing and construction sectors.

Analysis at the departmental scales still camouflages much of importance if we wish to examine urban areas and it is useful to look separately at cities of 100,000 or more inhabitants. Of the 36 cities in this category in 1982, 13 had more than

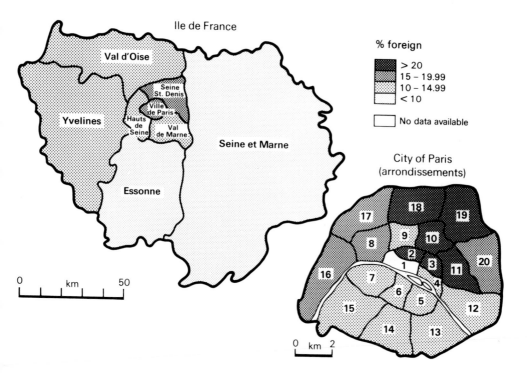

Fig. 3: Percentage of population foreign in (a) departments of the Ile de France and (b) arrondissements of Paris in 1982

(Source: INSEE, 1984, Recensement général de la population de 1982. Principaux résultats. Sondage au 1/20 e. Unpublished data)

10% foreigners in their population and a further 10 more than 7% (the average figure for the whole of France was 6.8%). Whilst the highest absolute numbers were obviously to be found in the three major cities of Paris, Marseille and Lyon, the highest proportional figures were in the northern and eastern industrial cities. Beyond the half-dozen largest cities, location and economic structure were more important than size in determining the contribution made by immigrants to urban populations. Table 4 presents data for four size categories. Paris is clearly in a class of its own: 1 in 6 Parisians is of foreign nationality and, in absolute terms, the city has nearly as many foreigners as the next two size categories, which cover 18 cities, combined. It has a relatively small proportion of North Africans amongst its foreigners, reflecting its extraordinary magnetism for a wide variety of immigrants. In the remaining three groupings of cities, the proportion foreign is broadly similar, but the notable characteristic is that both the overall proportion foreign, and the contribution of the North Africans, varies greatly within each category. For example, amongst those cities of 150–300,000 people, the contribution of foreigners varies from 13.4% (St. Etienne) to 2.4% (Rennes); in the fourth category, from 19.3% (Roubaix) to 3.1% (Le Mans). The contribution of North Africans to the foreign population varies greatly too: from 72.2% in Toulon (category 3) to 19.9% in Clermont Ferrand (category 2). Perhaps more significantly, the contribution of the North Africans to the total city populations varies from 10.4% (Roubaix) to under 2% in cities like Nantes, Bordeaux, Rennes, Brest, Clermont Ferrand and Caen. As the table shows, the proportion of North Africans (both in the foreign and in the total population) is more clearly related to city size than is the overall population of foreigners. Generally, through, the marked geographical concentrations shown in figure 2 are reflected in the regional cities themselves: the centre, west and south-west have relatively few immigrants in contrast to the north-east, east and south.

Concentration within cities is also of great importance. In the larger cities in particular, there are distinct ethnic concentrations particularly of the more recent immigrants. A city like Marseille with one in ten of its population foreign (and of these, 69% are North African) has very high and increasing concentrations in the central and northern arrondissements (A.M. Jones, 1984, 32). Paris, however, provides perhaps the best example, as preliminary data from the 1982 census are available for its twenty arrondissements. The overall proportion of foreigners is shown in figure 3 b: it is over 10% in all districts but is particularly high in the central (2 and 3), western (8, 16) and north-eastern areas (10, 11, 18, 19, 20). It is in this last set of districts that the North African concentration is particularly marked – always well over one third of the foreign population. More than half of all Algerians in the city, for example, are to be found in these five arrondissements. In the western districts, though the population of immigrants is high, this is made up of southern European (Spanish and Portuguese) or northern European immigrants. These results for 1982 reflect the underlying social structure of the city – the division between the prosperous west and the working-class east and north-east, with its implications for housing and job-opportunities – which has been fully described elsewhere for the 1960s and 1970s (Ogden, 1977).

Table 4: Proportion foreign in cities with populations > 100,000 by size category

Category	n	Total Population	Foreign Population %	Max.	Min.		North African Population % in (1) foreign pop.	Max.	Min.	% in (2) tot. pop.	Max.	Min.
I Paris	1	2,188,960	366,660	16.7	–	–	108,160	29.5	–	–	4.9	–	–
II 300– 900,000	6	2,593,640	227,820	8.8	10.7	6.4	115,400	50.7	68.9	19.9	4.5	6.4	1.7
III 150–<300,000	12	2,323,360	179,180	7.7	13.4	2.4	85,840	47.9	72.2	23.6	3.7	8.2	0.6
IV 100–<150,000	17	2,041,160	181,040	8.9	19.3	3.1	75,320	41.6	61.8	21.7	3.7	10.4	1.0
ALL CITIES >100,000	36	9,147,120	954,700	10.4	19.3	2.4	384,720	40.3	72.2	19.9	4.2	10.4	0.6

1 Percentage of North Africans in foreign population
2 Percentage of North Africans in total population

Source: Recensement général de la population de 1982.
1/20 sample tables (unpublished microfiches, INSEE, Paris)

By the early 1980s, therefore, the immigrant population was at a relatively high level, the balance of nationalities had moved decisively towards the North African groups and marked urban concentrations were apparent. Above all, it had become evident — and the 1982 census results on the number of 'foreigners' born in France confirm this — that a degree of permanency had come to characterise the 'immigrants' of the 1960s. In other words 'immigrants' had turned into 'ethnic minorities' and it is to the political climate and debate surrounding this issue that we must now turn.

II. The Political context of the immigration issue

'La France aux français', 'les français d'abord', the slogans of the National Front in France, disguise only thinly the racist sentiments which underlay the party's notably successful electoral campaigns in 1983 and 1984. Led by the irrepressible Jean-Marie Le Pen, ignored or belittled by most of the other political groupings, the Front succeeded in taking 11% of the vote and 10 of the 81 French seats in the European parliamentary elections in June 1984. This was a significant event in French politics, not least because Le Pen's score was only 0.25% behind that of the Communists, who at that time were still part of the governing majorité, and because the rise of the far Right has brought a new, acrid, tone to the already strained politics of the middle years of Mitterrand's presidency.

Whilst attempting to avoid further justifying Le Pen's own view of the 'pseudo-intelligensia . . . which gives (the) movement a carricatured and insulting image', (La Croix, 12 June 1984) the remainder of this chapter analyses the results of the European parliamentary vote and places them within the debate on immigration and immigrants in France. It does not aim to refute or support Le Pen's analysis and is concerned less with the National Front itself — which may well, like its British counterpart in the 1970s, prove a transitory phenomenon — than with the power of the immigration issue, not least in shaping a very distinctive geography of voting behaviour.

The potential importance of the National Front is clearly indicated by the fact that some 2.2 million votes (out of 19.9 million in total) were cast in its favour in June 1984. Despite an abstention level of 43:3%, the proportion of the vote secured by the Front was remarkable: 15% in Paris, 17% in Lyon, up to 21% in Marseille and almost 23% in Nice (all results quoted here are from Le Monde, 1984, pp. 68–102). Clearly, the voters were well aware that they were not voting for a national government and, though much may doubtless be attributed to the vagaries of the protest vote and to the level of abstentions, Le Pen's score, and its geographical spread, highlight widely-voiced social concerns. National Front voters, questioned as they left the polls (Le Nouvel Observateur, 1984, 27–29) confirmed that the two chief issues for them were law and order and immigration (Table 5), a markedly different balance from electors as a whole. A third issue — 'liberty' — was much proclaimed by Le Pen himself and was an indicator of the political capital he — and the Opposition more generally — made from the participation of the Com-

Table 5: Motivations of electors voting for the National Front in European Parliamentary elections in France in 1984

	All voters %	National Front %
Law and order	15	30
Social inequality	16	10
The building of EEC	25	8
Unemployment	24	17
Education	10	14
Immigration	6	26
Liberty	19	19
France's role in the world	16	11
Inflation	10	6
No response	15	18

Note: Voters were asked which two problems were most important for them; percentages therefore add up to more than 100

Sources: Le Nouvel Observateur, 22–28 June 1984, 27–29.

munists in an unpopular government. For the essential context of French politics in 1984 was that, after the heady days of his victory in 1981, Mitterrand's Socialist presidency had rapidly bred disillusion.

Although the scale of the Front's vote was not anticipated, the rise of the extreme Right had been heralded in a series of previous bye − and local elections during 1983 and early 1984, for example at Dreux and Aulnay-sous-Bois or in the Morbihan in Brittany. In the case of Dreux, a book (Gaspard and Servan-Schreiber, 1984) by the defeated Socialist Mayor of Dreux, Françoise Gaspard, and an associate reveals how the National Front played upon, and subtly interrelated, the familiar issues of crime, delinquency, unemployment and the easily perceived cultural threat posed by immigration. The success of their approach is well reflected by the declared motivations of voters in the European elections.

For various reasons, the time was ripe for Le Pen's nationalist, xenophobic message to strike an electoral chord: both the established political groupings of Left and Right had difficulties in their policies over the immigration issue. Since the ban imposed on new labour migration in the wake of the oil crisis in 1974, immigration had surfaced at successive elections as a contentious issue, although Le Pen injected more venom than previously experienced. For the Right, the record of the government under successive Presidents, and latterly under Giscard d'Estaing, had not been a happy one. Whilst from 1977, to his defeat in 1981, Giscard had imposed a more repressive and openly anti-immigrant policy, the vast majority of the four million or so foreigners resident in France by the early 1980s had, of course, been admitted under successive Right-wing governments (Kennedy-Brenner, 1979). Immigrants were very much 'theirs', the product of a period of rapid economic growth and buoyant demand for cheap labour. The Right had also presided over the significant shift in the national origins of immigrants documented above.

Both Giscard and Chirac, having held out the prospect of a decline in the number of resident immigrants, made the link at the time of the 1981 Presidential election between the '1.8 million employed foreigners and the 1.8 million unemployed French'. Yet, as we have seen, numbers had risen overall (despite some fall in the immigrant labour force) because of a relatively high rate of natural increase and because migration of immigrants' families has been partly relaxed during the 1970s. In addition, covert, illegal immigration — though by its nature difficult to assess — had certainly been increasing (Marie, 1983). Giscard had recognised the electoral importance of the immigration issue, but had succeeded by clumsy efforts at repatriation payments (Lebon, 1979; Poinard, 1979) and expulsion for illegal aliens in inflaming racial tensions. The overall impression of the Giscard years was that handling of immigration issues had been messy, an uneasy and indigestible combination of misjudged political expendiency and an uncertain feel for the role of immigrants and their families in French economy and society (see, for example, Briot and Verbunt, 1981).

Part of the platform on which François Mitterrand was elected in 1981 was a more sensitive treatment of the immigrant question. As in other social and economic spheres, the first year of his Presidency saw new initiatives in the field of immigration (Deley, 1983; Ogden, 1982). Whilst reaffirming tight control of new immigration of workers, family re-unification was to be continued and both repatriation payments and expulsions were to be stopped. The aim was to see the approach to immigration as part of wider foreign policy changes, particularly with respect to the Third World, and to recognise that France was likely to retain a large immigrant community, which had literally earned its right to full social participation. Most significantly, however, the new government authorised a 'regularisation' programme, whereby illegal migrants in work but with no papers were offered an 'amnesty' and given residence and work permits. By early 1982 well over 100,000 had been issued (Tribalat, 1983).

Yet the limitations of the new liberal attitude, at least towards immigrants and their families already resident, were soon exposed. A suggestion from Government ministers that immigrants be allowed the vote in local elections was quickly dropped after enraged protests of offended nationalism from all sides. Similarly, in 1983 and 1984 revised versions of repatriation payments and expulsion for the remaining unemployed, illegal migrants were mooted. For the parties of the left have the difficulty that it is precisely in the areas where their political support is greatest, in the working-class, urban and suburban districts, that the largest concentrations of immigrants are to be found and where xenophobia has been growing. Just before the 1981 Presidential elections, indeed, several Communist-controlled local councils in suburban Paris had taken a very severe line on immigrant concentration in their areas. The problem for the Left was that it had made humanitarian moves, not in any case universally popular, without seeming to come to terms with the immigrant question as a whole. Thus, 'it did not give the impression that it knew how to handle the questions of unemployment, literacy, education and training amongst immigrants. Innovation in policy is not enough. The problem must be managed intelligently, despite an unfavourable social climate' (quoted in Thépaut, 1984, 12).

The changes in the nature of the foreign community documented above demanded a wholly new and integrated set of policies (see, for example, Marangé and Lebon, 1982; Bastide, 1982).

III. Jean-Marie Le Pen and immigration

It is not difficult to see, then, that Le Pen's ideas were likely to find eager ears, in the midst of an economic crisis, with the Left in power and with the centre-right opposition in an unsteady state. Le Pen's ideas were less notable for their originality than for the attention they attracted. The level of support recalled that of the Poujadistes who in January 1956 (with Le Pen as a candidate) took 11.5% of the votes, but rarely in the intervening years did the far Right attract support. Throughout the 1970s, for example, the groups on the extreme Right had remained fragmented, with much rivalry between the National Front and the PFN (Parti des forces nouvelles) (Bell, 1976). Only from 1981, with the collapse of the latter, did Le Pen obtain a stranglehold on the extreme Right (Llaumett, 1984). Husbands (1981) has recently provided a broad review of the far Right in Europe which sets the French case in context.

Le Pen's views on immigrants were set within a wider social view. For example, the joint external threats were seen to be two-fold: Soviet hegemony and the take-over of France by 'barbarous races'. Thus, 'we cannot share the heritage of France with anyone. Our heritage is our nationality transmitted by our ancestors'; His campaign was for 'the defence of the indigenous French' who must, indeed, be encouraged to multiply by an avidly pronatalist policy (see Ogden and Huss, 1982), including the repression of homosexuality (which, 'if it develops, would lead to the end of the world') and of abortion (quotes from a speech by Le Pen in Lyon reported in la Croix, 12 Jun 1984). Law and order should be assured by the re-introduction of the death penalty and harsher prison sentences and conditions. Le Pen's oft-repeated claim was to say 'what the majority of French people were thinking but dare not utter'.

On immigration, Le Pen plotted a careful course between expressed and implied views. For example, whilst declaiming that France was for the French, he vehemently denied his opponents' charges of racism. His prescriptions to solve the immigrant problem were threefold. First, all illegal immigrants should be sent home, since they were 'for the most part on social security'. He assured his audiences — a sure vote-catcher amongst those Frenchmen who had returned from North Africa in the 1960s — that 'we shall be more tactful in sending them home than they were in sending back our "pieds-noirs" '. Secondly, whilst those immigrants in work deserve a certain respect, they should be encouraged to leave since two-thirds of jobs currently occupied by them could be carried out by Frenchmen. Thirdly, social security funding for immigrants should be separated from the general 'French' system: all family allowances for immigrants should be stopped (population growth to be encouraged among 'native' French only) and an autonomous social fund for immigrants should be met from payments by the migrants themselves and the firms for which they work (See *Le Monde* 12 June and 22 June 1984, based in part on Le Pen's (1984) book). It is significant that what Le Pen was really talking about was not the foreign population as a whole, but the 'Arab-Muslim', particularly North African, groups who as Table 1b shows, in fact constitute a good deal less than half the total. Further, Llaumett (1984) shows from a careful study of Le Pen's speeches that he develops an equation not only between immigration and the 'swamping' of French culture and employment, but also crime and delinquency, terrorism (through a liberal refugee policy) and even technological backwardness (since recourse to migrant labour in the 1960s had stultified the search for more efficient methods of production).

The extent to which Le Pen had chosen a suitably sensitive political issue was revealed by an opinion poll in April-May 1984: 58% thought that the number of foreigners in France was too high, 23% thought it was not, while 19% did not express a view. In terms of voting intentions, those in the first category were in the majority in all political groupings, and their numbers rose to 91% amongst Le Pen voters (reported in L'Express, 8—14 June 1984): Table 5 has shown that these concerns were, indeed, reflected at the vote itself.

IV. The geography of voting behaviour and the immigrant question

Analysis of the geographical pattern of voting may tell us a good deal about the relative success of Le Pen's message and about the importance of the immigrant issue. Is there a simple correlation, for example, between the distribution of the foreign population and the National Front vote at the department, city or intra-city scale? It should be noted here that the analysis must rely on the census-based administrative divisions, rather than upon the electoral 'circonscriptions', because we do not have social data for the latter. Foreigners themselves, of course, do not have the right to vote.

Table 6 gives the general division of votes by major parties. In terms of social or occupational categories, support for the National Front was widely spread, although with more support from men than women; slightly more in the older age-groups than the younger and an equal spread amongst educational and religious groups. In occupational groups, the strongest support — recalling the Poujadiste days — was from the small shopkeepers, tradesmen, artisans and lower middle class in general (Table 7).

Table 6: Voting in the European Parliamentary elections in France, June 1984

Main political groups	Votes (millions)	%	Seats	Change in seats 1979—1984
Communist	2.26	11.28	10	− 9
Socialist	4.16	20.76	20	− 2
Opposition	8.59	42.88	41	+ 1
National Front	2.20	11.00	10	+10

Table 7: National Front voting by occupational group

% voting Le Pen

Farmers	8
Shopkeepers/artisans	15
Managers/professionals	14
Junior managers/employees	10
Workers	9
Retired/unemployed	10

Source: sample survey reported in Le Nouvel Observateur 22–28 June
        1984, p 28.

Yet the way support varied geographically tells us a great deal more about the variable appeal of the Le Pen philosophy. Figure 4 shows the vote by department. It is notable, first, that in all but three areas (in the Massif Central) Le Pen secured over 5% of the vote, a remarkable national vote by previous standards of the extreme Right. Yet geographical concentration of the vote was marked and, indeed, the main areas of support are contiguous. In general, it is the west and south-west where the vote is least and the Paris basin, east and south-east where support is concentrated. Thus, on the Mediterranean littoral, Le Pen scores over 15% in most departments from the Pyrénées Orientales (15.9%) to the Bouches du Rhône (19.5%) round to the Alpes Maritimes, where the score at 21.4% is the highest in France. Other areas where the vote exceeds 15% are in the Rhône department (around Lyon), in southern Corsica and in parts of the Paris basin.

In this general pattern, two factors emerge as of striking importance. First is, indeed, the correlation with the distribution of the foreign population (Fig. 2). In all ten departments with the lowest proportion of foreigners the National Front vote was below average and, conversely, the ten departments with the most foreigners all scored above average (Thépaut, 1984). This is not the product of the foreigners themselves voting for the Front (an unlikely eventuality in any case) because they do not have the right to vote, (for the contrasting case of Britain, see McAllister and Studlar, 1984; and for a European perspective on immigrant political involvement, Miller, 1982). These correlations are tested in more detail for large cities below, but the national picture seems to be that, while Le Pen struck a chord in most areas it was in those districts where the immigrant 'threat' was most evident or where the presence of immigrants coincided with wider social problems that his message was taken to heart. For example, in the Ile de France the two departments of greatest immigrant concentration (Paris itself and Seine St. Denis, see Table 3 b) are those with the highest level of voting for the Front (15.24% and 15.98% respectively). A second factor of importance in shaping the pattern of Figure 4 is the presence of 'pieds-noirs' — those French people repatriated from the former North African colonies, largely in the late 1950s and 1960s, who settled in the Mediterranean departments and who have clearly responded with gusto to the anti-Arab tone of the Le Pen message. Husbands (1981, 80) hinted at the likely importance of the 'pieds noirs' and the 1984 results provide ample evidence.

In general terms, Figures 2 and 4 suggest that like immigrant settlement the Le Pen vote was predominantly an urban phenomenon. The urban effect becomes clearly apparent if we look at more detailed voting patterns within each department. In France as a whole, the National Front seems to have obtained 3 or 4 more percentage points in the chief town of the department than in the surrounding districts (see Le Monde 1–2 July 1984). It did badly in the rural areas but scored 9% in small towns of 3,500 people or fewer and 10.3% in towns of 3,500–9,000 people. Of the thirty-six cities of 100,000 or more inhabitants, twenty-five scored over the national average vote for Le Pen (Fig. 5). There is a clear geographical distribution which reflects, and indeed determines to an extent, that shown in Figure 4. The careful inter-weaving by Le Pen of immigration with other social issues meant that almost all cities in the north, east and south-east registered high extreme-

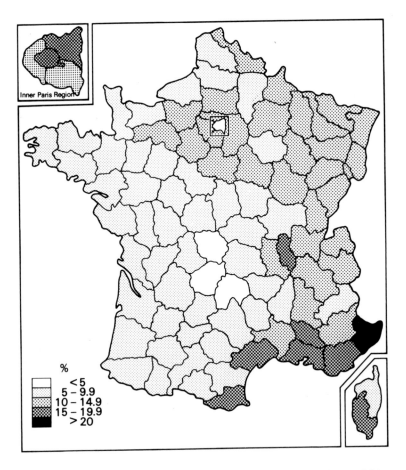

Fig. 4: Percentage of votes cast for National Front, June 1984

(Data source: Le Quotidien de Paris, 19 June 1984)

Right votes, compared to the calmer waters of the centre and west (for example, Limoges 6.5% or Brest 8.4%). Thus, there is considerable variation within each of the size categories identified in Table 4. In the cities of 300–900,000 people, the proportion voting for the Front ranged from 22.90 (Aix-en-Provence) to 9.71% (Clermont Ferrand); in the category 150–300,000, from 22.30% (Toulon) to 8.41% (Brest); in the category 100–150,000, from 21.50% (Perpignan) to 6.34% (Le Mans).

A simple statistical analysis illustrates that factors other than size are clearly at work: we may correlate support for the National Front in each of the thirty six cities with, first, the proportion of immigrants and second, the proportion of North Africans in the total population. In the first case, a clear positive association emerges (r = +0.50). Of particular interest is the pattern of positive residuals, that is cities where support for the National Front was well in excess of the general rela-

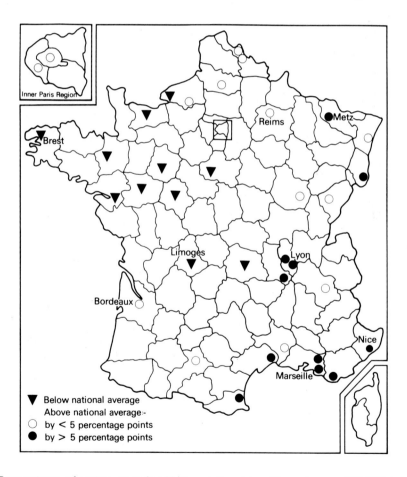

Fig. 5: Percentage of votes cast for National Front in cities of over 100,000 inhabitants (Data source: as Figure 4)

tinship. Six cities are particularly noteworthy: Marseille, Nice, Montpellier, Toulouse, Aix and Perpignan, all southern cities with a high proportion of pieds noirs and where support for the Front generally exceeded 20%. The second relationship, with the proportions of North Africans, is also strongly positive (r = +0.57) indicating that Le Pen's specifically anti-Arab message found a ready audience in those cities where North African settlement had been concentrated.

Yet the detailed distribution of the city vote is a reminder that the Le Pen appeal spread beyond the simple immigrant question to the wider issues of industrial decline and unemployment. In cities like St. Etienne (17%), Metz (16.9%) or Roubaix (19.1%), not normally associated with Right wing voting, a major influence was the unpopularity of government policies which had done little to stem the decline in heavy industry and to halt the rise in unemployment (on the municipal elections in Roubaix, see Etchbarne, 1983). This was matched by a large immigrant population (19.3% of the total population in Roubaix was immigrant and 10.4% North African in 1982).

The particular appeal of Le Pen meant that the pattern of voting did not simply replicate, more intensely, previous voting behaviour. It is true that he secured his largest votes in some areas where M Tixier-Vignancour, also of the extreme Right, had found greatest support in the Presidential elections of 1965. Yet in other traditional bastions of the 'established' Right in the west or in the Massif Central, Le Pen made relatively little headway. Rather, there was s sizeable transfer of votes from the Left in many of the areas pinpointed on figures 4 and 5: one in four of those who voted for the National Front in 1984 had voted for Mitterrand in 1981. The evidence is less clear about the transfer of votes from the Communists: only 2% of those who voted for Marchais in 1981 transferred to Le Pen in 1984. Jaffré's analysis *(Le Monde,* 1–2 July 1984) shows that in the 15 departments where the Communist Party's vote declined most sharply, Le Pen obtained below his party's national average vote. In the Communist cities of more than 100,000 inhabitants, the National Front obtained 9.7% of the vote, compared to 13.2% in the Socialist cities and 15% in the cities run by the 'Opposition'. Similarly, in the towns and cities of more than 30,000 inhabitants and with a high concentration of immigrants (over 16% of the population) the respective votes for Le Pen were 14.9%, 16.2% and 18.9%. It is, thus, the vote against Mitterrand, rather than the Communists, that appears to count. Jaffré quotes two examples both in the Isère department: St. Martin d'Hères, a Communist municipality, with 19.3% of the population immigrant, registered only 9.9% for Le Pen; Grenoble, a former Socialist city now in the hands of the Opposition, with 10.8% immigrants, registered 12.1%.

The detail of the urban vote and its motivations may be further refined by looking at patterns within the large cities. In Marseille, for example, the overall vote of 21% was spread fairly evenly over the city, but with the highest vote of 26% in the quarter of La Cayolle with a very high immigrant population (Thépaut, 1984, 9). Analysis of voting in the twenty arrondissements of Paris shows that all recorded votes for Le Pen above the national average, indicating that the law and order, anti-immigrant theme appealed, as one would expect, beyond the areas where immigrants were concentrated. It is a measure of the Front's success that in every arrondissement it also secured a higher proportion of the votes than the Communists. We may again establish simple correlations between the National Front vote and both the overall importance of immigrants in the population of each arrondissement (Figure 3b) and the proportion of North Africans. In the first case, a positive relationship exists (r = +0.54): the northern and eastern arrondissements with high proportions of immigrants had a vote for Le Pen of over 16%. Yet the correlation is not perfect, since the National Front message appeals also in those traditionally Right-wing residential areas where the threat posed by crime, unemployment or immigration is less immediately in evidence. Indeed, support for the National Front certainly cuts across traditional social-geographical cleavages in voting patterns in the city (see Ranger, 1977; Sarramea, 1984) and suggests a considerable extension of the appeal of the far Right parties identified by Bell (1976) and Husbands (1981) well beyonds their traditional bourgeois heartlands.

The study of positive residuals from this general relationship is revealing. There are two distinct cases where support for the National Front was in excess of the general expectation suggested by the relationship. First, in the well-off, middle-class residential districts of the west – the 8th, 9th or 17th and to some extent the 7th and 16th – the National Front still scored well over the city average. The highest vote of all for Le Pen was in the eighth arrondissement where the Communists and Socialists together took only 11% of the vote and where it seems middle and upper class voters decided to show their disillusion with government and with the official Opposition by providing Le Pen with 19% of all votes cast. Secondly, in the 18th and 20th arrondissements a different phenomenon is evident: a large vote amongst small shopkeepers and artisans has clearly been supplemented by a large working-class vote. Le Pen had himself stood in the municipal elections in the 20th arrondissement in 1983 and his vote then of 11.26% rose to 17.98%, playing in both instances on the fact that immigrants made up almost 20% of the area's population. Similarly, the 18th includes the well-publicised immigrant quarter of the Goutte d'Or (see chapter by P. White – this volume). Thus, Le Pen was able to draw support from widely differing parts of the city, with differing traditions of electoral behaviour.

A second correlation, between National Front support and the presence of North Africans, reveals a positive, although weaker, relationship (r = +0.35). It is certainly true that in the 10th, 11th, 18th, 19th and 20th arrondissements, North Africans accounted for over 7% of the total population and the National Front gained over 16% of the vote in all cases. Yet, as in the first case, the general validity of the relationship was weakened by the strength of support in the more prosperous areas where the 'threat' of North Africans could be perceived only at a distance (only 2% of the population in the 8th was North African, for example) and where the other aspects of the Le Pen campaign may have assumed greater importance.

A final comment on the Parisian pattern must be made for two cases where the support for the National Front was significantly below the general expectation. In both the 5th and the 13th arrondissements, the RPR (Rassemblement pour la République) fought a vigorous campaign. In the 5th, Jacques Chirac's political base, the National Front scored its lowest vote in any of the twenty arrondissements.

Neither arrondissement has a high immigrant or North African population, although a well-publicised, recently-installed Chinese community in the 13th seems to have provoked relatively little protest: a National Front vote of 11.7% is well below the city average.

V. CONCLUSION

This chapter has sought to illustrate the urban political significance of immigration. It has deliberately aimed to emphasis the character and evolution of immigration rather than to embark upon a fully-fledged electoral geography of the National Front. It may well be that Jean-Marie Le Pen and the National Front prove transitory features of the French political landscape. The element of protest voting in the European Parliamentary elections encourages caution in interpreting their importance. However, in the local elections in March 1985 the Front obtained 11% in the cantons where it stood (Johnson, 1985, 436), and the change to proportional representation for the legislative elections in March 1986 ensured a strong parliamentary presence for the front. Yet, for the immigration issue in particular, the importance of Le Pen lies in the influence he has brought to bear on the other political parties: the tone of debate about immigration has shifted perceptibly to the right. This both reflects, and is reflected in, public opinion: a poll held in November 1984 indicated the extent to which the issues raised by Le Pen have gained support: 27% were in favour of his general campaign on immigration; 37% were against mixed marriages; 68% in favour of a complete stop on new arrivals including family members; and 74% were against the franchise being extended to immigrants (Le Nouvel Observateur, 30 November − 6 December 1984, 38−39).

The first section of this chapter has shown that the nature of immigration itself has changed over the last decade: new entrants have been reduced and limited largely to family members; there is a growing permanency of immigrant settlement and the new 'ethnic minorities' are both highly concentrated and frequently socially disadvantaged. North Africans, at whom the Le Pen message has been directed, have grown in number but still constitute considerably less than half of the total.

Clearly, a much more detailed analysis is needed of voting patterns to isolate the importance of the immigration issue and the appeal of the National Front across traditional divisions of class and geography. This would be particularly appropriate for the parliamentary elections in 1986, but the present more cursory analysis of the European elections has shown nevertheless the way in which the careful mixing of a narrow range of sensitive issues has been turned to electoral advantage by a resourceful party leader. Given the many other factors involved in influencing the geographical spread of voting decisions, immigration still emerges as a powerful influence. As Thépaut (1984) suggests, Le Pen managed to see, and to fill, an ideological gap since the established parties of neither Left nor Right were prepared to address directly the National Front's crude message that immigration, unemployment and increasing lawlessness were inter-related. It was certainly in large urban

Cartoon from Le Monde, 16 October 1985, p. 1.

areas with high proportions of migrants that the message received its most fervent support, although the discussion has indicated that other factors such as the presence of *pieds noirs* or threats to particular industries helped to secure a high vote for the National Front. Thus, Le Pen achieved such startling progress because he was able to appeal both to the traditional French Right of Vichy days, with support from the older age groups, practising Catholics and the upper middle classes; from the *pieds noirs* who were greatly attracted by le Pen's nationalistic, anti-North African stance; and, thirdly, the "younger, heavily male and working-class group, recruited on specifically racist themes within the decaying inner cities" (Johnson, 1985, 346).

Immigrant distribution is, of course, only one of several correlates which might have been used to explain how Le Pen broadened his support. The example of Paris showed powerfully how the combined message of the National Front struck a strong chord both in the wealthy western arrondissements and in the eastern and north-eastern districts of strong immigrant concentrations. Whatever the long-term future for the National Front, the strident message of Le Pen certainly found a sufficiently wide audience to influence the general debate on the role of immigrante in French society.

THE MIGRANT EXPERIENCE IN PARIS

PAUL WHITE (SHEFFIELD)

Introduction

Paris has the largest immigrant population of all mainland Western European cities and it is also one of the leading cities in terms of the proportionate importance of the immigrant element in the total population. The 1975 French census identified 1.025 million foreigners in the Paris agglomeration, or just under 12 per cent of the total population. The 1982 enumeration produced a total of 1.254 million foreigners, or 14.4 per cent of the total population. Census results for the city of Paris itself indicate that the population of foreign origin (both foreigners and those naturalized as French) rose from 17.8 per cent in 1975 to 21.2 per cent in 1982 (or from 13.7 per cent to 16.6 per cent if only those of foreign nationality are counted).

It is, however, virtually impossible to produce completely accurate data on the immigrant population, and the census results are far from showing the complete and true picture. Definitions of immigrants are blurred. For example, those from the French overseas departments *(départements d'outre-mer)* hold French citizenship and are therefore not identified as foreign in the French census. Many Algerians who arrived in France before 1962 retain French citizenship, whilst an increasing number of the second and third generation are now legally French having accepted French nationality at the age of 18. Further difficulties over data inevitably arise from the presence of large numbers of illegal immigrants in France and especially in the Paris area (Ogden, 1985; Ogden and Winchester, in press). Merlin (in press) has suggested that a true estimate of the population of foreign ethnicity in the Paris agglomeration in 1982 might be 19 per cent if all definitional difficulties and under-enumerations were eliminated; that implies that about one-quarter of the population of the city of Paris was ethnically not French.

The city that closest approaches the immigrant levels of Paris is London. Peach (1985) has estimated at 960,000 the coloured population of Greater London in 1981, to which must be added a significant number of non-coloured immigrants. The coloured population formed just under 14.5 per cent of Greater London's population. No other city remotely approaches Paris and London in terms of absolute numbers of immigrants although several smaller cities exceed them in terms of their proportionate importance, for example Brussels, Geneva, Frankfurt or Stuttgart (White, 1984; Noin *et al.,* 1984).

It is the objective of this chapter to examine two closely related aspects of immigrants in Paris. The first concerns the experiences of individual migrant groups in the city. Increasingly, of course, such groups must be relabelled as ethnic minority groups since a decreasing proportion of the group members has direct experience of immigration, having been born in France. In looking at this question particular stress will be placed on housing experiences and on spatial location at a macro-scale level. The second question concerns the experience of Paris as an environment witnessing immigration: to what extent have neighbourhoods dominated by minority group activities evolved, how stable are they, and what possible changes may develop in the future? In looking at these two aspects it is essential to recognize that different migrant groups have had different experiences within Paris.

The Parisian Context

The context of migration to France, and to Paris in particular, has been somewhat different from the circumstances surrounding migration to other Western European countries, especially West Germany, Switzerland and Austria. The result is the existence of several strong contrasts between Paris and cities elsewhere in Western Europe.

The first of these contrasts occurs in terms of migrant ethnicity or origin. There is no one migrant community in Paris; instead there are a large number of migrant groups of very varied origin. This variety is much greater than that experienced in cities such as Vienna, Stuttgart or West Berlin where one or two national origins predominate (Lichtenberger, 1984; Borris et al., 1977). Table 1 shows the diversity of nationalities of foreigners present in the city of Paris in 1982. In addition to the groups shown (which total approximately 63 per cent of the enumerated foreigners) there are significant additional groups of West Africans, Chinese and other South-East Asians along with growing numbers of Turks (just under 19000 in 1982) (Bastié, 1984; 61).

Table 1: Nationalities of Foreigners in the City of Paris, 1982

	Absolute number	Per cent of total foreign population
Algerian	53 784	14.9
Portuguese	53 472	14.8
Spaniards	35 028	9.7
Tunisians	29 344	8.1
Moroccans	24 360	6.7
Italians	12 368	3.4
Other EEC countries	19 472	5.4

Source: Recensement Général de la Population de 1982,
Résultats du Sondage au 1/4, Ville de Paris, Table D11.

Although at a crude level, for example in the campaigning of the right-wing National Front, all immigrants are grouped together, in practive surveys have shown that the French do not normally hold the same view of all ethnic minorities. A se-

ries of distinctions are made and a series of prejudices held which differ from group
to group. Opinion surveys conducted in the 1970s (Girard, 1977; Castles and Castles, 1971) showed that the Italians were the most preferred group, followed by the
Spanish and Portuguese. Then came the West Africans and West Indians (these latter being predominantly French citizens from Martinique and Guadeloupe); below
them were the Moroccans and Tunisians with the Algerians being the most dis-
trusted and disliked, and therefore most subjected to prejudice in everyday life.

Another important point of context is that France has a history of immigration
that has been relatively unregulated in comparison with other Western European
countries such as West Germany or Switzerland (Böhning, 1972). Although the
guest worker phenomenon certainly existed in France it was less predominant than
elsewhere. France, and Paris in particular, saw the creation of ethnic minority communities of migrant origin at least a decade earlier than elsewhere (with the obvious
exception of the UK), with the existence of significant numbers of dependants
amongst the immigrant populations from an early date. By the mid 1960s such
communities were developing strongly in Paris at a time when the rotation principle
was still dominating migration policies elsewhere. The halting of labour immigration in 1974 was specifically followed a year later by detailed conditional guarantees for the further admission of dependants, and by moves to legalize clandestine
immigrants in 1981 after the accession of Francois Mitterrand to the French Presidency.

In part as a result of the large scale and unregulated nature of immigration in the
1950s at a time when rural-urban movement was also strong, there occurred around
Paris and other large French cities the development of shanty-towns or *bidonvilles*
in a manner that did not occur in other central or north-west European countries.
The French urban housing market was unable to meet the high level of demand
which included a need for family housing for migrants (not present in such large
numbers elsewhere) and which also, at the time, had a low level of employer-
provided housing schemes, unlike the West German case. This was also a reflection
of the fact that immigration in France was generally immigrant-determined rather
that job-specific.

Finally in this set of contextual points, it is significant that from 1960 onwards
with the first drives to eliminate the *bidonvilles* public agencies became involved in
immigrant housing to a much greater extent than elsewhere, for example Vienna
where foreigners are virtually entirely absent from public sector housing (Lichtenberger, 1984; Leitner, 1983). Part of the reason for the high rate of social housing
amongst immigrants lies in the extent of the clearance schemes that have progressively eliminated much other migrant housing (not just the *bidonvilles* but also slum
rented property). But in recent years the increase in social housing amongst immigrants has been influenced also by the reluctance of the French to move into certain newly-completed estates (for example at Porte de Choisy, discussed later in this
chapter) and by their departure from some of the earlier grands ensembles in favour
of owner-occupied housing (White and Winchester, 1984). In France as a whole in
1982 24 per cent of households with the household head of foreign nationality
lived in social housing: in Paris the figure was low for the city itself (6.8 per cent of

foreigner-headed households in social housing) but reached a maximum level of 31 per cent in the suburban *département* of Seine-Saint-Denis. It is probable that a higher proportion of the ethnic minority population of the Paris agglomeration is now housed in some sort of aided or social dwelling than is the case in any other European city.

In terms of many of these contextual features, Paris is clearly different from other Western European cities where immigration has been less complex in origin, more regulated in flow, and has had different repercussions in the housing market. In certain respects there are similarities with migration into the USA at the turn of the century or the UK during the later 1950s, certainly in terms of the way in which in all these cases immigration was in large part immigrant-determined. However, certain aspects of the French situation remain unique, most notably the experience of the *bidonvilles.*

Life Paths of Migrants

In tracing the experience of the migrants in Paris it is most useful to focus on the housing market and to consider migrants' life paths through it. Following the work of Rex and Moore (1967) in Birmingham, the housing market may be seen as being composed of a number of sub-markets or housing classes. Such classes are composed of groups households sharing a common set of opportunities or constraints linking them to a common housing type (the type generally being defined in terms of tenure): the link of household to housing is structured by a variety of bureaucratic forces, collectively operating as urban managers, as well as by economic considerations. Rex and Moore's initial statement of housing classes was based on consideration of immigrant housing and community in the Sparkbrook district of Birmingham – an area that Rex (1968) characterised as a zone in transition. The concept has since been taken up by many other researchers and subjected to a strong measure of critical evaluation (Pahl, 1975; Bassett and Short, 1980). In particular its utility in the analysis of immigrants in the city has been broadened by those who have added a temporal dimension to the classification (Haddon, 1970).

The strength of the concept of housing classes lies not in the universality of the classes recognised from city to city – Rex and Moore's classes were specific to Birmingham and not intended to be definitive for other cases (Knox, 1982) – but in the recognition of the possibility of producing groups within the population in terms of similar market situations in relation to housing supply of various types. The housing classes or sub-markets so defined are distinguished by a degree of closure whereby movement within the sub-market is easier than movement between sub-markets, for which new criteria of access become applicable (Bourne, 1976; Ley, 1983).

The concept of housing classes has proved useful in studies of immigrant populations because of the ways in which the status of being an immigrant affects access to specific housing sectors. Immigrant status may be important in economic terms (via the competitive power of the immigrants in the housing market), in length-of-residence terms (often important as a qualification for the social housing market), or in terms of managerial policies that result in biases in housing allocations (for example of mortgages or of tenancies).

Analysis of the housing classes of relevance in the study of immigrants in Paris displays the existence of certain classes, such as the *bidonvilles* or purpose-built housing, that are of no significance elsewhere. A short classification of immigrant housing situations might be as follows:

i) Provided by industrial employers. In Paris such accommodation has only been important in connection with major construction and public works programmes (such as the building of suburban motorways). It is peripheral in location. The workers employed have been male, generally Southern European and especially Portuguese.

ii) Domestic service accomodation. The employment of domestic servants and concierges is now diminishing in Paris but even in 1982 there were still significant numbers of resident female domestic servants in the city, the vast majority of them undoubtedly foreign. They are generally Spanish, Portuguese or Italian and live in the richer Western parts of the city (Brettell, 1981). Most are housed by their employers under some form of agreement linking employment and accomodation, although the payment of rent is not uncommon. The employment of migrants as concierges occurs in other European cities, for example Vienna (Leitner, 1983).

iii) Rented property on the private housing market. This is inevitably a very broad class with a great variety of housing situations in it. At one extreme are the appalling slum properties in which single males were housed by the so-called sleep merchants in the 1950s and 1960s, with beds used on a shift basis. As these situations of exploitation in *meublés* and *garnis* have been tightened up (although they still exist for illegal immigrants) a greater proportion of those living in open-market property are now composed of family groups in ordinary apartments, although still of below average amenity levels.

iv) The *bidonvilles*. These have now been virtually entirely eliminated around Paris, although leaving an unknown number of *micro-bidonvilles* housing less than 80 people. A census of *bidonvilles* carried out in 1966 by the Ministry of the Interior gave their total population in the Paris agglomeration as 46827 (Benoît, 1980).

v) Institutional housing specifically for immigrants. This is of two types. Firstly there are the *cités de transit* − governmentally-financed purpose-built low standard housing designed specifically for immigrant families moved out of the *bidonvilles*. It was the intention that this should provide a half-way stage between the *bidonvilles* and normal social housing: in practice much longer stays on an apparently permanent basis have become common (Gokalp and Lamy, 1977) and the external environment of the *cités* has come to resemble the *bidonvilles* themselves (Lefort, 1980). The second type of institutional housing is comprised of the *foyers-hôtels:* hostels of single workers, without the connotations of social engineering that underlie the *cités de transit*. In recent years both types of institutional housing have been used for the temporary accommodation of the boat people refugees from south-east Asia.

vi) Normal social housing rented from one of the regional social housing organizations, and predominantly suburban in location.

vii) Owner-occupied accommodation. There has recently been a rapid increase in the proportion of immigrants in such property, especially Spaniards, Italians and Portuguese buying small houses in suburban locations.

Table 2: Housing of Foreigners, Paris agglomeration, 1982

| Percent in: | Foreigner-Headed Households | | | All |
	Paris	Suburban départements[1]	Total	households, Total[2]
Unfurnished open-market rentals	51.5	41.4	46.2	41.4
Furnished rentals	15.5	8.4	11.6	3.9
Social housing	6.8	24.8	16.2	16.4
Employer-provided accommodation	11.7	5.2	8.3	4.6
Rent free	3.7	2.0	2.8	3.8
Owner-occupying or purchasing	11.2	18.2	14.9	29.9

Notes: 1 Départements of Hauts-de-Seine, Seine-Saint-Denis, Val-de-Marne
2 Paris plus suburban départements

Source: Recensement Général de la Population de 1982, Résultats du Sondage au 1/4, Table D18.

Housing data from the 1982 census do not, unfortunately, exactly match this classification of immigrant housing. Nevertheless (Table 2) they do provide some indication of the importance of different sectors of housing for immigrants in that year. The greatest distinctiveness of immigrant households from all households occurs in terms of their much greater frequency in furnished rented property (including here both open-market rentals and the institutional foyers mentioned above), and in their much lower level of owner-occupancy. These are findings which correspond closely to those observed in many British cities (P. N. Jones, 1979). As already indicated, however, the rate of social housing tenancies is now relatively high amongst immigrants in Paris, and here there is a similarity between the immigrants and the total population. Table 2 also shows important housing class differences between Paris and its suburbs, particularly in terms of furnished accommodation and employer-provided accomodation. There is little social housing within the city of Paris: only 11.4 per cent of Paris households occupy such property.

It is possible to look at the life paths of various migrants through these different housing types, using as information sources various published or unpublished inter-

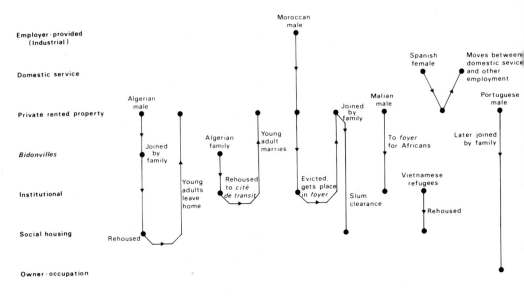

Fig. 1: Migrant life paths in Paris

Sources: Charef, 1983; Lefort, 1980; Anglade, 1976; Mallet - Joris, 1970; Lemieux, 1983; Rocha Trindade, 1977.

views, autobiographies and works of creative literature (White, 1985). Certain examples of such life paths are rendered in diagrammatic form in Figure 1. The first of these is a life path derived from a novel written by an Algerian living in France, and recently filmed (Charef, 1983). This describes the arrival in France of an Algerian worker in the 1950s, living then in inner-city slum housing in an overcrowded room — the sort of accommodation also described in a well-known novel by Claire Etcherelli (1967) who set part of her book in the Goutte d'Or area of inner Paris. In Charef's book the Algerian is joined by his family in about 1960 and they take up residence in a *bidonville* in Nanterre, the only housing he can find for the family unit. With the destruction of the *bidonvilles* the authorities rehoused the family to a nearby social housing estate. For adolescents of families such as this a normal next step is back into inner Paris to a slum flat on the open market. Such a move into the normal rented market is also shown in the second case in Figure 1, although here the young adult concerned leaves the family home in a *cité de transit* and, with his new wife, rents a tiny suburban property (Lefort, 1980). These life paths involving North Africans also apply to certain Portuguese (Anglade, 1976), but are not representative of the experience of other nationalities: the Spanish and Italians were never of significance in the *bidonvilles* and *cites de transit* whilst West Africans, Chinese and Turks arrived in large numbers only after the clearance of the *bidonvilles* had begun. Thus the life path of a Malian male in Figure 1 shows six years spent in a privately-owned and grossly overcrowded inner city lodging-house followed by a move to an institutional hostel (Anglade, 1976). The most recently-arrived group, the Vietnamese refugees, have, in this example, moved straight from their reception hostels into social housing made specifically available to them, just as it was for the French settlers repatriated, effectively as refugees, from Algeria in 1962 (Guillon, 1974).

The final two representative life paths from Figure 1 give two Iberian examples. The first is of Spanish female domestic servants who move between living-in with employers and working in other employment, for example as shop assistants, living in normal rented accommodation. It appears that, except for older women, a high degree of mobility, both occupational and residential, is typical of such individuals (García Hortelano, 1967). The second is of Portuguese males, arriving in the 1960s and living then in lodging-houses, later joined by their families and taking other rented accommodation, finally moving into house purchase: throughout their location has been suburban.

This limited set of life paths is, of curse, only a very small sample of those that might be observed amongst migrants in the Paris area. Those illustrated here have been chosen because they are representative of many other lives described in a wide variety of written accounts and in what have been termed 'documents of life' (Plummer, 1983). Little official data exist on immigrant movement within the housing market: the most useful can be derived from the applications made by single workers for permits for family reunification within France (P. C. Jones, 1984), but these relate only to the recent period of tighter immigration controls and are unrepresentative of vast sections of the immigrant community. Consequently analysis of biographical literature is perhaps the most useful means of investigation of movement between housing sub-markets.

It is possible to put forward a number of generalizations on the basis of such an analysis. Firstly there is a great diversity of routes through the housing environment of Paris: no single pattern exists of transfer between different housing sectors. Secondly this diversity is in part related to the period of arrival and initial occupation of the migrants. Thirdly, the pivotal sector for almost all life paths is that of private rented property: it is commonly an entry point to the urban housing market either for new arrivals or for the first independent housing of the second generation. And fourthly the significance of public authority intervention shows up in terms of the roles of institutional and social housing and in slum clearance and subsequent rehousing.

There is a tendency towards the concentration, over time, of foreign immigrants in a limited number of accommodation types. Since such accommodation types tend to be geographically concentrated this produces the mechanism for the emergence of significant levels of spatial segregation amongst the immigrants. The most important housing sub-market is that of unfurnished property on the open market, which included 46 per cent of foreign-headed households in 1982: over half of these lived in Paris itself and the remainder in the inner suburbs. Much of this property is old and degraded. The other housing sub-markets of some importance were social housing in the suburbs (13 per cent of foreign households), owner-occupation in the suburbs (10 per cent), furnished rentals in Paris (7 per cent), and employer-provided accommodation in Paris (6 per cent). In total these housing situations included over 80 per cent of all foreigner-headed households in the Paris area in 1982. There is definitely some convergence of housing experience through time between the immigrant and indigenous populations, but notable differences still exist, particularly between immigrants of different nationalities and dates of arrival in the city.

The Evolution of Immigrant Neighbourhoods

As in other cities, the immigrant populations of the Paris agglomeration are not evenly spread across the built-up area. It is the perception of ordinary Parisians, verifiable by analysis of location quotients, segregation indices and so on, that certain parts of the city have high degrees of concentration of immigrants. Whether or not such areas are dominated by their immigrant populations is a more complex question. It has been commonly held that in Western European cities ethnic segregation occurs on a house-by-house level, less frequently at a block-by-block level, and never at the scale of a district as a whole (O'Loughlin and Glebe, 1984; White, 1984, p 132). Nevertheless in Paris the term 'ghetto' is frequently used by a variety of people — academics, planners, immigrant leaders, immigrants themselves and indigenous Parisians — to describe certain areas of the city: the term, although being used differently from its meaning in the U.S.A., is much less pejorative than it is in West Germany.

The most segregated and ghetto-like or exclusive communities have now disappeared in Paris. These were the *bidonvilles,* inhabited entirely by immigrants and with, in many cases, very little national mixing: thus the *bidonvilles* of Champigny-sur-Marne and other suburbs south-east of Paris were almost entirely Portuguese in population (Allal *et al.,* 1977) while those north-west of the city were predominantly Algerian (El Gharbaoui, 1971; Hervo and Charras, 1971). The *cités de transit* are much smaller in scale, whilst suburban dispersion has been effected with the immigrant's accession to social housing, although certain *communes,* for example Saint-Denis, have high concentrations of immigrants in certain social housing estates.

If areas of immigrant concentration are to be found today they must be looked for in inner Paris itself. The French geographer Jean Bastié (1984) identifies certain zones of high immigrant presence on the basis of quantitative data, along with "true foreigner neighbourhoods" (Bastié, 1984: 62) identified more qualitatively in three specific locations — the Goutte d'Or, Belleville and the Porte de Choisy.

Figure 2 shows the proportion of foreigners in each of the eighty *quartiers* of Paris in 1982. Being based on a census definition and population is has all the drawbacks outlined at the start of this chapter, but it provides a useful general indication of overall distributions. The greatest concentrations exist in a series of districts in the north (Goutte d'Or) and north-east (Belleville) of Paris, along with two small central districts of relatively low populations. The high concentration in one southern district is brought about by the presence there of university accommodation specifically for foreign students and can be discounted. Moderately high foreigner

Fig. 2: Foreign resident population of Paris, 1982

Source: Census, unpublished tabulations.

presences are also recorded in a series of rich western districts, in the centre (but not in the gentrifying Marais area) and in the east.

It must be stressed, however, that this is a composite distribution made up of a variety of different patterns for different nationalities. In the rich Western areas of the city the dominant foreign nationalities are the Spanish and Portuguese as they also are in the city centre. In the areas of greatest concentration in the north and north-east it is North Africans, and above all Algerians, who are predominant. It is notable that despite the large numbers of Iberians in the western parts of the city (totalling 9.9 per cent of the population of the Champs Elysées district, 8.8 per cent of the Chaillot district) this area betrays few signs of their presence and is not perceived as an Iberian area in any sense by Parisians. Here a significant proportion of the immigrants are employed in domestic service, are female (60 per cent of the active Iberian population in the Champs Elysées district is female) and are living in employer-provided accommodation in isolation from others of the same nationality. It is certainly arguable that an immigrant community does exist but that it is largely a non-place community with no visible manifestations, operating largely through regular social meetings between its members. A high degree of apparent immigrant concentration does not, therefore, necessarily result in a distinctive, segregated and visible presence.

Those real immigrant community neighbourhoods that do exist and have significance in Paris concern the more ethnically differentiated populations who are anyway, as shown earlier, the least liked by the French. Such areas do not display the levels of minority group concentrations witnessed in American cities, but they qualitatively play a very similar role in the mental images of city neighbourhoods held by both native Parisians and the immigrants themselves.

Chief among these areas is the Goutte d'Or (or Barbès as many of its inhabitants call it) just north of the Gare du Nord. In the census district as a whole in 1982 39.85 per cent of the resident population was of foreign nationality or origin (in other words naturalised as French), but the real ethnic concentration occurs only in the southern half of the *quartier* where, by implication, they form the majority of the residents. The boundaries of the area are extremely well defined. To the west is the hill of Montmartre with its conservation area; to the south is an overhead *métro* line, one of the most efficient neighbourhood divides in Paris as Chombart de Lauwe (1952) recognized; to the east is a railway line and to the north a block of industrial land use. The district is not penetrated by major roads and consists of a dense pattern of narrow streets. The existence of a minority community in the area is reflected in a wealth of territorial indicators and distinctive street-scapes: shop names and graffiti are often in Arabic, the commercial organization in part reproduces conditions in North African cities (Paddison *et al.*, 1984), and political activity in the area is a reflection of the extension of the domestic politics of the Maghreb into the French arena.

Of these features it is the streetscapes that probably contribute most to the identification of the Goutte d'Or as an area of immigrant concentration. And foremost here is the fact that in certain streets, particularly in the southern part of the area, observation at any time of day shows that over 90 per cent of street users and other visible people are ethnically not French. The Goutte d'Or does not fulfil only a residential function: it is also the commercial, leisure and community centre for many immigrants living elsewhere in Paris (Vuddamalay, 1984; Allal *et al.*, 1977).

In total the dominance of the Goutte d'Or by the visible manifestation of an immigrant population is a feature that distinguishes the experience of Paris from that of many other continental European cities. In Vienna, Munich, Düsseldorf or Zürich, and in many other cities, immigrant concentrations have not produced distinctive streetscapes which have become part of the customary mental map of the city cognized by its inhabitants. The Marolle district of Brussels, with its largely Moroccan population, is a partial replication of the Goutte d'Or, but one has to look further afield — to Southall in London or to U.S. cities — to find the closest parallels. It is in the ghettos of New York and Chicago in the early years of this century that certain images also representative of the Parisian Goutte d'Or in the 1980s can be found. The ethnic minority communities of turn-of-the century northern U.S. cities were built on migration, just as in Paris, and on a migration that was voluminous enough, intendedly permanent enough, and distinctive enough to generate in its wake a full range of tertiary and business activities solely orientated towards supplying the needs of the immigrant community. Movement was also, as in Paris, largely unrestricted but with the placing of the migrants in the destination housing markets being highly constrained. The initial development of an area of concentration provides a trigger to the identification of a mental construct of segregation resulting in either institutionalised discrimination (as in Chicago or New York) or in avoidance strategies on the part of the indigenous population (as in Paris). The process becomes self-fuelling, especially with the accretion and development of ethnic business and entertainment activities. The streetscape, smells, noises and impressions of the Goutte d'Or in Paris differ only in detail from those described by Wirth (1928) in Maxwell Street in Chicago or by Pred (1976) in 47th Street in the same city.

However, two important points must be added about the Goutte d'Or, qualifying its identification as an area dominated by an immigrant community. Firstly there is a very great deal of real cultural or ethnic differentiation within the district. Despite the general belief among Parisians that North Africans are the sole residents of the area, they in fact only predominate in the southern part of the district and even there an increasing number of other ethnicities are represented, particularly West Africans. In total there are known to be over 40 different ethnic groups in the district (Vuddamalay, 1984), with the balance between them in a constant state of flux, particularly in the northern part of the district. Although their presence is not a very noticeable one, there are also significant numbers of elderly French in the area, generally living in rented property still affected by the rent control legislation of 1948. In total, therefore, the Goutte d'Or is thus not a single minority neighbourhood but a multicultural area of transition and change. Interestingly, this diversity is reminiscent of Louis Wirth's description of the Chicago ghetto of the 1920s (Wirth, 1928).

The second point is that the Goutte d'Or does not have an assured future as an immigrant concentration area. The district only became the home of immigrants in the 1950s, and then only in the southernmost streets (currently most strongly Arab). In late 1984 the first of a series of public inquiries was held on the future of the area and these will almost certainly result in official designation as a priority redevelopment area. Already some demolition has taken place and some of the worst slum properties are boarded up awaiting clearance. The result of redevelopment will be the elimination of the furnished lodging houses and cheap rented property and their replacement by social housing and by new open-market apartments at much higher rent levels. The immigrants will be driven out or re-housed outside the city in publicly-financed housing, and the existing informal community organisation, which can aptly be characterised, following Suttles (1968) work in Chicago, as the 'social order of the slum', will be eliminated. The slum clearance of the Goutte d'Or will reproduce the clearance of the bidonvilles of the 1960s in terms of creating greater institutionalization of the housing of many immigrants whilst leaving others in situations of increasing marginalization.

Such a development can already be seen in one of the other major immigrant concentration areas of the recent past — Belleville. Belleville was, until the 1960s, the most 'Parisian' of Paris districts in terms of the origins of its population (Ceaux et al., 1979; Jacquemet, 1975). With the expectation of urban renewal, planning blight occurred and during the 1960s there was a rapid increase in the district's immigrant population and Belleville became, like the Goutte d'Or, a focus of community life for immigrants (chiefly North African) from other parts of the city (Ben Sassi, 1968). The demolition of Belleville commenced at the end of the 1970s, with the inhabitants either being rehoused in the suburbs or moving west into the next *quartier* of Folie-Méricourt in which, by 1982, immigrants were already a greater proportion of the total population than in Belleville. Foreigners in Paris have a higher rate of intra-urban mobility than do French citizens of the city, and it is moves within the city by foreigners that have recently been instrumental in increasing the proportion of foreigners in certain districts that, until the 1970s, had very small immigrant populations. The intra-urban migrants are moving from areas of demolition to the next most marginal areas which, themselves, are likely to be threatened in the future.

The only significant exception to this marginalization of the immigrant population of the city of Paris lies in the Chinese and South-East Asian populations who, arriving in Paris in the years since 1975, have obtained stable housing in the city very quickly, partly because of the status of many of them as refugees and partly because of their domestic financial arrangements of pooling resources which have enabled them to pay the higher rents needed for the new blocks that have replaced the slums. Ironically, therefore, the reconstruction of Belleville has in part resulted in the initiation of a Chinese community, although the more extensive, visible and, to Parisians, recognized Chinese concentration is that around the Porte de Choisy on the south-eastern edge of the city, in an area of tower block redevelopment. Here, because of the recency of the environmental fabric, a stable community may well develop.

Paris appears to stand part-way between the experiences of North American cities and those of West Germany, Austria or Switzerland. On the one hand Paris has seen the evolution of distinctive ethnic community districts in a way that German cities have not. But on the other hand such districts do not, in general, appear to have the long-term potential for permanence that has been characteristic of the American ghetto. Ethnic community neighbourhoods have evolved in Paris out of the spatial concentration of particular processes within specific housing sub-markets containing immigrants — degeneration of slum property in the Goutte d'Or, planning blight in a slum area in Belleville, new housing at the Porte de Choisy. But many significant minorities in Paris, such as the Southern Europeans, have created no such neighbourhoods at all. It is only the more ethnically and racially distinctive groups who have produced levels of concentration and the associated elements of community artifacts and streetscapes that lead to a perception of dominance over a limited and defined territory. And, with the exception of the Chinese, it is because of their status as the lowest regarded of the immigrant groups with the weakest position on the housing market, that it is the most distinctive ethnic groups that have been most limited to a single corner of that housing market. Paris is gentrifying rapidly, and in the process undergoing demographic and social polarization between the well-to-do and immigrant communities (Merlin, in press). The most distinctive immigrant groups in Paris (such as the North and West Africans) are the most economically marginal and are therefore limited to the most marginal housing classes — rented open-market property and lodging houses, inevitably of very poor conditions. Such property is progressively disappearing in Paris and the marginalization of the immigrants dependent upon it will therefore increase. And despite the continued removal of many immigrant families to suburban housing estates the demand for inner city property is kept up by young adults of the second generation.

This scenario, however, only applies to the most ethnically distinct immigrant populations. For others, suburbanization, integration and, effectively, social invisibility could be argued to be developing strongly. However, although the *grands ensembles* of the Paris suburbs generally have mixtures of various ethnic groups within them that would appear to show a high degree of housing integration, it is also an obvious observation by anyone visiting such estates that segregated behaviour patterns are the norm. Inter-group antipathy, both between French and immigrants, and between immigrants of different origins, is common (Charef, 1983; Anglade, 1976, pp 162–3).

CONCLUSIONS

The experiences of immigrants in Paris, and the experiences that Parisians have of immigrants, are of considerable interest for a number of reasons. Large-scale immigration has occurred over a longer period of time into Paris than into many other European cities. True communities, as opposed to groups of single male guest-workers, occurred at a much earlier date. The numbers involved and their significance have also been much greater than in many other cities.

In certain respects Paris is rather more like the cities of the U.K. and the U.S.A. than are the cities of other Western European countries such as West Germany or Switzerland. Even so there are important distinctive features to immigration in Paris which are not replicated elsewhere, such as the experience of the *bidonvilles*. It is not plausible to compare cities elsewhere with a Parisian 'model'. The discussion here has shown that features of the local political economy, political culture, social attitudes and general context are of vital importance in determining the evolution of migrant experience, especially in spatial terms. In particular the housing structure is of overwhelming importance, both through the operation of distinctive housing sub-classes specifically catering for immigrants and through institutional involvement in immigrant housing both directly (through the *cités de transit* for example) and indirectly (through slum clearance policies). These factors all differ from city to city, so that any study of immigration experiences must be well-grounded in a consideration of local circumstances.

It is also essential to consider immigrant experiences not as a whole but through the disaggregation of the immigrants into separate national, ethnic, racial or functional categories. The case of Paris clearly demonstrates that immigrants of different nationalities, periods or occupations have had very different life paths in the city, and that the creation of concentration areas of segregated activity space has been far from universal for all groups. There is a distinct need now to consider different immigrant community groups, to look at the ways in which these operate, to elucidate the meanings and values that they attribute to surrounding urban space and housing, and to look at the respective impacts of their behaviour on the landscape and neighbourhood patterns of the city.

THE DYNAMICS OF IMMIGRANT SETTLEMENT:

Surinamese, Turks and Moroccans in Amsterdam 1973–1983

HANS VAN AMERSFOORT AND LEO DE KLERK (AMSTERDAM)

1. Introduction

Housing has always been an important field of research in the study of immigrants and minority groups. The way a particular group fulfils this basic need is an expression of its social position. At the same time the way a particular group is housed influences its participation in society and thereby shapes its future social position. In this study we will analyse changes in the settlement patterns of three immigrant groups in Amsterdam, the Surinamese, the Turks and the Moroccans. These groups are the most numerous of all immigrant groups in the Netherlands and also in Amsterdam, moreover, they are most clearly defined as 'problem groups' by Dutch society.

Of course, we do not pretend that Amsterdam is a micro model of Dutch society. Between Dutch cities considerable differences in housing stock, in municipal housing policy and in the number and composition of their immigrant groups exist. Amsterdam may even be deemed a fairly extreme case, having the oldest housing stock, a comparatively tight bureaucratic control, and, by Dutch standards, a large number of immigrants. However, in many other respects these differences are only minor variations within a general pattern, the forces behind the process are the same as elsewhere in the Netherlands.

Before turning to these settlement patterns and housing of immigrants in Amsterdam, we will first give some general backgrounds on the Surinamese, Turkish and Moroccan immigration to the Netherlands and to Amsterdam. Next, we will give a short review of the literature on immigrant housing in the Netherlands and from this we will develop the rationale of our particular approach. As immigrants entering the housing market have to fit in into an existing system, a large section is given to the structure of the housing market of Amsterdam and to developments within this market during the nineteen seventies. In the next section, changes in the settlement patterns of immigrants are described and analysed. In our final paragraph we will return to the relationship between housing and the overall social position of immigrants within the Dutch society.

2. Immigrants in the Netherlands

Though small and densely populated, like all industrialized countries the Netherlands have a number of immigrants. However, their overall figure is not very high; they only form 5 percent of the total population and this aggregate is composed of very different categories. For instance, there are 43,000 Germans and about the same number of citizens from the United Kingdom living in the Netherlands. Next to citizens from other industrial countries there are various group of international refugees. Here, however, we will consider only groups that are commonly described as 'ethnic minorities': the Surinamese as the most striking example of (post-) colonial immigrants, and the Turks and Moroccans as the two most important categories of labour migrants from the Mediterranean area.

2.1. Surinamese migration to the Netherlands

Surinam is a Caribbean country that shares many characteristics with its neighbour Guyana and the West Indian islands. The country had a flourishing plantation economy till the end of the eighteenth century but has never really recovered from the crisis of the Napoleonic era. The European planter class was never very numerous and left the country in the nineteenth century. After the abolition of slavery the mulatto and negro population, locally called Creoles, concentrated in the country's only city, Paramaribo. The agricultural population consisted more and more of contract labourers from 'British India' (locally known as Hindustanis) and Java. These three main population groups comprise to date roughly forty, forty and fifteen per cent of the population respectively. They are complemented by small numbers of Chinese, Lebanese and Europeans (van Amersfoort, 1982 a).

The leading Creole families had to thank their entry into the Dutch school system for their socio-cultural position. They had a strong orientation to Dutch culture and to Holland. Already during the nineteenth century they had started to migrate to the Netherlands. Up to World War Two this was a migration of a small number of middle-class persons, whose presence was hardly noticed by Dutch society. Their orientation to Holland and their migration towards the mother country spread after World War Two to the lower-middle class and, during the recovery of the Dutch economy during the 1960s, the whole Creole population became involved. The Hindustani population participated more widely in Surinamese society in the second and third generations and adopted the migration pattern of their Creole compatriots after 1965. In this way the migration increased in numbers and the Surinamese population in the Netherlands also became more and more heterogeneous in terms of social class, ethnicity and duration of stay.

How many Surinamese there were in Holland at a particular time (or are at present) is difficult to tell. Until the independence of Surinam in 1975 all Surinamese had Dutch citizenship. The great majority of the Surinamese are therefore Dutch citizens and cannot be identified statistically. In the first years of the post-war migration it was to a certain extent possible to avoid this difficulty by defining the Surinamese as 'Dutch citizens born in Surinam'. But with the settlement of the Surinamese population, and the birth of a second and to a limited extent already a third generation, this definition has become less and less satisfactory. This is the reason why we can only estimate the number of Surinamese in the Netherlands. Up till 1974 about 50,000 Surinamese had come to the Netherlands and their number was increasing steadily. This was already causing great concern among Dutch politicians, even before the economic crisis made itself felt. It was the main reason why Surinam was strongly encouraged to become independent. Just as had been the case with the New Commonwealth migration to England, however, the fear that it would become difficult, if not impossible, to migrate to the Netherlands caused a rush to beat the date of independence. Within two years another 50,000 Surinamese arrived in the Netherlands. In the first years after independence the rare of migration was very small but after 1977 it again increased sharply. The Dutch government was alarmed and introduced strict immigration controls in 1980, and this brought the migration more or less to an end. At present there are 141,000 people born in Surinam in the Netherlands. We can therefore estimate the number of Surinamese at 190,000 if we include all people born of a Surinamese mother in the definition.

The rush years of 1974 and 1975 in particular brought many Hindustanis and Javanese of rural backgrounds and also poorly educated Creoles to the Netherlands, categories that previously had played only a moderate part in the migration. They came at a time when the unemployment rate was rising every month. Small wonder many found it difficult, if not impossible, to get employment, so a certain subproletariat has developed, especially in the three main cities. The almost automatic incorporation into Dutch society of the earlier migrants, who were fewer in number and had, in general, better qualifications for participating in an industrial society, no longer exists. Discrimination, which in the past played only a limited role, has become in the present condition of high unemployment a serious issue (Bovenkerk, 1978). The Surinamese are more and more defined as a problem by Dutch society. This has contributed further to the stereotyping of the Surinamese as a lower-class black population, though in reality the Surinamese are a highly heterogeneous immigrant group in terms of level of education and ethnic composition.

2.2. Turkish and Morrocan migration to the Netherlands

Mediterranean migration to the Netherlands is part of the more general migration from the Mediterranean area towards the industrial countries of Western Europe. We will describe it somewhat shorter than the Surinamese migration, because this migration follows the more familiar pattern of other labour migrations (Van Amersfoort, Muus and Penninx, 1984).

In the nineteen sixties the Dutch started to recruit labour for their older industries (textiles, shipyards, coal mining and the like) requiring vast numbers of unskilled workers. However, the influx of foreign labour remained modest, and Turks and Moroccans made their appearance on the Dutch labour scene relatively late. In 1965 only 8,802 Turks and 4,506 Moroccans were in the Netherlands (Penninx, 1979). Both by the Dutch government and by the foreign workers involved this migration was seen as a temporary phenomenon. It turned out to be a typical labour migration. It started with men leaving their families behind and intending to return after a few years of working hard and living frugally to invest their savings in the family farm or shop. Especially the Moroccans have long maintained this traditional pattern of circular migration (Van Amersfoort, 1978, De Mas and Haffmans, 1985). But as is usual with this type of migration, the perceptions and aspirations of the migrants change. Instead of returning after a few years they bring their families over. For legally settled immigrants the Dutch law makes it relatively easy (as compared to Germany and Switzerland) to bring over direct dependents. This family re-unifying migration was unconnected to the demand on the labour market but originated from the internal dynamics of this particular migration process.

Labour migration as such practically came to a standstill with the oil crisis of 1973. Afterwards, the Dutch government issued hardly any new work permits. But the migration continued and even increased due to the influx of women and children. The migration of the nineteen seventies dramatically changed the demographic structure of the Turkish and Moroccan populations in the Netherlands.

After 1980 the migration figures dropped quickly; apparently the migration process has reached its final stage. At present 80 per cent of the Turkish and 65 per cent of the Moroccan husbands have brought over their families; in 1985 156,000 Turks and 111,000 Moroccans were living in the Netherlands. Whether these figures would have been higher if the economic crisis had not caused high unemployment among young Turks and Moroccans, is a matter of speculation. However, clearly this would not have changed the basic character of this type of migration. The high migration figures of the seventies were no part of an ever swelling wave, threatening to overflood Dutch society, as the popular press would have it. They just show the completion of a labour migration process that had started in the nineteen sixties.

As with the Surinamese immigration the increase in Turkish and Moroccan immigration came at a very unsuitable period. Though the reasons for coming to the Netherlands were very different, the results were somewhat similar. In the expectation that they would contribute to the family income, Turkish and Moroccan fathers sent for their teenage children. These young immigrants had little or no skills to offer on a labour market on which unemployment was rising rapidly anyhow. Having arrived too old to profit in any way from the Dutch school system, this 'in-between' generation hardly stands a change in the labour market and has little to hope for in Dutch society (Brassé a.o., 1984).

3. Immigrants in Amsterdam

Of all Dutch cities, Amsterdam has the largest proportion of foreign-born inhabitants among its population: over 18 per cent by 1983. However, these immigrants come from a great number of countries; many from other members of the E.E.C. and a significant number from Northern America, while small groups from a host of countries elsewhere in the world add up to a considerable number. Nevertheless, the largest single group is formed by the Surinamese (5.8 per cent), followed by the Moroccans (3.5 per cent) and the Turks (2.3 per cent).

The immigration of Moroccans and Turks into Amsterdam follows the pattern sketched above for the Netherlands with only a slight variation. Contrary to the

Table 1: Turks, Moroccans and Surinamese in Amsterdam, 1973–1982
(absolute and as a percentage of the total population)

Year	Turks		Moroccans		Surinamese	
1973	4508	(0.59%)	4655	(0.61%)	16381*	(2.15%)
1978	10751	(1.52%)	13907	(1.96%)	24307*	(3.43%)
					32672**	(4.61%)
1982	16863	(2.35%)	23732	(3.45%)	39675**	(5.88%)

* only those born in Surinam and with the Dutch nationality.
** including marriage partners and children born in the Netherlands, and those holding the Surinamese nationality.

other big cities in the Netherlands, more Moroccans than Turks settled in Amsterdam. This is related to the nature of the local labour market. The Turks, who on the average entered the Dutch labour market a few years earlier than the Moroccans, primarily found employment in the 'classical' (heavy) industries; the Moroccans were more frequently engaged in the light industries and the 'general services'. As the Amsterdam economy is more dominated by the latter kind of employment than is the case in other Dutch cities, it now harbours a relatively small Turkish, but the biggest Moroccan community in the Netherlands.

At the beginning of the period we study, the second stage of labour migration – the immigration of women and children – was right on its way. An impressive rise in absolute numbers went along with rapid change in the demographic composition, especially during the first years. The percentage of women among the immigrant populations gives a fair indication here: it rose from 36 in 1973 to 43 in 1978 among the Turks, and from 23 to 36 among the Moroccans. After 1978 migration had less impact, both due to the greater size of the settled population and to the sharp decline in the absolute number of immigrants from 1981 onwards. By 1983 the Turkish community counted 44, and the Moroccan 42 per cent women. This demographic changeover had very important consequences for the housing needs of these immigrant groups.

Amsterdam has always functioned as an important entry port for Surinamese immigrants. In 1965, one half of the Surinamese in the Netherlands lived in Amsterdam. During the high tide of immigration in the years 1973–1975 the number of Amsterdammers born in Surinam rose from 16,000 to 28,000, however, at the same time Amsterdam lost its absolute predominance as the main Surinamese centre in the Netherlands; the majority of immigrants settled elsewhere. By now, the city harbours nearly 20 per cent of all Surinamese.

In the years after 1975, the number of Surinamese leaving Amsterdam slightly surpassed the number entering. Suburban developments like Lelystad and especially Almere attracted a considerable number of Surinamese. Nevertheless, if we include children born from one or two Surinamese parents in the Netherlands, their number in Amsterdam rose from 33,000 in 1978 to 40,000 in 1983.

Table 2: Turks, Morrocans, Surinamese and Dutch by age as a percentage of the
total group, Amsterdam, 1982

Age group	Turks	Moroccans	Surinamese	Dutch
0– 5 years	17.6	22.3	12.1	3.9
6–19 years	29.5	27.2	27.2	13.7
20–29 years	19.2	18.5	26.5	19.5
30–44 years	24.5	24.3	20.7	20.5
45–64 years	8.9	7.6	10.2	23.3
65 years and over	0.0	0.0	3.4	19.2

As compared to the Dutch population of Amsterdam, the three immigrant groups described here are all very young with many children. The modal Turkish or Moroccan household is a married couple with (by Dutch standards) many children; especially among the Moroccans the birth rate is high, though quickly falling now. Next to married couples, one parent families are very common among the Surinamese (though actually an unmarried partner may be living in with the family). The Surinamese birth rate is only slightly higher than the Dutch one, but as proportionally far more women are of child-bearing age, natural growth is still considerable.

4. Housing and Settlement Patterns in the Netherlands

So far, several studies have been made on settlement patterns of immigrant groups in Dutch cities. The most valuable general source is Van Praag's monograph (1981), while studies of a more limited scope are made of Utrecht (De Smidt, 1980, Bovenkerk a.o., 1985), Tilburg (Musterd, 1984), Rotterdam (Mik a.o., 1980) and Amsterdam (Van Amersfoort and Cortie, 1973, Van Amersfoort, 1982b). Recently, immigrant housing has been analysed by Serail (1984) using data from a national housing survey, while Prinsen (1983) focused on allocation by public housing authorities.

As a general approach, these studies compare immigrant housing to that of the Dutch population. From their results, a fairly clear picture emerges. Usually, Mediterranean immigrants are worst off. They tend to occupy the smallest dwellings (though their families are the largest) and the oldest ones, often lacking amenities like bathrooms and central heating. The Surinamese, though their situation still compares unfavourably with the Dutch population, are in a markedly better position, however, at the price of paying very high rents. Especially, they have been far more successful in gaining access to public housing.

Though with different emphases, there is a general consensus on explanations for the weak position of immigrants on the housing market. Their low socio-economic position and their generally large families, taken together with a limited supply of adequate housing pose unfavourable conditions; discrimination (wittingly or unwittingly committed) and problems of communication add to this, while some particular aspirations among immigrants (especially the stated reluctance of Moroccans and Turks to pay substantial rents) provide another stumbling block.

In many ways, however, the global consensus sketched above is not very satisfactory. Aggregating, amongst others, Italians and Moroccans to 'Mediterraneans' is in our view not always contributing towards a better understanding. These groups represent quite distinct migration movements and quite different previous experiences with an urban and industrial society. Even within one nationality important differences may exist. So we know that the Moroccan immigration to the Netherlands consists out of three different streams of which the one from the Northern Riff area is the most important. In their behaviour these Riffians may be significantly different from their countrymen from the urbanized Atlantic coast. However, in our data we have no way to differentiate beyond nationality. But compounding different nationalities in one single category tends to obscure our view on the nature and timing of the immigration movements even more, and so this should be avoided.

The main weakness of the studies on immigrant housing in the Netherlands done so far is that they tend to focus more on differences with the native Dutch at any one moment than on changes occurring over time. One more static comparison would elucidate little beyond what we do already know: immigrants like Turks, Moroccans or Surinamese tend to start at the bottom of society. This held true for nineteenth century Europe and early twentieth century Chicago, it still holds true for the comparatively egalitarian Dutch society during the nineteen seventies. However, it is equally important to know if immigrant housing is improving, at what rate and why or why not. Changes in the settlement patterns may give us an important clue towards understanding the social position of immigrants, now and in the near future, within Dutch society.

5. Housing in Amsterdam

In the beginning of the nineteen seventies immigrants looking for a house were still pioneers; they were as much baffled by the complexities of the Amsterdam housing market as the authorities were by these new groups seeking admittance in an already tight and overburdened system. Gradually, all parties concerned got used to one another, and by now immigrant housing has turned more or less into a routine. However, the final outcome of this development was influenced by many causes.

5.1. The Amsterdam housing stock

The housing stock of Amsterdam is largely an inheritance from the past. It is older and smaller than in any other Dutch city. But its 305,000 dwellings are, of course, differentiated according to size, quality and price. Because Amsterdam was not destroyed during the war we can take the historical development of the city as a lead in giving a general idea of its social areas.

The present day city centre closely follows the outlines of the seventeenth century city, whose boundaries were not revised until 1867. It is characterized by the great heterogeneity of its dwellings. The segregation between house and work and between rich and poor that has developed since the nineteenth century, alongside the development of transport and the growth of industrial cities, was still unknown. Undoubtedly, there was spatial variation, but no segregation as it is known today.

This multi-functional character from the past gives the area even today a great diversity. Alongside the more attractive canals seventeenth century (ware-)houses have been converted into luxury appartments. In the small backward streets there are still many tiny, and presently sub-standard, houses. It is also the area where both cheap lodging houses and luxury hotels for international jet-set tourism may be found.

By the end of the seventeenth century the Dutch economy, and that of Amsterdam in particular, had lost much of its vigour. After a long decline it only recovered in the second half of the nineteenth century. Dutch cities, in particular Rotterdam, but Amsterdam as well, started to grow again. The old city walls soon proved to be an obstacle for modern times, and Amsterdam spilled over them. The prestigious monuments of the new era, the Rijksmuseum and the Concertgebouw, were built in the new fashionable district just outside the former city walls.

However, the mass of the new citizens were people of small means, usually rural migrants who had become superfluous in the rationalizing agriculture or who had been driven out by the agrarian crisis in the last decades of the nineteenth century. This new population was housed in badly constructed new outlays. The development of transport and technological innovations in the production process made separation between work and living possible and necessary. The office as a separate location was invented. Due to these developments the housing district as a more or less homogeneous area made its appearance. The more well-to-do started to live in distinct neighbourhoods, or even left the city altogether to live in the wooded Gooi-area. Modern railway transport could bring fathers to their jobs every day.

The poor quality of the dwellings constructed to house the 'labouring classes' caused the government to interfere at the turn of the century. Uncontrolled city growth was checked by the passage of the Housing Act of 1902. This act made it possible for the municipalities to plan future developments, to enforce certain minimum standards on housing, and to construct subsidized housing, the so-called 'Woningwetwoningen'.

From 1906 onwards the influence of the new act became visible in all newly constructed dwellings. The 'Woningwetwoningen' (built by the municipality, but administered by non-profit, membership based organizations, the Housing Federations) were constructed in relatively large streams of whole blocks or even neighbourhoods. Their share in the total output of new buildings became increasingly important. Nevertheless, 30 per cent of all houses in Amsterdam is constructed before 1906, and so before state legislation became operative. Of the present stock, 27 per cent consists of 'Woningwetwoningen', whereas of the stock constructed after 1971 this is even 65 per cent, with another 30 per cent subsidized according to newer regulations that supplement the Housing Act. Today, there is hardly any building but subsidized building in Amsterdam.

Of course, the standards of the 'Woningwetwoningen' have been upgraded through time. The newer ones are more spacious and have central heating, but even the older ones have a certain minimum of amenities and cannot be considered substandard.

For administrative purpose Amsterdam is divided into a number of neighbourhoods that vary widely in their size and the number of their dwellings (from about 1,500 to over 20,000). However, this division offers one great advantage (apart from the availability of data on this level): as a rule the housing stock within one neighbourhood is fairly homogeneous as to quality, age, size and type of its dwellings. Between neighbourhoods important differences exist in age (ceteris paribus reflecting quality), social status and prices, and, to a lesser extent, physical outlay, although the peripherally located 'garden-villages' dating from the nineteen twenties still have a distinctive character. With this as a starting point we have divided Amsterdam into ten 'quality zones'; this division forms the main point of reference for our analysis.

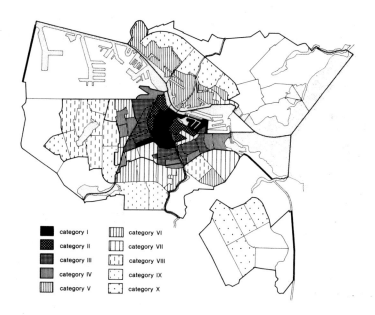

category I
category II
category III
category IV
category V
category VI
category VII
category VIII
category IX
category X

Map 1: Amsterdam divided in ten 'quality zones'

(The zones are described in table 3)

Clearly, not only quality is at stake on a housing market; of equal importance is what it costs to rent or buy. And here the picture becomes really complicated, because in Amsterdam there is only a weak relationship between rent on the one hand and quality on the other.

Table 3: Amsterdam in ten quality zones (see map 1)

Zone	Rent	No. of bedrooms	Type of building	Residential mobility
1. Inner city – business districts	low to some high	0, 1, some many	appartments 4-storied	high
2. Inner city – residential areas	low to some high	0, 1, some many	appartments 4-storied	high
3. Nineteenth century residential areas	low	0, 1	appartments 4-storied	high
4. Central location built 1906–1930	low to moderate	2 to 3	appartments 4-storied	high
5. Peripheral location built 1906–1930	low to moderate	2 to 3	detached to 2-storied	low to moderate
6. Resiential areas built 1930–1945	moderate	3	appartments 4-storied	moderate to high
7. Upper-class areas built 1906–1945	moderate to high	2 to many	appartments, some villas	moderate
8. Residential areas built 1945–1960	moderate	2 to 3	detached to 4-storied	low
9. Residential areas built 1960–1970	moderate to high	2 to 3	detached to high rise	low to moderate
10. Bijlmermeer built 1970-now	high	3	high rise	high

Immediately after the second world war an acute housing shortage occurred. To protect the population against black marketeering, a system for the distribution of vacancies (see section 5.3) and a rent freeze was introduced. Rent nowadays depends primarily on the building costs at the moment of construction, not on rebuilding or maintenance costs. In a period of inflation and rising construction costs this means a de facto lowering of the rents in the existing stock each year. On the other hand, new houses become comparatively expensive, while in the old stock maintenance, both by private owners and by non-profit organizations, is strongly discouraged and consequently brought down to its barest minimum.

Under these circumstances it was inevitable that the liberal 'market-idea' became less important than a politico-bureaucratic idea of 'social needs'. Inevitably too, this system primarily protected the interests of the settled population, and worked adverse to all newcomers to the housing market, like young couples, students and immigrants.

Another consequence of this system was the withdrawal of private investments from middle and lower-class housing. Construction within the rent sector became a near hundred per cent government affair. And while owner-occupation surged in the Netherlands during the sixties and the seventies, the Labour dominated City

Council of Amsterdam discouraged this development. Housing for the common citizen, the 'Woningwetwoning', was preferred at the exclusion of all other categories. Although owner-occupation increased from 4 per cent in 1971 to 7 per cent in 1981, this was entirely brought about by conversions in the existing stock from rent or industrial usage to owner-occupation. Those who earned to much to qualify for the 'distribution houses' (see 5.3), but not enough to be able to pay the inflated prices in the small private sector, had no choice but to leave the city altogether.

5.2. The population of the city

Houses are one side of the coin, the other are the people who do or should occupy them. The population of Amsterdam has declined substantially since the Second World War, and its composition has changed dramatically. Between 1971 and 1981 Amsterdam even lost 133,000 of its inhabitants, though international migration showed a positive saldo of 78,000. As there was only a very small excess of deaths over births, this means that migration of Dutch-born people showed a negative saldo of around 200,000 persons. For a city with 800,000 inhabitants in 1971 this loss is tremendous.

The general causes for this exodus are the same as everywhere else in the industrial world. So the question is not why suburbanization occurred, but why a city of modest size like Amsterdam had so much of it. Between 1972 and 1982 the total housing stock increased by 16,000 dwellings to a total of 305,000. As in the same period 18,000 dwellings were demolished, the construction of new ones was far higher: 34,000. However, this addition was highly selective as to type of dwelling: 94 per cent in the rent sector and 93 per cent in high rise buildings, and did not reflect market demand, but the policy of the City Council to build in an urban way and primarily for low-income households. Meanwhile, single-family houses for owner occupation, very popular among middle class families, were built in large numbers in the surrounding municipalities. As a result, the classical pattern of suburbanization, the departure of upper and middle class family life from the city, was strongly reinforced.

This development strengthened the political position of an already powerful interest group: young adults rejecting the traditional, family oriented way of life. Their counterpart, the Dutch-born married couple with children, was by 1982 only one of the many minorities in the city: approximately 13.5 per cent of all households fell into this category. Between 1971 and 1982 the age composition of the population changed rapidly: at the beginning of this period, children up to 15 years old made up 19 per cent of the city's inhabitants, by the end this had fallen down to 14 per cent. Conversely, the age group between 25 to 35 years rose from 13 to 19 per cent. The outmigration of Dutch families coincided with the immigration of Moroccan, Turkish and Surinamese families. By now, the children of Amsterdam are for a large part immigrant children.

These population movements led to a housing demand at the end of the seventies that was quite different from that of the earlier decades. In 1982, 34 per cent

Table 4: The Amsterdam population by ethnic origin and age, 1982
(percentage of total age group)

Age group	Turks	Moroccans	Surinamese	Dutsch	Others
0– 5 years	7.1	13.5	12.3	55.5	11.6
6– 9 years	6.3	10.1	11.7	62.8	9.1
10–14 years	4.6	6.1	11.2	71.8	6.3
15–19 years	3.4	4.2	8.9	79.1	4.4
0–19 years	5.2	8.1	10.9	68.3	7.5
All ages	2.3	3.5	5.8	81.8	6.6

of all dwellings were occupied by only one person, another 34 per cent by two. The elderly and a substantial part of the young people have, be it for different reasons, only a modest income, but as their households are small, they can manage with one and two bedroomed houses. Only among the Moroccans, the Turks and, to a lesser extent, the Surinamese, we still find large families. For these immigrants housing that is both cheap and spacious is still very important.

5.3. Housing allocation

In Amsterdam, we can use the concept of a housing market only in a meta-phorical sense. Since the Second World War, access to housing has been subjected to bureaucratic rules established by the City Council. Immediately after the war, this municipal allocation system was applied very strictly. War experiences had made the idea of a just distribution of scarce goods acceptable to the population at large. As a result, private owners and the Housing Confederations saw their power to pick and choose tenants drastically hemmed in. Although the housing shortage diminished in the course of time and the cheapest houses of very low quality and the most expensive ones were returned to the free market, the basic principles of the system have been retained up till now (Van Amersfoort, 1982b).

The core idea of the system is that housing need can be objectively established by relating the number of persons in a household to the number of rooms available. Discrepancies between available living space and the norm qualifies households for entry into a waiting list and, in due course, for assignment of fitting housing by the municipality. To this end, the municipality claims a considerable share of the vacancies in the rent sector for distribution among its clients, while the other vacancies only can be filled with households satisfying the norms.

At first, actual norms were definitely family oriented. In the frugal post war years people did not bother very much about the housing needs of singles, and especially not if these needs were deemed to be only temporary, like those of students. It took more than ten years before unmarried people could qualify for independent housing, and then only when they were least 27 years of age.

Of course, the practice of the system diverged somewhat from its theoretical aims. Its weakest point was that it tried to apply a kind of socially defined 'need' to the allotment of vacancies, whereas the main benefactor from the system at large was the settled population. The rent control in particular was very favourable for everybody who already had a house (see before). The decreasing rent quote these people experienced stiffled movement on the housing market; e.g. widows living in a four bedroomed house tend to be far better off by staying than by moving, since every (smaller) alternative tends to be newer and so far more expensive. Secondly, the system was tuned to the 'real Amsterdamer' because duration of residence gave a clear preference. Even more disturbing were the possibilities for owners or administrators to manipulate the system, especially when they administered great quantities. These possibilities arose from a gradual slackening of the severeness with which the system was applied. Private administrators and the housing corporations claimed that they could work quicker and with less red tape than the municipal housing authorities. They asked (and got) the right to allocate houses to persons qualifying under the rules of the municipality, however, according to priority rules of their own. Due to a continuous 'upgrading' of the norms, registered demand always widely surpassed the supply of houses, and within this large pool of qualified households private administrators and housing federations could select to a greater or lesser extent the more 'desirable' tenants, and offer these the best of their housing stock, turning the worst part in for allocation by the municipality. As especially immigrants had to turn to the municipal authorities, they only obtained housing in the least desired part of the market. This situation was exposed in several publications (Van Amersfoort and Cortie, 1973, Valkonet-Freeman, 1978), which led to a heated public debate; finally, the Council strengthened its grip on the allocation system.

However, by the end of the seventies the system was already eroded in other ways. The growing housing stock and the declining population made an ever more liberal definition of need possible; by now, everybody aged 18 years can claim a house. This redefinition widened the discrepancy between the existing stock and the recognized needs. The stock primarily reflects ideas of planners building for families; the waiting lists are crowded by young singles and unmarried couples. This resulted in the paradoxical situation that while 53,000 households are officially waiting for adequate housing, in the high rise Bijlmermeer Estate several thousands of (admittedly rather expensive) three and four bedroomed houses are vacant.

Related to this development, the allocation system lost its general support among the population, and became a bone for political contention. In the resulting legitimation crisis especially the young started to define their rights themselves. At first, squatters only occupied houses and old stores that for one reason or another were empty for many years. But soon illegal occupation became less discriminating and affected the housing stock subjected to the municipal allocation system. Young mobile persons actively squatting could run the risk of being put on the street again; at the same time they waged a rather succesful battle to get squatting accepted as a fair practice. The municipal government gave in and tended to legalize accomplished facts (Priemus, 1983). Obviously, this alternative right of the strongest works at the disadvantage of (immigrant) families with children too vulnerable to use this tactic. Moreover, these groups lack the political contacts with councillors, the churches and the press that helped the squatter movement to get what it wanted.

As a result of the developments sketched above an entirely new type of competition for housing has emerged. During the nineteen sixties and early seventies family houses were the most wanted items and (institutionally and practically) 'protected' against immigrants. Nowadays, competition is far more about those parts of the city that are attractive to young singles and unmarried couples: the small but cheap stock in and immediately around the inner city. Though — be it ageing — Dutch families still dominate the outskirts of the city, family housing somewhat out of the city centre is far less in demand.

6. Immigrant Settlement in Amsterdam

Between 1973 and 1982, the pattern of immigrant settlement within Amsterdam has been far from static. This holds especially true for the Turks and Moroccans. By 1973 the majority of them lived in or closely around the inner city; ten years later, their point of gravity has decisively shifted towards the neighbourhoods built between 1900 and 1940, with the neighbourhoods built during the nineteen fifties becoming increasingly important.

The pattern of Surinamese settlement is far more stabile and quite distinctive from the Turkish and Morrocan pattern in one major respect: a huge number of Surinamese lived and live in the south-eastern part of the city; the newly constructed Bijlmermeer area. Otherwise, the Surinamese pattern shows a rough resemblance to that of the other immigrant groups, though concentrations tend to be far less pronounced.

However, maps can only give a first and rough impression of the changes that occurred. In a more thorough analysis we will first turn our attention to the quality of the housing involved, next, we will relate these findings to the changing settlement pattern of the native Dutch population.

The settlement patterns of Turks and Moroccans are very similar. The minor differences that occur reflect the fact that the latter started to bring their families to the Netherlands a few years after the Turks did so, and that they still have more males among their number who did not do so as yet. As the Turks offer a more typical case of a population that has completed the second stage of labour migration, for brevity's sake we will only present data on this group. The Moroccan story is very much the same.

6.1. Changes in immigrant housing

Although by 1973 already a considerable number of Turkish women and children had come to Amsterdam, the majority of men still lived without their families

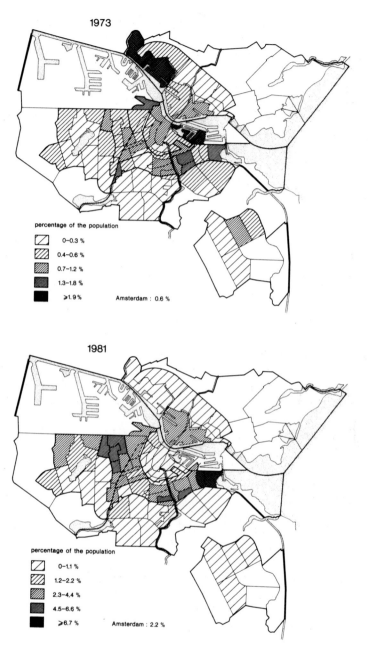

Map 2: The development of the Turkish settlement pattern in Amsterdam

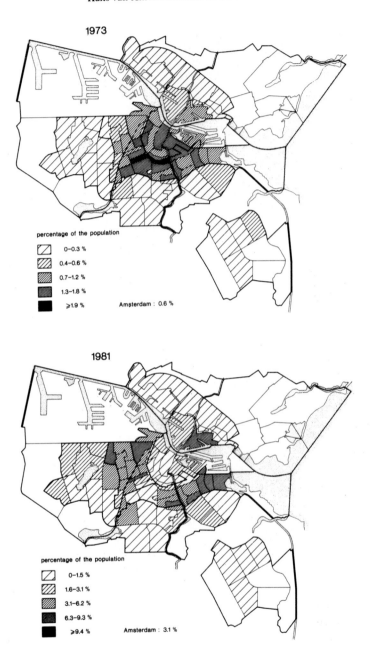

Map 3: The development of the Moroccan settlement pattern in Amsterdam

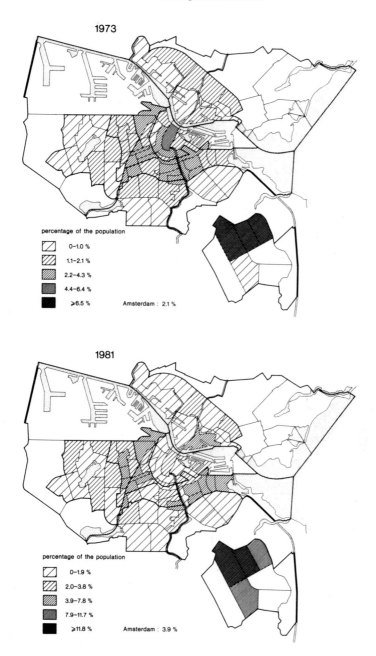

1973

percentage of the population

- 0–1.0 %
- 1.1–2.1 %
- 2.2–4.3 %
- 4.4–6.4 %
- ⩾6.5 %   Amsterdam : 2.1 %

1981

percentage of the population

- 0–1.9 %
- 2.0–3.8 %
- 3.9–7.8 %
- 7.9–11.7 %
- ⩾11.8 %   Amsterdam : 3.9 %

Map 4 : The development of the Surinamese settlement pattern in Amsterdam

in barracks (most prominently in a large Turkish camp north of the river IJ) or in lodging houses in and around the inner cities. Family housing was concentrated in the nineteenth century neighbourhoods and in the adjoining working-class districts built between 1900 and 1930.

In the next few years, the shift from lodging house areas towards neighbourhoods with old (though not obsolete) but cheap family housing continued, and by 1978 hardly a Turk was living anymore in the inner city or in the pre-war neighbourhoods with spacious dwellings built for the upper-class and now often converted into lodging houses. As such, this movement did not constitute any change in the opportunities for Turks on the housing market; it merely reflected the change from a population of single male adults towards a population consisting overwhelmingly out of families. However, in the meantime the Turks increasingly got access to the neighbourhoods built between 1930 and 1940 and even, be it just marginally, in the early post-war housing estates at the western edge of the city.

Because after 1978 immigration and the change in the demographic composition of the Turkish population resulting from this were far less important (at first only relatively, later on absolutely as well), the Turkish settlement pattern became more stable too. However, the same tendencies prevailed. Contrary to the public image, the concentration in the nineteenth century neighbourhoods started to decline at least relatively, but in some cases even absolutely, while the influx of Turks into the housing estates built between 1945 and 1960 gathered momentum.

So between 1973 and 1983 the Turks got access to ever newer, and ever better houses. By and large, this progress did not result from intra urban mobility; Turks bringing over their families around 1980 just got better housing in newer neighbourhoods than their compatriots some years earlier. However, the movement towards the post war housing estates is brought about by families leaving old and overcrowded dwellings in the pre-1930 neighbourhoods for the more spacious and better equipped apartments at the western edge of the city (Vijgen en De Klerk, 1986).

The most conspicuous feature in the Surinamese settlement pattern is the high concentration in the Bijlmermeer area, the south-eastern part of the city. This is a consequence of the development spelled out previously. The Bijlmermeer was constructed by the municipality for citizens who did not want to go there. They preferred to become owner-occupier of a single-family house in the suburbs. However, Surinamese families with no other option than public housing and pressed by bad circumstances in lodging houses were quite ready to grasp this opportunity. As they were almost alone in competing for this kind of housing, and as vacancies abounded, one could get a house in the area very quickly. And once a certain number of Surinamese families lived there, the word got around and attracted others. Presently, about 10,000 Surinamese out of the city's 35,000 live in the Bijlmermeer.

Within this area, however, an important change took place. The newest outlays, built from 1978 onwards, were no more in high-rise and even contained a considerable number of single-family houses. These parts became far more popular among the native Dutch; nevertheless, a considerable number of Surinamese succeeded in exchanging their high-rise appartment for a terraced dwelling in these new projects.

Table 5: Concentration and change in Turkish settlement by quality zone, Amsterdam, 1973–1982*

Zone	Patterns			Changes	
	1973	1978	1982	73–78	78–82
1. Inner city – business areas	54	−74	−70	−116	0
2. Inner city – residential areas	−34	−68	−72	− 59	−24
3. 19th century – residential areas	37	60	46	49	−33
4. Central location built 1906–1930	93	150	149	120	20
5. Peripheral location built 1906–1930	−8	−32	−36	− 33	−15
6. Residential areas built 1931–1944	−43	31	45	60	48
7. Upper-class areas built 1906–1944	−71	−81	−81	− 53	−14
8. Residential areas built 1945–1959	−36	−12	7	6	56
9. Residential areas built 1960–1970	−77	−73	−73	− 43	−12
10. Bijlmermeer built 1970 – now	−21	−89	−87	− 90	−11

As a result, the proportion of Surinamese in the oldest part of the Bijlmermeer dimiished from 29 per cent to 20 per cent, while in the newest parts it rose from nearly nothing in the first blocks being completed to 10 per cent in 1983.

In the rest of the city, Surinamese settlement between 1973 and 1978 followed approximately the same pattern as the Turkish. Hotels and lodging houses in and around the inner city that had been very important to provide temporary shelter for the vast wave of immigrants in 1974 and 1975, still functioned in 1978, though their importance was declining. The majority of the Surinamese got housing in the pre-war residential districts. After 1978, however, the Surinamese started to move into a wide range of districts, the only exception being the inner city and the neighbourhoods immediately around it.

Elsewhere, we have analyzed the settlement pattern in 1982 by way of regression analysis (Van Kempen en De Klerk, 1984). The results indicate that Turks, and to a somewhat lesser extent the Moroccans, are living in neighbourhoods with abundant family housing of moderate rent, while for the Surinamese the rent level is of no importance. However, the factor that explained most of all three settlement patterns is the number of vacancies that occurred in recent years. So the underrepresentation of Turks and Moroccans in the post-war housing estates may be ascribed to different causes. The rents may be too high, which is a likely explanation

Table 6: Concentration and change in Surinamese settlement by quality zone,
Amsterdam 1973–1982

Zone	Patterns			Changes	
	1973	1978	1982	73–78	78–82
1. Inner city – business areas	20	6	−60	−20	−154
2. Inner city – residential areas	−26	−51	−53	−53	−8
3. 19th century residential areas	11	19	10	18	−20
4. Central location built 1906–1930	2	36	51	63	32
5. Peripheral location built 1906–1930	−61	−73	−61	−38	15
6. Residential areas built 1930–1945	−31	−14	−1	23	21
7. Upper-class areas built 1906–1945	−31	−50	−62	−44	−33
8. Residential areas built 1945–1960	−50	−48	−27	−11	49
9. Residential areas built 1960–1970	−37	−57	−45	−48	16
10. Bijlmermeer built 1970 – how	313	310	341	88	140

for the estates built after 1965 (into which the Surinamese, who are prepared to pay far higher rents, entered on a large scale) but not for the estates built between 1945 and 1965, or not enough vacancies occurred. Patterns of invasion and succession are very important to explain the settlement pattern of immigrants in Amsterdam.

6.2. Immigrants and Dutch residential mobility

The degree of spatial segregation between different groups gives some indication about their respective positions on the housing market. Although comparisons between different cities are somewhat dangerous, the degree of segregation of immigrants in Amsterdam from its other inhabitants seems fairly low. The segregation of Turks and Moroccans is somewhat higher than that of the Surinamese, which may be a reflection of the fact that the first two groups tend to operate on a more limited segment of the housing market than the latter.

Up till 1978, the segregation of Turks and Moroccans increased. This growth seems primarily due to the rapid immigration combined with the change in the demographic composition of these groups. Lodging house areas, still very important

Table 7: Index of dissimilarity between Turks, Moroccans and Surinamese
and the remaining population, Amsterdam, 1973–1981.
(75 neighbourhoods)

Year	Turks	Moroccans	Surinamese
1973	29.3	37.2	29.5
1974	29.8	35.7	31.4
1975	30.9	36.0	32.7
1976	34.6	37.2	31.2
1977	36.0	37.9	29.2
1978	36.9	38.8	27.7
1979	36.9	39.2	27.0
1980	36.2	38.0	27.6
1981	35.9	36.5	28.8

in 1973, dwindled to insignificance, while areas with family housing, already important in 1973, were absolutely dominant by 1978. The result is an increase in segregation. After 1978 segregation tended to decrease, which may reflect the move towards the post-war neighbourhoods, but this decrease is only very slight.

The Surinamese segregation rose during the years of mass immigration, 1974 and 1975. Then, it started to decline, which may be attributed to the gradual dispersion of Surinamese households over a large part of the housing market, including the suburban developments outside Amsterdam, which is, however, not visible in these figures. The slight rise in segregation in 1980 and 1981 is entirely due to the rapid Surinamese migration to the newest parts of the Bijlmermeer area, and so is, somewhat surprisingly, part of the same process that initially led to desegregation.

However, these overall segregation figures have some important shortcomings. First, they obscure the fact that immigrants anno 1982 live as (lowly) segregated from the population at large as in 1973, but in different neighbourhoods. The movement towards increasingly newer and better housing remains hidden behind these overall measures. Secondly, by comparing the position of immigrants to that of the Dutch population at large an important point is missed. As we outlined before, Dutch families are moving out of the city, while young singles and unmarried couples are now exerting a very active demand for the small and usually cheap dwellings in the older parts of the town. Immigrant housing should be related to this development.

Residential mobility in Amsterdam follows a familiar pattern. It tends to be very low in neighbourhoods for the first thirty years after their completion. Then, the first generation of inhabitants reaches old age and their number starts to decline. Up till 1965, the replacement population coming in to fill the vacancies tended to be of a somewhat lower socio-economic position and was of course much younger, but otherwise it was no different from the settled population. However, as families started to leave the city altogether, after 1965 these newcomers increasingly adhered to a different lifestyle, either by being young and unmarried, or by being immigrants.

The young were especially attracted to the city centre and its immediate surroundings, areas that had little to offer by way of family housing and so to immigrants. As increasingly newer neighbourhoods away from the city centre came in for a second cycle of habitation, immigrants could move into these areas without severe competition, neither from the young non-family households nor from Dutch families. At the outskirts of the city (with the Bijlmermeer area as the major exception), far less entries were possible for them, both because the mobility of the settled Dutch families was much lower, and because of protective policies of the managers of the housing stock.

Table 8: Index of dissimilarity between Turks, Morrocans, Surinamese and
selected Dutch population categories, 1982 (9 districts)

	(2)	(3)	(4)	(5)	(6)
1. Dutch married couples 30–65 years	43.2	12.7	37.9	38.1	35.2
2 Dutch singles 20–30 years	–	30.8	34.4	28.3	33.9
3. All Dutch	–	–	32.5	29.5	28.3
4. Turks	–	–	–	7.0	30.1
5. Moroccans	–	–	–	–	28.2
6. Surinamese	–	–	–	–	–

These developments led to a pattern of segregation that is quite remarkable. The segregation between Dutch families and young Dutch non-family households is far higher than that between the Dutch and any immigrant group. In and around the inner city young adults, rejecting the traditional family oriented way of life, congregate, whereas elsewhere Dutch family life still holds sway. Between these two groups a niche has developed into which immigrants have entered.

7. Prospects

The general conclusion of our analysis is that the situation of immigrants in Amsterdam as far as their housing is concerned has improved considerably during the past decade. This is remarkable because this period is characterized by heavy unemployment, while the political scene has been dominated recently by the sudden rise and fall of the Centrum Partij, a party based on racist anti-immigrant propaganda.

Usually, the position of immigrants on the housing market is depicted far more gloomily. They are seen as a replacement population, getting the least desirable housing on a market dominated by the indigeneous population, and remaining in this position at the end of the queue for many years.

For the Turks and Moroccans in Amsterdam, this description still has some value. They got housing not longer wanted by Dutch families and for which the young non-family households showed little interest. But due to the particular circumstances in Amsterdam, this position at the end of the queue did not imply that the worst kind of housing was allocated to them. Especially after 1978 many Turks and Moroccans got houses well above the minimum standards. Moreover, by moving into this better housing they are rapidly filling the gap that previously existed between their position and that of the Dutch.

To describe the position of the Surinamese as at the bottom of the housing market is even more inadequate. Undeniably, this was the point from which many Surinamese started immediately after their entry into the Netherlands. But within a few years an impressive number of them had gained access to much better parts of the market, and even competition from Dutch households could not stop this movement.

In a recent overview on immigrant housing and housing policy Shadid and Kornalijnslijper (1985) come to a similar conclusion. However, in view of the public housing policy and the trends in the socio-economic position of immigrants they expect an end to the gradual improvement of their housing situation. We cannot share this pessimistic view. Recent research indicates that there is only a very weak relationship between the socio-economic position of immigrants in Dutch cities and their housing career (Vijgen and De Klerk, 1986), and while the major policy instruments that helped immigrants to get along, the municipal housing allocation system and the system of rent grants, may become somewhat less generous, they will not wither away within the next few years.

Most importantly, however, the major force that helped the immigrants to improve their situation is largely outside political control: the decline of the Dutch family opened up opportunities that were unforeseen even a decade ago. In Amsterdam this demise has progressed further than anywhere else in the Netherlands, but the same process is going on in all cities. Whatever other social consequences this development may have, to immigrants it proved to be a windfall.

Acknowledgements

The data presented in this article were collected in the course of the research project 'Woongeschiedenis geimmigreerde minderheden'. The authors wish to thank all collaborators on this project, but especially Ronald van Kempen, Jacques van de Ven and Jacqueline Vijgen.

Technical note

For administrative purposes Amsterdam is divided into 89 neighbourhoods ('buurtcombinaties') forming 11 urban districts ('stadsdelen'). 14 neighbourhoods having a population of less than 1500 were not included in the analysis, while detailed population data on two (small) districts were not available, so these have been omitted in the analysis on the level of districts as well.

The index of concentration (tables 5 and 6) was constructed by first computing the average percentage of immigrants per neighbourhood for the city as a whole (X_u) and its standard ⇔ deviation (S_u), and the average number of immigrants per neighbourhood for each quality zone (X_z). The index was computed by this formula:

$$I = \frac{X_z - X_u}{S_u} \times 100$$

Change in the percentage of immigrants in some period per neighbourhood was measured as the degree to which the percentage in some later year had grown (or declined) faster than that of the city as a whole. The expected percentage in some later year was established by means of regression, with the first year acting as a predictor; change is taken as the deviation of the observed value from the regression estimate. The index of change is constructed according to the same formula as the index of concentration.

The index of dissimilarity is somewhat more familiar (Lieberson, 1981). It can be interpreted as the percentage of one population group that would have to move to get a spatial distribution is similar to that of some reference group. It takes a highest value of 100 (complete segregation) and a lowest of 0 (no segregation). It is computed according to the following formula:

$$ID = .5 \times \Sigma \; |a_i - b_i|$$

in which a_i = members of a group A in neighbourhood i as a percentage of the total membership of group A in the city, and b_i is the same for some reference group B.

THE RESIDENTIAL LOCATION OF IMMIGRANT WORKERS IN BELGIAN CITIES:

an ethnic or a socio-economic phenomenon?

CHRISTIAN KESTELOOT (LEUVEN)

1. Introduction

Since the results of the 1970 census in Belgium were issued, geographers are able to study the distribution of foreigners according to their dwelling place in the cities. Indeed statistical sectors, or census tracts were first introduced in this census, and this enables the researcher to look at the spattial patterns on a fine scale. The results of the 1981 census concerning foreigners are currently being released, and as far as possible, we shall refer to these data in the paper. Before looking at the results of these studies, it is useful to stress some peculiar features of foreign workers immigration in Belgium. In a second part, the empirical evidence yielded by the studies on Belgian cities will be reviewed, in order to provide possible explanations in a third part. The general framework in which these explanations must be understood will also be briefly discussed. In a last part, the two main alleys of explanation, termed here the ethnic and the socio-economic explanation will be examined.

2. Foreign workers in Belgium: Some generalities

On January 1983, 891.244 foreigners lived in Belgium or 9 % of the total population. This figure results from a sharp increase of foreigners coming from other than adjacent countries during the postwar period. This growth of the foreign population is essentially due to immigration till 1974, while natural increase in the foreign population is the dominant factor since then.

When looking at the nationalities represented (table 1), three groups can be discerned. Neighbouring countries show quite normally an important presence in Belgium. But also Americans are among the ten most important nationalities. This points to the presence of important groups of top managers and civil servants of both border countries and the USA, related to the location of the EEC, the NATO and the SHAPE, as well as the European headquarters of many multinational corporations and financial institutions in Belgium.

Thirdly the Mediterranean nationalities appear to form together the dominant group of foreigners. They are workers who immigrated in Belgium between the fifties and the early seventies. Broadly speaking the Italians came first, followed by the Spaniards between the early fifties and the sixties. Moroccans and then Turks followed at the end of the sixties and the beginning of the seventies. It must be

Table 1: Foreigners per nationality in 1981

Nationalities	Total	%	Regional distribution in %		
			Flanders	Wallonia	Brussels
Italians	279.700	31,8	11	76	13
Moroccans	105.133	12,0	29	16	55
French	103.512	11,8	17	58	25
Dutch	66.233	7,5	82	11	7
Turks	63.587	7,2	49	26	25
Spaniards	58.255	6,6	19	33	48
West-Germans	26.756	3,0	41	44	15
British	23.080	2,6	45	24	31
Greeks	21.230	2,4	18	37	45
Americans	11.536	1,3	33	44	23
Algerians	10.796	1,2	17	62	21
Portuguese	10.482	1,2	21	33	46

Source: N.I.S., Volkstelling 1981.

Table 2: Working population of foreign nationality by economic sector and by sex in Belgium – Situation in 1977

Activity sector	Men		Women	
	Abs.	%	Abs.	%
Agriculture, forestry, fishing	1.846	0,9	326	0,5
Energy and water	11.226	5,5	171	0,3
Extraction of non-energy minerals	28.485	13,9	1.743	2,6
Chemical industry	4.970	2,4	1.461	2,2
Metal manufacturing and engineering	30.589	14,9	5.435	8,0
Other manufacturing industries	21.213	10,4	11.244	16,6
Building industry	30.020	14,7	801	1,2
Trade, hotel, restaurants	36.279	17,7	20.583	30,5
Transport and communication	10.016	4,9	1.147	2,7
Finance and services to industries	6.965	3,4	2.506	3,7
Other services	14.033	6,9	19.862	29,4
Not defined activities	9.193	4,5	2.327	3,4
Total	204.796	100,0	67.566	100,0

Source: MOULAERT & MARTENS, 1982.

stressed that familial immigration was favoured by the Belgian authorities, essentially for demographic reasons (see Martens, 1976; Martens & Moulaert, 1985). One must also notice that the number of Spaniards declined in the last decade with 14 %, while the total number of foreigners increased. This is partly due to the democratization of Spain in 1975, and to better economic prospects during the seventies.

The fact that each national group of foreign workers arrived in Belgium in a determined period, is also reflected in their occupational structure (table 2), and the location of these groups at the regional level. One has to know that in order to be employed, foreigners need a permit delivered by the Department of Labour and Employment. During the first year this permit is linked to a specific employer who asked for foreign employees, while during the following three years at least, it is linked to a specific activity sector. Only after four or five years are the foreigners free to choose any employment. Although there are a series of exceptions to this rule, it is the cornerstone of the foreign labour policy (including the fact it was actually not applied between 1962 and 1967) and results in the relation between period of arrival, economic activity and regional location of the foreigners (see for more details Moulaert, 1983).

Italians who were attracted here to work in the Walloon mining sector, are dominantly located in the Walloon industrial axis. Spaniards came later and are more dispersed in different industries: among them construction and services (trade, catering and personal services). They show therefore a stronger presence in Brussels. The same applies even more to the Moroccans who are dominantly located in the Brussels region. The Turks came later and found jobs in the Limburg mines and the textile industry. They show therefore a concentration in Flanders (see Grimmeau, 1984).

This spatial pattern (see more details van der Haegen, 1981) points to the position of the foreigners in production together with the spatial structure of the production activities. It is typical to find them in backward regions where traditional industries like mining, steel and metal manufacturing or textile are in difficulty, or in central areas where an important secondary labour market is flourishing for construction industries, transportation, catering and personal services.

It must be stressed that foreigners were attracted as a replacement labour force, for jobs the Belgians did not want and were not forced to accept because of the general level of skill and the full employment situation during the sixties and the early seventies. Only at the end of the sixties did the trade unions ask for an immigration stop. This resulted in a tighter application of the immigration regulations from 1967 on and a post-factum official immigration stop in 1974 (see Moulaert & Derycke, 1985).

We will come back to this position of immigrant workers in production when looking at explanations of the residential location of these minorities within cities.

3. The spatial distribution of foreign workers in Belgian cities — Empirical evidence

Research in Brussels (De Lannoy, 1975, 1977, 1978; Gonzalo, 1979; Hofman, 1984; Kesteloot, 1977, 1980; De Lannoy & Kesteloot, 1985), Antwerp (De Winter & Kesteloot, 1983, Janssens, 1985), Liege (Bolinne-Govaerts, 1974, Laloux, 1980), Ghent (Vanneste, 1980, 1981, the smaller mining towns in Limburg (Schroe, 1979; Van Krunkelsven, 1979), and Mechelen (Knops, 1977), lead to four general conclusions, which are outlined below. Whenever illustration is appropriate, the Brussels case is referred to — as far as data are available —, since the migrant phenome-

Map 1: Percentage of Turks in total population, Brussels –1981

		Statistical sectors
0 %		275
0.01 - 0.49 %		194
0.50 - 1.99 %		99
2.00 - 3.99 %		24
4.00 - 6.99 %		13
7.00 - 9.99 %		11
10.00 - 14.99 %		5
15.00 - 19.99 %		3
20.00 - 24.99 %		4
25.00 - 33.43 %		3

0   3.75 km

Cartography: J. P. Grimmeau

Map 2: Percentage of Italians in total population, Brussels – 1981

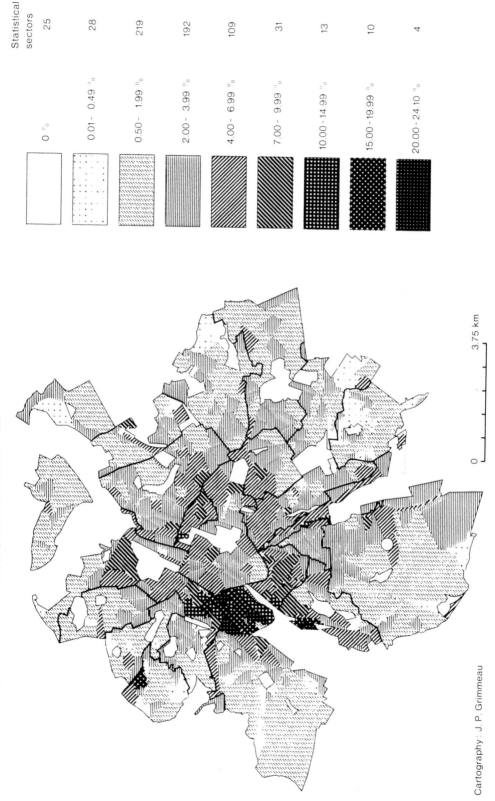

		Statistical sectors
	0 %	25
	0.01 - 0.49 %	28
	0.50 - 1.99 %	219
	2.00 - 3.99 %	192
	4.00 - 6.99 %	109
	7.00 - 9.99 %	31
	10.00 - 14.99 %	13
	15.00 - 19.99 %	10
	20.00 - 24.10 %	4

0   3.75 km

Cartography: J. P. Grimmeau

non is strongest in this city. Indeed in 1981, 23,8 % of the Brussels population was foreign (but not all immigrant workers), against 7,7 % in Antwerp, 19,4 % in Liege or 5,5 % in Ghent.

1. Immigrant workers are not located over the whole urban area, but are strongly concentrated in certain zones of the city, generally near the city center.

2. This concentration of foreigners varies according to the different national groups. Groups which recently immigrated, like the Turks and the Moroccans — which show by the way the largest cultural differences with the Belgian population in terms of language, religion and way of life —, are less dispersed than groups arrived earlier as Italians and Spaniards (see maps 1 and 2).

3. This concentration of foreigners does not entail spatial segregation. National groups stick together in certain neighbourhoods, but by no means are spatially isolated from other national groups. Even in the neighbourhoods with the highest concentration of foreigners, several national groups are present, while each national group appears as a foreign group to another (not to speak about the existence of different communities within a national group). In each of these neighbourhoods, the Belgian population forms always one of the most important national groups (in 1970 the Belgian population was the largest group in every neighbourhood). Most of these Belgians are old and poor. They appear as a residual population compared to the continuous decrease of Belgian population in these neighbourhoods since the interwar period (see for some figures about the Brussels case Jouret, 1972 and Van der Haegen et al., 1983). Table 3 illustrates this phenomenon. It gives the population per nationality for the three statistical sectors with the highest proportion of foreigners in Brussels.

However one should add that spatial segregation can be observed at another geographical scale, namely at the level of street segments or housing blocks. Vanneste (1980) has shown the complete separation of Belgians and Turks in the backyards of a single neighbourhood in Ghent. In studies of deprived neighbourhoods in Mechelen (Knops, 1977) and Anderlecht (Kesteloot, 1977) maps of nationalities show cases of segregation at the level of buildings and street segments (see map. 3).

This spatial pattern, common in all Belgian cities, of concentration without segregation at the neighbourhood level and segregation at the street segment or housing block level, is similar to what is observed in the other West-European countries, as far as forced segregation (through social housing allocation, employers' housing or "bidonvilles") is absent (see Castles & Kosacks, 1985, pp. 312–314). Although social housing in the Belgian mining towns has a similar role, since access to it is determined by an employment in the mines, no segregation at the neighbourhood level can be observed, mainly because of the multinational composition of the employees (Schroe, 1979; Van Krunkelsven, 1979).

4. It has also been well documented that the foreign workers live in very bad housing conditions and in neighbourhoods poorly provided with social amenities. At the neighbourhood scale, one can only point to similarities between the location of foreigners and the distribution of housing characteristics (see e.g. De Lannoy,

Map 3: Distribution of nationalities in the Rosee neighbourhood (Anderlecht, Brussels) – 1974

Nationalities

Italian
Spanish
Greek
Turkish
Moroccan
Belgian and Others

• depreciated dwelling
— accessibility line

0 25 50 75 100 m

Source: Kesteloot, 1977, p. 125

1978 or Kesteloot, 1980b), but the abundance of the literature on this topic can be an illustration in itself (see a.o. Martens & Wolf, 1974; Campanelli & Delcourt, 1975; De Lannoy, 1975; Delcourt, 1975; Panciera & Plevoets-Quivy, 1976; Kieffer, 1978 et 1982; Marques-Balsa & Martins-Boudru, 1978; Kesteloot, 1980). The Belgian National Institute for Housing has also issued two reports on this problem in 1981 and 1984. Janssens has published some comparative figures, drawn from the 1981 census, for the Antwerp agglomeration (1985) — see table 4.

4. Competing explanations of immigrant settlement

One finds in the Belgian literature, often implicity, two types of explanations for these spatial patterns. Each of them is linked to a different theoretical framework on the functioning of society. The first one is individual and behavioural, the second collective and structuralist.

These two views stem from a concern for social problems in geography which appeared in the second half of the seventies in Belgium. The first one was linked to an interest in perception geography which lead to a broader acceptance of behavioural and humanistic philosophies. The second view is related to the discovery of Marxian works by an handful of geographers (see Kesteloot, 1985b), and later to the influence of Weberian sociology and geography flourishing in the Anglo-Saxon world. Thus both types of explanation have common grounds with competing approaches in the wider social sciences. They therefore also show some internal variations (Marxian versus Weberian, humanistic versus behavioural frameworks). However these theoretical issues are only weakly addressed in the Belgian literature under study (see Jackson & Smith, 1981; Peach, 1981, Brown, 1981 for a discussion of the problem in the Anglo-Saxon literature).

4.1. The explanation on the individual level or the ethnic explanation

This explanation stems from the idea that the spatial distribution of social groups results from individual decisions and behaviour, possibly influenced by group belonging. The spatial concentration of the immigrant workers and their possible segregation is thus a result of location processes on the individual and group level.

On the individual level decisions and behaviour are guided by people's tendency to safeguard ones own identy regarding to different people. This is manifest through suspicion against different individuals, generalisation of this suspicion to entire social groups and through the assertion of own peculiarities. These attitudes lead to a residential location choice that favours proximity to similar people and separation from different people, in this case the host society or other nationalities.

The same mecanisms can be reinforced at the level of the social group. Indeed concentration and possible segregation are conditions for an efficient social control in the group in order to maintain its cohesion and identity. Groups maintain their existence with the transmission of a specific set of values, norms and behaviour among their members. Social control makes sure that these values and norms are adopted and respected by the group members. In order to be efficient, it requires spatial proximity of the members, while the separation of other groups makes the adoption of new characteristics, which could bring the existence of the groups into question, more difficult.

These processes at the individual and group level can explain the concentration of immigrant workers in the cities. They apply as well to the Belgians and thus show why natives avoid neighbourhoods with strong foreign concentration. They also explain why different national groups show varying concentration levels according to the length of their stay in Belgium and the importance of their cultural differences with the Belgians (language, religion, food and clothing habits, raising of children . . .), because these factors influence the degree of integration or assimilation of these groups with the Belgian society.

The interaction between the different groups and individuals must also be taken into account within this framework. Each group will not only avoid the neighbourhoods with a strong concentration of other national groups. As far as they have the means to do so, they will also discriminate against the other groups in order to keep them out from their neighbourhood (this is evidently the case on the housing market where landlords are reluctant to let to foreigners).

On the other hand, self-identity of foreign groups can be strengthened by the fact they feel discriminated in the host society, thus reinforcing group behaviour leading to spatial concentration. One could interpret the well developed retail, cultural and religious networks of each national group in Brussels, Ghent and Antwerp as a manifestation of this process of protective self-assertion (on these networks, see Vanneste, 1980; Hofman, 1984 and Janssens, 1985).

This type of explanation stresses the ethnic differences between national groups, including the Belgians. To simplify, one can call this an ethnic explanation of the distribution of foreigners in urban space. It implies that choices and decisions of individuals, possibly influenced by group attitudes, are fundamental in the explanation of social facts.

This explanation is often associated with choice (versus constraint) in ethnic residential location (see debates in Peach, Robinson & Smith eds., 1981 and Jackson & Smith eds., 1981). However one should note that in this view constraints appear when social control is considered (on the point of view of the individual, social control can hardly be seen as a choice), and when interaction between different social groups is taken into account. The translation of different explanations in terms of a 'choice versus constraints' debate is thus an oversimplification of the problem.

4.2. The explanation on societal level or the socio-economic explanation

This type of explanation stresses the idea that the position of individuals in society — and more precisely their position within the economic system —, is the decisive factor for their residential location. This reasoning starts from the fact that immigrant workers are in a marginal position on the labour market. They are employed in declining industrial activities, or they are trapped in the secondary labour market for urban service activities (see Castles & Kosack, 1985; Moulaert & Martens, 1982 on the Belgian situation and Basteniers, 1979 on the Brussels case).

A consequence of this economic position is a low and fluctuating income, and therefore a marginal position on the housing market. The great majority of immigrant workers have incomes that are too low and uncertain to have access to home-ownership. This is even more evident when their family structure is taken into account: they need large and therefore expensive dwellings, while a large part of their incomes must be spent on sustaining their children. Moreover this fact is reinforced by their propensity to save money. This attitude is linked to the myth of a return to their homeland, which was first sustained by the principle of rotation of foreign workforce, now by the threat of a forced return to their homeland because of the economic crisis.

Access to social housing is very limited, except for miners where it is linked to the occupation. As a matter of fact, immigrants have no voting rights and do not belong to the electoral clients of the managers of the social housing associations who are in general local politicians or linked to local political party sections. While they qualify for social housing in terms of income and while there are priority rules for access (taking income, household composition, previous housing conditions into account), a whole set of formal and informal means are used to keep foreigners out of social housing estates. But more fundamentally the insufficient social housing supply is at stake (in Brussels e.g. social housing forms 7 % of the housing stock; foreigners are 25 % of the population and something like 2 or 3 % of social housing is occupied by foreigners). This problem is reinforced by the fact that large social dwellings, needed by immigrant families, are even scarcer.

It follows that the main group of foreign workers faces the supply of housing on the private rental market with a specific demand, cheap housing, adapted to their family structure. Since the logic of landlords is to let in order to obtain a revenue from their assets, they are not keen to adapt the rents to the financial possibilities of the immigrants. Moreover they often refuse to let their dwellings to large families with children, and especially foreign families, because they have the reputation of causing higher maintenance costs and of bothering the other tenants. Lastly one must consider that large dwellings are in short supply in the cities and that many landowners reject foreign tenants simply for xenophobic reasons (one must notice that the Belgian act against racism, issued in 1981, does only apply to written documents or racist attitudes in presence of witnesses. The refusal of housing or a job is not prohibited in itself. As a result xenophobism in housing and labour matters is hardly restrained by the law).

There is no quantitative shortage of housing in Belgium, but a serious qualitative shortage. Moreover land ownership is very atomized and many landlords are reluctant to put some energy and money in the rehabilitation of their houses. They prefer to leave them inhabitated and wait for a good opportunity to sell them (see on the Brussels situation, Noel, 1984).

It is easy to see that with their specific demand and their weak financial means, immigrant workers face a systematically short supply on the urban housing markets. It forces them to pay more for a similar dwelling than Belgians, and to live in relatively — and often absolute —, bad housing conditions. Overpopulation in dwellings is also a possible response to this situation. These facts are in turn the basis for their reputation of causing blight and housing dereliction.

It appears from this view that immigrant workers are submitted to a double pressure: one coming from the employers on the labour market and one coming from the landlords on the housing market. These pressures force them to seek accommodation in a specific sector of the housing market, namely the private rental market, with relatively cheap but bad housing conditions. One could term this housing market sector 'residual' because it is the only one which remains accessible to social groups which are rejected from the other sectors. A second meaning of this term points to the low rents which are only possible because they concern old dwellings which are already paid off. In other words, rents only correspond to maintenance costs (as far as the landlord has any costs), future demolition costs and interest. These dwellings are, in that sense, residuals of earlier investments in housing. The latter helps to understand why this housing market sector is located in a specific zone of urban residential space, namely the central city which corresponds to the 19th century part of the urban region.

One can summarize this reasoning in a schema (see schema 1).

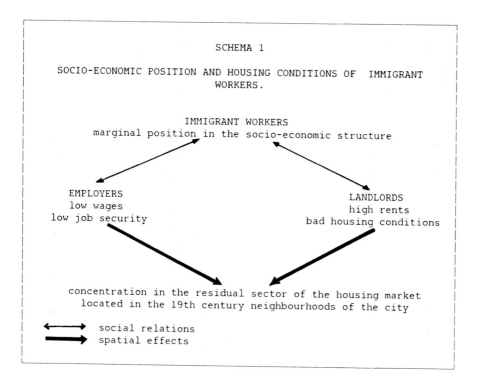

SCHEMA 1

SOCIO-ECONOMIC POSITION AND HOUSING CONDITIONS OF IMMIGRANT
WORKERS.

IMMIGRANT WORKERS
marginal position in the socio-economic structure

EMPLOYERS
low wages
low job security

LANDLORDS
high rents
bad housing conditions

concentration in the residual sector of the housing market
located in the 19th century neighbourhoods of the city

social relations
spatial effects

The same logic can be applied to the rich foreigners, working in multinational corporations, the EEC and the NATO, to explain their concentration in some parts of the urban periphery. They are linked to a specific housing market sector because of their position on the labour market, and in turn this sector is located in specific areas of the urban regions (see for Brussels Grimmeau & David-Valcke, 1978).

De Lannoy (1975) has shown with 1970 data that the Americans in Brussels had a segregation index nearly as high as the Turks (61.3 % against 68.3 %), while Moroccans, Spaniards and Italians have lower indices (respectively 58.1, 50.6 and 34.9 %).

This type of explanation does not stress so much the needs, aspirations or choices of the individuals, but mainly the constraints and limits inherent to the organization of society, more precisely the labour and the housing market. The position of the individuals in these structures is determining, and in this sense one can speak of a socio-economic explanation.

This kind of explanation is sometimes summarized as the 'constraints' point of view (see Peach, 1981 on this). We have already pointed to the fact that choice and constraint concepts are too simple to deal with the problem. Moreover choices or constraints at the scale of the individuals should not be compared with constraints or choices at the level of social groups or society as a whole. This points to the fact that the balance between choice and constraint is unimportant, but that the nature of the social relations in which the power of choice and/or constraint is embedded, is critical.

In this sense one must emphasize that the societal explanation relates to the broader framework of social reproduction theory. This means that the backward position of the immigrant workers is maintained in the long term, and adapted to evolutions in the total structure of society and that their residential location and the life conditions linked to it are part of this reproduction process. Three elements can be put forward as links between residential location and the reproduction of the societal position of foreign workers.

1. Their poor housing conditions make their low wages possible since housing costs are calculated in the wages. One could even say that the presence of foreigners holds down the wage costs for all workers, since rents are part of the official cost of living index, the evolution of which is linked to wage increases. (However the automatic wage increases with inflation had been temporarily abolished and then reintroduced in a weaker form during the eighties).

   Anyway, as long as the housing conditions of foreign workers are socially accepted, there is no pressure for higher wages according to this component of the cost of life. In turn these low wages are the cause of bad housing conditions. Thus labour and life conditions, production and reproduction are linked.

2. Foreign workers are located in neighbourhoods with very poor social infrastructure. Education especially is of low quality. In fact if spatial segregation is nonexistent, functional segregation appears to be very strong in education. This leads to a degeneration of the schools in these neighbourhoods and therefore a condamnation of the children of foreign workers to subordinate positions in their later life.

More generally all social amenities in these neighbourhoods are more or less submitted to the same process. The location of foreigners in these neighbourhoods limits their access to other or better amenities. Thus their location determines what is sometimes called their social consumption (the use of collective goods and services like education, health care, sporting and cultural equipments . . .), which because of its spatial differentiation is a strong means of social reproduction in the longer term.

3. The relative isolation of the foreign communities from other social groups has also a reproduction effect on the ideological level. In fact they are separated from groups with which they could potentially integrate because of similar interests on the labour and the housing market. In other words there is a kind of ideological or political segregation. Clearly this prevents seriously the emancipation of the foreign communities and reproduces their ideological and political position in the Belgian society. Solidarity can appear on a common workplace, but it is weakened by separate living places and conditions.

5. Confronting the ethnic and the socio-economic explanations

A close look at the existing studies on foreign minorities in Belgium yields some elements to challenge both types of explanation.

It is also often supposed that the analysis of the evolution of settlement patterns will yield some answer to the assessment of each approach. Stronger concentration would show ethnic forces working against integration. Dispersion would show the spatial expression of such an integration while its extent would be determined by the socio-economic forces. This kind of assumption points also to the idea that the balance between ethnic and socio-economic forces changes over time. The first results of the comparison between the 1970 and 1981 census are currently under analysis. It appears, as far as known that the evolution pattern is a rise of the proportion of foreigners in the neighbourhoods concerned and a simultaneous expansion of this concentration area (see Janssens, 1985 and compare map 4 with map 1). In order to understand this phenomenon, one has to remember that increase in foreign population between 1970 and 1981 are still important and essentially due to natural growth. Thus within each urban region, the effects of natural growth and of national and international immigration should be eliminated in order to assess the importance of internal migration. But even then concentration or dispersal do not tell much about ethnic versus socio-economic forces, as long as the motives or reasons for internal migration are not understood.

Other facts show the socio-economic, structural explanation to be preponderant and the ethnic explanation to be part of it.

1. Studies of the total social structure of urban space in Belgian cities show that the location of foreigners fits extremely well in the socio-economic structure of that space, rather than being an independent component of it. Foreign workers of the mediterranean countries live in the poorest neighbourhoods of the cities; the rich foreigners live in the richest parts of the cities. This has been established for

Map 4: Percentage of Turks in total population, Brussels–1970

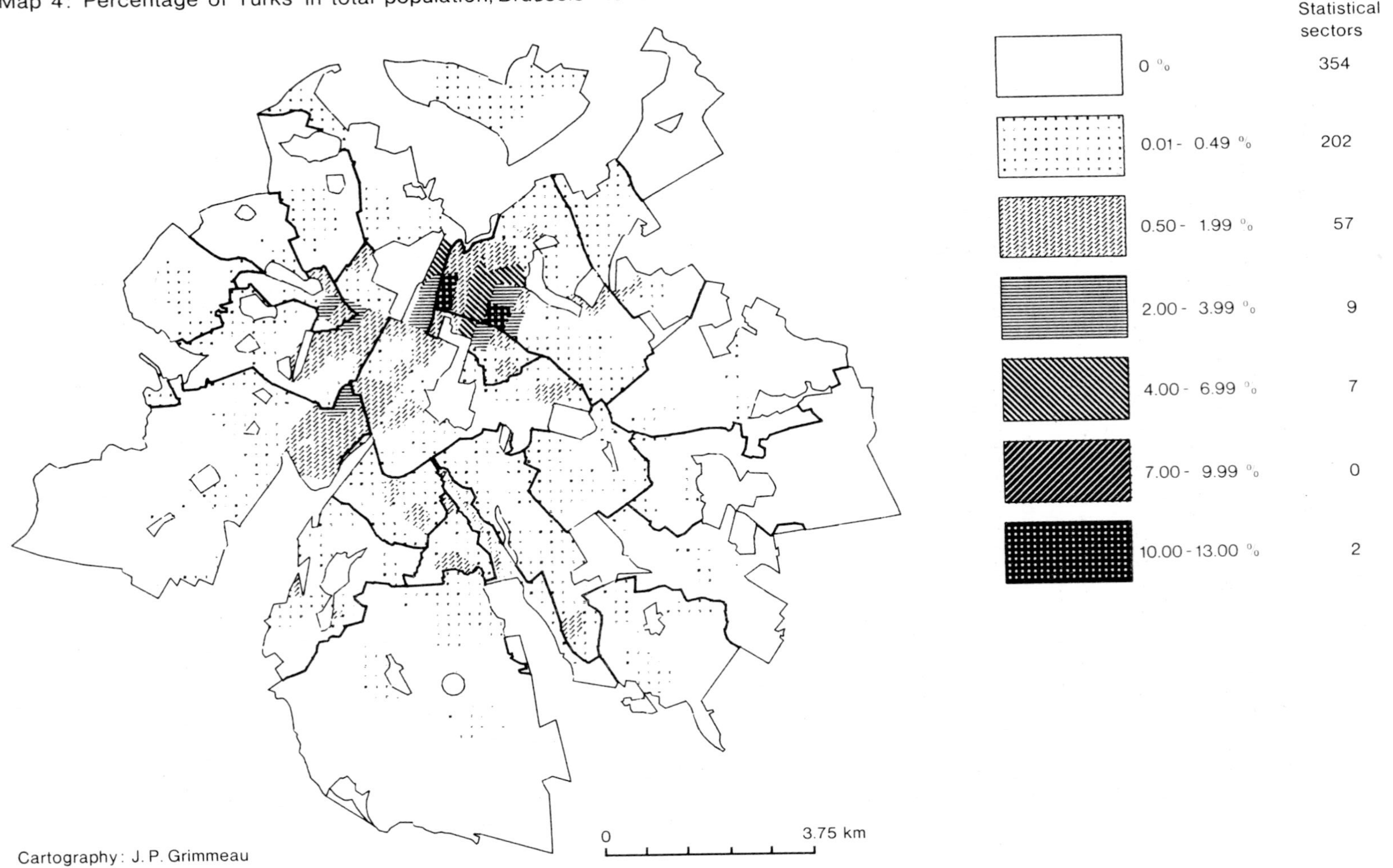

		Statistical sectors
	0 %	354
	0.01 - 0.49 %	202
	0.50 - 1.99 %	57
	2.00 - 3.99 %	9
	4.00 - 6.99 %	7
	7.00 - 9.99 %	0
	10.00 - 13.00 %	2

0   3.75 km

Cartography: J. P. Grimmeau

Brussels (De Lannoy, 1977, Kesteloot, 1980a), Ghent (Vanneste, 1982) and Antwerp (De Winter & Kesteloot, 1983).
2. Each national group is itself quite strongly differentiated. This differentiation is also translated in space, according to the socio-economic dimension. Gonzalo (1979) has shown that rich Spaniards in Saint-Gilles (Brussels) live in the rich part of the municipality, while poorer Spaniards live in the poorest part. Socio-economic position rather than ethnic belonging determines also the perception of the neighbourhoods in this case. In the same study, Gonzalo analysed mental maps of Spanish schoolchildren, and found separate neighbourhoods according to socio-economic position.

In a study on Ghent, Vanneste (1980) found no difference between the mental maps of Turkish and Belgian childs who shared the same neighbourhood. Thus ethnicity is not a differentiating factor in this respect, while the similar socio-economic position of Turks and Belgians could explain their identical perception of the neighbourhood.

Table 3: Population per nationality in some Brussels neighbourhoods – Situation in 1981 (in percentage)

NEIGHBOURHOODS (stat. sectors)	NATIONALITIES						
	BELG	ITAL	SPAN	MORO	GREE	TURK	OTHER
Rosée-Est Anderlecht B10	23,5	21,0	7,5	32,8	4,1	7,5	3,6
Rue de l'Olivier Schaerbeek A04	26,6	3,2	4,8	20,4	2,0	33,4	9,5
Saint-François Saint-Josse A10	27,8	6,3	1,6	32,8	0,5	26,5	4,5

Source: N.I.S. Volkstelling 1981.

Table 4: Housing conditions of Belgians, Maroccans and Turks in the Antwerp agglomeration – Situation in 1981

	BELG	MOROC	TURKS
% owner occupied dwellings	45	14	13
% dwellings built before 1919	17	39	48
% dwellings built after 1945	55	14	13
% dwellings with central heating	59	14	13
% dwellings with bathroom or shower	84	58	55
% dwellings with telephone	69	10	13
% dwellings with thermal insulation	27	5	4
Mean number of rooms per person	1.91	0.93	0.96
Mean area per person (sq. meters)	31.2	13.9	14.1

Source: JANSSENS, 1985

A last piece of evidence concerning the preponderance of the socio-economic rather than ethnic dimension in the areas with concentration of foreigners is given by Leman: in Anderlecht (Brussels) Sicilians who improve their socio-economic position move out from their neighbourhood (see Roosens, 1979; Leman, 1980).

3. Last but probably most important, as illustrated in table 3, the neighbourhoods with a strong concentration of foreign population are pluri-ethnical. There is no area of the size of a census tract in the Belgian cities where one nationality is in the majority. Should the ethnic processes operate at this spatial level, one would find mono-ethnic neighbourhoods.

Of course this is not to say that the ethnic explanation has no object. Individual behaviour and group phenomena on ethnic grounds do exist. However, as far as residential location is concerned, they apply as we have shown, on an intra-neighbourhood scale in the Belgian cities. Ethnicity is also an important, but subordinated component in the processes of social reproduction. In this case, Belgians act as an ethnic group with the effects of reinforcing the processes described by the socio-economic explanation. The xenophobic attitude of landowners and social housing companies, the lack of solidarity from Belgians experiencing the same life and labour conditions and their avoidance of schools with a large foreign population are such behaviours.

6. CONCLUSIONS

The confrontation between those two explanations is not only a scientific matter. To emphasize one of them has political consequences. Should the ethnic explanation be self-sufficient, the spatial concentration of foreigners and the perceived or real problems this involves, would be inevitable phenomena, since nobody can escape the need to protect his own identity and to maintain social control within the group he belongs to. This explanation does not put social structures into question, because it sticks to the individual and group level. It follows that the only way to modify the explained reality would be to change the behaviour of the individuals and groups involved — which can very often only be obtained through coercive measures. (The most classical repressive ones are forced return of the foreigners to their homeland or forced ethnic mix in housing allocation — see e.g. Flett, 1979 for England, Kok, 1982 for the Netherlands, Espaces et Societes, 1984 for France).

The socio-economic explanation, on the contrary, points directly to a set of societal problems: the residential location of foreign minorities is a result of their marginal position on the labour market and the absence of the right to decent housing. These problems imply that significant changes would appear only if societal relations are altered. More precisely the relations between foreign workers (and Belgians living and working in the same conditions) on the one hand, the employers, the landowners and the State (which intervenes in these matters) on the other hand, should change in a sense giving more power to the former. This change in power balance should be a prerequisite to any form of a viable pluri-ethnic society.

Different actions could be possible in this line, like the political organisation of foreign communities (the second and third generation members can be expected to have greater awareness of the problems and some of them will accede to better education, putting them in a potential leader position for their community); voting rights for foreigners (which are denied at the present time in Belgium), better education facilities in the concerned neighbourhoods or a social housing and urban renewal policy geared to the needs of their inhabitants. They should be evaluated in terms of changing power relations between the ethnic minorities as belonging to socio-economic groups, and the opposite actors on housing and labour market.

Both tendencies exist in the Belgian society. Right wing and centrist parties defend coercive measures against foreigners not willing to integrate. On the other hand a minority of organisations fight for voting rights or better housing conditions for the foreigners (among them self-managed tenants cooperatives, renting houses both on the private and public rental market and subletting them to their members). Up to now, research could confront the advocates of the first tendency with the weakness of the justifications provided by reality. The second tendency could gain from the research findings and even more from further research on social action and change in this field. More fundamentally, this illustrates that there is nothing such as a neutral position in this matter when coming down to explanations. Although many geographers are aware of this today, there is still much to do in order to confront different explanations on scientific grounds, rather than on a devotion for neutrality.

Acknowledgements

This paper his based on an overview of the literature produced by Belgian geography on the topic (see Kesteloot, 1985a). I would like to thank John O'Loughlin for his comments and questions on a first draft of the paper and Jean-Pierre Grimmeau for his help in producing some maps.

GUESTWORKERS – LIFE IN TWO SOCIETIES[1]

ELISABETH LICHTENBERGER (WITH HEINZ FASSMANN[2] WIEN)

1. On the Theory: Guestworkers – Life in Two Societies

Numerous investigations, written from the point of view of receiving countries, focus on the questions of immigrant segregation, integration or assimilation. In these works, guestworkers are regarded as immigrants. Guestworkers are, however, not immigrants, but temporary itinerants, because of the job market policies of the receiving countries. Foreign workers are issued temporally limited labour and residence permits. Although there are considerable differences between various European receiving countries with respect to visa and residence permits, this does not alter the fact that guestworkers embody a life-style which is marked by insecurity in connection with the most important life-decisions regarding family, housekeeping, location of accommodation and job possibilities.

This dual and insecure life-style does not mesh with Marginality Theory in sociological research, according to which guestworkers in Western European industrial countries have developed a social system marginal to the indigenous population. The usual criteria of marginality are measured, such as below-average education, residual position on the job market, and discrimination in the accommodation market. In this light, guestworkers are judged by the status criteria of education and job training as attributes imported from their countries of origin, thus justifying their residual position compared to the indigenous population.

Guestworkers live in and between two societies. The partial view of the theory of the formation of a substratum must therefore be replaced by a bilateral stratification theory, with being a member of a substratum in the receiving country is, somehow, compensated by belonging to a new top class in their home provinces. Guestworkers are therefore assigned two roles whereby especially the second social role, that in their place of origin, is often more important than the in many cases marginalised 'underdog' position in the receiving society. The knowledge, abilities, experience and savings acquired through working abroad enable the guestworker to raise himself in prosperity and status above the population of his place of origin who did not go abroad. It is understandable that this possibility of a social advancement in their home country offers an important, often underestimated, compensation for the various deprivations and voluntary constraints in Northern, Western

---

1 The paper is based on the book: E. Lichtenberger (1984): Gastarbeiter – Leben in zwei Gesellschaften. (Unter Mitarbeit von H. Fassmann, EDV-Technologie.) Verlag Böhlau, Wien, Köln, Graz.

2 H. Fassmann was responsible for data processing.

and Central Europe. One can assume that this second social role constitutes a considerable part of the personal identity of the guestworker. It can further be assumed that, only after the discarding of this possibility of identification through breaking away from their country of origin, a cultural and identity crisis is induced, and it is especially pronounced in guestworkers' children.

A change from such origin-bound social roles presupposes the existence of two households, or at least two habitats, between which functional interweaving exists and toward which different forms of investment are made. Even if the aforementioned condition does not apply, there is at least a splitting of life into two territories, into two spheres of perception, information and action, which are interconnected through the rhythmic phenomena of the return journeys. In a wider social perspective, in which the separation of residential locations of urban societies depends upon the new possibilities of individual transport, certain analogies between migrant workers and second-home owners in large cities become apparent. In both cases, complementary forms of accommodation exist: rented and owner-occupied.

The concept of a bilateral stratification theory corresponds with the classification of bilateral household types. At the same time, it proved necessary to relate two spatial systems, namely, the urban system of Vienna and the settlement system of the places of origin of the migrant workers in Yugoslavia, in order to understand the consequences of life in two societies in the spatial context.

2. Organisation and Methodology of the Bilateral Research Projects in Vienna in 1974 and 1981

The concept, execution and documentation of the two bilateral research projects on Yugoslav guestworkers in Vienna in 1974 and 1981 has a number of outstanding attributes, such as repeated surveys, a bilateral concept and co-operation, the unusually wide thematic spread, and the fortunate choice of time: 1974 at the end of the main immigration phase and 1981 after 7 years' recession, concurrent with the national census, at a time before Austria was affected by serious economic slumps and, therefore, began to take measures to reduce the guestworker quota.

The isolation of clearly defined elements is, for natural scientists, an obvious prerequisite for an analysis. This is difficult to achieve with social scientific research. It succeeded with the study of Yugoslav guestworkers in Vienna insofar, as in both 1974 and 1981, they constituted the absolute majority of all guestworkers. The organisation of both inquiries was in the form of a short-term (14 days) major inquiry within the teaching organisation at the Geographical Institute of Vienna University in co-operation with the Institute of Migration Research in Zagreb (under the then Director Prof. Dr. Ivo Baučić) with 100 co-workers in total. The information was gathered in the homes of the guestworkers. Communication was in the form of a language triangle whereby the Austrian and Croat students spoke English to each other and in their respective mother tongues with the guestworkers. The travel expenses of the Yugoslav colleagues and co-workers were met in 1974 by UNESCO and in 1981 by the VW-Foundation and the Foundation for the Advancement of Scientific Research in Austria. The rapid processing of the inquiry results in 1981 was only possible due to the institutionalising of the project within the Commission for Regional Research of the Austrian Academy of Sciences.

3. The Derivation of Bilateral Household Types

Bilateral household types form the central classification instrument of the bilateral strata theory. They are an indicator of the process of change and at the same time a regulator for all socially relevant dimensions such as work and living conditions in Vienna, functional relationships to the origin, imitation of the consumer habits of Vienna society, willingness for cultural assimilation, etc. The derivation of bilateral household types had to meet two methodological requirements:

1. It was necessary to overcome the problem of multilevel analysis (see Fig. 1).
2. The simplest possible classification system was established whose results allow precise comparison and possess the greatest selectivity.

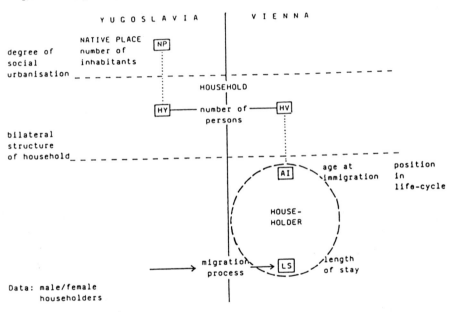

Fig. 1: Bilateral types of household and multi-level analysis (results of a cluster analysis)

According to the research topic in the 1981 inquiry, 'Life in Two Societies', a symmetrical multilevel-structured questionnaire was chosen as the organisational instrument. The central information level focussed on the bilateral household structures and the respective residential locations in Yugoslavia and Vienna. Data on the dwelling premises in Vienna and the native places in Yugoslavia (every 7th household) was collected on a higher level of aggregation. On the lower level of persons in the Vienna households, about one-third of the female guestworkers questioned were asked further questions on cultural assimilation and concerning schoolchildren. For further details on the methodological problems of multi-level analysis, see H. Faßmann, 1984.

As a statistical instrument a non-hierarchical cluster analysis was used, into which four theoretical constructs with five operational definitions were entered: bilateral household structure (number of persons in the household in Vienna and in Yugoslavia), life cycle concept (age of the head of household), phases of the migration process (year of immigration of the head of household), degree of social urbanisation of the place of origin (number of inhabitants).

After several test-runs, six types of guestworker households were identified and labelled according to specific attributes of the heads of households: 1. city dweller, 2. older late migrant, 3. older guestworkers from villages, 4. older guestworkers from mixed settlements, 5. young guestworkers with small households in Vienna, and 6. young guestworkers with families in Vienna (see Fig. 2).

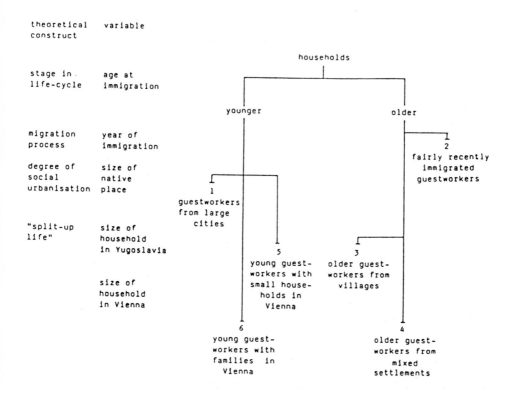

Fig. 2: Types of households – the results of a cluster analysis

By means of a cluster analysis and a factor analysis accompanying it, some key results were isolated: The main element of household classification is the age at immigration and thus in which phase of life the decision to move was made. In the factor analysis, the age factor accounted for 45 percent of the explained variation and, thus, for even more than the household size variables which were split into two factors, together accounting for 43 percent. (All statements refer to the male heads of households.) In the systematic layout of the dendrogram (Fig. 2), the variables immigration and household sizes in Vienna and Yugoslavia overlap regarding the dichotomisation of the contrasting pairs older-younger and the sizes of the constituent parts of the household in Vienna or in Yugoslavia.

Quite surprising, however, is the minimal effect of the degree of social urbanisation and, likewise, that of the stage in the migration process. The dichotomy of town versus country is of little use in a description of the native places of the Yugoslav guestworkers in Vienna. Here, it is changed to a dichotomy between guestworkers from cities and those from other communities and, therefore, the determinant is a step higher up the scale as far as settlement size is concerned. The reasons for this can be sought in the settlement structure in Yugoslavia, where the intermediate level of central places, i.e., for example, the many small towns in Austria and West Germany, is only weakly developed.

The grouping of the immigration process into pre-, high- and late-phases is reduced to two phases in the typology: the growth phase and the recession phase, whereby a considerable structural change in the guestworker society from a predominantly male society to a normal population only takes place during the late-phase.

4. Household Types and Age Structure of the Population and the Employed in Yugoslavia and Austria

The concept of the bilateral household types is based upon the assumption that the migration process is controlled decisively by familial conditions. As reasons for fetching or not fetching individual members of the family to Vienna, one continually heard stereotyped formulae such as 'because my father died', 'because my mother fell ill', 'because my husband (my brother) moved to Vienna'. It was determined from many informal conversations that the analysis of the bipartite system of households and families of guestworkers offer a key explanation to the behaviour of guestworkers in all the socially relevant dimensions, in Vienna and in Yugoslavia. Basically, bilateral household types form a complex demographic typology, which is also capable of specifically illustrating the generational bonds, the characteristics of Vienna guestworker households and the members of the family remaining behind in Yugoslavia. Thus, the individual household types possess very disparate bilateral age structures.

At a more specific level two household types, the older guestworkers from villages and the young guestworkers with families in Vienna, are graphically documented. For the villagers, from the point of view of ideal types, this group constitutes the link between the traditional seasonal migrants and the modern guest-workers. Their family life is certainly burdened by the long absence of the men, though it is a problem which is traditional in the affected areas, and, through adaptation, it is not felt to be too great a hardship. The possibility of frequent journeys home, usually by means of public transport, also shortens the period of separation, which formerly had lasted not just months but years. In spite of the long period of stay of ten years on average, the members of this group left their families in Yugoslavia. Only a few have fetched their wives to Vienna. Thus the villagers create a markedly male society in Vienna. The high quota of employed in Vienna of 65.2 percent supports the population in Yugoslavia, which has an employed quota of only 22.9 percent. The villagers usually come from small rural communities, predominantly from agriculture, and their children also remain mostly in agriculture. Therefore, one can consider work abroad in this group as a kind of secondary or additional income to the agricultural industry at home. The next generation, the 'children' mentioned in the household questionnaires as living in Yugoslavia, are mostly grown up and married, while the grandchildren are already growing up in the farmhouses which have been renovated and extended with the savings of the grandfathers in Vienna (see Fig. 3).

At the other end of the scale are the young guestworkers with families in Vienna (see Fig. 4). They come from larger rural communities, often from the suburbs surrounding the larger towns. Even before migration to Vienna, a breakup of the three-generations household had begun. As can be seen from the diagram, less than half of the households had left grandparents or other relatives behind in the place of origin. The age structure of this group largely approximates that of an average population. Although there is a moderate male surplus in Vienna and a slight female excess in Yugoslavia, the employed quota in Vienna almost matches the average of the population of Vienna. 40 percent of the guestworkers in this group living in Vienna are already second-generation guestworkers.

5. Living in Vienna and Yugoslavia

Earlier in this paper, the division of residences was isolated as an important process in guestworker migration, the comparison with second-home owners drawn up and a social advancement-hypothesis formulated. With the slogan 'they live to build', the new building activity in the Yugoslav guestworkers' places of origin can be identified as the most important result of the guestworker migration. This is a 'peripheral phenomenon' of rural areas, and a very definite negative correlation with the size of settlement can be seen. If one takes the number of completed one-family dwellings as a yardstick, the percentage sinks from 62.5 percent in communities of less than 1,000 inhabitants to 45.5 percent in communities of between 1,000 and 5,000 inhabitants and in larger communities reaches barely 20 percent. This peripheral effect is partly correlated to the bilateral household structure (see the discussion above). No less then 33.3 percent of the households with no members left in Yugoslavia are building houses. We can, however, ascertain that even

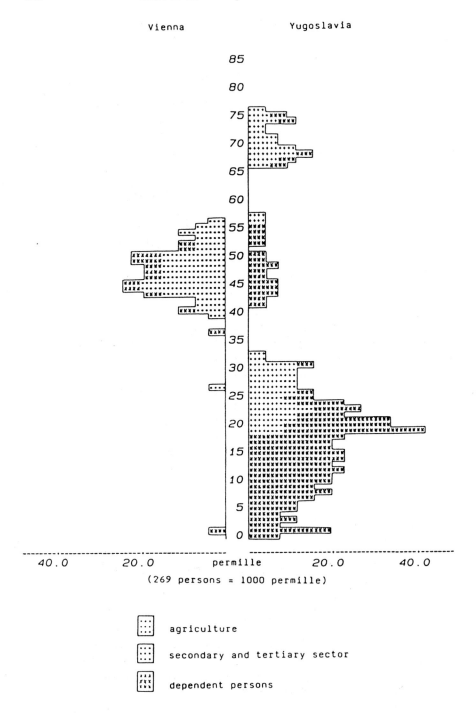

Fig. 3: The bilateral age structure of the older guestworkers from villages in 1981

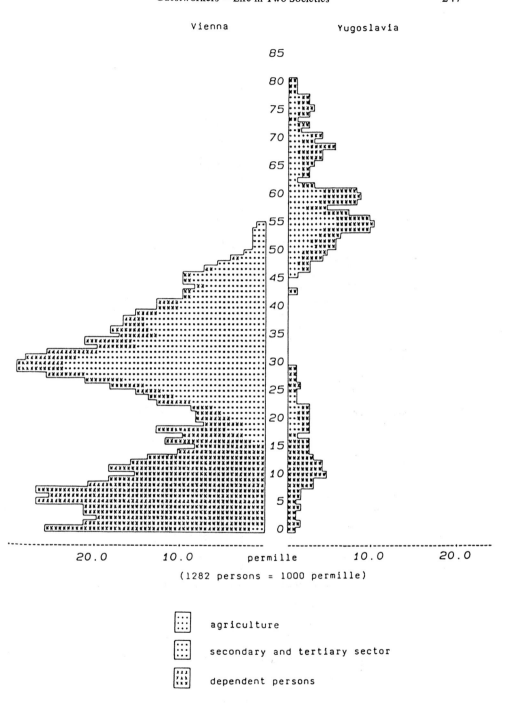

Fig. 4: The bilateral age structure of the young guestworkers with families
in Vienna in 1981

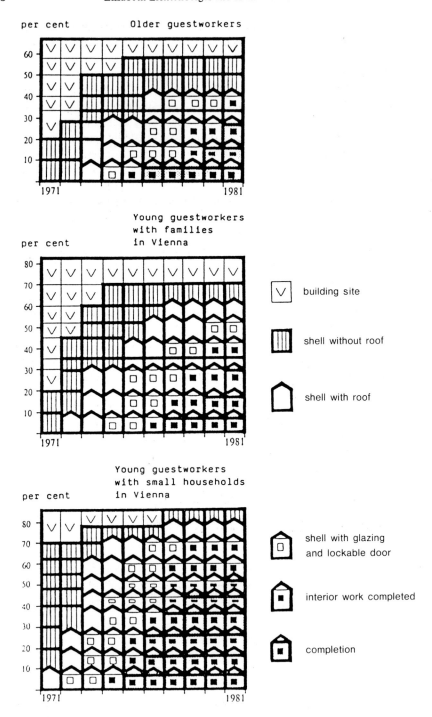

Fig. 5: Building activity and types of households

with large households in Yugoslavia, one third of the guestworkers did not decide to begin construction of a new dwelling or had not finished construction yet.

The building activity is an extremely long-term procedure, which extends over many years. Figure 5 attempts to portray the living in makeshift accommodation, the frequent travelling to and from, the stage-by-stage building development, from which it can be seen how extensive the quota of carcase structures with or without roof, half-finished and fully completed dwellings was in the past decades. In the 1981 inquiry for the older guestworkers, one-half of the dwellings were still in the early building stage, of which two-thirds were empty structures without roof. A similar situation, only on a broader basis, existed with young guestworkers with families in Vienna. The slowing-down of building development during the recession because of the fall-back of investment and reduction of transfer payments is visible in the diagram, as is the effect of the reunification of family members with young guestworkers.

Let us now relate these developments in the Yugoslav origin with the Vienna residential situation. Guestworkers who have not built houses in Yugoslavia are not different in their living standards in Vienna from the house builders. While guestworkers in Vienna are quite generally living in small dwellings, the number of rooms in the newly-built homes in Yugoslavia covers an unusually wide range, reaching from three to ten and more rooms. A great range of variation in residences is evident in Yugoslavia because the building stock is composed of older houses, older self-built structures, half-finished and finished new buildings. Similarly there is variation in the quality of the modern conveniences, which, in almost half the cases, are of a temporary nature, as are the type and range of the fixtures, fittings and furnishings. Figure 6 demonstrates that the quality of the furniture in Vienna bears no relation to that in Yugoslavia. Around half of the guestworkers who had bought new bed-

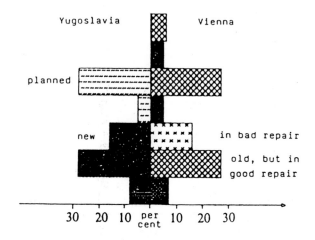

Fig. 6: Discrepancies in furniture purchases with double households
    in Vienna and Yugoslavia

room suites for their dwellings in Yugoslavia lived with old but well-preserved furniture in Vienna; a further one-third, despite a long stay, had invested nothing in the Vienna fixtures and fittings and were satisfied with heavily-worn furniture. Barely one-sixth had new furnishings in both Yugoslavia and Vienna. In part, the reduced economic expenditure on the Vienna home furnishings is a result of the investment at home. In those households which are not yet planning the furnishing of a house in Yugoslavia, the furnishings of the Vienna home are better than the average, and the category of heavily-worn furniture is missing. The accent on new furnishings at home in Yugoslavia is further evidenced through the fact that in addition to the bedroom suites, in 90 percent of the cases a new fitted kitchen and fitted living room were bought whereas in the Vienna milieu this furnishing combination is missing except for a few individual cases.

The better furnishings and fixings in Vienna are connected with an 'advancement syndrome' which can be measured by means of the usual indicators such as better education, higher aggregate household income, and a higher percentage of television sets, washing machines and new furniture. This 'advancement syndrome' is generally independent of building activity in Yugoslavia. On the other hand, the readiness for investment and transfer home of money represents phenomena dependent on the 'peripheral effect' and the level of involvement in agriculture. To those with their own home both in Vienna and in Yugoslavia, which comprise a half of all guestworker households, some 20 percent are to be added who have not yet completed their houses. A further 30 percent have a dwelling with their parents or in their own older houses in their homeland.

The social advancement hypothesis can be verified with regard to the location of the dwelling in the homeland. We can regard the overgenerous dimensions of the houses as an architectural symbol of the higher social status, as they are, attained through work in Vienna, in many cases, in excess of the actual living space requirements. As it is, this realisation of the objective of a social upgrading as to building structure produces problems for the future. High tax burdens for the house-owner have now come into effect, and the question of 'domicile loyalty' of the oncoming second generation cannot as yet be answered. It is likely that a considerable number of the houses, which are already standing completely or partly empty during the stay abroad, will also stand empty in the future.

6. Working in Two Societies: Work at Home and Work Abroad and the Plans for the Return Home

The succession of the 'Work in Two Societies', i.e., the change of work in the homeland to work in Vienna and the plans for the return home, is dependent upon the persistence of home-orientated work patterns and the creation of new work patterns in Vienna.

The idea behind the analysis of successive jobs types is that — in spite of the widely prevailing classification of the guestworker as labourer — no perfect substitution of the job role is possible. Even at the lowest level of the division of labour, certain manual knacks and acquired skills are necessary so that the opportunities to change jobs and to move up the occupational ladder are limited to some extent. The statistical analysis identified the following order of the persistence of job types: skilled workers in industry 60 percent, skilled workers in the building trade 50 percent, agricultural workers 42 percent, industrial workers (labourers and skilled workers) 36 percent and building labourers 19 percent. New job types resulted

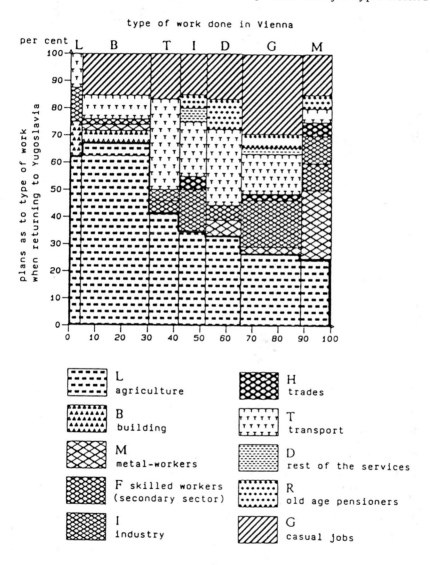

Fig. 7: Type of work done in Vienna by former agriculturalists and their job plans after returning to Yugoslavia

from the influence of the Vienna job environment. Among these the employment in the field of transport is especially prominent, thus exerting a dominant influence on the objectives of the guestworkers. The percentages of guestworkers in the transport industry in Vienna who wish to continue in similar employment in Yugoslavia are: former agricultural workers 65 percent, previously unemployed 46.3 percent, former building labourers 45.5 percent and former industrial workers 33.3 percent. The extremely complex situation is demonstrated by means of the matrix diagram for former agricultural workers (see Fig. 7).

The flight from agriculture, which appears as an explanatory element of Yugoslav guestworker migration, is an irreversible feature of the normal urbanisation process. Things are different with guestworker migration. Even so the question remains open as to how many guestworkers who come from agriculture are actually prepared to return to agriculture. On this point, the 1981 Vienna inquiry brought out the interesting result that 17.6 percent of the male heads of households would take up agriculture again as their main occupation in the event of a return to Yugoslavia. This percentage of potential agricultural workers is roughly the same as that of guestworkers possessing 5 hectares or more of agricultural land. The preparedness to return to agriculture is however dependent to a large extent on the employment in Vienna. Thus, two-thirds of the agricultural workers who work in the building industry in Vienna want to be engaged again in agricultural in Yugoslavia. This percentage is almost double that of all other fields of work of guestworkers in Vienna. One explanation for this is that guestworkers in the Vienna building industry often live in accommodation provided by the firm and have little contact with other fields of employment. In contrast, more than a third of those former agricultural workers employed in the metal and transport industries indicate that they are influenced in their job expectations by their Vienna employment.

The comparative readiness of guestworkers to return to agriculture is also due to the economic conditions in Yugoslavia, where unemployment in the secondary and tertiary sectors during the 1980s' recession has increased rather than decreased. With the growing level of education of job-hunters, people with poor education qualifications, which agricultural workers are as a rule, have now less chance of being considered for a job back in the homeland than before they left. Due to the generally low rates of pay in Yugoslavia, agricultural jobs can, moreover, easily 'compete' with those in industry. In other respects, because of the deterioration in food supplies in Yugoslavia, the increasing demand for agricultural products would offer good chances of a revitalisation of the agricultural industry. The actual development of agriculture will depend in the first instance on Yugoslavia's future agrarian-political climate for the private agricultural sector.

All the above statements relate to male guestworkers. The strictly job-specific role apportionment between male and female guestworkers cannot be examined in detail here, but it should be borne in mind that at a time when cleaners and catering workers are still in demand in Vienna, the wives can ensure the continuation of the household, even when the husbands are unemployed for a considerable time because of rationalisation measures in industry. The acceptance of working wives cannot only be seen as an important result of the guestworker migration, but also has a value not to be underrated from the point of view of workplace requirements in Yugoslavia. The possibility for wives to work in Yugoslavia will no doubt influence the readiness to return home.

7. The Functional Relationship between Place of Origin and Workplace

The peculiarities of the life-style of the guestworker, the double living location and the building activity at the place of origin lead to the phenomenon of rhythmic movements of persons and goods between the two locations and capital transfer from place of work (Vienna) to place of origin (Yugoslavia). Within the scope of the 1981 inquiry, an effort was made to measure the intensity of the relationship between place of origin and place of work by means of the following indicators: existence of transfers and amount of same, savings in a Yugoslav bank, and the number of return journeys to the place of origin. In this sequence of indicators, a weighting is already expressed. It can be stated that these behavioural dimensions are guided by differing influences. While the transfer was determined to a large extent by the household types (see Table 1), the manner of savings (see Table 2) showed itself to be dependent on the sociocultural milieu of the republic of origin. The frequency of travel is however best interpreted by means of a distance model (Fig. 8).

The money transfer of Yugoslav guestworkers to the homeland is considerable. It should be noted that in 1981, the yearly turnover of 'Shopping City South', a large shopping centre south of Vienna, was as high as the cash transferred by Yugoslav guestworkers to the homeland. 43 percent of the guestworkers questioned stated that they were able to make transfer payments to members of the family living at home and gave the amounts. Former villagers lead the money transfer home, transferring almost half of their earnings to Yugoslavia, and they thus display a remarkable renunciation of consumer goods in Vienna. Secondly, the ethnocultural pluralism of Yugoslavia offers an explanatory background for the disparity in cash transfer in that guestworkers from Croatia send very much less money than those from Serbia, Bosnia or Macedonia. While the household types play a decisive role in money transfers, they are only of secondary importance with regard to savings habits. Whether a guestworker opens his savings account with an Austrian or a Yugoslav bank, depends primarily on the sociocultural milieu in the home republic and not on bilateral household types. This result demands special notice, as it demonstrates that, when examining guestworkers' problems, the influence of Yugoslav federalism and the resultant diversity must not be ignored.

The frequency of the return journeys is determined fundamentally by distance to home; Macedonians and Bosnians provide an almost perfect contrasting pair with regard to travel habits. Macedonians (from Southern Yugoslavia) travel home usually once per year, whereas Bosnian guestworkers travel six times or more per year. Although the travel habits depend only secondarily on the household structure, this does however determine the mode of transport. 80 percent of city-dwellers travel

| money transfer (per cent) | householders men | | | | | | | women |
| | guest-workers from large cities | fairly recently immigrated guest-workers | older guestworkers from | | young guestworkers with | total | |
			villages	mixed settlements	small/large households in Vienna			
regular transfer	26.1	52.6	70.7	36.3	63.1	22.9	43.1	28.9
irregular transfer	12.5	20.0	19.2	28.8	23.9	19.9	21.9	23.8
amount transferred per month (AS):								
up to 500	28.6	10.0	....	4.3	1.6	5.3	3.6	15.6
500-1 000	14.3	20.0	5.4	34.8	21.4	41.3	25.5	31.1
1 000-2 500	28.6	20.0	21.6	39.1	39.7	32.0	34.2	40.0
2 500 and more	28.6	50.0	73.0	21.7	37.3	21.3	36.7	13.3
	100.0	100.0	100.0	100.0	100.0	100.0	100.0	100.0
mean (AS)	1 750	2 890	3 994	2 004	2 862	2 113	2 693	1 718

AS = Austrian schillings

n=275   n= 44

Table 1: Monthly money transfer of the various household-types of Yugoslav guestworkers in Vienna in 1981

way of saving	householders men							women
	guest-workers from large cities	fairly recently immigrated guest-workers	older guestworkers from		young guestworkers with small/large households in Vienna		total	
			villages	mixed settlements				
per cent depositors with account:								
with bank in Yugoslavia	61.5	55.6	48.8	75.0	66.5	75.1	68.4	58.7
with bank in Yugoslavia and in Austria	31.3	40.0	68.2	61.1	52.7	34.3	42.9	34.3
with bank in Austria	18.8	20.0	13.6	25.9	21.4	18.8	19.9	10.0
	50.0	40.0	18.2	13.0	25.9	46.8	37.2	55.6
	100.0	100.0	100.0	100.0	100.0	100.0	100.0	100.0

n=454   n= 85

Table 2: Saving methods of Yugoslav guestworkers in Vienna according to household-types in 1981

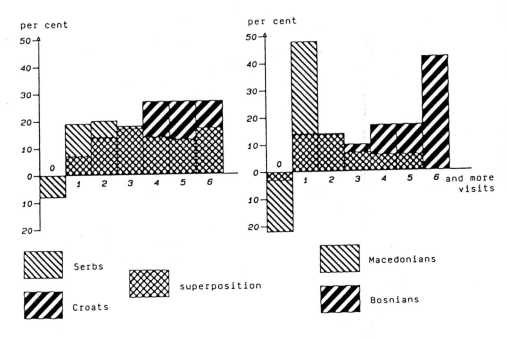

Fig. 8: The frequency of visits to Yugoslavia according to Republics in 1981

with their own car, late migrants and villagers predominantly use buses, while older guestworkers from mixed settlements and young guestworkers with small households use either a bus or their own car for the journey home. As a form of transport to the homeland, railways play a very small role.

8. Quo Vadis ?

The important question is still open: Where will guestworkers' settlement in Vienna lead and how long are guestworkers going to maintain their double existence? As an adaptation strategy for this divided life, they have developed ambivalent habits which partially replace the workplace- or home-orientation and aim at securing and perpetuating this double existence. Of these habits the following deserve special notice: the building activity of around one-third of the guestworkers without family members in Yugoslavia; a further third of the guestworkers who, although they have no direct relatives in Yugoslavia, transfer money and travel back frequently to the homeland; guestworkers who have brought their children to Vienna and have developed a strategy to cover themselves in the homeland through the opening of foreign currency accounts in Yugoslav banks; as contrast to that, Austria-oriented savers who have left their children in the homeland. Finally, the established guestworkers with farm and family in Yugoslavia have tried to develop secure living conditions in Vienna, with the very strong tendency to get a foothold in apartment-building caretaker positions. The analysis showed that guestworkers with ambivalent attitudes and behaviour already constitute an absolute majority (about 55 percent of the total), while the proportion of 'potential Viennese' is just 6 percent, that of the 'returners' amounts to 39 percent.

During the recession, politicans of all ideological shades in the receiving countries learnt that guestworkers cannot be substituted by the native unemployed. There are several reasons for this. Guestworkers and the unemployed belong partly to separate regional systems, namely, densely populated urbanized areas (guestworkers) and rural peripheries (native unemployed). The subsidized building of private homes in league with job guarantees and traditional property ideals have led to an immobilisation of the population in structurally weak regions. The close-knit social security system combined with ossified professional roles and the traditional importance attached to prestige have reduced the readiness of native Austrian job-seekers to take up low-qualified work. The coordination between educational politics and job market politics in Austria is insufficient in that 'buffer' manpower prepared to take over dangerous, dirty, badly-paid work with irregular hours is not provided.

A notable stabilisation of the guestworker households has taken place in the dual labour market due to the coming-together of the family and the wife taking over traditional sex-specific occupations in personal service and in the catering and cleaning industries. This finds its parallel among the Black in the United States, where similarly the wife is better able to avoid unemployment when, during rationalisation measures in large industrial plants, the men are made redundant.

The process of the inner tertiarisation of businesses appears to be especially important. Guestworkers are already represented in surprisingly high numbers in all manipulative activities in warehousing, in transport, in distribution and sales. Their way is open in the service society, if only in subordinate positions.

With the continous return of guestworkers to their countries of origin in the 1980s, in spite of a continuing demand for foreign labour in Northern, Western and Central Europe, there naturally exists a very fundamental problem in the host society: An increase in ethnocultural distance coincident with a further segmentation of the job market is continuing so that an accentuation, rather than a weakening, of the ethnocultural segregation effect is to be expected in the urban areas of Northern, Western and Central Europe in the future.

FOREIGN WORKERS IN SWITZERLAND
AND IN THE CANTON OF ZÜRICH

AYSE EVRESNEL (ZÜRICH)

1. Introduction

The purpose of this contribution is to present an empirical overview of foreign employment in Switzerland and in the canton of Zürich. The growth in the number of foreign workers, as well as their concentration in certain sectors and branches of industry defines importance of the topic. From information on foreign workers in Europe that has been collected for more than 20 years, we know, however, that the "foreign-worker problem" cannot be examined solely on the basis of statistical data. For this reason, the employment of foreigners in Switzerland will be subsequently examined as a social problem, whose roots lie in the varied makeup of the foreigner groups as well as in their treatment by the host society.

In this chapter I will first of all look at the host society, in this case, Switzerland. I wish to demonstrate what the social context looked like for the employment of foreigners and why it created problems (section 2). The discussion of the social context will make it possible to give us a better understanding of the subsequent growth in the number of foreigners (section 3). The next section (section 4) will be concerned with the question of why the employment of foreigners was considered such a problem. Lastly, the group of workers will be investigated empirically using the case of Turkish workers in Zürich (section 5). This section illustrates the social-economic situation of the Turkish workers themselves made on the basis of their own statements.

2. Complexities of the foreign worker — host society relationship

In this section I would like to examine the foreign worker problem in a social context, by the method of determining the social framework which the host society provides foreign workers. This goal of illustrating the foreign worker problem in a social context requires the choice of a model of society as a whole. For that purpose I adopt the three-way classification of Hoffmann-Nowothny/Hondrich and Offe: the economic-subsystem (economy), the political-subsystem (government) and the normative-subsystem (community) (see Figs. 1 and 2). These subsystems characteristics will be related to foreign workers. For purposes of illustration, Swiss society was chosen.

Subsystem "government" and Swiss policy regarding foreign workers

The political-administration system is responsible for the regulation of events in the social system as a whole. It is often viewed as the "source of all problems" in society or the common codeword, government failure. The state regulation of foreign workers was distinguished by different phases. We can accept that "foreigners

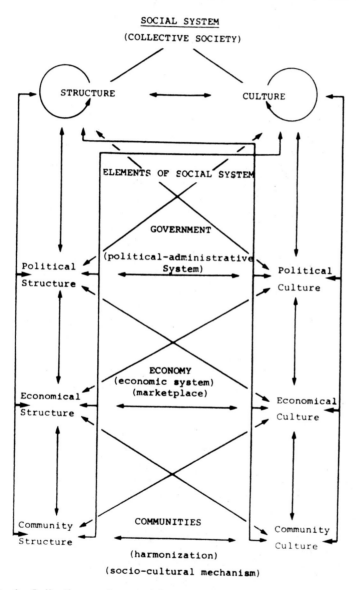

Fig. 1: Collective society and its sub-systems (Source: HOFFMANN-NOWOTNY – HONDRICH; 1981)

in Switzerland before 1914, between the two extremes of naturalization on the one hand and deportation on the other, could live completely free" (Haug 1980). In contrast, the policy regarding foreigners during and between the 1st and 2nd World Wars became extremely restrictive. In the post-World War II era, this restrictive policy was no longer adhered to because of the work force needs of Swiss economy. Foreign workers were actively recruited. The government found itself in a difficult situation, characterized by the necessity to make the labour force needs of the economy clear to a population heretofore well-acquainted with the "foreign peril". In spite of this difficulty the immigration restrictions were further dismantled. In the Federal Council's 1958 report on business, the needs of the economy were viewed as directing the foreign worker policy, "as far as the economic needs coincided the needs of the nation as a whole" (Haug 1980).

In the late 1960's and early 1970's popular initiatives were proposed to set limitations on the numbers of foreign workers, which forced the government to give up its liberal open door policy regarding foreign workers. In December 1964 a "plebiscite against the infiltration of foreigners" was launched by the Democratic Party of the canton of Zürich, but was later rejected by the voters. With the argument that an acceptance of the plebiscite would ruin the economy, it was mainly the employers' organizations that fought against it. Shortly after the defeat of the first "initiative against the infiltration of foreigners", a body consisting mainly of representatives of the "National Front against the foreign penetration of people and home" decided to launch a second plebiscite which was named after one of its main proponents, Schwarzenbach. This plebiscite had the intention of prohibiting the dismissal of any Swiss citizen because of rationalization measures as long as there were foreigners working in the same company or professional organization. Moreover, its plan was to reduce the number of foreigners by 265,000 in the four years to December 1968. The plebiscite, which according to the employers' organizations would have led to "economic suicide", was rejected by a narrow majority of the Swiss voters. In order to satisfy both the business community and the skeptics and to head off further initiatives, a scheme of state-wide limitations of foreigners with cantonal quotas was introduced. In accordance with this scheme the national labour market officials determine the overall limit for Switzerland. The apportionment, however, is regulated by the individual cantons (Niederberger 1981).

Economic-subsystem and the attitude of the Swiss business organizations towards foreigner employment

The Swiss economic-subsystem is distinguished by its clear goal-conception and its ability to adjust to changing conditions. As we will see later, these two characteristics often cause problems for the other subsystems in society (government and community) (Hoffmann-Nowothny/Hondrich 1981 and Offe 1973). The attitude of business organizations generally favoured foreigner employment. The need for foreign workers was first evident in the textile industry. In 1945 the Swiss knitting factory association suggested that national officials and relevant trade circles should meet to discuss current problems. The associations saw the solution in the employment of foreign workers. This suggestion met with heavy resistance from the labour unions. In 1945, in spite of the union resistance, the Federal Council approved the employment of foreign workers with the condition that it would be on a limited basis and, therefore, it would prevent inflation in the industry (Doleschal 1977).

The attitude of both organizations in the following years remained unchanged. While management organizations found foreigner employment troublefree, the unions viewed it, in the long term, as undesirable.

Community-subsystem and the attitude of the community towards foreigners

"Harmony" describes the fundamental need of the community. "Communities can hardly bear the intrusion of an direct contact with dissimilar values, norms, lifestyles and practices" (Hoffmann-Nowothny/Hondrich 1981). The need for social harmony can lead to attitudes of prejudice and discrimination towards foreigners. Why is the native population prejudiced? Why does the native population discriminate against foreigners? Prejudice provides a pseudo-orientation in a complex society. An individual is either not able to seek the reasons for his/her own failure (or that of society) or this is tied together with considerable complexity, i.e. alienation. Transference offers a solution to personal and/or social problems by shifting the blame to other groups or persons, i.e. foreigners.

We can say that "discrimination", like prejudice, is not merely a personal matter. In the function of discrimination, the desire to secure one's own position is recognizable. Native groups (or, more precisely, members of these groups) reflect their own insecurity with regard to their position in society by that of feelings of power. Using the thesis of superiority, the group legitimizes discrimination towards foreigners. In this way problems are shifted somewhere else. In this sense, the "strangeness" or "foreignness" of the ethnic groups is of great significance. One can postulate that the dissimilarity of cultures contributes to the legitimization of discrimination (ESSER 1980).

From Hoffmann-Nowothny's research (1973), with empirical data based on interviews with Swiss and Italians, we learn that, especially, the lower and lower middle classes of the native population are inclined toward prejudice and discrimination. This research confirmed the assumptions regarding the complexity of the prejudice-discrimination problem. This problem has a social aspect that extends beyond the personal (psychological). Attitudes of prejudice and discrimination against foreigners are connected with the social status of the native group.

Summarizing the previous discussion of foreigner problems in the host society, we recognize that the societal sub-systems have differing goal conceptions. While the economic system is not disturbed by the foreignness of immigrant labour, this same dissimilarity can be very disruptive to the community. The position of the government in this situation is especially difficult. On the one hand the government depends on the business community for support and the economy for revenue: on the other hand, it is directed by the loyalty of the community (see Fig. 2). The gov-

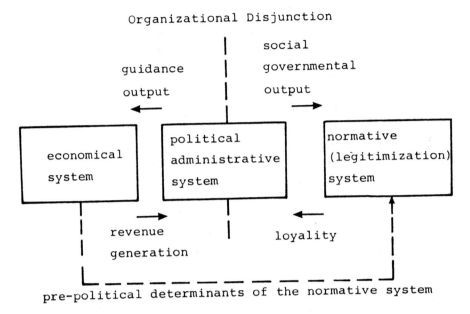

Fig. 2: Subsystems of society and their relation to one another (Source:
OFFE; 1973)

ernment, in Switzerland as well as in the Federal Republic of Germany, sought to
master the difficult situation regarding foreign worker policy, in that it fulfilled the
demands of the economy for almost 10 years and only later took into consideration the opposition of the community (after the fear of an over-influx of foreigners
increased). (See Leitner's chapter in this book.)

3. Foreign workers in Switzerland and in the canton of Zürich

Between 1959 and 1963, the population of foreigners living in Switzerland rose
form 430,000 to 756,000. In 1974, the foreign-resident population reached its peak
and totaled 1,065,000. Since 1979, this numerical growth has shown a declining
trend. The initial increase in the number of foreigners can be seen as the result of
the early liberal policies towards foreigner immigration. The decrease which one can
see starting in 1979 can be explained by the fact that these immigration policies became more and more restrictive.

For persons gainfully employed within the foreign-resident population, we can
say that between 1959 and 1982 this group constituted approximately half of the
total foreign-resident population (see Fig. 3). Examining the share of gainfully-
employed foreigners to the gainfully-employed Swiss, we find that the foreigners,
between 1970 and 1982, constituted approximately one-fourth of the total number
of gainfully-employed persons in Switzerland (see Fig. 4).

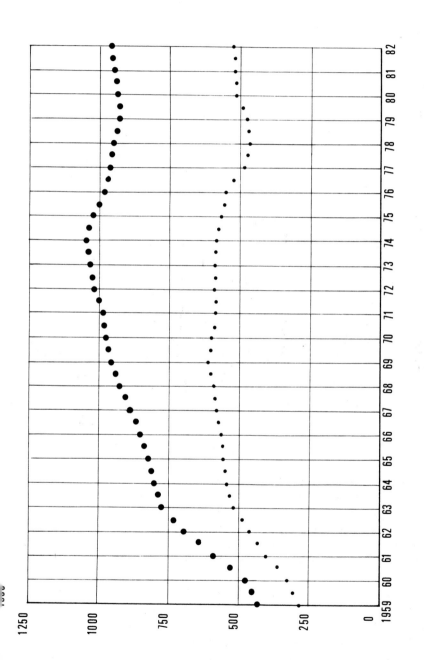

Fig. 3: Foreign-resident population in Switzerland 1959-1982

Source: Data based on SCHWARZ, 1984, Tabl. 2-2, p. 13

● resident population
• gainfully-employed

Ayse Evrensel

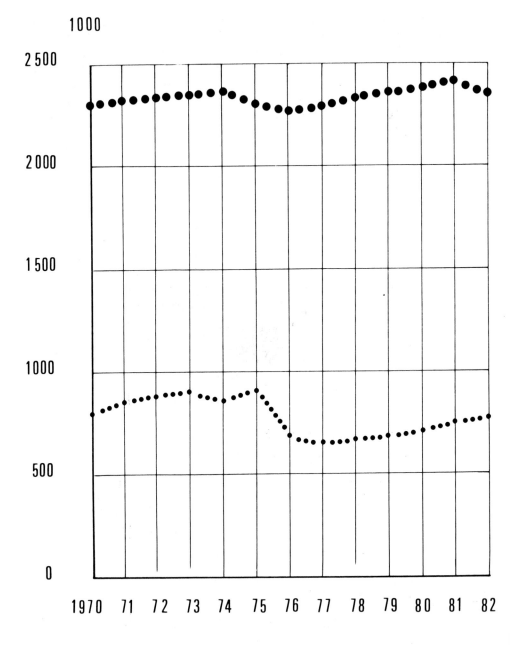

Source: Data based on SCHWARZ, 1984,
Tab. 4 - 4, p. 101

●●●● Swiss
•••• foreigners

Fig. 4: Gainfully-employed persons in Switzerland 1970-1982

The distribution of Swiss and foreign workers within the industrial sectors shows the following consistency. While the majority of the Swiss workforce (57 %) is employed in the tertiary sector, the majority of foreigners (59.7 %) works in the secondary sector (see Fig. 5). This shows that foreigners are filling the gaps in industry which resulted from the departure of the Swiss to the tertiary sector. Foreign employment, therefore, moderated the development of bottlenecks in the industry, and thereby stimulated increased productivity and growth. In addition, native workers were able to assume better positions (see Schwarz 1984).

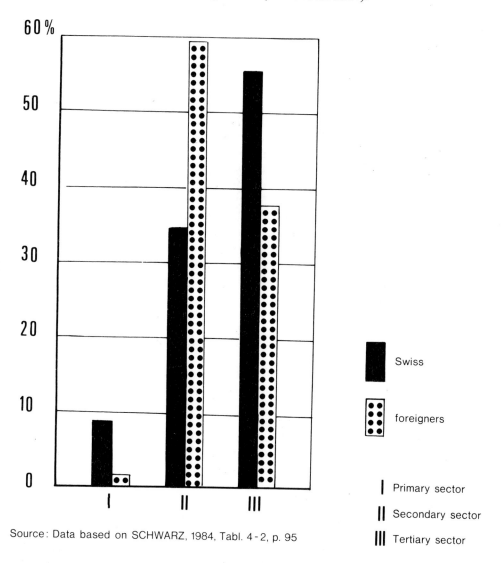

Source: Data based on SCHWARZ, 1984, Tabl. 4-2, p. 95

Swiss

foreigners

I   Primary sector

II Secondary sector

III Tertiary sector

Fig. 5: Distribution of Swiss and foreign workers by economic sectors, 1980

The spatial distribution of foreign workers by canton in the years 1950, 1960, 1970, and 1980 showed that the following cantons, Zürich (ZH), Glarus (GL), Solothurn (SO), Basel-land (BL), Basel-city (BS), Schaffhausen (SH), Aargau (AG), Thurgau (TG), Vaud (VD) and Geneva (GE), had foreign workers constituting one-third of the total employment. This is explained by the above-average representation of secondary and tertiary sectors in these cantons. Many international organizations are located in the canton of Geneva, which of course greatly influences the number of foreigners in that canton (see Fig. 6). Due to the existence of a liberal work-permit policy, the percentage of employed foreigners in each canton more than doubled between 1950 and 1960. The cantons, which in 1950 boasted a high percentage of foreign workers, belonged again in 1960 to that group of cantons with particularly high percentages.

The years between 1960 and 1970 were, after 1963, characterized by the establishment of quotas in business organizations. Although this represented a restrictive measure with regard to foreigner employment, its impact was delayed and the number of foreign workers further increased. Between 1960 and 1970, the distribution of foreign workers within the cantons showed no great changes. Largely because of the 1974/76 recession, foreigner employment decreased between 1970 and 1980, because now, the establishment of nationwide quotas regulated the number of foreign workers. During this decade the distribution of foreign workers within the cantons again did not change.

With regard to the distribution of foreign workforce by sector and job group in the canton and city of Zürich, the specific focus of this chapter, the distribution of the foreign workforce by job sector differs from that in other cantons in Switzerland because most foreign workers are employed in the secondary sector. It is in the manufacturing industry within the secondary sector that most foreign workers are employed (see Fig. 7 and 8).

4. Why has the employment of foreigners become a problem?

In the 1960's, when mass labourforce migration began, it was generally believed that the industrialized nations of Europe greatly profited from this migration. The acceptance of this view was largely due to the emphasis placed on the growth-promoting effects of foreigner employment.

In this light, as a result of the economic expansion, labour was needed. Qualified labour could be only partly recruited from the native population. Unqualified labour was brought in from abroad. In this way, the economy could best adapt itself to the new circumstances without having to suffer any losses, a major national advantage in the employment of foreigners.

Over time, because of growing economic and social problems, the wisdom of employing foreigners was called into question. Foreign workers were no longer only seen as "useful" but also as "problematic". Economic problems are generally viewed as a cost-profit question, in which the profitability of foreigner employment for the economy (banks, insurance companies, etc.) is weighed against the societal-

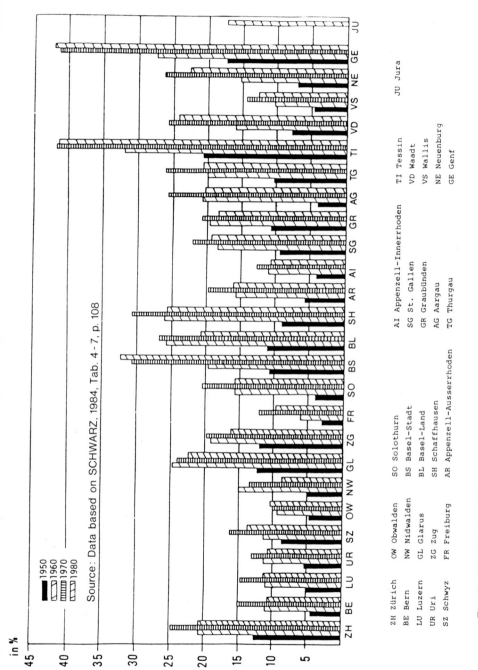

Source: Data based on SCHWARZ, 1984, Tab. 4 - 7, p. 108

ZH Zürich   OW Obwalden   SO Solothurn   AI Appenzell-Innerrhoden   TI Tessin   JU Jura
BE Bern   NW Nidwalden   BS Basel-Stadt   SG St. Gallen   VD Waadt
LU Luzern   GL Glarus   BL Basel-Land   GR Graubünden   VS Wallis
UR Uri   ZG Zug   SH Schaffhausen   AG Aargau   NE Neuenburg
SZ Schwyz   FR Freiburg   AR Appenzell-Ausserrhoden   TG Thurgau   GE Genf

Fig. 6: Distribution of employed foreigners by canton in the years 1950, 1960, 1970 and 1980

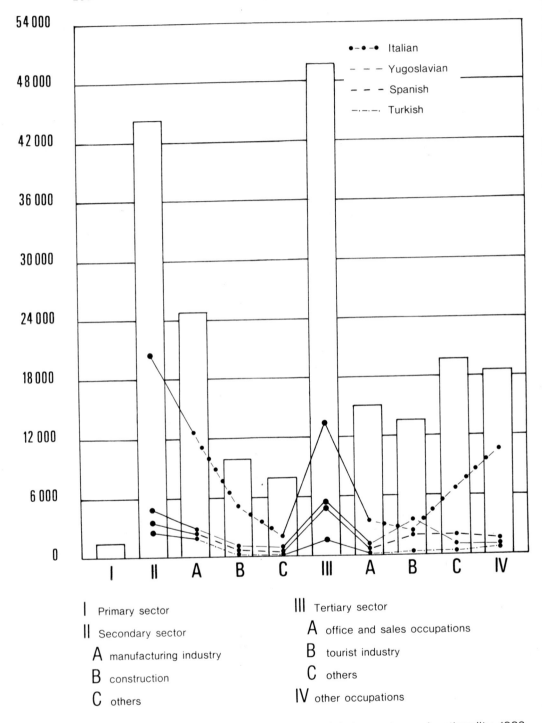

Fig. 7: Foreign workers in the canton of Zurich by sector and nationality, 1983

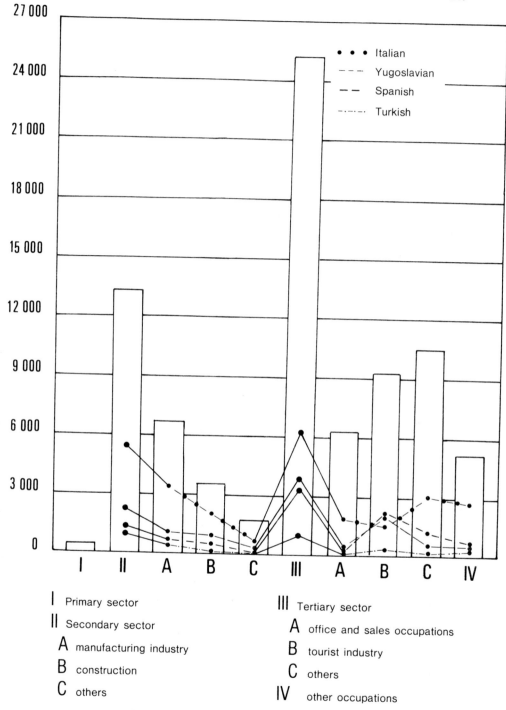

I Primary sector   III Tertiary sector

II Secondary sector   A office and sales occupations

   A manufacturing industry   B tourist industry

   B construction   C others

   C others   IV other occupations

Fig. 8: Foreign workers in the city of Zurich by sector and nationality, 1983

infrastructure costs (living quarters, schools, etc.). Of central importance among the social problems caused by foreigner employment is the problem of "integration". The term "integration" is the center of numerous discussions about the foreigner employment problem. The differences between foreign workers and the native population (Turks are strongly perceived as most dissimilar) strengthens the demand for integration. The native population expects, therefore, that foreign workers will integrate themselves into society or leave the country. However, we must take into account that the foreign workers were, at the beginning, looked upon as guest-workers, who come in during a favourable economic time, but have to leave again during an unfavourable one. This so-called "conjunctural-buffer theory", which as accepted in 1948/49, could not however be put into practice along the desired lines in the sixties, as the expected slack in the economy did not arrive. Foreign workers stayed on in Switzerland for more than 10 years. This generated the expectation amongst the natives that foreigners should integrate themselves. (By integration, the natives meant the learning of the 'respective' language, not to look strange, etc.)

Among the groups of foreign workers the Turks are the least interested in integration, as the native population defines it. Research has shown, however, that the return of foreign workers to their native land (especially with regard to Turks) is time and again postponed. Because of this contradiction, the question is often asked whether foreign workers are "immigrants" or temporary "guest" workers. This question, which has both general and scientific interest, is not examined by political authorities, because their objective is to solve problems politically regardless of how the problems arose.

5. The foreign worker group — neither integration nor repatriation

The goal in this section is to determine the expectations of the foreign worker group. To reach this goal, foreigner employment will be presented from the point of view of foreign workers presently residing in a host country, Switzerland. The motives for immigration, intentions regarding repatriation and problems of integration represent the most important elements of the foreigner employment problem.

I would like to introduce briefly the relevant results from my own research, which I carried out in late 1982 and early 1983. This empirical study was part of my dissertation, which tried to elucidate the problem of foreigners in the immigrant society using the example of Turkish workers in the city of Zürich. This part of the study considers the situation of the Turkish workers. I will introduce the workers' attitudes on certain subjects such as expatriation/repatriation. The other part of the study looks at the immigrant society (of Switzerland). In this context the subsystems of society (the state, the economy, and the community) will be analysed about their attitudes towards employment of foreigners. The aim of this study was to illustrate the conflict of interests between these two parts (immigrant society and foreign workers) and to emphasize the complexity of the problem.

The first part of the study is based upon results of interviews made with 65 Turkish workers in the city of Zürich. In the following, some of the most important results are introduced.

Motives for expatriation

Table 1: Motives for moving to Switzerland (main reason)

economic problems at home	19
better pay	16
to be able to live in Europe	9
the family was in Switzerland	6
adventure	4
other	11

While 29 % of the interviewees emigrated because of economical problems, nearly 25 % of them declared their motive for emigration as "better pay" (Table 1). There it must be remembered that it is not only the poor and unemployed who emigrate. The interviews showed that nearly half of the interviewees state their pay in Turkey was ,"average" to "very good" (Table 2).

Table 2: Assessment of the pay formerly received in Turkey

not good	25
average	21
good	11
very good	4
no statement	4

What should also be taken into account is the influence of information which the workers obtained from their relatives/acquaintances working abroad while they were still in Turkey (Table 3 and 4):

Table 3: Relatives/acquaintances abroad

yes	45
no	20

Table 4: Informational conversations

yes	37
no	8

Nearly 70 % of the interviewees had relatives or acquaintances abroad while they were still in Turkey. And more than half of this group had held talks concerning the employment abroad with those still in Turkey. What kind of information they obtained through these discussions concerning employment abroad, is shown in Table 5:

Table 5: Contents of the informational conversations

good pay	12
demonstrative effect*	7
beautiful country	5
civilized country	3
educational opportunities	2
opportunities for saving	2
other	2

* their relatives/acquaintances always showed their acquired goods.

As we can see this information carries the message of economic advantages and other positive statements about the country. The interviewees, therefore, came to Zürich with a positive image of Switzerland (Table 6):

Table 6: Former image of Switzerland

civilized country	31
highly developed country	8
beautiful country	8
agricultural country	4
mountains	3
offers all kinds of opportunities	3
did not know much	8

From the Table 7 it is apparent that nearly two thirds of the interviewees presumed that their stay would be only a temporary one before they left.

Table 7: Originally planned length of stay

1 – 3 years	14
4 – 7 years	12
more than 7 years	5
until enough capital is acquired	6
for a short time	3
did not think about it	13
others	5
no statement	7

The situation of the interviewees in Zürich

Nearly two thirds of the interviewees declared themselves satisfied with their pay. Although the situation at work was more or less satisfactory, the rather distant relations with the Swiss presents a problem. Nearly 70 % of the interviewees have no close relations (friendship etc.) with the Swiss. This can be explained partly by the fact that these interviewees only have an elementary knowledge of German.

Intentions to repatriate and investments

Over 70 % of the interviewees have been in Zürich for more than 7 years, despite their original intention of staying only for a few years and in spite of having no close ties to their social surroundings. One reason for this longer stay are investments which generated higher demands for the workers. Over 80 % have made investments in Turkey. The different types of investments are illustrated by Table 8:

Table 8: Types of investments

real estate / land	8
house	8
apartment	6
business	2
real estate + apartment + etc.	30

Both because the financing of these investments needed time and because the workers felt they had to invest more and more, they stayed longer in Zürich than originally planned. We can assume that an important part of the interviewees decision to remain longer is that they have been unable to secure a permanent means of livelihood in Turkey. Over 60 % of the interviewees plan to make further investments in Turkey, mostly with the intention of opening up a business (Table 9):

Table 9: Future planned investments

business	25
house	7
apartment	3
apartment + business + etc.	5
no further investments	14
do not know	5
no statement	6

Because of these investment plans, the return home is further delayed (Table 10):

Table 10: Desired length of stay

1–3 years	8
4–7 years	10
more than 7 years	2
do not know	43
will probably settle permanently	2

The assessment of the difficult economic situation in Turkey is one of the reasons why over 65 % of the interviewees do not know when they are going to return home. Nearly 63 % of the interviewees evaluate the situation as "not good" and this induces them to make further investments in order to secure their means of livelihood in Turkey. This however, means that they will stay longer in Zürich.

Although the interviewees consider themselves alien and discriminated against in Zürich (Table 11), they prize the economic opportunities here, which leaves their intentions of returning home unfulfilled.

Table 11: Problems of the employment abroad

far away from home and the family	10
foreign culture	6
one feels oneself a stranger, here	10
the Swiss are cold-hearted	4
the Swiss treat the Turks badly	20
others	4
see no problem	11

Table 12: Positive side of the employment abroad

economic opportunities	42
self-development	11
no positive side	12

Illustrating the problem in relation to foreigner employment and through the study of foreign groups and also that of the host society, it has been demonstrated that the widespread opinion "that the foreign workers problem is a problem of foreign workers" is unrealistic. We have seen that the host society, through its structures, has reinforced the problem. This analysis shows the futility of the formation of conventional solutions, i.e., "Foreigners should integrate themselves into society", and "The native population should be more tolerant toward foreigners". I would suggest that the scientific community avoid hasty solutions and continue to engage in analyses of the actual situation, both of foreigner lifestyles and Swiss society. The study of the conflicting causes of a social problem advances understanding of the problem which is not the case for approaches which concentrate on finding solutions.

Summary

The results of the study show that for more than 70 % of the Turkish interviewees in Zürich the term "integration" means a change in the norms and values as well as their religion. Based on this appreciation the majority resolves not to change their culture, i.e. not to integrate. This fact poses longterm difficulties in accommodating the desires of the foreigners to remain separate and the Swiss wish for their integration by adopting Swiss norms.

Economic reasons emerged as the most frequent motive for migrating. The goal of the immigrant workers was the improvement of their standard of living in their native country, which was planned as a temporary stay abroad. The positive side of foreign employment, namely better earning potential, represented the most important incentive for immigration. Problems of living in a foreign country were not addressed before the workers left for Switzerland and this reinforced the fixed idea of better earning potential. During the stay, this goal remained the most important. The majority of foreign workers in Europe come here, therefore, to improve their standard of living in their native country while remaining generally unaware of the possible consequences of foreign employment. This attitude affects their adjustment vis-a-vis the society of the host country.

During the stay in the host country, material goals will be reached and the living standard in the immigrants' native lands improved through investments. The scheduled returns to the homeland, however, do not take place and are postponed indefinitely. Because of the demands of their improved life style, the foreign workers find their homeland prospects to be economically unsound. Financial considerations bind them to the host country. However, in that they are "foreigners" and they always perceive their legally restricted position in society. They compensate for their lack of social position in the host country with investments in and other connections with their native country.

While the continually postponed return to the homeland calls into question the temporary immigration status of today's foreign workers in Europe, the ties to the land of origin calls into question a permanent immigration status. The situation is characterized by no decision to return to the homeland and no decision to definitely stay in the host country. We recognize what a prolonged stay in the host country has nothing to do with "integration" and with cultural adjustment. Integration is a requirement of the host society motivated by deep social beliefs. The majority of foreigners do not want to integrate, not least because it means for them a type of self-alienation. Researchers often attempt to understand complex social problems with mono-causal explanations. "Those who become integrated remain in the country, and those who do not, repatriate". Countless definition and stages of integration (assimilation), acculturization, adaptation, accommodation, etc.), created by social scientists, do not help much in dismantling the common, stereotypical attitudes such as: "Swiss are hostile to foreigners" or "Turks are not capable of adjustment".

Among foreign workers there is a so-called "unintegrated mass", especially among the Turks. My research revealed that the majority of foreign workers view integration as a type of conversion from deeply-held convictions. Observing the way of life of Turkish workers in Europe, it can be seen that this conception (or better expressed – this fear) dominates their life, regardless of whether social scientists define integration as adaptation or something else. Social problems are much more than a matter of social science definitions. Labels such as "integration" and "repatriation" attach a definitional character to the problem, giving the impression that a solution to the dilemma is generally possible.

We must continue to ask whether foreign workers are "temporary guest workers" or "immigrants". From the point of view of Swiss society, integration is a requirement. Measures and requirements to promote integration are ineffective, however, because they overlook the expectations, problems and fears of foreign workers. The actual situation of foreign workers can be expressed as "neither integration nor repatriation".

Illustrating the problem in relation to foreigner employment and through the study of foreign groups and also that of the host society, it has been demonstrated that the widespread opinion "that the foreign workers problem is a problem of foreign workers" is unrealistic. We have seen that the host society, through its structures, has reinforced the problem. This analysis shows the futility of the formation of conventional solutions, i.e., "Foreigners should integrate themselves into society", and "The native population should be more tolerant toward foreigners". I would suggest that the scientific community avoid hasty solutions and continue to engage in analyses of the actual situation, both of foreigner lifestyles and Swiss society. The study of the conflicting causes of a social problem advances understanding of the problem which is not the case for approaches which concentrate on finding solutions.

BIBLIOGRAPHY

Adams, J. S. (1984): The meaning of housing. in: Annals, Association of American Geographers 74, 515–526.

Akinci, A.U. (1982): Differentation of capital and international labor migration: constructing a working hypothesis. in: International Migration 20, 35–44.

Allal, T. et al. (1977): Situation migratoires. Paris: Galilee.

Amersfoort, H. van (1974): Immigrate en minderheidsforming: een analyse van de Nederlandse situatie 1945–1973. Alphen A.D. Rijn: Sansom.

Amersfoort, H. van (1978): Migrant workers, circular migration and development. in: Tijdschrift voor Economische en Sociale Geografie 69, 17–26.

Amersfoort, H. van (1982a): Immigration and the formation on minority groups. The Dutch experience 1945–1975. Cambridge: Cambridge University Press.

Amersfoort, H. van (1982b): Immigrant housing in a welfare state: the case of the Netherlands in the 1970s. in: Research in Race and Ethnic Relations 3, 49–77.

Amersfoort, H. van et al. (1984): International migration, the economic crisis and the state. in: Ethnic and Racial Studies 7, 238–268.

Amersfoort, H. van; Cortie, C. (1973): Het patroon van de Surinaamse vestiging in Amsterdam 1968 t/m 1970. in: Tijdschrift voor Economische en Sociale Geografie 64, 283–294.

Anglade, J. (1976): La vie quotidienne des immigrés en France de 1919 a nos jours. Paris: Hachette.

Arend, M. (1982): Sozialökologische Analyse der kleinräumigen Ausländerverteilung in Zürich. in: Hoffmann-Nowotny, H.J.; Hondrich, K.O. (Eds.): Ausländer in der Bundesrepublik Deutschland und in der Schweiz. Frankfurt: Campus Verlag, 294–374.

Bach, R.L. (1978): Mexican immigration and the American state. in: International Migration Review 12, 536–558.

Badcock, B. (1984): Unfairly structured cities. Oxford: Basil Blackwell.

Bade, K.J. (Ed.) (1984): Auswanderer, Wanderarbeiter, Gastarbeiter: Bevölkerung, Arbeitsmarkt und Wanderung in Deutschland seit der Mitte des 19. Jahrhunderts. Ostfildern (Scripta Mercaturae Verl.).

Bähr, J. (1971): Regionalisierung mit Hilfe von Distanzmessungen. in: Raumforschung und Raumordnung 29, 11–19.

Bähr, J. (1983): Bevölkerungsgeographie, Verteilung und Dynamik der Bevölkerung in globaler, nationaler und regionaler Sicht. Stuttgart: Ulmer-Verlag.

Bähr, J.; Gans, P. (1985): Differences in migration behaviour of Germans and foreigners in selected cities of the Federal Republic of Germany. in: Espace-Populations-Societes 1, 201–214.

Banton, M. (1955): The coloured quarter. London: Jonathan Cape.

Barou, J. (1978): Travailleure Africains en France. Grenoble: Presses Universitaires de Grenoble.

Bartels, D. (1968): Türkische Gastarbeiter aus der Region Izmir. in: Erdkunde 22, 313–324.

Bassett, K.; Short, J. (1980): Housing and residential structure. London: Routledge and Kegan Paul.

Bastenier, A. (1979): L'immigration ou l'avenir d'une ville pluri-ethnique. La Revue Nouvelle 70.11, 339–348.

Bastide, H. (1982): Les enfants d'immigrés et l'enseignement français. Enquête dans les établissements du premier et du second degré. Paris: Presses Universitaires Française (Cahier de l'INED, 97).

Bastié, J. (1984): Géographie du Grand Paris. Paris: Masson.

Baumgartner-Karabak, A.; Landesberger, G. (1978): Die verkauften Bräute – türkische Frauen zwischen Kreuzberg und Anatolien. Reinbek bei Hamburg: Rowohlt (rororo aktuell).

Bell, D. (1976): The extreme right in France. in: Kolinsky, M.; Paterson, W.E. (Eds.): Social and Political Movements in Western Europe. London: Croom Helm.

Ben Sassi, T. (1968): Les travailleurs Tunisiens dans la region Parisienne. in: Hommes et Migrations. 109.

Benoît, J. (1980): Dossier E . . . Comme esclaves; Paris: Alain Moreau.

Bentham, G; Mosely, M. (1980): Socioeconomic change and disparities within the Paris agglomeration: does Paris have an innercity problem? in: Regional Studies 14, 55–70.

Berlin, Regierender Bürgermeister (1980): Wohnraumversorgung von Ausländern und Entballung überlasteter Gebiete durch städtebauliche Maßnahmen. Berlin: Der Regierende Bürgermeister.

Berry, B.J.L. (1981): The open housing question: Race and housing in Chicago 1966–1976. Cambridge, MA: Ballinger Publishing Co.

Binder, J.; Simoes, M. (1980): Psychische Beschwerden bei ausländischen Arbeitern: Eine Untersuchung bei portugiesischen Arbeitsemigranten. in: Zeitschrift für Soziologie 9.3, 262–274.

Bingemer, K. et al. (Eds.) (1970): Leben als Gastarbeiter. Köln, Opladen.

Blanchet, D. (1985): Intensité et calendrier du regroupement familial des migrants: Un essai de mesure à partir de donées agrégées. in: Population 40.2, 249–266.

Blotevogel, H.H.; Hommel, M. (1980): Struktur und Entwicklung des Städtesystems. in: Geographische Rundschau 32, 155–164.

Boal, F.W. (1981): Ethnic residential segregation, ethnic mixing and resource conflict: a study in Belfast, Northern Ireland. in: Peach, C.; Robinson, V.; Smith, S. (Eds.): Ethnic Segregation in Cities. London: Croom Helm, 235–251.

Boehning, W.R. (1970): Foreign workers in post-war Germany. in: New Atlantis 2, 12–38.

Boehning, W.R. (1972): The migration of workers in the United Kingdom and the European Community. London: Oxford University Press.

Bonacker, M. (1982): The social community of immigrants. in: Friedrichs, J. (Ed.): Spatial disparities and social behaviour. Hamburg: Christians Verlag, 102–113.

Borris, M. (1973): Ausländische Arbeitnehmer in einer Großstadt: eine empirische Untersuchung am Beispiel Frankfurt. Frankfurt a.M.: Europäische Verlagsanstalt.

Borris, M. et al. (1977): Les etrangers à Stuttgart. Paris: Editions du C.N.R.S.

Bourne, L.S. (1976): Housing supply and housing market behaviour in residential development. in: Herbert, D.T.; Johnston, R.J. (Eds.): Social areas in cities. Vol. 1: Spatial processes and form. Chichester: Wiley, 111–158.

Bourne, L.S. (1981): The geography of housing. London: Edward Arnold.

Bovenkerk, F. (1978): Odmat zij anders zijn; patronen van rasdiscriminatie in Nederland. Meppel: Boom.

Bovenkerk, F. et al. (1985): Vreemd volk, gemengde gevoelens. Meppel: Boom.

Brasse, P. et al. (1984): Jonge Turken en Marokkanen op de Nederlandse arbeitsmarkt. Amsterdam: Instituut voor Sociale Geografie.

Braun, R. (1970): Sozio-kulturelle Probleme der Eingliederung italienischer Arbeitskräfte in der Schweiz. Zürich.

Brettell, C. (1981): Is the ethnic community inevitable? A comparison of the settlement patterns of Portuguese immigrants in Toronto and Paris. in: Journal of Ethnic Studies 9, 1–18.

Briot, F.; Verbunt, G. (1981): Immigrés dans la crise. Paris: Editions Ouvrières.

Brown, K. (1981): Race, class and culture: Towards a theoretization of the 'choice/constraint' concept. in: Jackson, P.; Smith, S. (Ed.): Social interaction and ethnic segregation. London: Academic Press (Institute of British Geographers; Special Publications 12).

Bucher, H. et al. (1983): Ausgewählte aktuelle Trends in der räumlichen Entwicklung. in: Informationen zur Raumentwicklung, 1149–1189.

Bühler, D. (1982): Individuelle Determinanten der residentiellen Verteilung von Ausländern im städtischen Raum. in: Hoffmann-Nowotny, H.-J.; Hondrich, K.-O. (Eds.): Ausländer in der Bundesrepublik Deutschland und in der Schweiz. Frankfurt a.M.: Campus Verlag, 375–448.

Bundeszentrale f. politische Bildung (Ed.) (1983): Ausländer. Informationen zur politischen Bildung 201.

Burgess, E. (1926): The growth of the city. in: Park, R.E.; Burgess, E.W. (Eds.): The city. Chicago: University of Chicago Press, 47–62.

Burtenshaw, D. et al. (1981): The city in West Europe. Chichester: John Wiley.

Butcher, I.; Ogden, P.E. (1984): West Indians in France: Migration and demographic change. in: Ogden, P.E. (Ed.): Migrants in modern France: four studies. Occasional Paper 23. Dept. of Geography and Earth Science. London: Queen Mary College.

Campanelli, V.; Delcourt, J. (1976): Nomadisme institute I et II. Brussels: Editions du Cerse.

Castells, M. (1975): Immigrant workers and class struggles in advanced capitalism: the Western European tradition. in: Politics and Society 5, 33–66.

Castells, M. (1977): The urban question. London: Edward Arnold.

Castells, M. (1983): The city and the grass-roots. London: Edward Arnold.

Castles, G.; Castles, S. (1971): Immigrant workers and class structure in France. in: Race 12, 303–315.

Castles, S. (1985): Postscript to the second edition. in: Castles, S.; Kosack, G.: Immigrant workers and class structure in Western Europe. London: Oxford University Press, 486–506.

Castles, S. et al. (1984): Here for good. Western Europe's new ethnic minorities. London: Pluto Press.

Castles, S.; Kosack, G. (1973): Immigrant workers and class structure in Western Europe. London: Oxford University Press.

Castles, S.; Kosack, G. (1985): Immigrant workers and class structure in Western Europe. 2nd ed. London: Oxford University Press.

Cater, J. (1981): The impact of Asian estate agents on patterns of ethnic residence. in: Jackson, P.; Smith, S. (Eds.): Social interaction and ethnic segregation. London: Academic Press, 163–184.

Ceaux, J. et al. (1979): Images et réalités d'un quartier populaire: le cas de Belleville. in: Espaces et Sociétés 30–31, 71–107.

Chaney, E. (1981): Migrant workers and national boundaries: the basis for rights and protections. in: Brown, P.G.; Shue, H. (Eds.): Boundaries. National autonomy and its limits. Totowa, New Jersey, 37–77.

Charef, M. (1983): Le thé au harem d'Archi Ahmed. Paris: Mercure.

Chauvire, Y.; Noin, D. (1980): Typologie socio-professionelle de l'agglomération Parisienne. in: Bulletin de l'Association de Géographes Français, 467, 51–61.

Chombart de Lauwe, P.H. et al. (1952): Paris et l'agglomération Parisienne. 2 Vol. Paris: Presses Universitaires Française.

Clark, J.R. (1975): Residential patterns and social integration of Turks in Cologne. in: Krane, R.E. (Ed.): Manpower mobility and cultural boundaries. Leiden, 61–76.

Cliff, A.D.; Ord, J.K. (1981): Spatial processes: models and applications. London: Pion.

Cox, K.R. (1983): Residential mobility, neighbourhood activism and neighbourhood problems. in: Political Geography Quarterly 2, 99–117.

De Lannoy, W. (1975): Residential segregation of foreigners in Brussels. in: Bulletin de la Société Belge d'Etudes Géographiques 44, 215–238.

De Lannoy, W. (1977): De residentiele differentiatie in de Brusselse agglomeratie. Brussels: unpubl. Ph.D. thesis, Vrije Universiteit Brussels.

De Lannoy, W. (1978): Atlas socio-geographique de Bruxelles-capitale. Brussels: Centrum voor Bevolkings- en Gezinsstudien (Studies en Documenten 11).

De Lannoy, W.; Kesteloot, C. (1985): La differenciation residentielle et les processus de ségrégation. in: La cité belge d'aujourd'hui, quel devenir? Special issue 154. Bulletin trimestriel du Credit Communal de Belgique, 137–150.

De Winter, L.; Kesteloot, C. (1983): De ruimtelijke sociale struktur van het Antwerpse stadsgewest. in: Acta Geographica Lovaniensia 23.

Delcourt, J. (1975): Le logement des travailleurs immigrés: un cas d'imprévoyance sociale. Brussels: Commission des Communautes Européennes.

Deley, M. (1983): French immigration policy since May 1981. in: International Migration Review 17, 196–211.

Dennis, R.; Clout, H. (1980): A social geography of England and Wales. Oxford: Pergamon Press.

Department of the Environment (1979): National dwelling and housing survey. London: HMSO

Department of the Environment (1980): National dwelling and housing survey 2, 3. London: HMSO

Desai, R. (1963): Indian immigrants in Britain. London: Oxford University Press.

Desplanques, G. (1985): Nuptialité et fécondité des étrangères. in: Economie et Statistique 179, 29–46.

Doherty, J. (1983): Racial conflict, industrial change and social control in post war Britain. in: Anderson, J. et al. (Eds.): Redundant spaces in cities and regions. London: Academic Press, 201–239.

Doleschal, J. (1977): Das Problem der ausländischen Arbeitskräfte in der schweizerischen Arbeitgeberpolitik der Nachkriegszeit. Unter besonderer Berücksichtigung der Jahre 1962 bis 1970. Bern: Peter Lang Verlag.

Drewe, P. et al. (1975): Segregation in Rotterdam: an explorative study on theory, data and policy. in: Tijdschrift voor Economische en Sociale Geografie 66.4, 204–216.

Droth, W.; Dangschat, J. (1985): Räumliche Konsequenzen der Entstehung 'neuer Haushaltstypen'. in: Friedrichs, J. (Ed.): Die Städte in den 80er Jahren. Demographische, ökonomische und technologische Entwicklungen. Opladen: Westdeutscher Verlag, 147–180.

Duclaud-Williams, R.H. (1976): The politics of housing in Britain and France. London: Heinemann.

Duncan, O.D.; Duncan, B. (1957): The Negro population of Chicago. Chicago University Press.

Duncan, O.D.; Lieberson, S. (1959): Ethnic segregation and assimilation. in: American Journal of Sociology 64, 364–374.

Economist (12.1.85): Private rented housing. 50–51.

Economist (2.2.85): Racial harassment: nasty neighbours. 22–23.

Economist (2.11.85): Immigration – fear of foreigners. 44–48.

El Gharbaoui, A. (1971): Les travailleurs Maghrébins immigrés dans la banlieue nord-ouest de Paris. in: Revue de Géographie du Maroc 19, 3–56.

Espaces Et Sociétés (1984): La cohabitation pluri-éthniques. Paris: Espaces et Sociétés 45.

Esser, H. (1980): Aspekte der Wanderungssoziologie. Darmstadt: Luchterhand (Soziologische Texte 119).

Esser, H. (1981): Aufenthaltsdauer und die Eingliederung von Wanderern zur theoretischen Interpretation soziologischer 'Variablen'. in: Zeitschrift für Soziologie 10, 76–97.

Esser, H. (1982a): Sozialökologische Bedingungen der Eingliederung ausländischer Arbeitnehmer im Ruhrgebiet – am Beispiel der Stadt Duisburg. Duisburg: Rhein-Ruhr-Institut für Sozialforschung und Politikberatung.

Esser, H. (1982b): Sozialräumliche Bedingungen des Spracherwerbs von Arbeitsmigranten. in: Zeitschrift für Soziologie 11, 279–306.

Esser, H. (1985): Ausländiche Bevölkerung und großstädtische Entwicklungen. in: Friedrichs, J. (Ed.): Die Städte in den 80er Jahren. Opladen: Westdeutscher Verlag, 117–146.

Etchebarne, S. (1983): L'urne et le xénophobe à propos des élections municipales à Roubaix en Mars 1983. in: Espaces, Populations, Sociétés II, 133–138.

Etcherelli, C. (1967): Elise ou la vraie vie. Paris: Denoel (Englisch translation 1970. London: André Deutsch).

Evans, D. J. (1984): The segregation of the new Commonwealth population in Wolverhampton Municipal Borough 1961–1981. North Staffordshire Polytechnic Dept. of Geography and Recreation Studies (Occasional Paper 3).

Evrensel, A. (1984): Ausländische Arbeiter in der Einwanderungsgesellschaft. Am Beispiel türkischer Arbeiter in der Stadt Zürich. Zürich: Dissertation im Geographischen Institut.

Fassmann, H. (1984): Mehrebenenanalyse − Fehlschlußproblem − Aggregierungsverzerrung. Wien (Geographischer Jahresbericht aus Österreich, XLI, 7−26).

Fincher, R. (1984): The state apparatus and the commodification of Quebec's housing cooperations. in: Political Geography Quarterly 3, 127−143.

Flett, H. (1977): Council housing and allocation of ethnic minorities. in: Working Papers on Ethnic Relations 5. SSRC Research Unit on Ethnic Relations.

Flett, H. (1979): Dispersal policies in council housing, arguments and evidence. in: New Community 7, 184−195.

Foner, N. (1979): West Indians in New York City and London: a comparative analysis. in: International Migration Review 13, 284−297.

Freeman, G.P. (1979): Immigrant labour and racial conflict in industrial societies. Princeton: Princeton University Press.

Friedmann, J.; Wolff, G. (1982): World city formation: an agenda for research and action. in: International Journal of Urban and Regional Research 6, 311−344.

Friedrichs, J. (1977): Stadtanalyse. Reinbek bei Hamburg: Rowohlt (rororo).

Friedrichs, J. (Ed.) (1982a): Spatial disparities and social behaviour: a reader in urban research. Hamburg: Christians Verlag.

Friedrichs, J. (1982b): Socio-spatial differentiation in the Hamburg region. in: Friedrich, J. (Ed.): Spatial disparities and social behaviour. Hamburg: Christians Verlag, 14−30.

Friedrichs, J. (Ed.) (1985): Die Städte in den 80er Jahren. Demographische, ökonomische und technologische Entwicklungen. Opladen: Westdeutscher Verlag.

Frisch, N. (1967): Öffentlchkeit als Partner. Frankfurt a.M.: Suhrkamp.

Gans, P. (1979): Bevölkerungsgeographische Veränderungen in der westlichen Unterstadt Mannheims zwischen 1970 und 1976. in: Mannheimer Geographische Arbeiten 2, 41−84.

Gans, P. (1981): Bevölkerungsentwicklung und Wanderungsverflechtungen in Ludwigshafen seit 1970. in: Mannheimer Geographische Arbeiten 10, 105−115.

Gans, P. (1983): Raumzeitliche Eigenschaften und Verflechtungen innerstädtischer Wanderungen in Ludwigshafen/Rhein zwischen 1971 und 1978. Eine empirische Analyse mit Hilfe des Entropiekonzeptes und der Informationsstatistik. Kiel: Kieler Geographische Schriften 59.

Gans, P. (1984): Innerstädtische Wohnungswechsel und -veränderungen in der Verteilung der Bevölkerung in Ludwigshafen: eine empirische Untersuchung über Wohnungsteilmärkte und Mobilitätsbarrieren. in: Geographische Zeitschrift 72, 81−98.

García Hortelano, J. (1967): Gente de Madrid. Barcelona: Seix Barral.

Gaspard, G.; Servan-Schreiber, C. (1984): La fin des immigrés. Paris: Seuil.

Gastarbeiter in Deutschland (1984): Gastarbeiter in Deutschland. Offenbach a.M.: Marplan Forschungsgesellschaft mbH. (Ausländerpolitische Themen).

Gatzweiler, H.-P.; Stiens, G. (1982): Regionale Mortalitätsunterschiede in der Bundesrepublik Deutschland. Daten und Hypothesen. in: Jahrbuch für Regionalwissenschaft 9, 36−63.

Gatzweiler, H.-P.; Meuter, H. (1983): Kleinräumige Raumbeobachtung − Informationen für Wohnungs- und Städtebaupolitik. in: Informationen zur Raumentwicklung, 1079−1106.

Geiger, F. (1975): Zur Konzentration von Gastarbeitern in alten Dorfkernen. in: Geographische Rundschau 27, 61−71.

Giddens, A. (1979): Central problems in social theory. London: Macmillan.

Giese, E. (1978): Räumliche Diffusion ausländischer Arbeitnehmer in der Bundesrepublik Deutschland 1960−1976. in: Die Erde 109, 92−110.

Giese, E.; Nipper, J. (1979): Zeitliche und räumliche Persistenzeffekte bei räumlichen Ausbreitungsprozessen. Analysiert am Beispiel der Ausbreitung ausländischer Arbeitnehmer in der Bundesrepublik Deutschland. Karlsruhe (Karlsruher Manuskripte zur Mathematischen und Theoretischen Wirtschafts- und Sozialgeographie 34).

Girard, A. (1977): Opinion publique, immigration et immigrés. in: Ethnologie Française 7, 219−228.

Glebe, G. (1984): Tendenzen ethnischer Segregation und Konzentration von Gastarbeiterminoritäten in Düsseldorf 1974–1982. in: Zeitschrift für Wirtschaftsgeographie 28, 91–111.

Globet, F. (1980): Distribution spatiale des revenus dans l'agglomération Parisienne. in: Bulletin de l'Association des Géographes Français 467, 63–68.

Gokalp, C.; Lamy, M.-L. (1977): L'immigration Maghrébine dans une commune industrielle de l'agglomération Parisienne: Gennevilliers. in: Les immigrés du Maghreb: études sur l'adaptation en milieu urbain. Paris: Presses Universitaires Française (Cahier de l'INED, 79), 327–404.

Gonzalo, A. (1979): L'immigration espagnole en Belgique, à Bruxelles et à Saint-Gilles. Leuven: unpubl. M.A. thesis, Katholieke Universiteit Leuven.

Good, D. (1984): Social processes at work in space: the distribution of immigrants in Luzern, Switzerland, 1980. Oxford: unpubl. Diss. for part of the B.A. Degree.

Gordon, M.M. (1964): Assimilation in American life. Oxford: Oxford University Press.

Gray, F. (1975): Nonexplanation in urban geography. in: Area 7, 228–235.

Gray, F.; Boddy, M. (1979): The origins and use of theory in urban geography: household mobility and filtering theory. in: Geoforum 10, 117–127.

Grimmeau, J.-P.; David-Valcke, A. (1978): Les cadres étrangers à Bruxelles. in: Revue Belge de Géographie 102.1, 33–41.

Gschwind, F.; Henckel, D. (1984): Innovationszyklen der Industrie – Lebenszyklen der Städte. in: Stadtbauwelt 82, 992–995.

Guillon, M. (1974): Les rapatries d'Algérie dans la region Parisienne. in: Annales de Géographie 83, 644–675.

Haddon, R. (1970): A minority in a welfare state: location of West Indians in the London housing market. in: New Atlantis 2, 80–123.

Haegen, H. van der (1981): Negenhonderdduizend vreemdelingen in Belgie: weerspiegeling van de recente sociaal-economische evolutie en de grensligging. in: Statistische Tijdschrift, 3–10.

Haegen, H. van der et al. (1983): The Belgian settlement system. in: Acta Geographica Lovaniensia 22, 251–363.

Hammer, T. (Ed.) (1985): European immigration policies. London: Cambridge University Press.

Hamnett, C. (1983): Housing and social change. in: Davies, R.L.; Champion, A.G. (Eds.): The future of the city centre. London: Academic Press, 145–164.

Harloe, M. (1981): The remmodification of capital. in: Harloe, M.; Lebas, E. (Eds.): City, class and capital. London: Edward Arnold, 17–50.

Harloe, M.; Martens, M. (1984): Comparative housing research. in: Journal of Social Policy 13, 255–277.

Harris, R. (1984): Residential segregation and class formation in the capitalist city: a review and directions for research. in: Progress in Human Geography 8, 26–49.

Harvey, D. (1973): Social justice and the city. London: Edward Arnold.

Haug, W. (1980): ', . . . und es kamen Menschen'. Ausländerpolitik und Fremdarbeit in der Schweiz 1914–1980. Basel: Z-Verlag.

Hegedus, J.; Tosics, I. (1983): Housing classes and housing policy: some changes in the Budapest housing market. in: International Journal of Urban and Regional Research 7, 467–494.

Helmert, U. (1982): Konzentrations- und Segregationsprozesse der ausländischen Bevölkerung in Frankfurt a.M. in: Hoffmann-Nowotny, H.-J.; Hondrich, K.O. (Eds.): Ausländer in der Bundesrepublik Deutschland und in der Schweiz. Frankfurt a.M.: Campus Verlag, 256–293.

Hervo, M.; Charras, M.-A. (1971): Bidonvilles. Paris: Maspero.

Heuer, H. (1985): Die veränderte ökonomische Basis der Städte. in: Friedrichs, J. (Ed.): Die Städte in den 80er Jahren. Demographische, ökonomische und technologische Entwicklungen. Opladen: Westdeutscher Verlag, 23–47.

Höllhuber, D. (1982); Innerstädtische Umzüge in Karlsruhe. Plädoyer für eine sozial-psychologisch fundierte Humangeographie. Erlangen (Erlanger Geographische Arbeiten 13).

Hoffmann-Nowotny, H.-J. (1973): Soziologie des Fremdarbeiterproblems: eine theoretische und empirische Analyse am Beispiel der Schweiz. Stuttgart: Ferdinand Enke Verlag.

Hoffmann-Nowotny, H.-J.; Hondrich, K.O. (Eds.) (1982): Ausländer in der Bundesrepublik Deutschland und in der Schweiz. Segregation und Integration. Eine vergleichende Untersuchung. Frankfurt a.M.: Campus Verlag.

Hoffmann-Nowotny, H.-J.; Hondrich, K.O. (1982): Zur Funktionsweise sozialer Systeme – Versuch eines Resümees und einer theoretischen Integration. in: Hoffmann-Nowotny, H.-J.; Hondrich, K.O. (Eds.): Ausländer in der Bundesrepublik Deutschland und in der Schweiz. Frankfurt a.M.: Campus Verlag, 569–635.

Hoffmeyer-Zlotnik, J. (1977): Gastarbeiter im Sanierungsgebiet. Hamburg: Christians Verlag (Beiträge zur Stadtforschung 1).

Hoffmeyer-Zlotnik, J. (1982): Community change and invasion: the case of Turkish guestworkers. in: Friedrichs, J. (Ed.): Spatial disparities and social behaviour. Hamburg: Christians Verlag, 114–126.

Hofman, M. (1984): Sociaal-geografische analyse van een Turkse etnische buurt in Schaarbeek. Brussels: unpubl. licence thesis, Vrije Universiteit Brussels.

Holzner, L. (1982): The myth of Turkish ghettos: a geographic case study of West German responses towards a foreign minority. in: The Journal of Ethnic Studies 9, 4, 65–85.

Hoorn, F. van (1984): De woonsituatie van Mediterranneen: veronderende woonstandigheden in Utrecht. Utrecht (Utrechtse Geografische Studie 34).

Hottes, K.-H. (1975): Die Integration der Gastarbeiter in die Stadt als soziales System. in: Esenstadt, M.G.; Kaltefleiter, W. (Eds.): Minoritäten in Ballungsräumen. Bonn: Eichholz Verlag (Sozialwissenschaftliche Studien zur Politik 6), 77–100.

Hottes, K.-H.; Meyer, U. (1976): Siedlungsstrukturelle Auswirkung der Verteilung ausländischer Arbeitnehmer in den Gemeinden. Ein Vorbericht. Bochum.

Hottes, K.-H.; Meyer, U. (1977): Siedlungsstrukturelle Auswirkungen der Verteilung von Ausländern in den Gemeinden. Integration ausländicher Arbeitnehmer. Siedlungs-, Wohnungs- und Freizeitwesen. in: Studien zur Kommunalpolitik, Schriftenreihe des Instituts f. Kommunalwissenschaften 16, 283–435.

Hottes, K.-H.; Pötke, P.M. (1976): Herkunft und Verteilung ausländischer Arbeitnehmer im Ruhrgebiet und Bergisch-Märkischen Lande. Bochum (Bochumer Geographische Arbeiten, Sonderreihe 6).

Hottes, K.-H.; Pötke, P.M. (1977): Ausländische Arbeitnehmer im Ruhrgebiet und im Bergisch-Märkischen Land. Paderborn: Ferdinand Schoeningh.

Husbands, C. (1981): Contemporary right-wing extremism in Western European democracies: a review article. in: European Journal of Political Research 9, 75–99.

Hussmanns, R. et al. (1983): Die demographische Lage in der Bundesrepublik. in: Zeitschrift für Bevölkerungswissenschaft 9, 291–362.

INED (1977): Les immigrés du Maghreb: etudes sur l'adaptation en milieu urbaine. Paris: Presses Universitaires Française (Cahier de l'INED, 79).

Ipsen, D. (1978): Wohnsituation und Wohninteresse ausländischer Arbeiter in der Bundesrepublik Deutschland. in: Leviathan 6, 558–573.

Ipsen, D. (1981): Segregation, Mobilität und die Chancen auf dem Wohnungsmarkt: eine empirische Untersuchung in Mannheim. in: Zeitschrift für Soziologie 10, 256–272.

Ipsen, D.; Mussel, C. (1981): Thesen zur Wohnungssituation, zur alten Wohnungspolitik und zur Notwendigkeit einer Neuen. in: Leviathan 9, 386–404.

Jackson, P.; Smith, S.J. (1981): Introduction. in: Jackson, P.; Smith, S. (Eds.): Social interaction and ethnic segregation. London: Academic Press (Institute of British Geographers, Special Publications 12), 1–17.

Jackson, P.; Smith, S.J. (1984): Exploring Social Geography. London: Allen and Unwin.

Jackson, P.; Smith, S.J. (Eds.) (1981): Social interaction and ethnic segregation. London: Academic Press. (Institute of British Geographers, Special Publications 12).

Jacquemet, G. (1975): Belleville aux XIXe et XXe siècles: une méthode d'analyse de la croissance urbaine à Paris. in: Annales: Economies, Sociétés, Civilisations 30, 819–843.

Jessen, J. et al. (1978): Untersuchungen zur Mobilität der Wohnbevölkerung in Stadtregionen, eine Kritik anwendungsorientierter Sozialforschung. in: Leviathan 6, 519–535.

Johnson, R.W. (1985): Who are Le Pen's legions? in: New Society. 21 March, 435–437.

Johnston, R.J. (1980): City and society. Harmondsworth; Penguin.

Johnston, R.J. (1984a): The world is our oyster. in: Transactions, Institute of British Geographers 9, 443–459.

Johnston, R.J. (1984b): Marxist political economy, the state and political geography. in: Progress in Human Geography 8, 473–492.

Joly, J. (1980): Evolution démographique et sociale de Grenoble, 1976–1979. in: Revue de Géographie Alpine 68, 5–20.

Jones, A.M. (1980): Spatial and social mobility of foreign immigrants in Marseille 1962–1975. Oxford: Dr. Phil. thesis.

Jones, A.M. (1984): Housing and immigrants in Marseille, 1962–1975. in: Ogden, P.E. (Ed.): Migrants in modern France: four studies, Occasional Paper 23, Dept. of Geography and Earth Science. London: Queen Mary College, 29–41.

Jones, P.C. (1984): International migration and demographic change: some evidence from the Rhone departement. in: Ogden, P.E. (Ed.): Migrants in modern France: four studies. Occasional Paper 23, Dept. of Geography and Earth Science. London: Queen Mary College, 9–28.

Jones, P.C.; Johnston, R.J. (1985): Economic development, labour migration and urban social geography. in: Erdkunde 39, 12–18.

Jones, P.N. (1978): The distribution and diffusion of the coloured population in England and Wales. in: Transactions of the Institute of British Geographers 3, 515–532.

Jones, P.N. (1979): Ethnic areas in British cities. in: Herbert, D.T.; Smith, D.M. (Eds.): Social problems and the city. Oxford: Oxford University Press, 158–185.

Jones, P.N. (1983): Ethnic population succession in a West German city, 1974–80: the case of Nuremberg. in: Geography 80, 121–132.

Jones, T.P.; McEvoy, D. (1978): Race and space in cloud-cuckoo land. in: Area 10, 162–166.

Jouret, B. (1972): La definition spatiale du phenomène urbain bruxellois. Brussels: Editions de l'Université de Bruxelles.

Kantrowitz, N. (1969): Ethnic and racial segregation in the New York metropolis. in: American Journal of Sociology 74, 685–695.

Kantrowitz, N. (1981): Ethnic segregation: social reality and academic myth. in: Peach, C.; Robinson, V.; Smith, S. (Eds.): Ethnic segregation in cities. London: Croom Helm, 43–60.

Keeble, D. (1978): Industrial decline in the inner city and conurbation. in: Transactions of the Institute of British Geographers 3, 101–114.

Kempen, R. van; Klerk, L. de (1984): Turken en Surinamers op de Amsterdamse woningmarkt 1973–1982. Amsterdam: Instituut voor Sociale Geografie.

Kemper, F.-J. (1984): Die Bedeutung des Lebenszyklus-Konzepts für die Analyse intra-regionaler Wanderungen. in: Colloquium Geographicum 18, 180–212.

Kennedy-Brenner, C. (1979): Foreign workers and immigrant policy: the case of France. Paris: Development Centre of the OECD.

Kesteloot, C. (1977): Some geographical aspects of proverty at the neighbourhood level. in: Acta Geographica Lovaniensia 15, 109–136.

Kesteloot, C. (1980): De ruimtelijke sociale struktuur van Brussel-Hoofdstad. Acta Geographica Lovaniensia 19.

Kesteloot, C. (1980): La structure sociale de l'éspace Bruxellois: revelateur des enjeux urbains. in: Contradictions 26, 91–121.

Kesteloot, C. (1985a): De geografische spreiding van de buitenlandse minderheden in Belgie; beschrijvingen en verklaringen. in: Martens, A.; Moulaert, F. (Eds.): Buitenlandse minderheden in Vlaanderen-Belgie. Kapellen: De Nederlandsche Boekhandel, 75–91.

Kesteloot, C. (1985b): La géographie radicale en Belgique. in: L'Espace Géographique, forthcoming.

Kiefer, L. (1978): Hoe huisvest Europa zijn gastarbeiders? in: Wonen 76, 22–25.

Kiefer, L. (1982): De woonomstandigheden can de gastarbeiders. in: Wonen 90, 40–47.

King, R. (1976): The evolution of international labour, concerning the EEC. in: Tijdschrift voor Economische en Sociale Geografie 67, 66–82.

Knops, G. (1977): De stadsvernieuwing in Klein Begijnhof-Heembeemd te Mechelen: een benadering ervan als geografisch probleem. in: Acta Geographica Lovaniensia 15, 137–145.

Knox, P. (1982): Urban social geography. London: Longman.

Kok, J.B. (1982): Het Rotterdamse spreidingsbeleid van ethnische minderheden. in: De Aardrijkskunde 3, 231–253.

Kommission 'Ausländerpolitik' (1983): Bericht vom 24. Februar 1983. Bonn: Der Bundesminister des Innern.

Korte, H. (1980): Einbürgerung oder Auswanderung? Ergebnisse und Interpretationen sozialwissenschaftlicher Forschung. in: Freund, W.S. (Ed.): Gastarbeiter: Integration oder Rückkehr. Grundfragen der Ausländerpolitik. Neustadt/Weinstraße, 40–55.

Korte, H. (1982): Politische Mitbestimmung von Ausländern. in: Schulerji-Hartje, U.K.; Schulz zur Wiesch, J. (Eds.): Beiträge zur Ausländerpolitik – Seminarberichte. Berlin: Deutsches Institut für Urbanistik (Materialien 4/82), 35–43.

Korte, H. (1983): Migration und ihre sozialen Folgen. Göttingen: Vandenhoek und Ruprecht.

Kreibich, V. (1982): Determinanten des Standortverhaltens von Haushalten. in: Wohnungspolitik und regionale Siedlungsentwicklung. Hannover. (Veröffentlichungen d. Akademie f. Raumforschung und Landesplanung, Bd. 146, Forschungs- und Sitzungsberichte), 19–43.

Kreibich, V. (1985): Wohnversorgung und Wohnstandortverhalten. in: Friedrichs, J. (Ed.): Die Städte in den 80er Jahren. Demographische, ökonomische und technologische Entwicklung. Opladen: Westdeutscher Verlag, 181–195.

Kreibich, V. et al. (1980): Wohnversorgung und regionale Mobilität am Beispiel München. Dortmund (Beiträge zur Raumplanung).

Kreibich, V.; Petri, A. (1982): Locational behaviour of households in a constrained housing market. in: Environment and Planning A 14, 1195–1210.

Kremer, M.; Spangenberg, H. (1980): Assimilation ausländischer Arbeitnehmer in der Bundesrepublik Deutschland. Königstein/Ts.: Hanstein (Materialien zur Arbeitsemigration und Ausländerbeschäftigung).

Kritz, M.M. (Ed.) (1983): U.S. immigration and refugee policy. Lexington, MA.: D.C. Heath.

Krunkelsven, M.L. van (1979): Vreemdelingen te Beringen, segregatie of niet? Leuven: unpubl. lincence thesis. Katholieke Universiteit Leuven.

Lambert, J. et al. (1978): Housing policy and the state: allocation, access and control. London: Macmillan.

Laumann, W. (1984): Ausländerhaushalte in öffentlich geförderten Wohnungen – Wirkungen und Grenzen der Belegungspolitik. in: Ausländerintegration – Politik ohne Alternative. Bochum: Deutscher Verband für Angewandte Geographie, DVAG (Materialien zur Angewandten Geographie 9), 63–71.

Le Monde (1984): Les deuxièmes élections Européennes. Paris: Dossiers et Documents.

Le Monde (12.3.85): La front nationale confirmé son implantation. p. 7.

Le Pen, J.-M. (1984): Les Français d'abord. Paris: Carrère Lafon.

Lebon, A. (1979): L'aide au retour des travailleurs étrangers. in: Economie et Statistique 113, 37–46.

Lebon, A. (1981): La contribution des étrangers a la population de la France entre le 1er janvier 1946 et le 1er janvier 1980. Paris: Ministère du Travail, Service des Etudes et de la Statistique.

Lebon, A. (1984): La population étrangère au recensement de 1982, problèmes économiques. in: Documentation Française. 16 august 1984, No. 1.886.

Lee, T.R. (1977): Race and residence: the concentration and dispersal of immigrants in London. Oxford: Clarendon Press (Oxford Research Studies in Geography).

Lefort, F. (1980): Du bidonville a l'expulsion. Paris: C.I.E.M.M.

Leitner, H. (1982): Residential segregation, socio-economic integration and behavioural assimilation: the case of Yugoslav migrant workers in Vienna. in: Cultural identity and structural marginalization of migrant workers. Strassburg: European Science Foundation (Human Migration II), 59–78.

Leitner, H. (1983): Gastarbeiter in der städtischen Gesellschaft. Frankfurt a.M.: Campus Verlag.

Leitner, H. (1986): The state and the foreign worker problem. A case study of the Federal Republic of Germany, Switzerland, and Austria. Environment and Planning C: Government and Policy 4 (forthcoming).

Leman, J. (1980): Un quasi-ghetto à Anderlecht. in: La Revue Nouvelle 72, 9, 191–194.

Lemieux, E. (1983): Qu'est-ce qu'elle a, ma Gueule? Paris: Le Hameau.

Leonhard, S. (1982): Urban managerialism: a period of transition. in: Progress in Human Geography 6, 190–215.

Ley, D. (1974): The inner city as a frontier outpost. Washington D.C.: Association of American Geographers.

Ley, D. (1983): A social geography of the city. New York: Harper and Row.

Lichtenberger, E. (1976): The changing nature of European urbanization. in: Berry, B.J. (Ed.): Urbanization and counter-urbanization. Beverly Hills, Ca., 81–108.

Lichtenberger, E. (1984): Gastarbeiter: Leben in zwei Gesellschaften. Wien: Hermann Böhlau Verlag.

Lieberson, S. (1963): Ethnic patterns in American cities. New York: Free Press.

Lieberson, S. (1981): An asymmetrical approach to segregation. in: Peach, C.; Robinson, V.; Smith, S. (Eds.): Ethnic segregation in cities. London: Croom Helm.

Llaumett, M. (1984): Politique et immigration ou 'l'effet le Pen'. in: Presses et Immigrés en France 115.

Loll, B.-U. (1982): Guestworkers' assimilation in West Germany. in: Friedrichs, J. (Ed.): Spatial disparities and social behaviour – a reader in urban research. Hamburg: Christians Verlag, 127–140.

Lomas, G. et al. (1975): The inner city. London: London Council of Social Service.

Malhotra, M.K. (1981): The psychological, social and educational problems of primary school children of different nationalities in West Germany. in: Ethnic and Racial Studies 4, 486–500.

Mallet-Joris, F. (1970): La maison de papier. Paris: Bernard Grasset. (English translation 1971. London: W.H. Allen).

Manhardt, M. (1977): Die Abgrenzung homogener städtischer Teilgebiete. Hamburg: Christians Verlag (Beiträge zur Forschung).

Marange, J.; Lebon, A. (1982): L'insertion des jeunes d'origine étrangère dans la société française. Paris: La Documentation Française.

Marie, C.-V. (1983): L'immigration clandestine en France. in: Hommes et Migrations. Documents 1059, 4–21.

Marplan GmbH (1984): Gastarbeiter in Deutschland 1984 – Ausländerpolitische Themen. Bonn: Bundesministerium des Innern.

Marques-Balsa, C.; Martins-Boudru, F. (1978): Besoins et aspirations des families etrangeres établies en Belgique. Brussels (Programme National de Recherches en Science Sociales. Vols. 20A et 20B. Services du Premier Ministre; Programmation de la Politique Scientifique).

Martens, A. (1976): Les immigrés, flux et reflux d'une main d'oeuvre d'appoint. Brussels: Editions Vie Ouvriere.

Martens, A.; Moulaert, F. (Eds.) (1985): Buitenlandes minderheden in Vlaanderen-Belgie. Kapellen: De Nederlandsche Boekhandel.

Martens, A.; Wolf, S. (1974): Buitenlandse werknemers op de huisvestingsmarkt. in: Bevolking en Gezin 3, 349–380.

Martens, M. (1985): Owner-occupied housing in Europe: postwar developments and dilemmas. in: Environment and Planning A 17, 605–624.

Mas, P. de; Haffmans, M. (1985): De gezinshereniging van Marokkanen in Nederland, 1968–1984. Den Haag: Ministerie van Soziale Zaken en Werkgelegenheid.

McAllister, I.; Studlar, D.T. (1984): The electoral geography of immigrant groups in Britain. in: Electoral Studies 3.2, 139–150.

Mehrländer, U. (1974a): Probleme der Ausländerbeschäftigung in der BRD, in Österreich und in der Schweiz. Bonn: Friedrich Ebert Stiftung.

Mehrländer, U. (1974b): Wohnverhältnisse ausländischer Arbeitnehmer in Deutschland. Berlin: Wissenschaftszentrum Berlin. (Seminar-Serien des Internationalen Instituts für vergleichende Gesellschaftsforschung).

Mehrländer, U. (1978): Bundesrepublik Deutschland. in: Gehmacher, E.; Kubat, D.; Mehrländer, U. (Eds.): Ausländerpolitik im Konflikt. Bonn: Neue Gesellschaft GmbH.

Mehrländer, U. (1981): Situation ausländischer Arbeitnehmer und ihrer Familienangehörigen in der Bundesrepublik Deutschland. Bonn: Bundesminister für Arbeit und Sozialordnung.

Merlin, P. (1986): Inner-city housing policies and the creation of ghettos of marginal groups: the case of Paris. in: Heinritz, G.; Lichtenberger, E. (Eds.): The crisis of the city and the rise of suburbia. Wiesbaden: Steiner Verlag (in press).

Mertins, G. (1983): Zwischen Integration und Remigration – die Gastarbeiterpolitik der Bundesrepublik nach 1973. in: Geographische Rundschau 35, 46–53.

Mertins, G.; Akpinar, U. (1981): Türkische Migratenfamilien. Familienstrukturen in der Türkei und in der Bundesrepublik. Angleichungsprobleme türkischer Arbeiterfamilien: Beispiel West Berlin. 3. Aufl. Bonn.

Mik, G. (1983): Residential segregation in Rotterdam. in: Tijdschrift vorr Economische en Sociale Geographie 74, 74–86.

Mik, G. et al. (1980): Segregatie in Rotterdam, feiten en beleid. Rotterdam: Erasmus Universiteit.

Miller, M. J. (1982): The political impact of foreign labor: a re-evaluation of the western European experience. in: International Migration Review 16.1, 27–60.

Moulaert, F. (1983): Labor migration and the role of the state. in: Moulaert, F.; Salinas, P. (Eds.): Regional analysis and the new international division of labor. Boston: Kluwer Nijhoff, 145–161.

Moulaert, F.; Martens, A. (1982): Arbeidsproces, sectoriale dynamiek en gastarbeid in Belgie (1970–1977). in: Amersfoort, J.M.M. van; Entzinger, H.B. (Eds.): Immigrant en samenleving. Deventer: Van Loghum Slaterus, 77–98.

Moulaert, F.; Derycke, P. (1984): The employment of migrant workers in West Germany and Belgium; a comparative illustration of the life-cycle of economic migration (1960–1980). in: International Migration 22.3, 178–198.

Muehlgassner, D. (1984): Der Wanderungsprozeß. in: Lichtenberger, E. (Ed.): Gastarbeiter: Leben in zwei Gesellschaften. Wien: Bohlau Verlag.

Munscher, A. (1979): Ausländische Familien in der Bundesrepublik Deutschland – Familiennachzug und generatives Verhalten. München: Deutsches Jugendinstitut. (Materialien zum Dritten Familienbericht der Bundesregierung).

Musterd, S. (1984): Buurten 'gesloten' voor Mediterranen? Enkele kanttekeningen bij Tilburgse woningmarkt. in: Geografisch Tijdschrift 18.4, 279–284.

Neef, R. (1981): Wohnungsversorgung und 'neue Wohnungsnot'. in: Leviathan 9, 332–353.

Netherlands Central Bureau Statistics (1984): Statistical yearbook of the Netherlands 1983. Den Haag: Staatsuitgeverij.

Niederberger, J.M. (1982): Die politisch-administrative Regelung von Einwanderung und Aufenthalt von Ausländern in der Schweiz. Strukturen, Prozesse, Wirkungen. in: Hoffmann-Nowotny, H.-J. Hondrich, K.O. (Eds.): Ausländer in der Bundesrepublik Deutschland und in der Schweiz. Frankfurt a.M.: Campus Verlag, 11–123.

Nipper, J. (1983): Räumliche Autoregressivstrukturen in raum-zeitvarianten sozioökonomischen Prozessen. Gießen (Gießener Geographische Schriften 53). .

Noel, F. (1984): De leegstand in de Brusselse agglomeratie. Brussels: Koning Boudewijnstiching.

Noin, D. et al. (1984): Atlas des Parisiens. Paris: Masson.

Nouvel Observateur (1984): Issue of 22–28 June.

Offe, C. (1973): 'Krisen des Krisenmanagement'. Elemente einer politischen Krisentheorie. in: Jaenicke, M. (Ed.): Herrschaft und Krise. Opladen: Westdeutscher Verlag, 197–233.

Offe, C. (1978): Political authority and class structures. in: Connerton, P. (Ed.): Critical sociology. London: Penguin Books, 388–421.

Office of Population (1981): OPCS monitor. in: General household survey, GHS 81/1. Preliminary results for 1980. London: HMSO.

Office of Population Censuses and Surveys (1974): Census 1971 Great Britain. Age, marital condition and general tables. London: HMSO.

Office of Population Censuses and Surveys (1975): Population trends. 2. London: HMSO.

Ogden, P.E. (1977): Foreigners in Paris: residential segregation in the nineteenth and twentieht centuries. in: Occasional Paper 11. Dept. of Geography. London: Queen Mary College.

Ogden, P.E. (1982): France faces immigration with difficulty. in: Geographical Magazine LIV, 318–323.

Ogden, P.E. (1985): France: recession, politics and migration policy. in: Geography 70, 158–162.

Ogden, P.E.; Huss, M.M. (1982): Demography and pronatalism in France in the nineteenth and twentieth centuries. in: Journal of Historical Geography 8.3, 282–298.

Ogden, P.E.; Winchester, H.P.M. (1986): France. in: Findlay, A.M.; Whithe, P.E. (Eds.): West Europe population in change. London: Croom Helm (in press).

O'Loughlin, J. (1980): Distribution and migration of foreigners in German cities. in: Geographical Review 70, 253–275.

O'Loughlin, J. (1983): Spatial inequalities in Western cities: a comparison of North American and German urban areas. in: Social Indicators Research 13, 85–212.

O'Loughlin, J. (1984): The geographic distribution of foreigners in West Germany. in: Regional Studies 19.4, 365–377.

O'Loughlin, J.; Glebe, G. (1980): Faktorökologie der Stadt Düsseldorf. Ein Beitrag zur Sozialraumanalyse. Düsseldorf (Düsseldorfer Geographische Schriften 16).

O'Loughlin, J.; Glebe, G. (1981): The location of foreigners in Düsseldorf: a causal analysis in a path-analytic framework. in: Geographische Zeitschrift 69, 81–97.

O'Loughlin, J.; Glebe, G. (1984a); Intra urban migration in West German cities. in: Geographical Review 74.1, 1–23.

O'Loughlin, J.; Glebe, G. (1984b): Residential segregation of foreigners in German cities. in: Tijdschrift voor Economische en Sociale Geografie 74.4, 373–384.

Oriol, M. (1981): Report on Studies of the human and cultural aspects of migration in Western Europe 1918–1979. Strassburg: European Science Foundation.

Ottens, H.F.L.; Ter-Welle, J.G.P. (1983): Recent urban research at Utrecht. in: Tijdschrift voor Economische en Sociale Geografie 74, 387–396.

Ozkan, Y. 1974): The legal status of foreign workers in the Federal Republic of Germany with special focus on Turkish laborers. Berlin: Wissenschaftszentrum Berlin. (Internationales Institut für vergleichende Gesellschaftsforschung: P/74–9a).

Paddison, R. et al. (1984:) Shop windows as an indicator of retail modernity in the Third World city: the case of Tunis. in: Area 16, 227–231.

Pahl, R. (1975): Whose City? 2nd ed. Harmondsworth: Penguin Books.

Pahl, R.E. (1980): Employment, work and the domestic division of labour. in: International Journal of Urban and Regional research 4, 1–20.

Paine, S. (1974): Exporting workers: the Turkish case. Cambridge: Cambridge University Press.

Paine, S. (1977): The changing role of migrant workers – the advanced capitalist economies in Western Europe. in: Griffiths, R.T. (Ed.): Government, labour and business in European capitalism. London: Europotentials Press, 195–225.

Palm, R. (1978): Spatial segmentation of the urban housing market. in: Economic Geography 54, 210–221.

Palm, R. (1983): The geography of American cities. New York: Oxford University Press.

Panciera, S.; Plevoets-Quivy, M. (1976): Les travailleurs immigrés dans l'agglomération bruxelloise. Brussels: Agglomération de Bruxelles.

Parker, J.; Dugmore, K. (1976): Colour and allocation of GLC housing. The report of the GLC Lettings Survey 1974–75. London: Greater London Council (Research Report 21).

Parker, J.; Dugmore, K. (1977/78): Race and allocation of public housing. GLC Service. in: New Community 6, 27–40.

Parkin, F. (1979): Marxism and class theory: a bourgeois critique. London: Tavistock Publications.

Patterson, S. (1963): Dark strangers. London: Tavistock Publications.

Peach, C. (1965): West Indian migration to Britain: the economic factors. in: Race 7, 31–47.

Peach, C. (1966): Factors affecting the distribution of West Indians in Great Britain. in: Transactions of the Institute of British Geographers 38, 151–163.

Peach, C. (1968): West Indian migration to Britain: a social geography. London: Oxford University Press for the Institute of Race Relations.

Peach, C. (1974): Ethnic segregation in Sydney and intermarriage patterns. in: Australian Geographical Studies 12, 219–229.

Peach, C. (1975a): Urban social segregation. London: Longman.

Peach, C. (1975b): Immigrant in the inner city. in: Geographical Journal 141, 372–379.

Peach, C. (1978/79): British unemployment cycles and West Indian immigration 1955–1974. in: New Community 7, 40–44.

Peach, C. (1981): Conflicting interpretations of segregation. in: Jackson, P.; Smith, S. (Eds.): Social interaction and social segregation. London: Academic Press, Special Publication of the Institute of British Geographers, 19–33.

Peach, C. (1982): The growth and distribution of the black population in Britain 1945–1980. in: Coleman, D.A., (Ed.): The demography of immigrants and minority groups in the United Kingdom. London: Academic Press, 23–42.

Peach, C. (1983): The dissolution and growth of ethnic areas in American cities. in: Patten, J.: The expanding city. London: Academic Press, 277–294.

Peach, C. (1985): Immigrants and the 1981 urban riots in Britain. in: Van der Knaap, G.A.; White, P.E. (Eds.): Contemporary studies of migration. Norwich: Geo Books, 143–154.

Peach, C. et al. (Eds.) (1981): Ethnic segregation in cities. London: Croom Helm.

Peach, C.; Shah, S. (1980): The contribution of council house allocation to West Indian desegregation in London, 1971–72. in: Urban Studies 17, 333–341.

Peach, C.; Winchester, S.W.C. (1974): Birthplace, ethnicity and the enumeration of West Indians, Indians, and Pakistanis. in: New Community 3, 386–393.

Peach, C.; Winchester, S.; Woods, R. (1975): The distribution of coloured immigrants in Britain. in: Urban Affairs Annual Review 9, 395–419.

Penninx, R. (1979): Voorstudie ethnische minderheden. in: Etnische minderheden (Rapport van de Wetenschappelijke Raad voor het Regeringsbeleid). The Hague: Staatsuitgeverij.

Petras, E. (1980): The role of national boundaries in a cross-national labour market. in: International Journal of Urban and Regional Research 4, 157–195.

Petri, A. (1984): Die Notlösung als Dauerzustand. in: Ausländerintegration – Politik ohne Alternative. Bochum: Deutscher Verband für Angewandte Geographie, DVAG (Materialien zur Angewandten Geographie 9), 55–62.

Phillips, D. (1981): The social and spatial segregation of Asians in Leicester. in: Jackson, P.; Smith, S.I. (Eds.): Social interaction and ethnic segregation. London: Academic Press, 101–122.

Philpott, S. (1977): The Montserratians: migration, dependency and the maintenance of island ties in England. in: Watson, J.L. (Ed.): Between two cultures: migrants and minorities in Britain. Oxford: Blackwell Scientific Press.

Philpott, T.L. (1978): The slum and the ghetto. New York: Oxford University Press.

Pinch, S.; Williams, A. (1977): Changes in the distribution of immigrants in the British urban system, 1961–1971. Paper presented to the Urban Studies Group. London: Institute of British Geographers, King's College, 13.5.77, Mimeo.

Piore, M. (1978): Birds of passage: migrant labor and industrial societies. New York: Cambridge University Press.

Plummer, K. (1983): Documents of life. London: G. Allen and Unwin.

Poinard, M. (1979): Le million des immigrés: analyse de l'utilisation de l'aide au retour par les travailleurs portugais en France. in: Révue Géographique des Pyrénées et du Sud-Ouest 50, 511–539.

Portes, A; (1978): Toward a structural analysis of illegal migration. in: International Migration Review 12, 469–484.

Portes, A.; Walton, J. (1981): Labor, class and the international system. New York: Academic Press.

Power, J. (1977): Western Europe's migrants. London: Pergamon Press.

Power, J. et al. (1979): Migrant workers in Western Europe and the United States. Oxford: Pergamon Press.

Praag, C.S. van (1981): Allochtonen, huisvesting en spreiding. The Hague: Sociaal Cultureel Planbureau.

Pratt, G. (1982): Class analysis and urban domestic property: a critical reexamination. in: International Journal of Urban and Regional Research 6, 481–502.

Pred, A. (1976): Business thoroughfares as expressions of urban Negro culture. in: Ernst, R.T.; Hugg, L. (Eds.): Black America: geographic perspectives. Garden City, N.Y.: Anchor, 178–199.

Price, C. (1969): The study of assimilation. in: Jackson, J.A. (Ed.): Migration. Cambridge: Cambridge University Press.

Priemus, H. (1983): Squatters in Amsterdam: urban social movement, urban managers or someting else? in: International Journal of Urban and Regional Research 7, 417–427.

Prinssen, J. (1983): Buitenlandse werknemers en de verdeling van huurwoningen. Nijmegen: Instituut voor Toegepaste Sociologie.

Ranger, J. (1977): Droite et gauche dans les élections de Paris (1965–1977). in: Révue française de Science Politique 27, 789–819.

Reimann, H. (1976): Die Wohnsituation der Gastarbeiter. in: Reimann, H.; Reimann, H. (Eds.): Gastarbeiter. München: Wilhelm Goldman Verlag, 131–148.

Reister, H. (1983): Ausländerbeschäftigung und Ausländerpolitik in der Bundesrepublik Deutschland. Berlin (Publikationen der Fachhochschule für Verwaltung und Rechtspflege, 38).

Repräsentativuntersuchung 1980 (1981): Situation der ausländischen Arbeitnehmer und ihrer Familienangehörigen in der Bundesrepublik Deutschland. Bonn: Der Bundesminister für Arbeit und Sozialordnung (Forschungsbericht Sozialforschung 50).

Rex, J. (1968): The sociology of the zone in transition. in: Pahl, R. (Ed.): Readings in urban sociology. Oxford: Pergamon, 211–231.

Rex, J. (1981a): A working paradigm for race relations research. in: Ethnic and Racial Studies 4, 1–25.

Rex, J, (1981b): Urban segregation and innercity policy in Great Britain. in: Peach, C.; Robinson, V.; Smith, S. (Eds.): Ethnic segregation in cities. London: Croom Helm, 25–42.

Rex, J. (1982): The 1981 urban riots in Britain. in: International Journal of Urban and Regional Research 6, 99–113.

Rex, J.; Moore, R. (1967): Race, community and conflict. Oxford: Oxford University Press.

Rex, J.; Tomlinson, S. (1979): Colonial immigrants in a British city. London: Routledge and Kegan Paul.

Rist, R.C. (1978): Guestworkers in Germany; the prospects for pluralism. New York: Praeger.

Robinson, V. (1979): The segregation of Asians within a British city: theory and practice. in: Research Paper 22. Oxford: School of Geography.

Robinson, V. (1980): Correlates of Asian immigration: 1959–1974. in: New Community 8, 115–122.

Robinson, V. (1981): The development of Asian settlement in Britain and the myth of return. in: Peach, C.; Robinson, V.; Smith, S. (Eds.): Ethnic segregation in cities. London: Croom Helm.

Rocha Trinidade, M.B. (1977); Structure sociale et familiale d'origine dans l'émigration au Portugal. in: Éthnologie Française 7, 277–284.

Rogers, R. (1981): Incentives to return: patterns and migrants' responses. in: Kritz, M.M.; Keely, Ch.B.; Tomasi, S.M. (Eds.): Global trends in migration: theory and research on international population movements. New York: Center for Migration Studies, 338–364.

Roosens, E. et al. (1979): Omtrent de achterstelling van immigranten in Belgie. Leuven: Acco.

Rothammer, D. (1974): Integration ausländischer Arbeitnehmer und ihrer Familien im Städtevergleich. Probleme, Maßnahmen, Steuerungsinstrumente. Berlin.

Runnymede Trust (1975): Race and council housing in London. London: Runnymede Trust.

Salah, A. (1973): La communauté Algerienne dans le Department du Nord. Paris: Editions Universitaires.

Salt, J. (1985): Europe's foreign labour migrants in transition. in: Geography 70, 151–157.

Santana, E. (1980): Les immigrés dans la ville: analyse d'un espace écologique à Toulouse. in: Révue Géographique des Pyrénées et du Sud-Ouest 51, 137–151.

Sarramea, J. (1985): Géographie électorale de la France. in: Information Géographique 3, 95–108.

Saunders, P. (1978): Domestic property and social class. in: International Journal of Urban and Regional Research 2, 233–251.

Saunders, P. (1980): Urban Politics. Harmondsworth: Penguin.

Saunders, P. (1983): Social theory and the urban question: a response to Paris and Kirby. in: Environment and Planning D, 234–239.

Scargill, I. (1983): Urban France. London: Croom Helm.

Schildmeier, A. (1975): Integration und Wohnen. Analyse der Wohnsituation und Empfehlungen zu einer integrationsgerechten Wohnungspolitik für ausländische Arbeitnehmer und ihrer Familien. Hamburg: Gesellschaft für Wohnungs- und Siedlungswesen (GEWOS) (Schriftenreihe. Neue Folge 14).

Schober, K. (1982): Les immigrés de la seconde génération en RFA: problèmes et perspectives. in: Documentes Françaises, 22.12.1982, 1803, 18–23.

Schrader, A. et al. (1979): Die zweite Generation. Sozialisation und Akkulturation ausländischer Kinder in der Bundesrepublik. Königstein/Ts.: Athenaeum.

Schroe, H. (1979): Vreemdelingen te Gent, segregatie of niet? Leuven: unpubl. licence thesis. Katholieke Universiteit Leuven.

Schuleri-Hartje, U.K. (1982): Ausländische Arbeitnehmer und ihre Familien. Teil 1: Wohnverhältnisse. Berlin: Deutsches Institut für Urbanistik.

Schuleri-Hartje, U.K. (1984): Ausländische Arbeitnehmer und ihre Familien. Teil 2: Maßnahmen im Städtevergleich. Berlin: Deutsches Institut für Urbanistik.

Schuleri-Hartje, U.K.; Schulz zur Wiesch, J. (Eds.) (1982): Beiträge zur Ausländerpolitik. Berlin: Deutsches Institut für Urbanistik (Seminarberichte).

Schwarz, H. (1984): Regionalwirtschaftliche Wirkungen der schweizerischen Fremdarbeiterpolitik. Bern: Arbeitsberichte der Programmleitung NFP (Nationales Forschungsprogramm) 'Regionalprobleme'.

Schwarz, K. (1983): Untersuchungen zu den regionalen Unterschieden der Geburtenhäufigkeit. in: Forschungs- und Sitzungsberichte der Akademie für Raumforschung und Landesplanung 144, 7–30.

Schwinges, U. (1980): Zur Integration von Zuwanderern: Aussiedler in Hamburg. in: Uni HH Forschung 12. Soziologische Stadtforschung in Hamburg. Hamburg, 52–57.

Serail, S. (1984): Huisvesting en verhuisgedrag etnische minderheden. Den Haag: Ministerie van Volkshuisvesting, Ruimtelijke Ordening en Milieubeheer.

Shadid, W.; Kornalijnslijper, N. (1985): The housing situation of ethnic minorities in the Netherlands. in: Muus, P. (Ed.): Migration, minorities and policy in the Netherlands. Report for SOPEMI 1985. Amsterdam: Institut voor Sociale Geografie, 23–39.

Shah, S. (1980): Aspects of the geographical analysis of Asian immigrants in London. Oxford: unpubl. Dr. Phil. thesis.

Shyllon, F.P. (1974): Black slaves in Britain. London: Oxford University Press for the Institute of Race Relations.

Simon, G. (1979): L'espace des travailleurs Tunesiens en France. Poitiers: Simon.

Slater, D. (1975): The proverty of modern geographical inquiry. in: Pacific Viewpoint 16, 159–170.

Smidt, M. de (1980): Concentratie, segregation en huisvestingsperikelen van gastarbeiders in de gemeente Utrecht. in: Blauw, P.W.; Pastor, C. (Eds.): Soort, beschouwingen over ruimtelijke segregatie als maatschappelijk probleem. Deventer: Van Loghem Slaterus, 160–172.

Socialdata (1980): Befragung deutscher und ausländischer Haushalte zur Ausländerintegration in Berlin. Berlin: Der Regierende Bürgermeister Senatskanzlei/Planungsleitstelle Berlin.

SOPEMI (1985): Continuous reporting system on migration, 1984. Paris: OECD.

Städte in Zahlen (1983): Ein Strukturbericht zum Thema Finanzen. Hamburg: Statistisches Landesamt (Verband Deutscher Städtestatistiker).

Statistisches Bundesamt (1966): Bevölkerung und Kultur. Fachserie Volks- und Berufszählung vom 6. Juni, 3. Stuttgart: Verlag Kohlhammer.

Statistisches Bundesamt (1984): Ausländer, 1983, Reihe 2, Bevölkerung und Erwerbstätigkeit. Stuttgart: Verlag Kohlhammer.

Statistisches Bundesamt (Ed.) (1972ff.): Statistisches Jahrbuch für die Bundesrepublik Deutschland. Stuttgart: Verlag Kohlhammer.

Statistisches Jahrbuch deutscher Gemeinden (1970–82): Köln: Deutscher Städtetag.

Statistisches Jahrbuch für die BRD (1984): Hrsg. v. Statistischen Bundesamt Wiesbaden. Stuttgart: Verlag Kohlhammer.

Statistisches Jahrbuch für die BRD (1985): Hrsg. v. Statistischen Bundesamt Wiesbaden. Stuttgart: Verlag Kohlhammer.

Statistisches Jahrbuch deutscher Gemeinden 1970–1982: Köln: Deutscher Städtetag.

Strukturatlas Kiel (1982): Der Magistrat der Landeshauptstadt Kiel (Ed.). Statistisches Bundesamt. Kiel.

Suttles, G.D. (1968): The social order of the slum. Chicago: University of Chicago Press.

Taeuber, K.E., Taeuber, A.F. (1965): Negroes in cities. Chicago: Aldine.

Tapinos, G. (1975): L'immigration étrangères en France, 1946–1973. Paris: Presses Universitaires Française (Cahier, No. 71).

Taylor, P.J. (1982): A materialist framework for political geography. in: Transactions. Institute of British Geographers, N.S. 7, 15–34.

Taylor, P.J.; Hadfield, H. (1982): Housing and the state: a case study and structuralist interpretation. in: Cox, K.R.; Johnston, R.J. (Eds.): Conflict, politics and the urban scene. London: Longman, 241–263.

Theodorson, G. (Ed.) (1961): Studies in human ecology. New York: Harper and Row.

Thépaut, F. (1984): Les élections européennes en France et l'immigration. in: Presses et Immigres en France 119.8.

Thomas B. (1954): Migration and economic growth. Cambridge: Cambridge University Press.

Thomas, E.-J. (1982): Immigrant workers in Europe: their legal status. Paris: The Unesco Press.

Tribalat, M. (1982): Chronique de l'immigration. in: Population 37, 131–157.

Tribalat, M. (1983): Chronique de l'immigration. in: Population 38, 137–160.

Tribalat, M. (1985): Chronique de l'immigration. in: Population 40, 131–154.

Valkonet-Freeman, M. (1978): De gesloten buurten van Amsterdam. in: Bovenkerk, F. (Ed.): Omdat zij anders zijn. Meppel: Boom, 58–77.

Vanneste, D. (1980): De Turkse gastarbeiders te Gent; segregatie of geen segregatie? Leuven: unpubl. license thesis. Katholieke Universiteit Leuven.

Vanneste, D. (1981): Sociaal-ruimtelijke in een stad: betekenis van de indicator 'gastarbeiders': een onderzoek van de Gentse situatie. in: Tijdschrift van de Belgische Vereniging voor Aardrijkskundige Studies 2, 161–174.